CASE CLOSED™

VOLUME 35

Gosho Aoyama

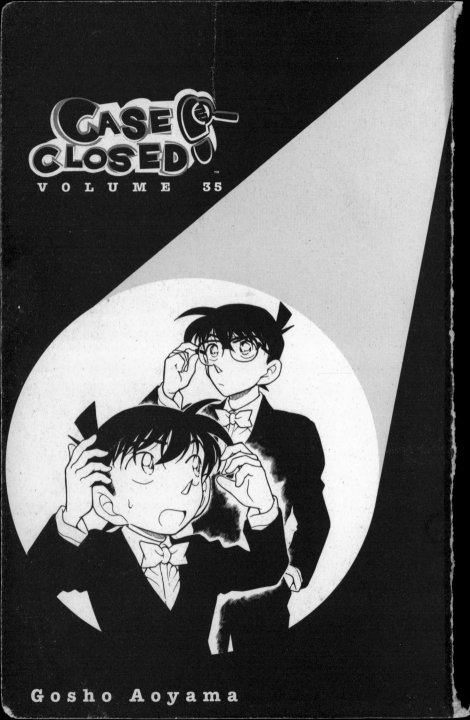

Case Briefing:

Subject:
Occupation:
Special Skills:
Equipment:

Jimmy Kudo, a.k.a. Conan Edogawa
High School Student/Detective
Analytical thinking and deductive reasoning, Soccer
Bow Tie Voice Transmitter, Super Sneakers,
Homing Glasses, Stretchy Suspenders

The subject is hot on the trail of a pair of suspicious men in black when he is attacked from behind and administered a strange substance which physically transforms him into a first grader. When the subject confides in the eccentric inventor Dr. Agasa, they decide to keep the subject's true identity a secret for the safety of everyone around him. Assuming the new identity of first-grader Conan Edogawa, the subject continues to assist the police force on their most baffling cases. The only problem is that most crime-solving professionals won't take a little kid's advice!

Table of Contents

CASE CLOSED

CONFIDEN

CASE CLOSED

Volume 35
Shonen Sunday Edition

Story and Art by GOSHO AOYAMA

© 1994 Gosho AOYAMA/Shogakukan
All rights reserved.
Original Japanese edition "MEITANTEI CONAN" published by SHOGAKUKAN Inc.

Translation
Tetsuichiro Miyaki

Touch-up & Lettering
Freeman Wong

Cover & Graphic Design
Andrea Rice

Editor
Shaenon K. Garrity

VP, Production **Alvin Lu**

VP, Sales & Product Marketing **Gonzalo Ferreyra**

VP, Creative **Linda Espinosa**

Publisher **Hyoe Narita**

Printed in Canada

Published by VIZ Media, LLC
P.O. Box 77010
San Francisco, CA 94107

10 9 8 7 6 5 4 3 2 1
First printing, July 2010

RATED
T+
FOR OLDER TEEN

PARENTAL ADVISORY
CASE CLOSED is rated T+ for Older Teen
and is recommended for ages 16 and up.
This volume contains realistic and graphic
violence.
ratings.viz.com

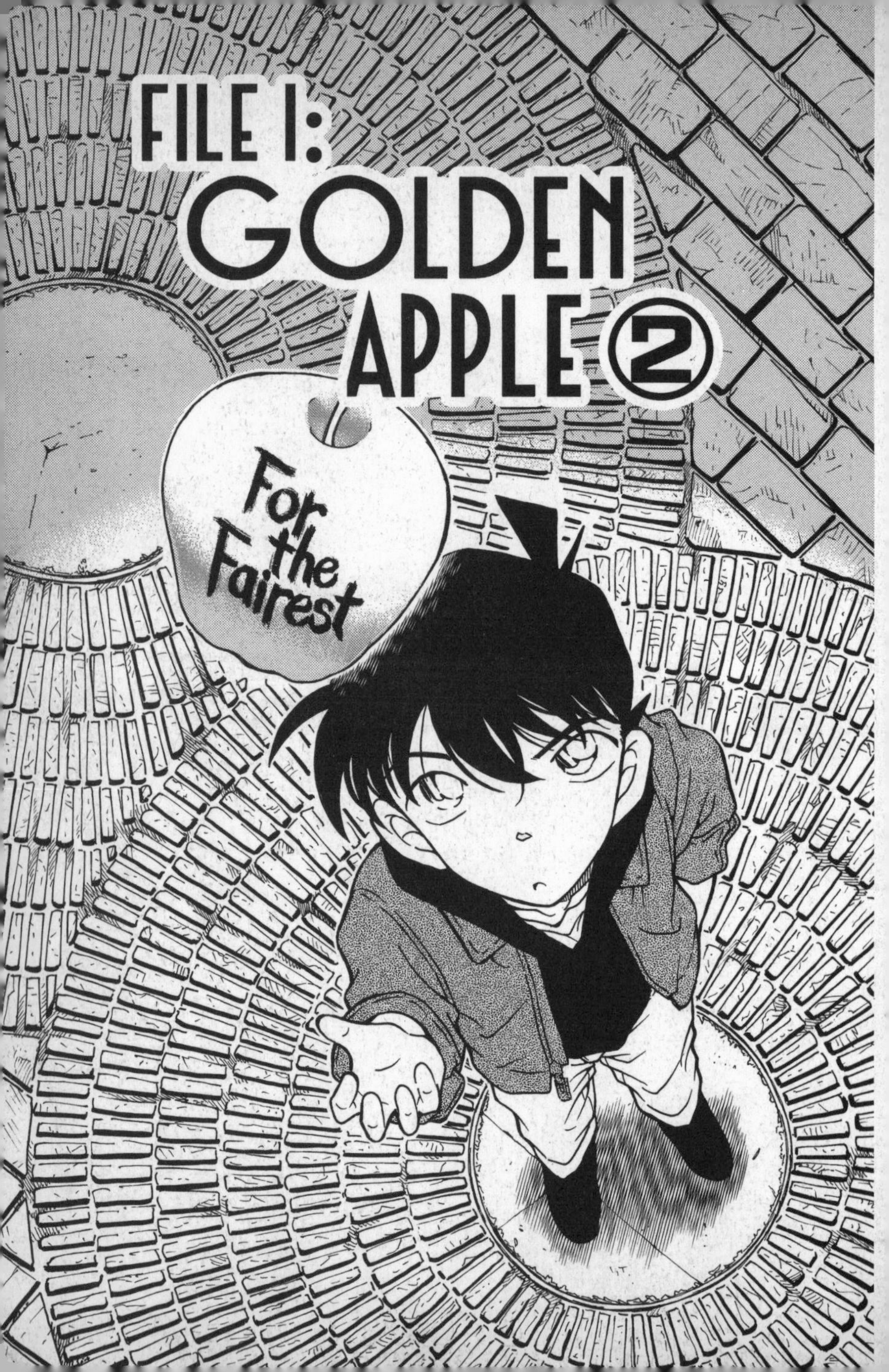
FILE 1:
GOLDEN
APPLE ②
For the Fairest

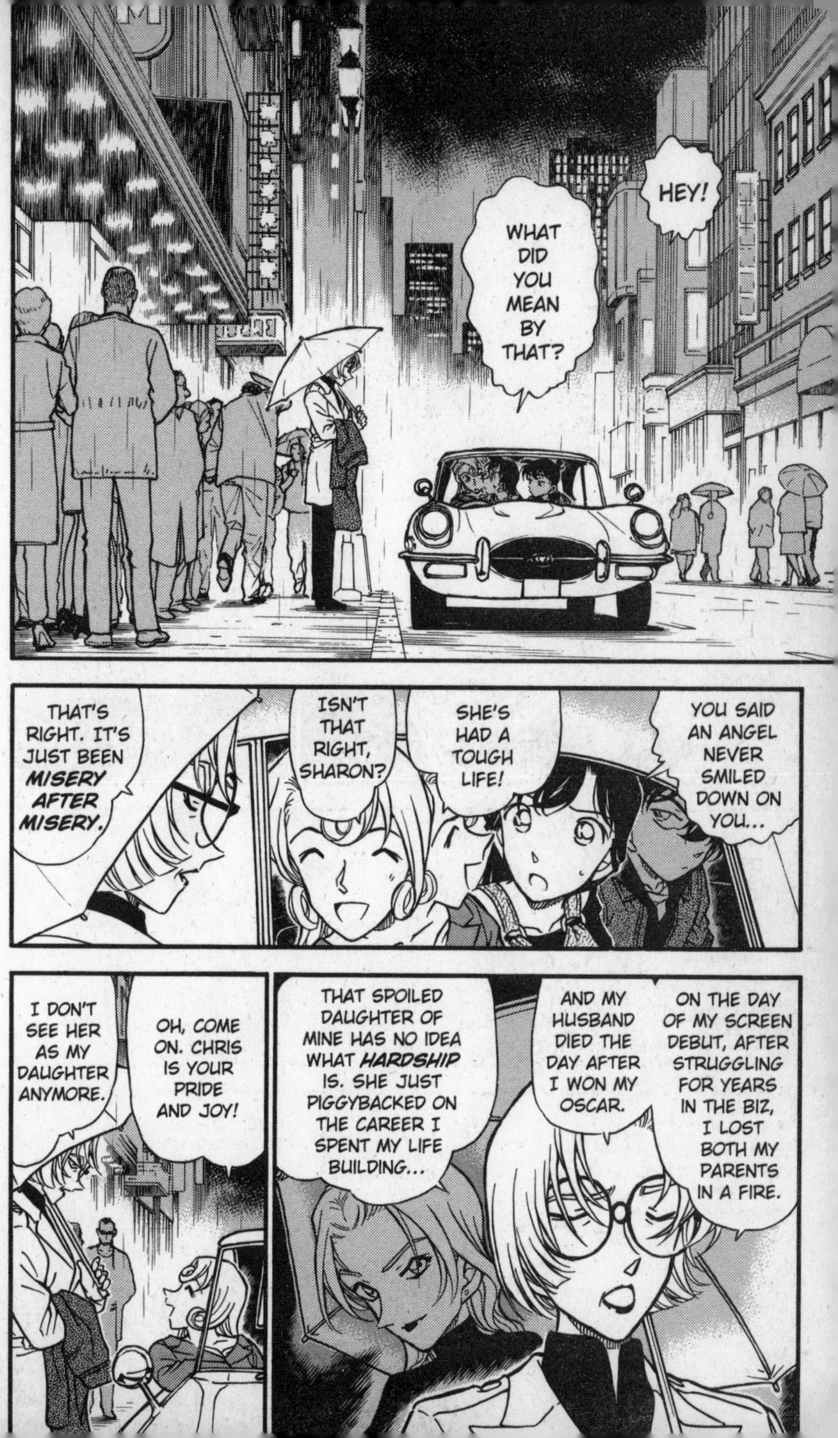
HEY!
WHAT DID YOU MEAN BY THAT?
YOU SAID AN ANGEL NEVER SMILED DOWN ON YOU...
SHE'S HAD A TOUGH LIFE!
ISN'T THAT RIGHT, SHARON?
THAT'S RIGHT. IT'S JUST BEEN ***MISERY AFTER MISERY***.
ON THE DAY OF MY SCREEN DEBUT, AFTER STRUGGLING FOR YEARS IN THE BIZ, I LOST BOTH MY PARENTS IN A FIRE.
AND MY HUSBAND DIED THE DAY AFTER I WON MY OSCAR.
THAT SPOILED DAUGHTER OF MINE HAS NO IDEA WHAT ***HARDSHIP*** IS. SHE JUST PIGGYBACKED ON THE CAREER I SPENT MY LIFE BUILDING...
OH, COME ON. CHRIS IS YOUR PRIDE AND JOY!
I DON'T SEE HER AS MY DAUGHTER ANYMORE.

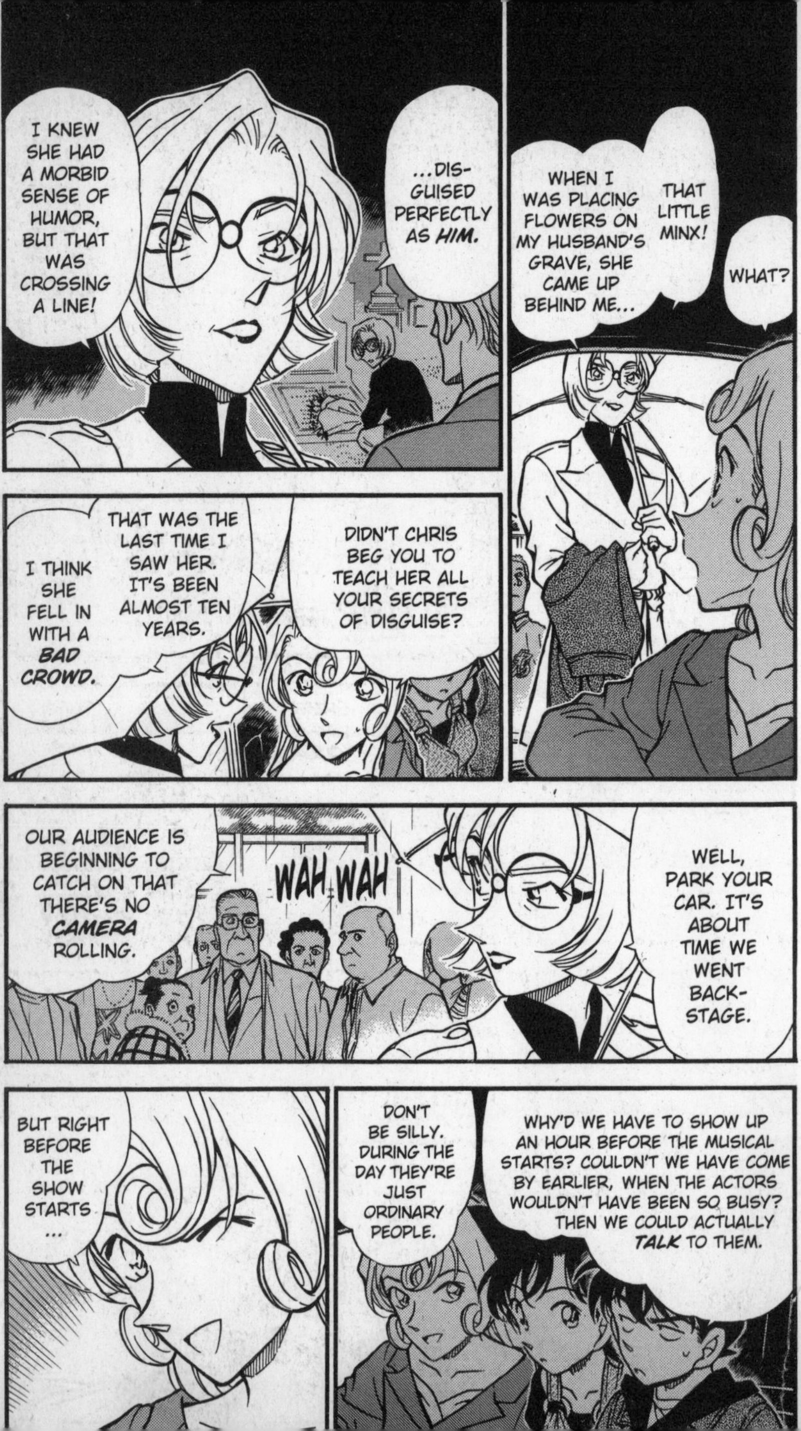
THAT LITTLE MINX!
WHAT?
WHEN I WAS PLACING FLOWERS ON MY HUSBAND'S GRAVE, SHE CAME UP BEHIND ME...
...DIS-GUISED PERFECTLY AS *HIM.*
I KNEW SHE HAD A MORBID SENSE OF HUMOR, BUT THAT WAS CROSSING A LINE!
DIDN'T CHRIS BEG YOU TO TEACH HER ALL YOUR SECRETS OF DISGUISE?
THAT WAS THE LAST TIME I SAW HER. IT'S BEEN ALMOST TEN YEARS.
I THINK SHE FELL IN WITH A *BAD CROWD.*
WELL, PARK YOUR CAR. IT'S ABOUT TIME WE WENT BACK-STAGE.
WAH WAH
OUR AUDIENCE IS BEGINNING TO CATCH ON THAT THERE'S NO *CAMERA* ROLLING.
WHY'D WE HAVE TO SHOW UP AN HOUR BEFORE THE MUSICAL STARTS? COULDN'T WE HAVE COME BY EARLIER, WHEN THE ACTORS WOULDN'T HAVE BEEN SO BUSY? THEN WE COULD ACTUALLY *TALK* TO THEM.
DON'T BE SILLY. DURING THE DAY THEY'RE JUST ORDINARY PEOPLE.
BUT RIGHT BEFORE THE SHOW STARTS ...

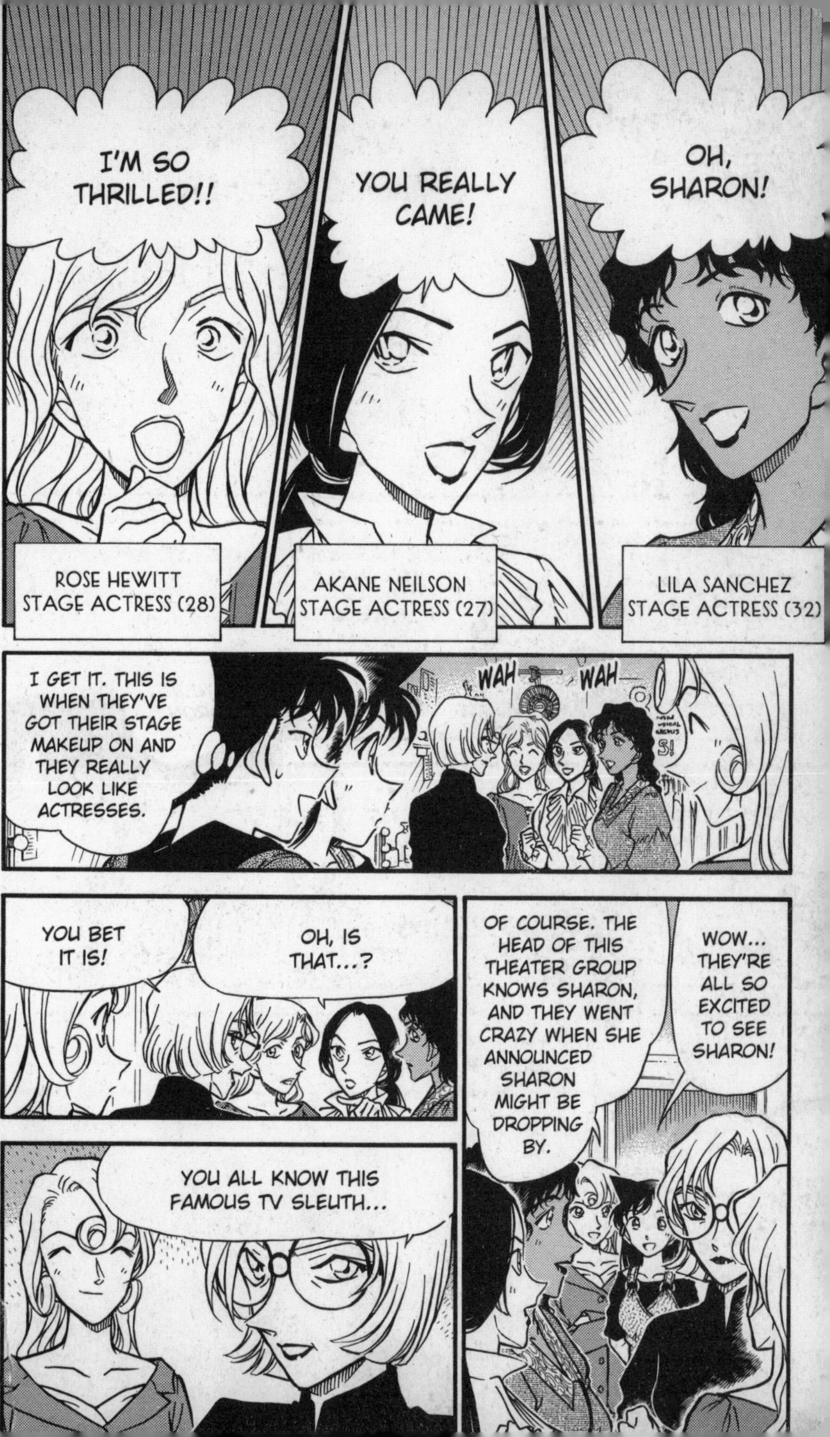
OH, SHARON!
LILA SANCHEZ STAGE ACTRESS (32)
YOU REALLY CAME!
AKANE NEILSON STAGE ACTRESS (27)
I'M SO THRILLED!!
ROSE HEWITT STAGE ACTRESS (28)
WAH
WAH
S!
I GET IT. THIS IS WHEN THEY'VE GOT THEIR STAGE MAKEUP ON AND THEY REALLY LOOK LIKE ACTRESSES.
WOW... THEY'RE ALL SO EXCITED TO SEE SHARON!
OF COURSE. THE HEAD OF THIS THEATER GROUP KNOWS SHARON, AND THEY WENT CRAZY WHEN SHE ANNOUNCED SHARON MIGHT BE DROPPING BY.
OH, IS THAT...?
YOU BET IT IS!
YOU ALL KNOW THIS FAMOUS TV SLEUTH...

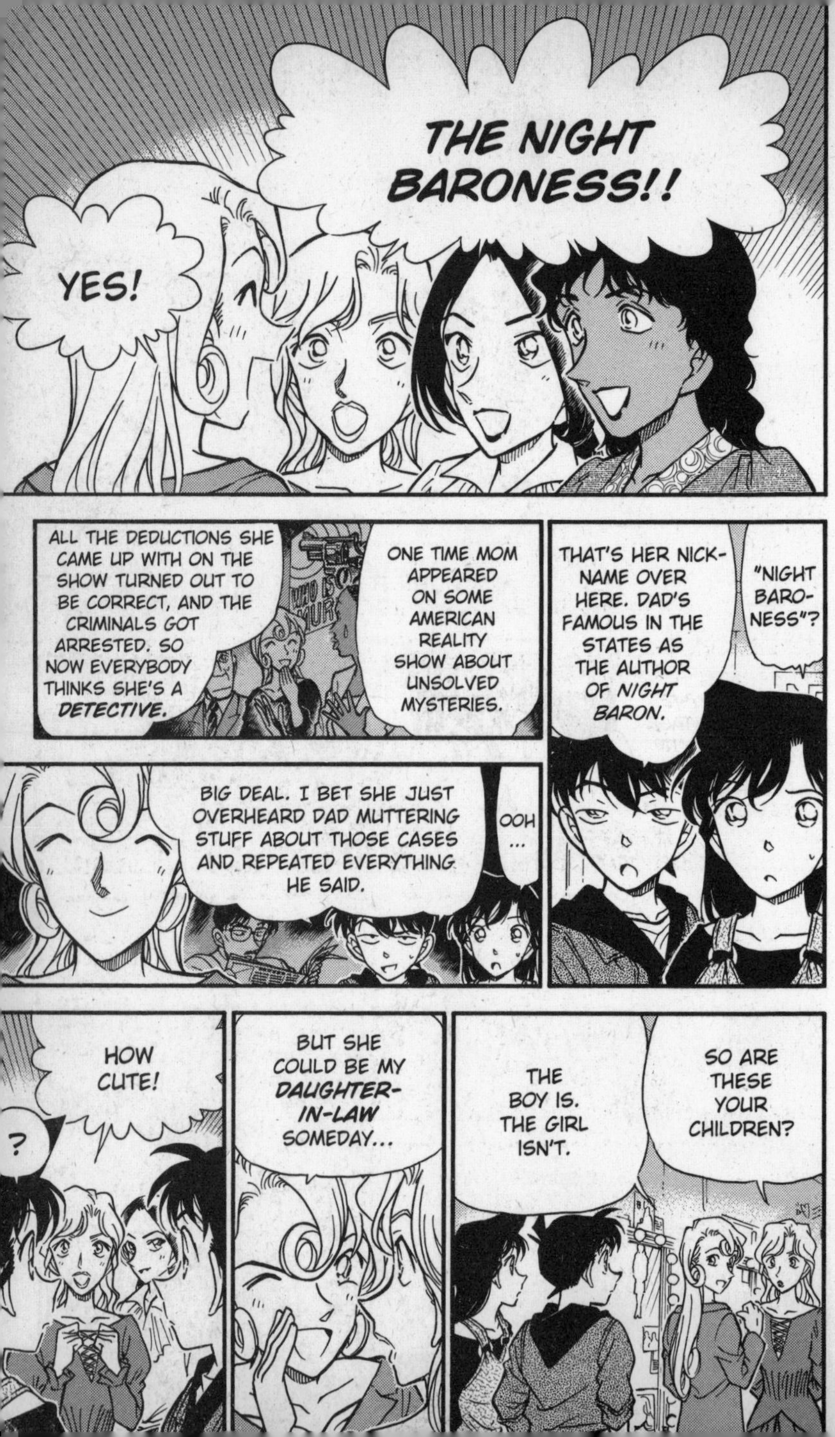
THE NIGHT BARONESS!!
YES!
"NIGHT BARONESS"?
THAT'S HER NICKNAME OVER HERE. DAD'S FAMOUS IN THE STATES AS THE AUTHOR OF *NIGHT BARON*.
ONE TIME MOM APPEARED ON SOME AMERICAN REALITY SHOW ABOUT UNSOLVED MYSTERIES.
ALL THE DEDUCTIONS SHE CAME UP WITH ON THE SHOW TURNED OUT TO BE CORRECT, AND THE CRIMINALS GOT ARRESTED. SO NOW EVERYBODY THINKS SHE'S A *DETECTIVE*.
OOH...
BIG DEAL. I BET SHE JUST OVERHEARD DAD MUTTERING STUFF ABOUT THOSE CASES AND REPEATED EVERYTHING HE SAID.
SO ARE THESE YOUR CHILDREN?
THE BOY IS. THE GIRL ISN'T.
BUT SHE COULD BE MY ***DAUGHTER-IN-LAW*** SOMEDAY...
HOW CUTE!
?

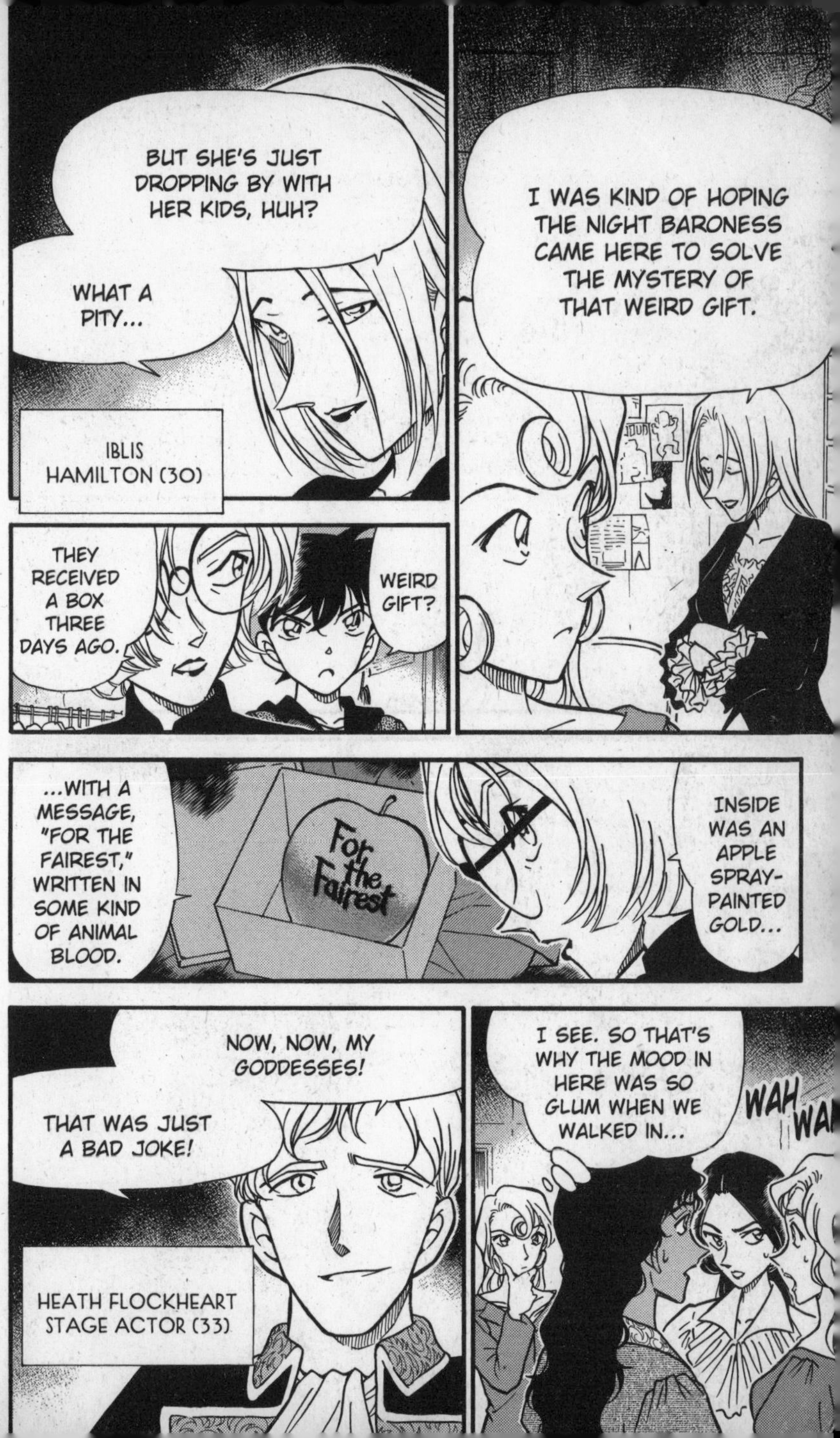
I WAS KIND OF HOPING THE NIGHT BARONESS CAME HERE TO SOLVE THE MYSTERY OF THAT WEIRD GIFT.
BUT SHE'S JUST DROPPING BY WITH HER KIDS, HUH?
WHAT A PITY...
IBLIS HAMILTON (30)
WEIRD GIFT?
THEY RECEIVED A BOX THREE DAYS AGO.
INSIDE WAS AN APPLE SPRAY-PAINTED GOLD...
For the Fairest
...WITH A MESSAGE, "FOR THE FAIREST," WRITTEN IN SOME KIND OF ANIMAL BLOOD.
I SEE. SO THAT'S WHY THE MOOD IN HERE WAS SO GLUM WHEN WE WALKED IN...
WAH
NOW, NOW, MY GODDESSES!
THAT WAS JUST A BAD JOKE!
HEATH FLOCKHEART STAGE ACTOR (33)

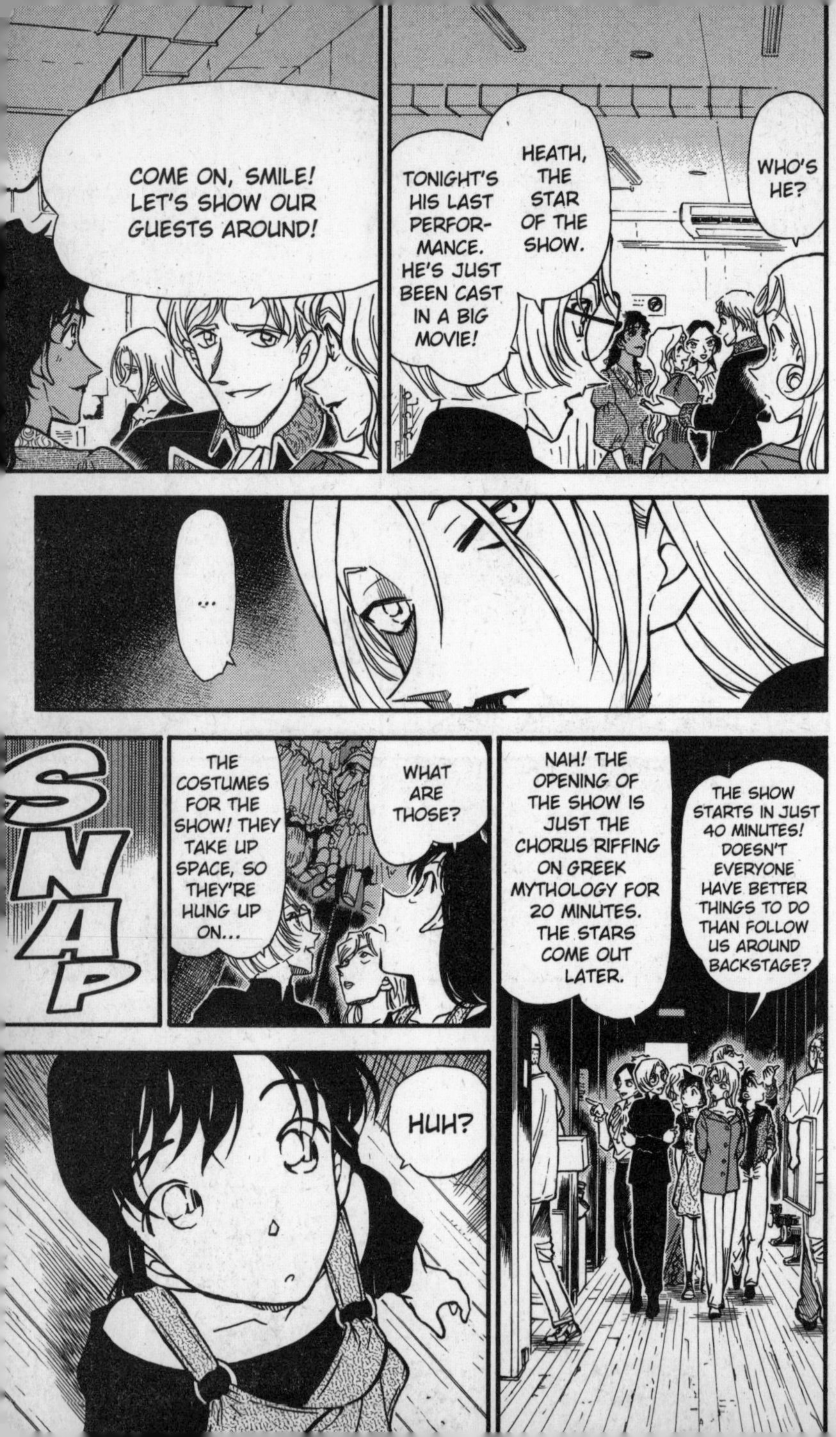
WHO'S HE?
HEATH, THE STAR OF THE SHOW.
TONIGHT'S HIS LAST PERFOR-MANCE. HE'S JUST BEEN CAST IN A BIG MOVIE!
COME ON, SMILE! LET'S SHOW OUR GUESTS AROUND!
...
THE SHOW STARTS IN JUST 40 MINUTES! DOESN'T EVERYONE HAVE BETTER THINGS TO DO THAN FOLLOW US AROUND BACKSTAGE?
NAH! THE OPENING OF THE SHOW IS JUST THE CHORUS RIFFING ON GREEK MYTHOLOGY FOR 20 MINUTES. THE STARS COME OUT LATER.
WHAT ARE THOSE?
THE COSTUMES FOR THE SHOW! THEY TAKE UP SPACE, SO THEY'RE HUNG UP ON...
SNAP
HUH?

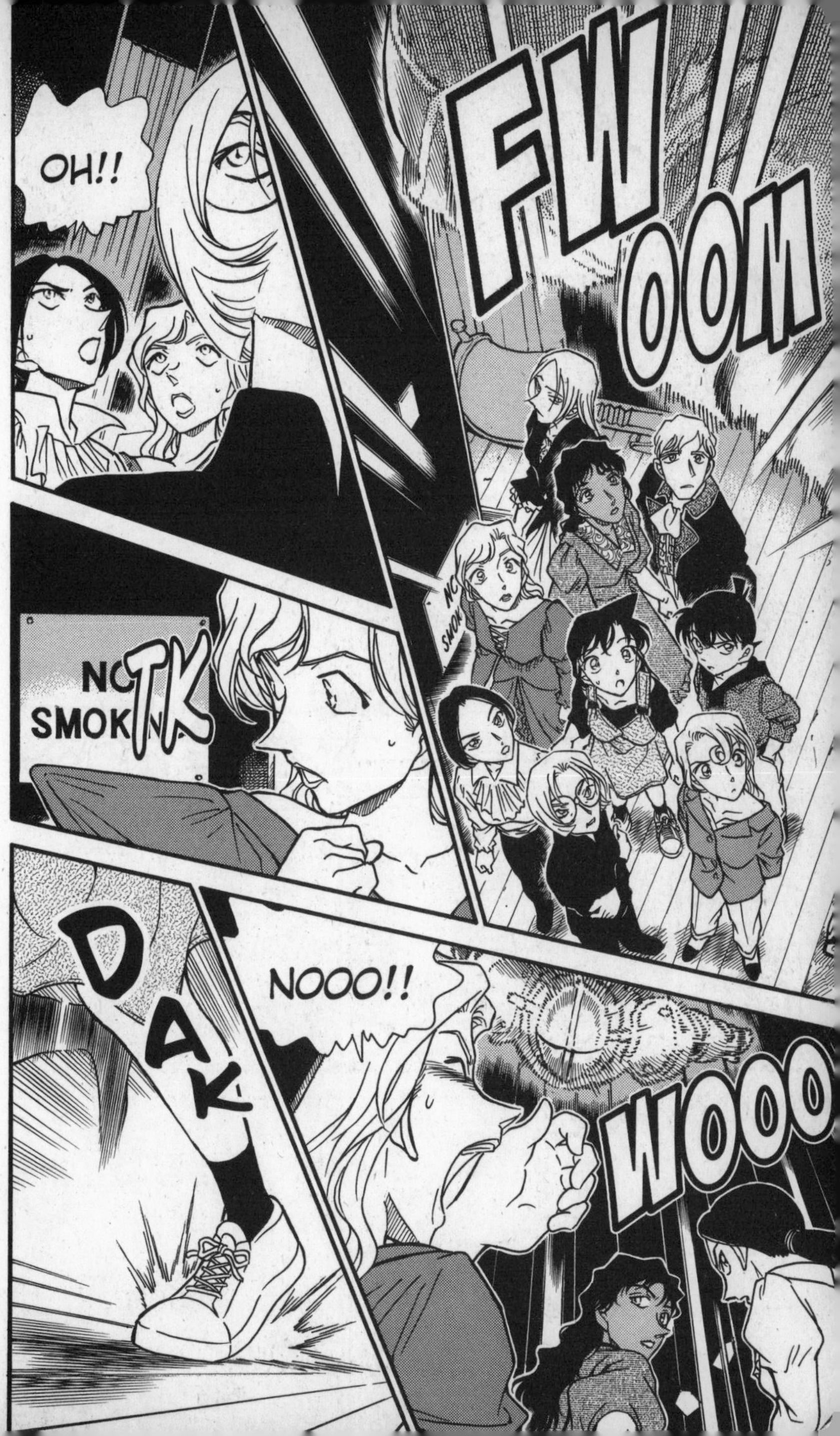
FWOOM
NO SMOK
OH!!
NO SMOK
TK
NOOO!!
WOOO
DAK

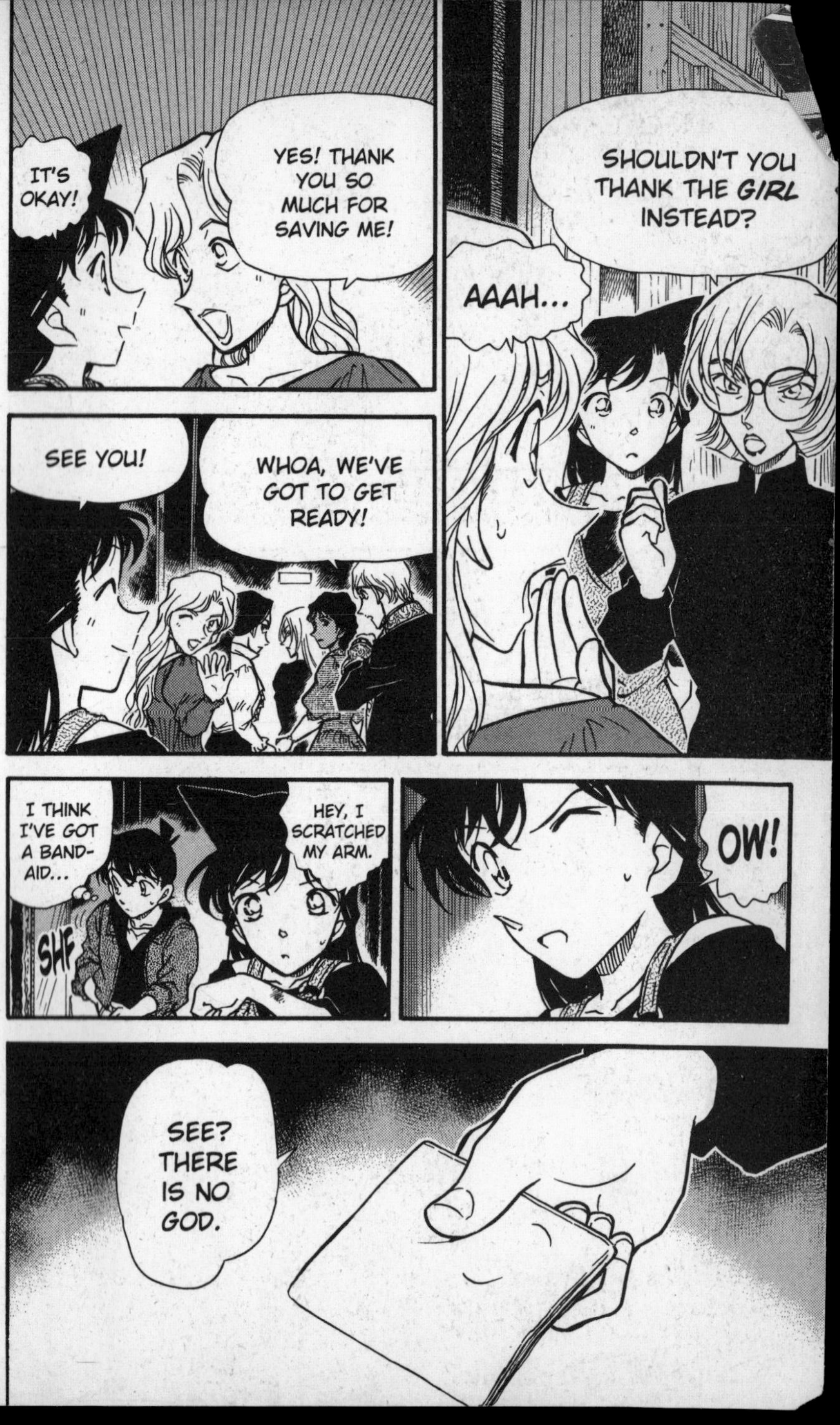
SHOULDN'T YOU THANK THE *GIRL* INSTEAD?
AAAH...
YES! THANK YOU SO MUCH FOR SAVING ME!
IT'S OKAY!
WHOA, WE'VE GOT TO GET READY!
SEE YOU!
OW!
HEY, I SCRATCHED MY ARM.
I THINK I'VE GOT A BAND-AID...
SHF
SEE? THERE IS NO GOD.

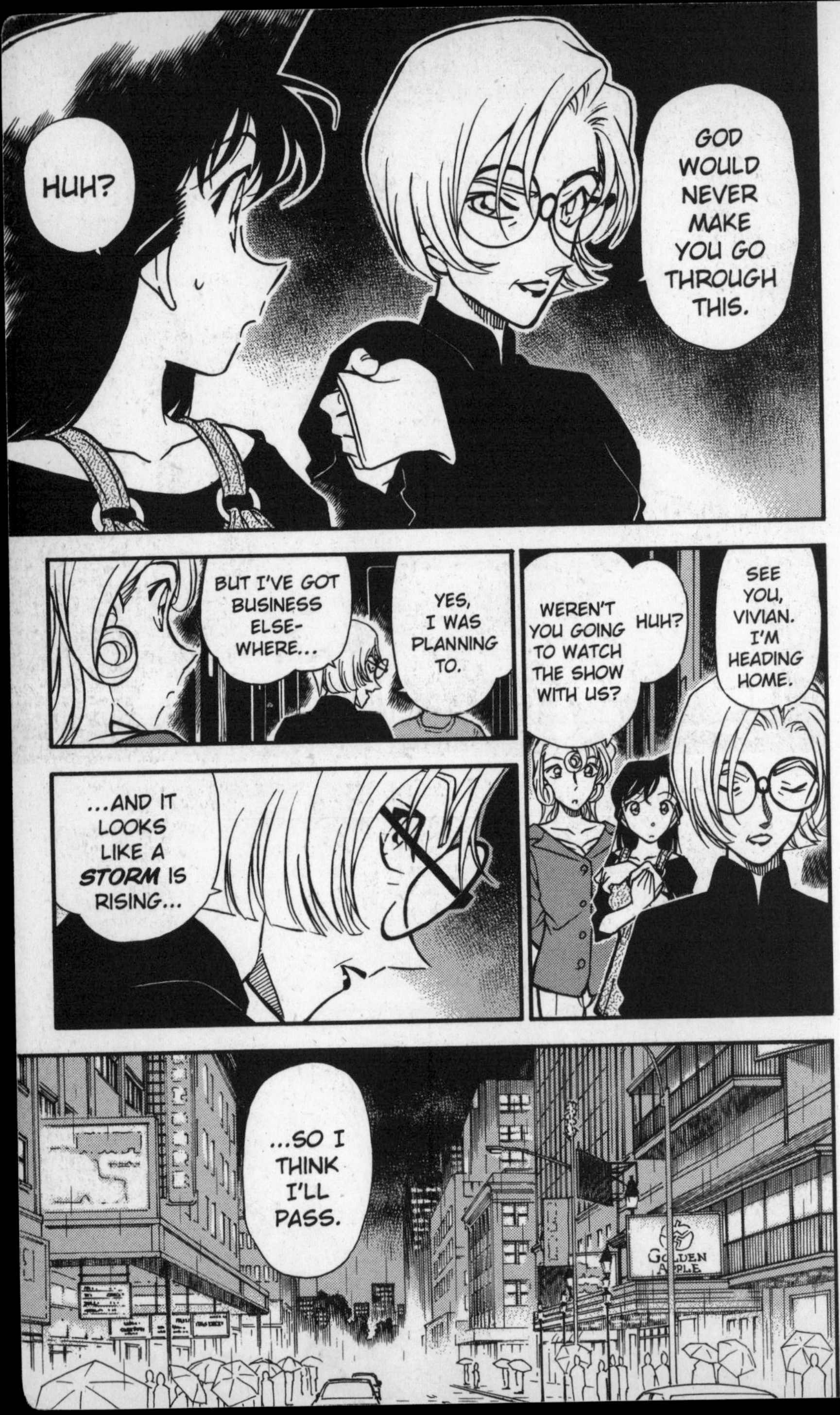
GOD WOULD NEVER MAKE YOU GO THROUGH THIS.
HUH?
SEE YOU, VIVIAN. I'M HEADING HOME.
HUH?
WEREN'T YOU GOING TO WATCH THE SHOW WITH US?
YES, I WAS PLANNING TO.
BUT I'VE GOT BUSINESS ELSE-WHERE...
...AND IT LOOKS LIKE A *STORM* IS RISING...
...SO I THINK I'LL PASS.
GOLDEN APPLE

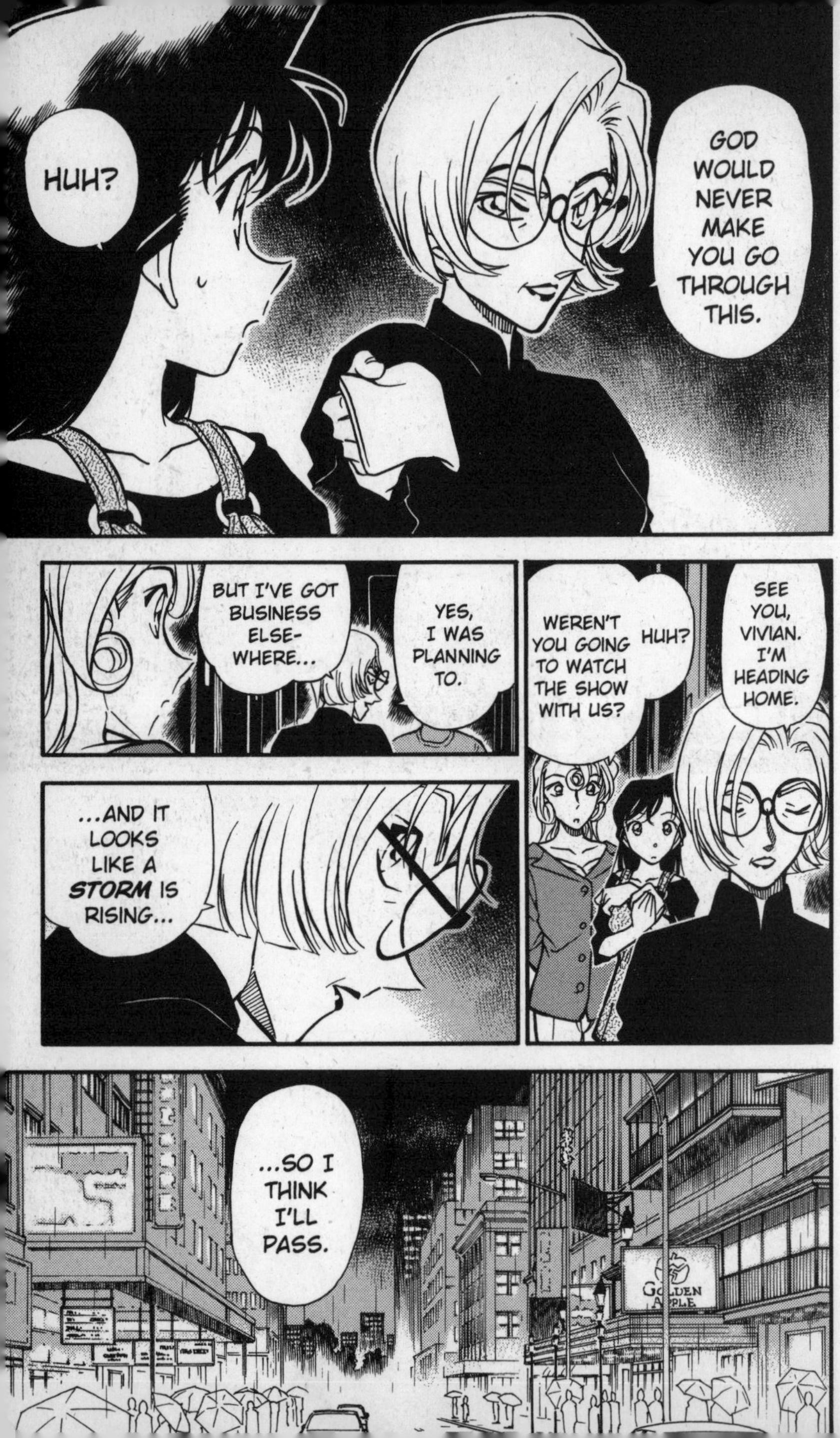
GOD WOULD NEVER MAKE YOU GO THROUGH THIS.
HUH?
SEE YOU, VIVIAN. I'M HEADING HOME.
HUH?
WEREN'T YOU GOING TO WATCH THE SHOW WITH US?
YES, I WAS PLANNING TO.
BUT I'VE GOT BUSINESS ELSEWHERE...
...AND IT LOOKS LIKE A **STORM** IS RISING...
...SO I THINK I'LL PASS.
GOLDEN APPLE

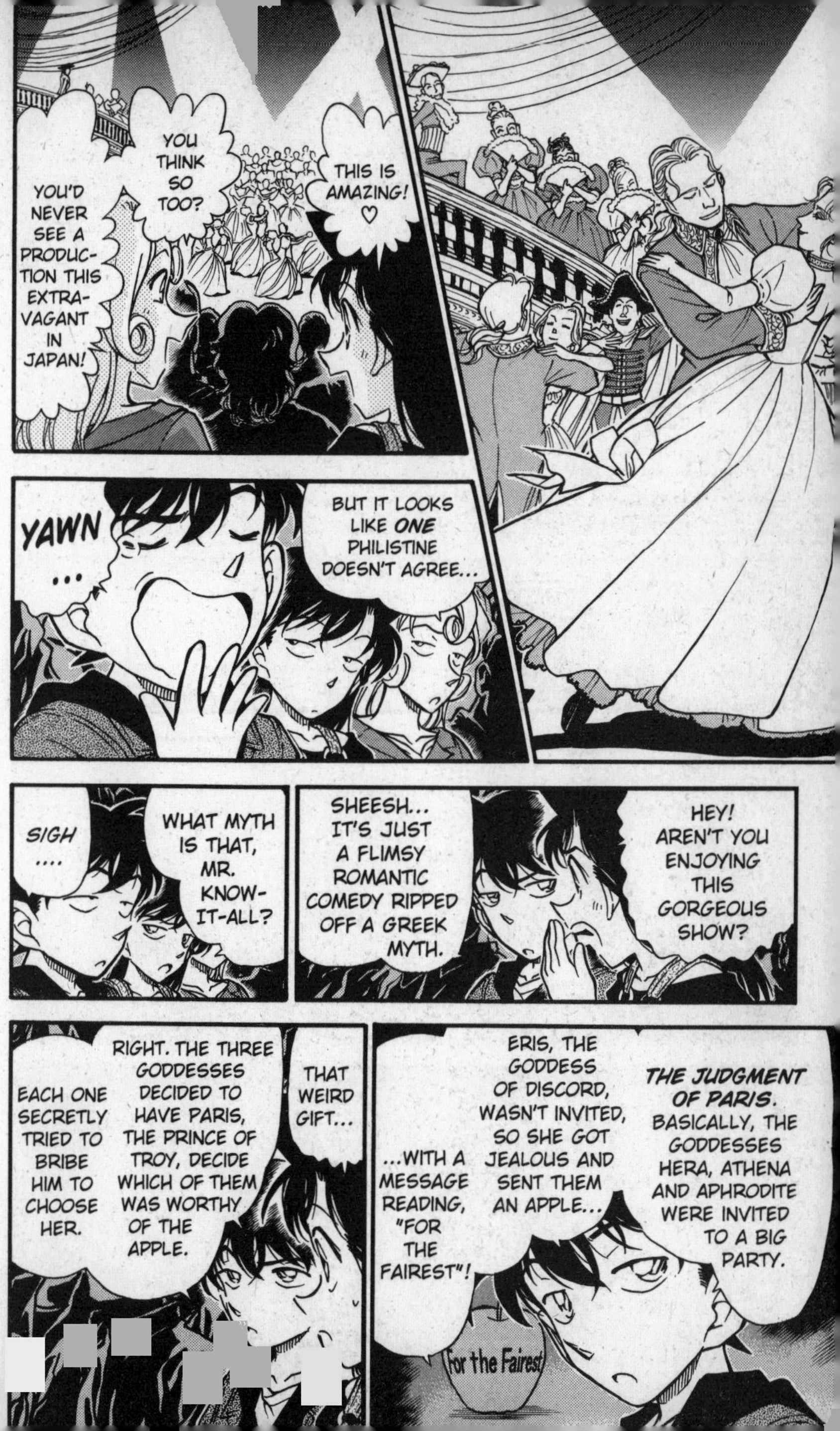
THIS IS AMAZING! ♡
YOU THINK SO TOO?
YOU'D NEVER SEE A PRODUCTION THIS EXTRAVAGANT IN JAPAN!
BUT IT LOOKS LIKE ONE PHILISTINE DOESN'T AGREE...
YAWN ...
HEY! AREN'T YOU ENJOYING THIS GORGEOUS SHOW?
SHEESH... IT'S JUST A FLIMSY ROMANTIC COMEDY RIPPED OFF A GREEK MYTH.
WHAT MYTH IS THAT, MR. KNOW-IT-ALL?
SIGH ....
THE JUDGMENT OF PARIS. BASICALLY, THE GODDESSES HERA, ATHENA AND APHRODITE WERE INVITED TO A BIG PARTY.
ERIS, THE GODDESS OF DISCORD, WASN'T INVITED, SO SHE GOT JEALOUS AND SENT THEM AN APPLE...
...WITH A MESSAGE READING, "FOR THE FAIREST"!
For the Fairest
THAT WEIRD GIFT...
RIGHT. THE THREE GODDESSES DECIDED TO HAVE PARIS, THE PRINCE OF TROY, DECIDE WHICH OF THEM WAS WORTHY OF THE APPLE.
EACH ONE SECRETLY TRIED TO BRIBE HIM TO CHOOSE HER.

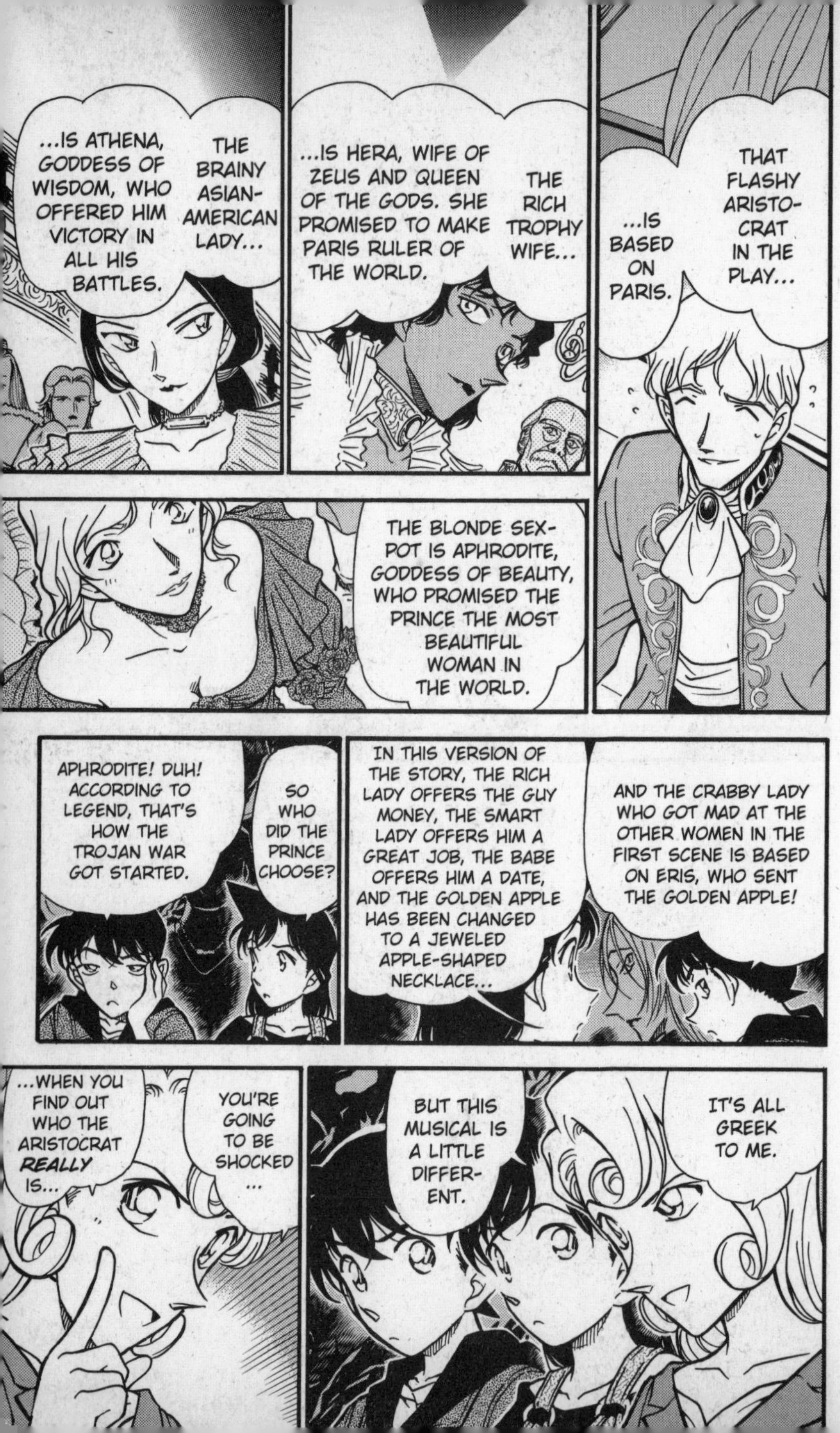
THAT FLASHY ARISTOCRAT IN THE PLAY...
...IS BASED ON PARIS.
THE RICH TROPHY WIFE...
...IS HERA, WIFE OF ZEUS AND QUEEN OF THE GODS. SHE PROMISED TO MAKE PARIS RULER OF THE WORLD.
THE BRAINY ASIAN-AMERICAN LADY...
...IS ATHENA, GODDESS OF WISDOM, WHO OFFERED HIM VICTORY IN ALL HIS BATTLES.
THE BLONDE SEX-POT IS APHRODITE, GODDESS OF BEAUTY, WHO PROMISED THE PRINCE THE MOST BEAUTIFUL WOMAN IN THE WORLD.
AND THE CRABBY LADY WHO GOT MAD AT THE OTHER WOMEN IN THE FIRST SCENE IS BASED ON ERIS, WHO SENT THE GOLDEN APPLE!
IN THIS VERSION OF THE STORY, THE RICH LADY OFFERS THE GUY MONEY, THE SMART LADY OFFERS HIM A GREAT JOB, THE BABE OFFERS HIM A DATE, AND THE GOLDEN APPLE HAS BEEN CHANGED TO A JEWELED APPLE-SHAPED NECKLACE...
SO WHO DID THE PRINCE CHOOSE?
APHRODITE! DUH! ACCORDING TO LEGEND, THAT'S HOW THE TROJAN WAR GOT STARTED.
IT'S ALL GREEK TO ME.
BUT THIS MUSICAL IS A LITTLE DIFFERENT.
YOU'RE GOING TO BE SHOCKED...
...WHEN YOU FIND OUT WHO THE ARISTOCRAT *REALLY* IS...

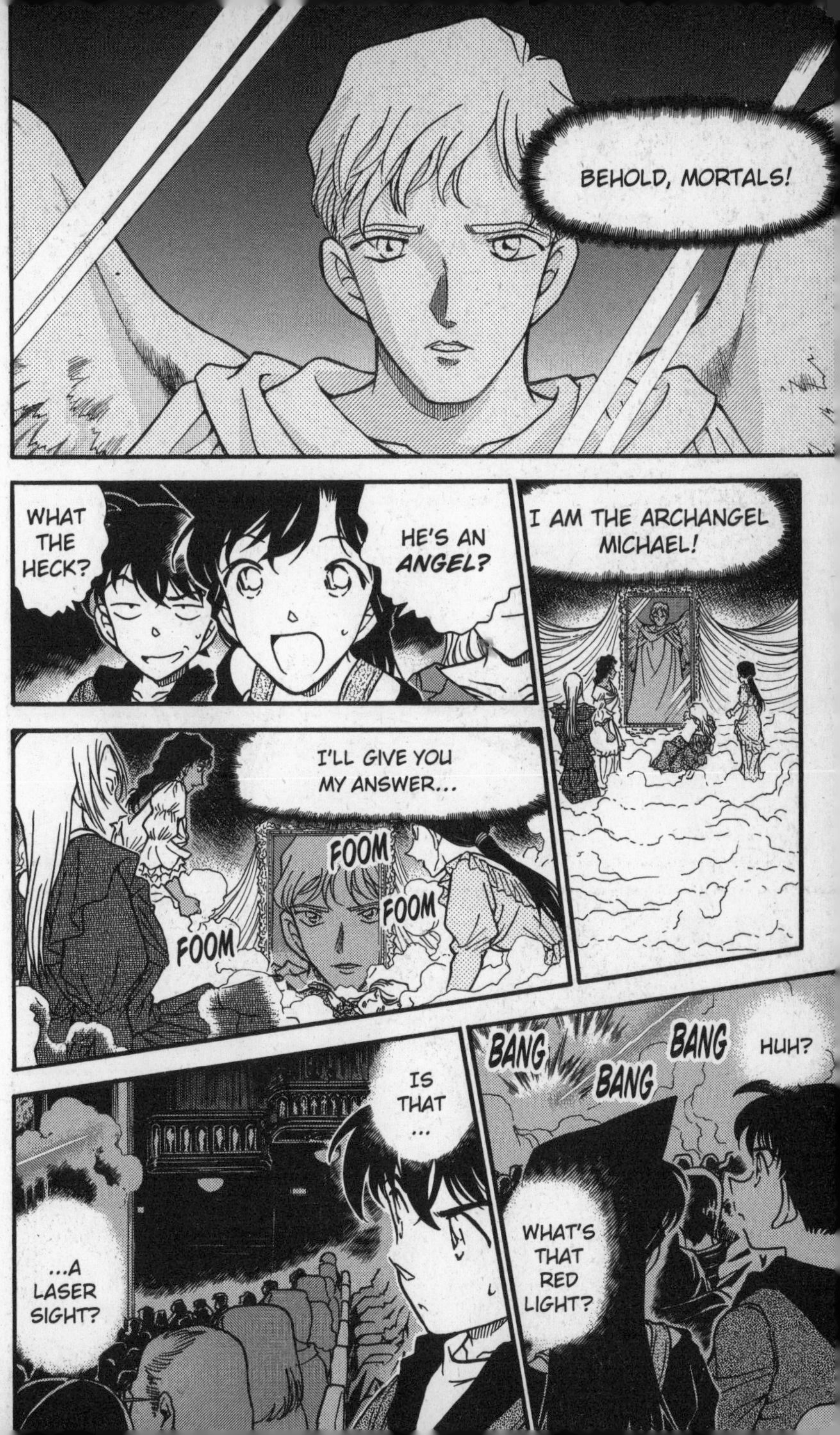
BEHOLD, MORTALS!
I AM THE ARCHANGEL MICHAEL!
HE'S AN *ANGEL?*
WHAT THE HECK?
I'LL GIVE YOU MY ANSWER...
FOOM
FOOM
FOOM
HUH?
BANG
BANG
BANG
WHAT'S THAT RED LIGHT?
IS THAT ...
...A LASER SIGHT?

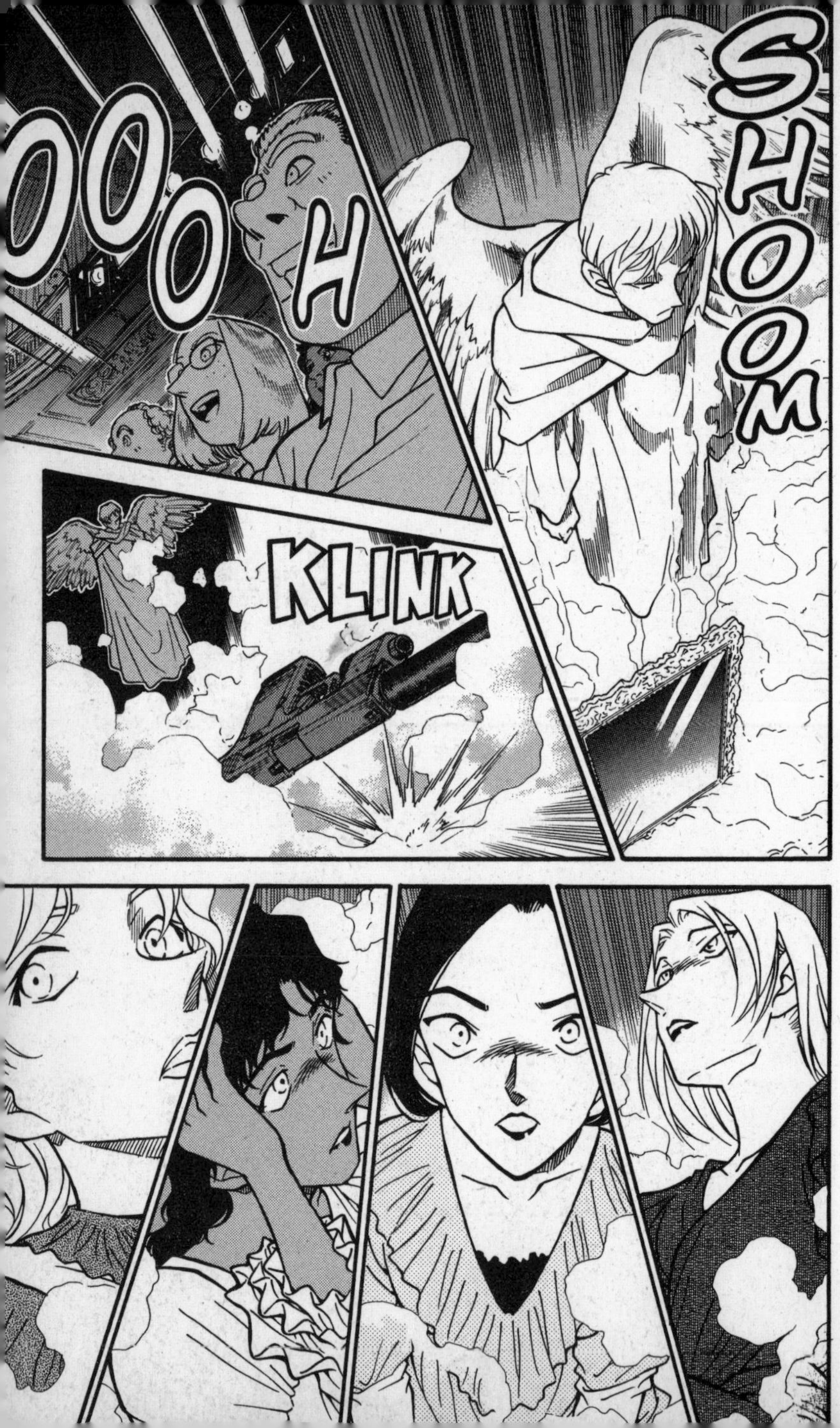
SHOOM
OOOOH
KLINK

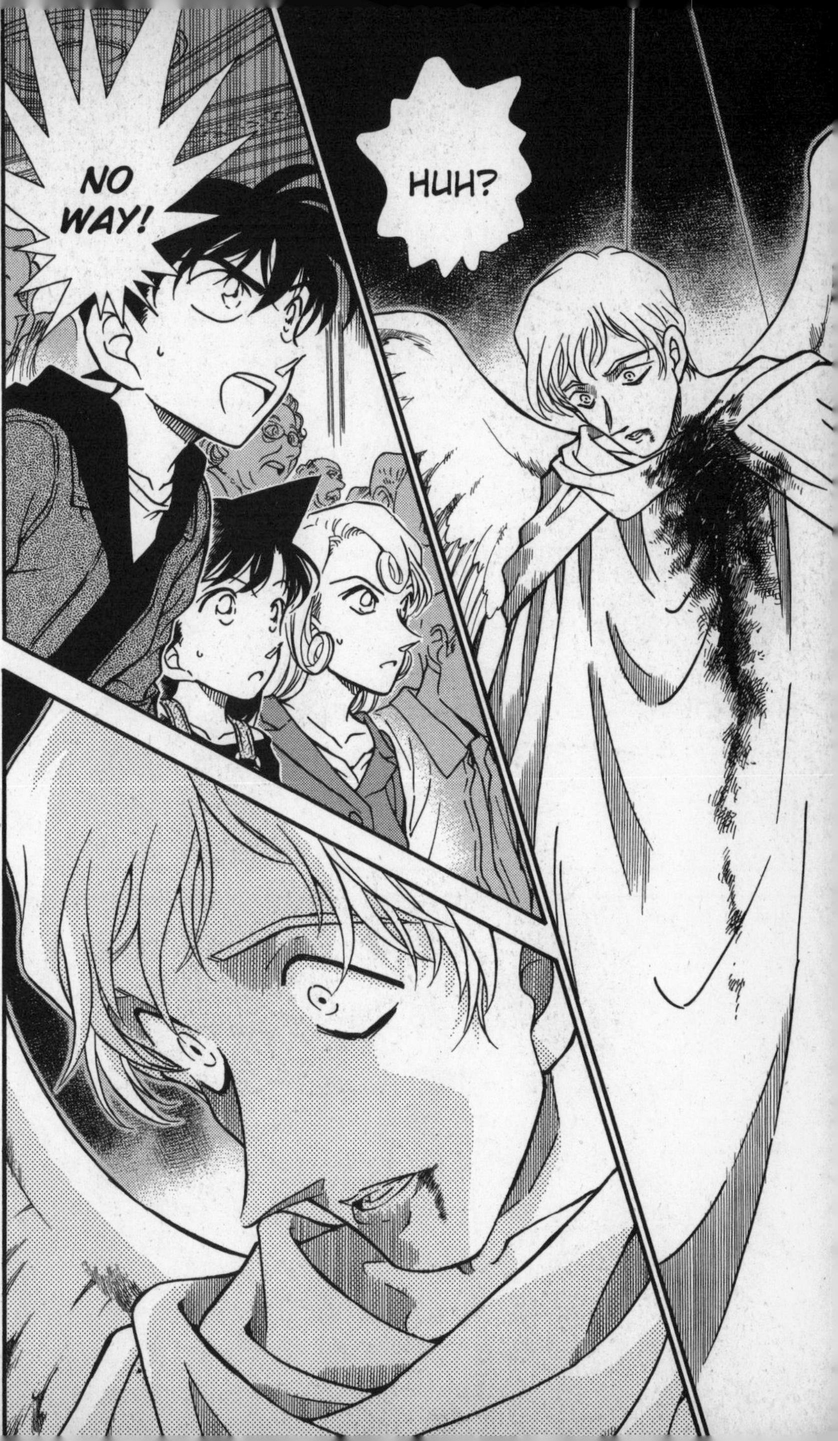
HUH?
NO WAY!

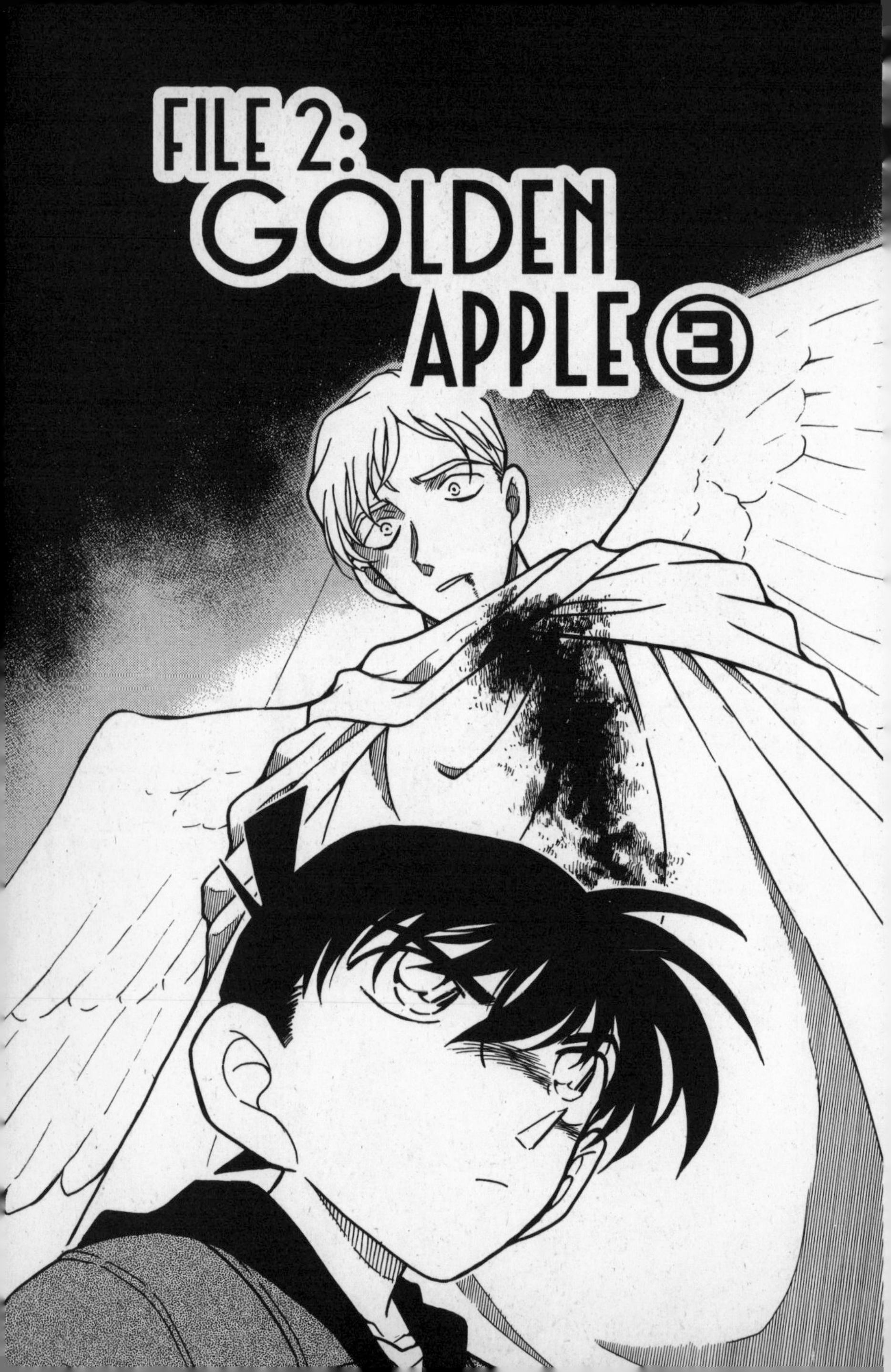
FILE 2:
GOLDEN
APPLE ③

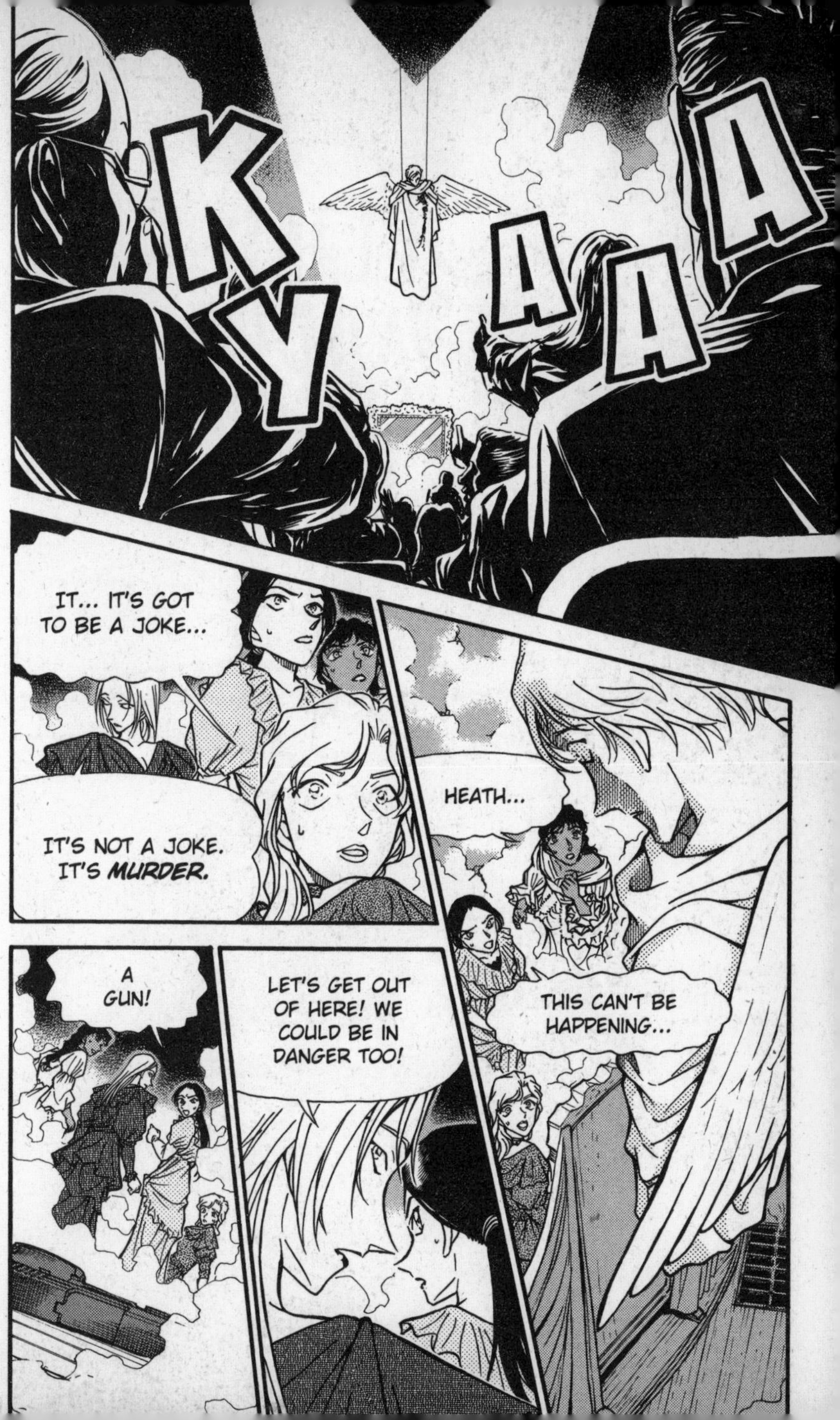
KYAAAA
HEATH...
THIS CAN'T BE HAPPENING...
IT... IT'S GOT TO BE A JOKE...
IT'S NOT A JOKE. IT'S *MURDER.*
LET'S GET OUT OF HERE! WE COULD BE IN DANGER TOO!
A GUN!

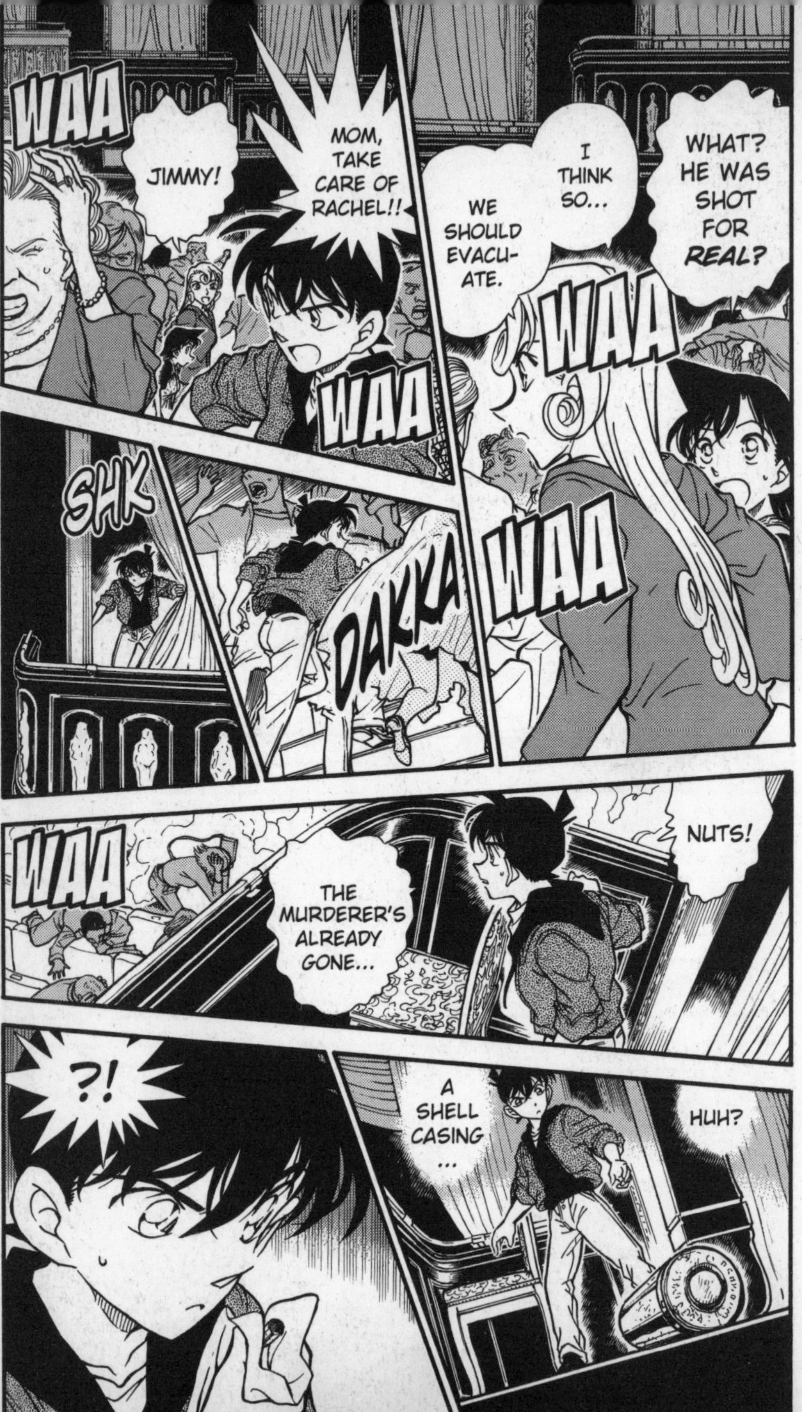
WHAT? HE WAS SHOT FOR REAL?
I THINK SO...
WE SHOULD EVACU-ATE.
WAA
WAA
MOM, TAKE CARE OF RACHEL!!
JIMMY!
WAA
WAA
DAKKA
SHK
NUTS!
THE MURDERER'S ALREADY GONE...
WAA
HUH?
A SHELL CASING ...
?!

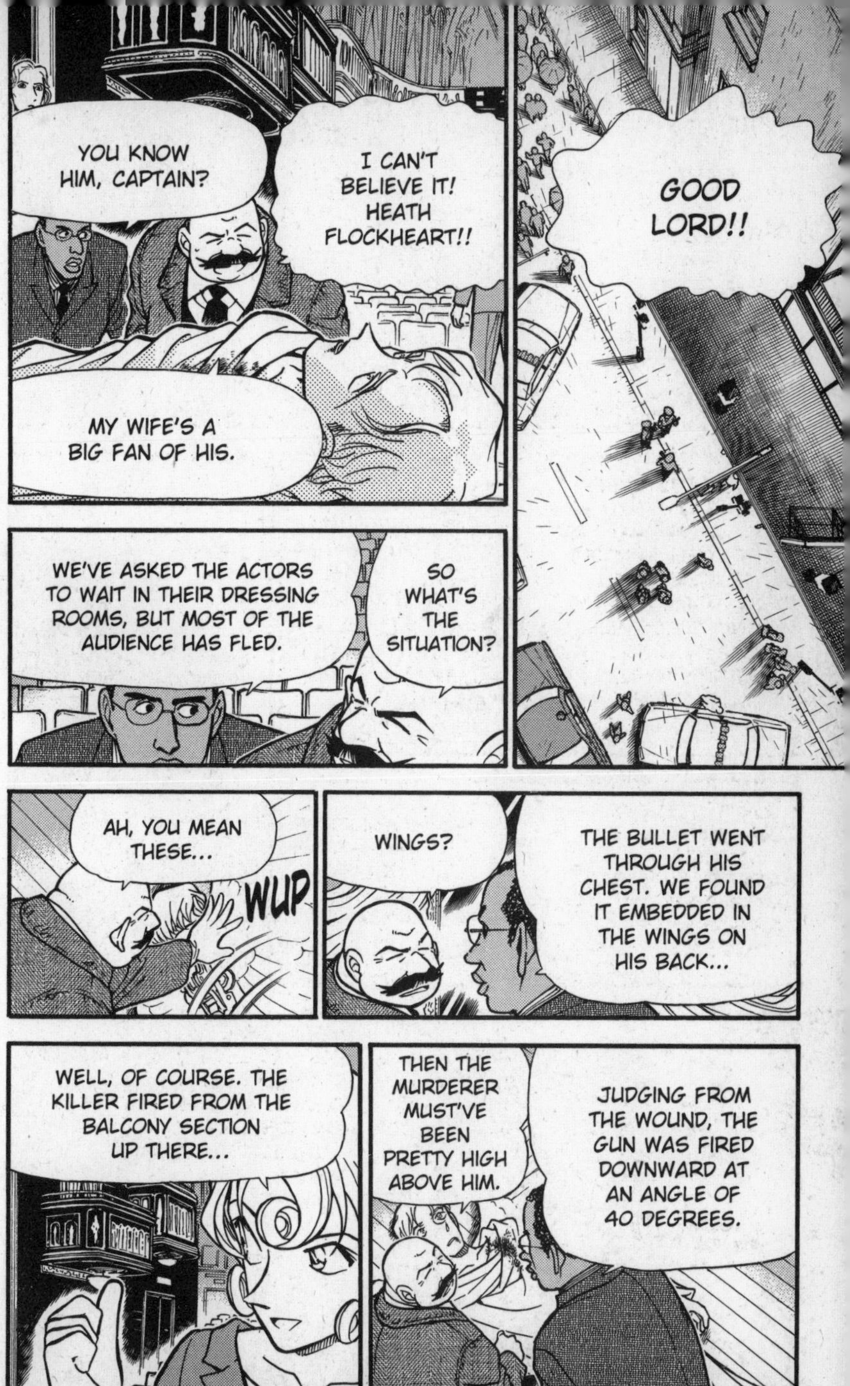
GOOD LORD!!
I CAN'T BELIEVE IT! HEATH FLOCKHEART!!
YOU KNOW HIM, CAPTAIN?
MY WIFE'S A BIG FAN OF HIS.
SO WHAT'S THE SITUATION?
WE'VE ASKED THE ACTORS TO WAIT IN THEIR DRESSING ROOMS, BUT MOST OF THE AUDIENCE HAS FLED.
THE BULLET WENT THROUGH HIS CHEST. WE FOUND IT EMBEDDED IN THE WINGS ON HIS BACK...
WINGS?
AH, YOU MEAN THESE...
WUP
JUDGING FROM THE WOUND, THE GUN WAS FIRED DOWNWARD AT AN ANGLE OF 40 DEGREES.
THEN THE MURDERER MUST'VE BEEN PRETTY HIGH ABOVE HIM.
WELL, OF COURSE. THE KILLER FIRED FROM THE BALCONY SECTION UP THERE...

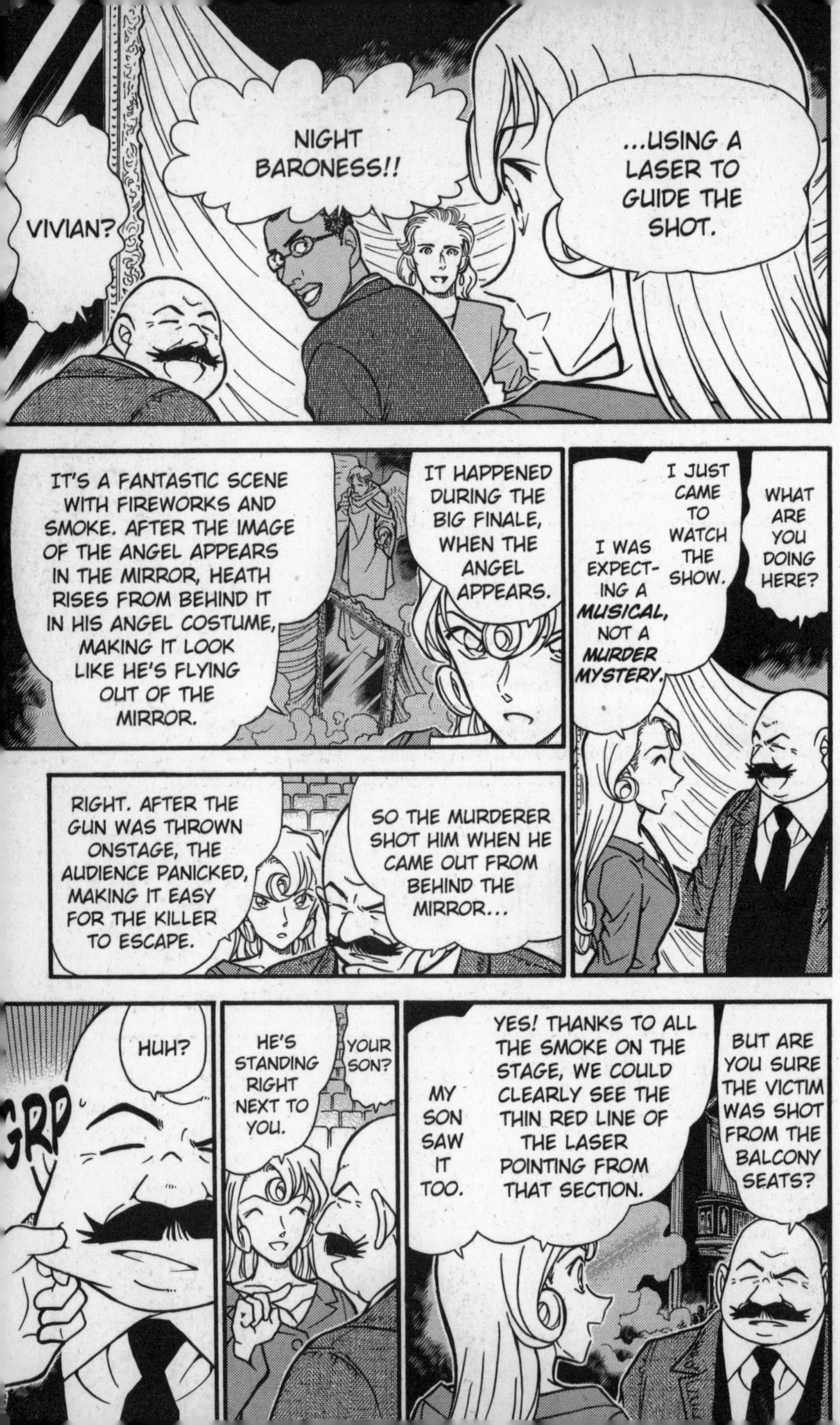
...USING A LASER TO GUIDE THE SHOT.
NIGHT BARONESS!!
VIVIAN?
WHAT ARE YOU DOING HERE?
I JUST CAME TO WATCH THE SHOW.
I WAS EXPECTING A *MUSICAL*, NOT A *MURDER MYSTERY*.
IT HAPPENED DURING THE BIG FINALE, WHEN THE ANGEL APPEARS.
IT'S A FANTASTIC SCENE WITH FIREWORKS AND SMOKE. AFTER THE IMAGE OF THE ANGEL APPEARS IN THE MIRROR, HEATH RISES FROM BEHIND IT IN HIS ANGEL COSTUME, MAKING IT LOOK LIKE HE'S FLYING OUT OF THE MIRROR.
SO THE MURDERER SHOT HIM WHEN HE CAME OUT FROM BEHIND THE MIRROR...
RIGHT. AFTER THE GUN WAS THROWN ONSTAGE, THE AUDIENCE PANICKED, MAKING IT EASY FOR THE KILLER TO ESCAPE.
BUT ARE YOU SURE THE VICTIM WAS SHOT FROM THE BALCONY SEATS?
YES! THANKS TO ALL THE SMOKE ON THE STAGE, WE COULD CLEARLY SEE THE THIN RED LINE OF THE LASER POINTING FROM THAT SECTION.
MY SON SAW IT TOO.
YOUR SON?
HE'S STANDING RIGHT NEXT TO YOU.
HUH?
GRP

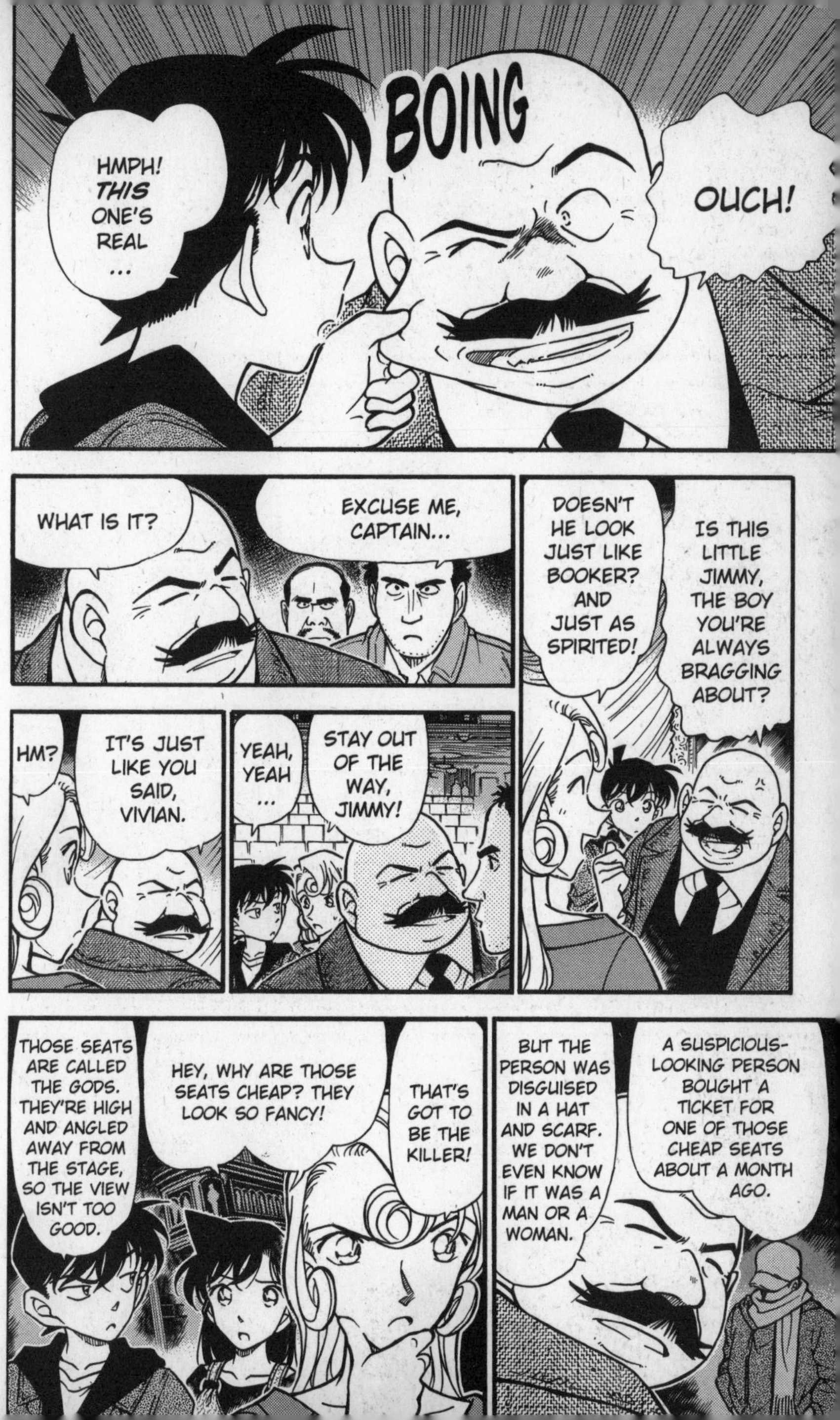
OUCH!
BOING
HMPH! THIS ONE'S REAL ...
IS THIS LITTLE JIMMY, THE BOY YOU'RE ALWAYS BRAGGING ABOUT?
DOESN'T HE LOOK JUST LIKE BOOKER? AND JUST AS SPIRITED!
EXCUSE ME, CAPTAIN...
WHAT IS IT?
STAY OUT OF THE WAY, JIMMY!
YEAH, YEAH ...
IT'S JUST LIKE YOU SAID, VIVIAN.
HM?
A SUSPICIOUS-LOOKING PERSON BOUGHT A TICKET FOR ONE OF THOSE CHEAP SEATS ABOUT A MONTH AGO.
BUT THE PERSON WAS DISGUISED IN A HAT AND SCARF. WE DON'T EVEN KNOW IF IT WAS A MAN OR A WOMAN.
THAT'S GOT TO BE THE KILLER!
HEY, WHY ARE THOSE SEATS CHEAP? THEY LOOK SO FANCY!
THOSE SEATS ARE CALLED THE GODS. THEY'RE HIGH AND ANGLED AWAY FROM THE STAGE, SO THE VIEW ISN'T TOO GOOD.

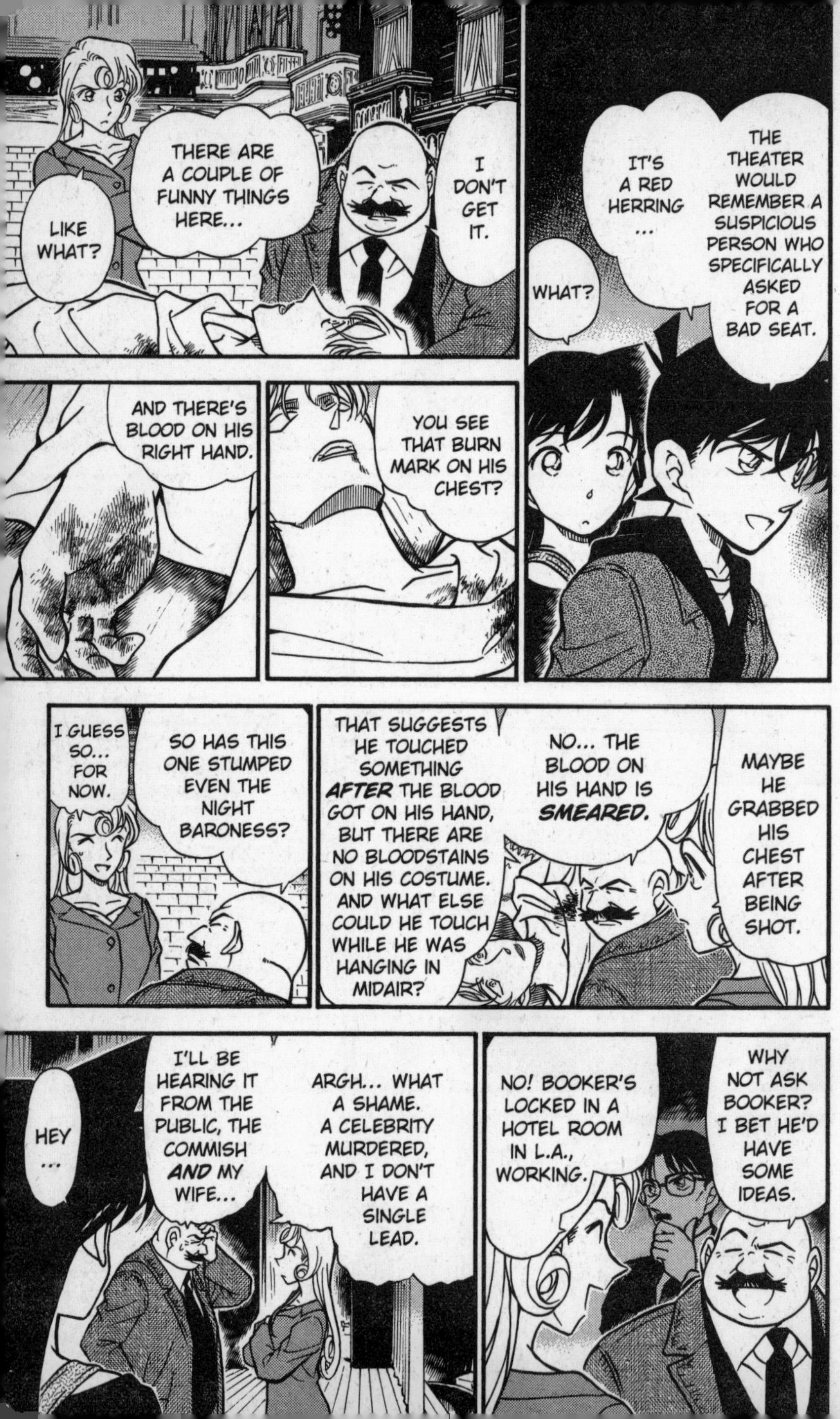
THE THEATER WOULD REMEMBER A SUSPICIOUS PERSON WHO SPECIFICALLY ASKED FOR A BAD SEAT.
IT'S A RED HERRING...
WHAT?
I DON'T GET IT.
THERE ARE A COUPLE OF FUNNY THINGS HERE...
LIKE WHAT?
YOU SEE THAT BURN MARK ON HIS CHEST?
AND THERE'S BLOOD ON HIS RIGHT HAND.
MAYBE HE GRABBED HIS CHEST AFTER BEING SHOT.
NO... THE BLOOD ON HIS HAND IS ***SMEARED.***
THAT SUGGESTS HE TOUCHED SOMETHING ***AFTER*** THE BLOOD GOT ON HIS HAND, BUT THERE ARE NO BLOODSTAINS ON HIS COSTUME. AND WHAT ELSE COULD HE TOUCH WHILE HE WAS HANGING IN MIDAIR?
SO HAS THIS ONE STUMPED EVEN THE NIGHT BARONESS?
I GUESS SO... FOR NOW.
WHY NOT ASK BOOKER? I BET HE'D HAVE SOME IDEAS.
NO! BOOKER'S LOCKED IN A HOTEL ROOM IN L.A., WORKING.
ARGH... WHAT A SHAME. A CELEBRITY MURDERED, AND I DON'T HAVE A SINGLE LEAD.
I'LL BE HEARING IT FROM THE PUBLIC, THE COMMISH ***AND*** MY WIFE...
HEY...

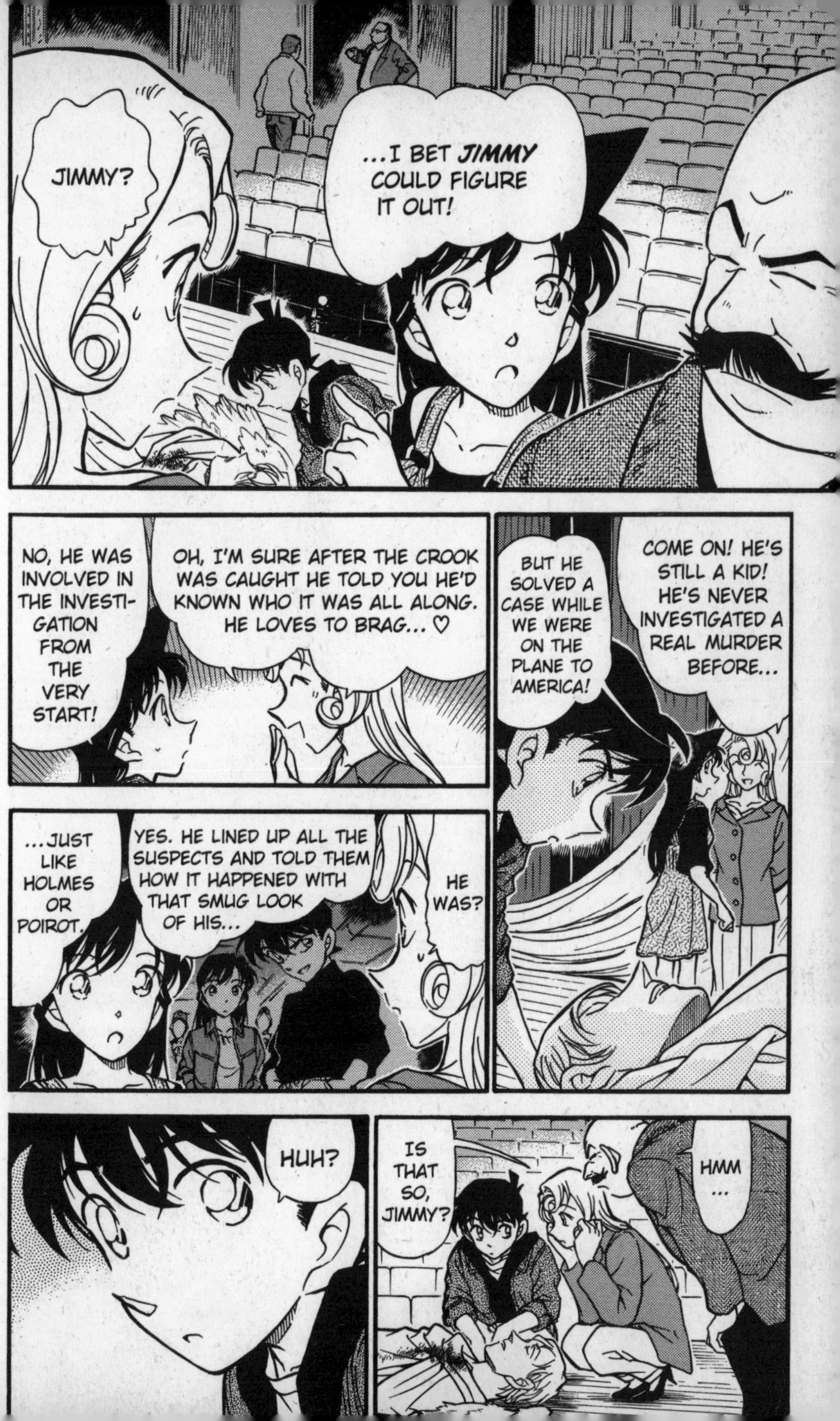
...I BET JIMMY COULD FIGURE IT OUT!
JIMMY?
COME ON! HE'S STILL A KID! HE'S NEVER INVESTIGATED A REAL MURDER BEFORE...
BUT HE SOLVED A CASE WHILE WE WERE ON THE PLANE TO AMERICA!
OH, I'M SURE AFTER THE CROOK WAS CAUGHT HE TOLD YOU HE'D KNOWN WHO IT WAS ALL ALONG. HE LOVES TO BRAG... ♡
NO, HE WAS INVOLVED IN THE INVESTIGATION FROM THE VERY START!
HE WAS?
YES. HE LINED UP ALL THE SUSPECTS AND TOLD THEM HOW IT HAPPENED WITH THAT SMUG LOOK OF HIS...
...JUST LIKE HOLMES OR POIROT.
HMM...
IS THAT SO, JIMMY?
HUH?

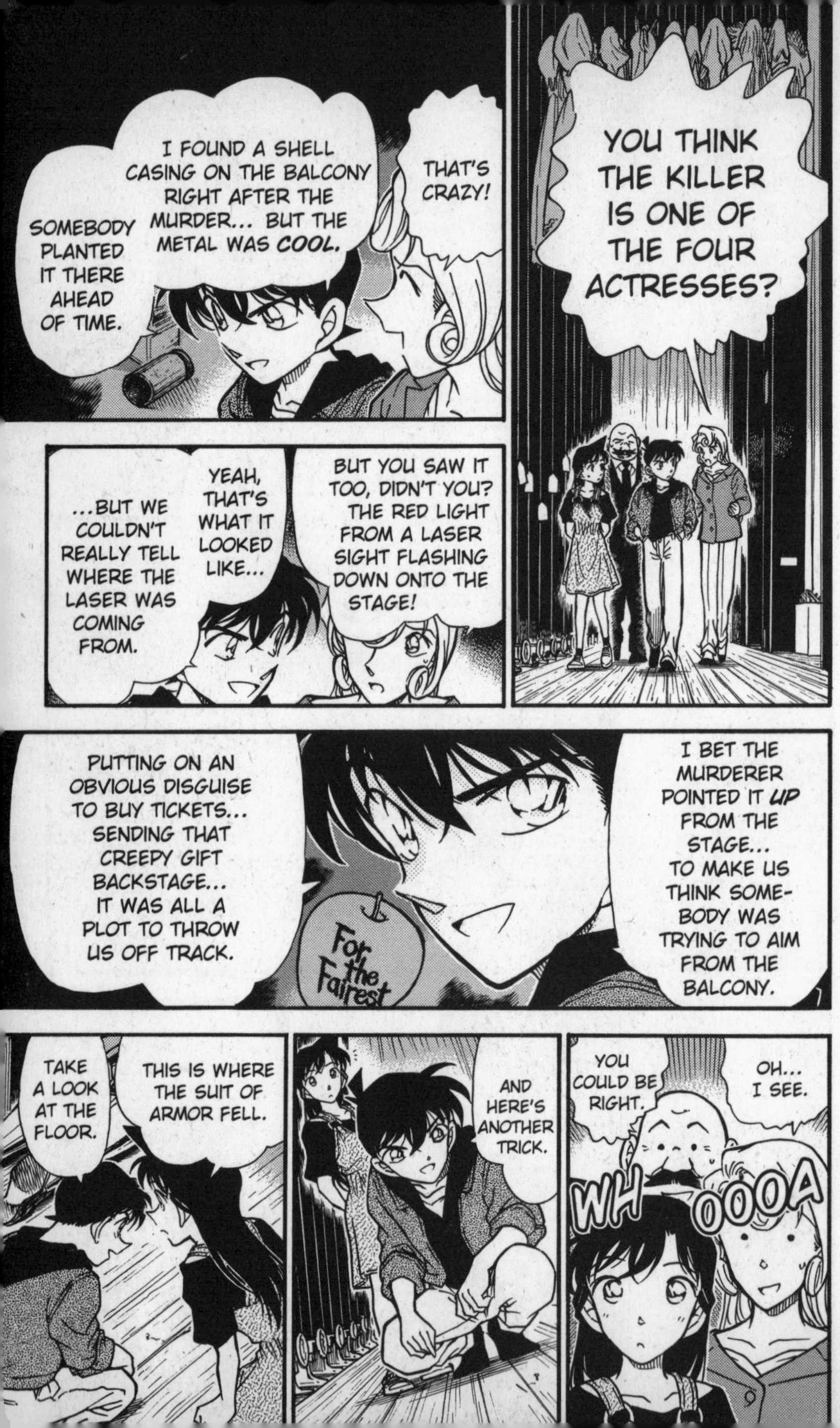
YOU THINK THE KILLER IS ONE OF THE FOUR ACTRESSES?
THAT'S CRAZY!
I FOUND A SHELL CASING ON THE BALCONY RIGHT AFTER THE MURDER... BUT THE METAL WAS *COOL.*
SOMEBODY PLANTED IT THERE AHEAD OF TIME.
BUT YOU SAW IT TOO, DIDN'T YOU? THE RED LIGHT FROM A LASER SIGHT FLASHING DOWN ONTO THE STAGE!
YEAH, THAT'S WHAT IT LOOKED LIKE...
...BUT WE COULDN'T REALLY TELL WHERE THE LASER WAS COMING FROM.
I BET THE MURDERER POINTED IT *UP* FROM THE STAGE... TO MAKE US THINK SOMEBODY WAS TRYING TO AIM FROM THE BALCONY.
For the Fairest
PUTTING ON AN OBVIOUS DISGUISE TO BUY TICKETS... SENDING THAT CREEPY GIFT BACKSTAGE... IT WAS ALL A PLOT TO THROW US OFF TRACK.
OH... I SEE.
YOU COULD BE RIGHT.
WHOOOA
AND HERE'S ANOTHER TRICK.
THIS IS WHERE THE SUIT OF ARMOR FELL.
TAKE A LOOK AT THE FLOOR.

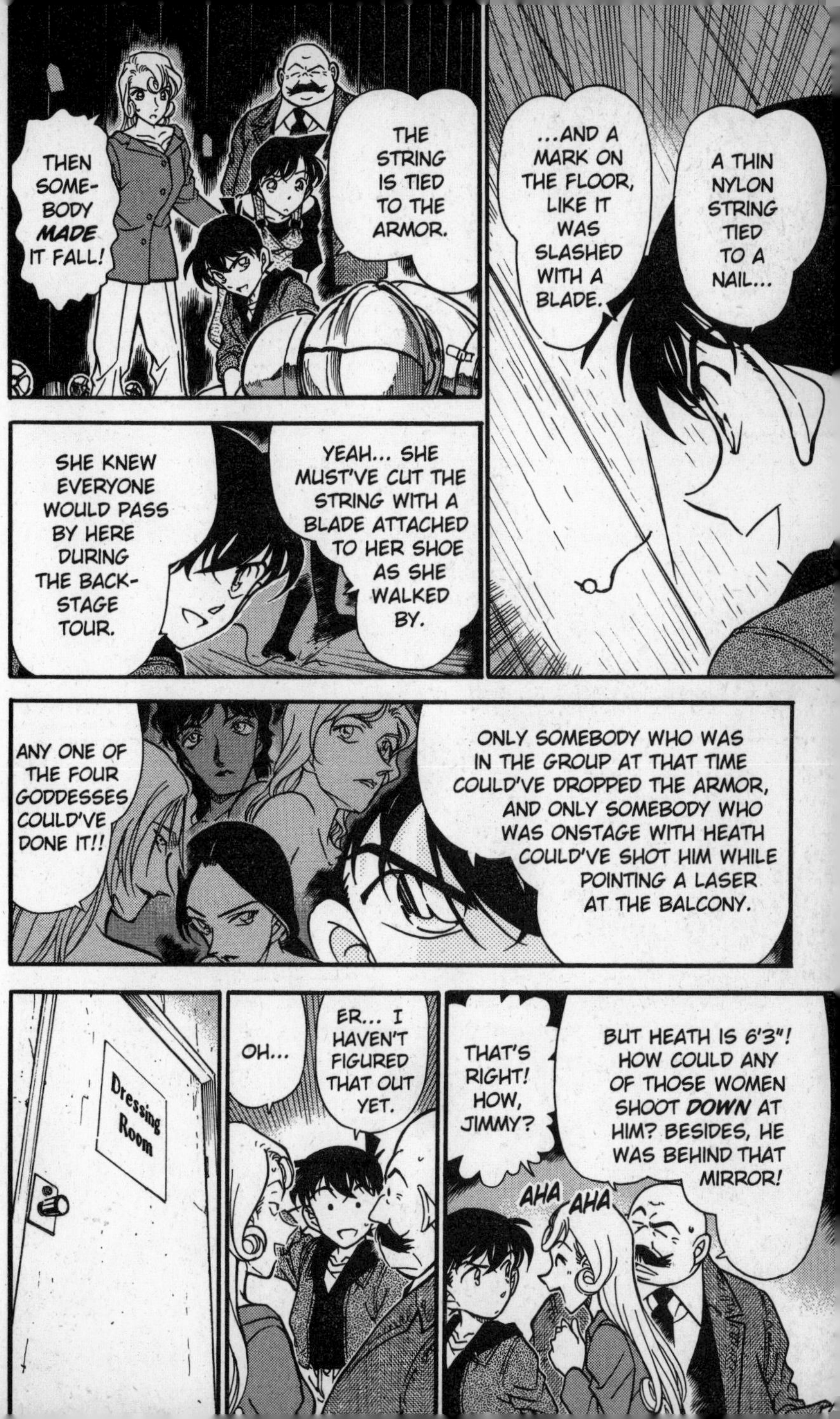
A THIN NYLON STRING TIED TO A NAIL...
...AND A MARK ON THE FLOOR, LIKE IT WAS SLASHED WITH A BLADE.
THE STRING IS TIED TO THE ARMOR.
THEN SOMEBODY *MADE* IT FALL!
YEAH... SHE MUST'VE CUT THE STRING WITH A BLADE ATTACHED TO HER SHOE AS SHE WALKED BY.
SHE KNEW EVERYONE WOULD PASS BY HERE DURING THE BACK-STAGE TOUR.
ONLY SOMEBODY WHO WAS IN THE GROUP AT THAT TIME COULD'VE DROPPED THE ARMOR, AND ONLY SOMEBODY WHO WAS ONSTAGE WITH HEATH COULD'VE SHOT HIM WHILE POINTING A LASER AT THE BALCONY.
ANY ONE OF THE FOUR GODDESSES COULD'VE DONE IT!!
BUT HEATH IS 6'3"! HOW COULD ANY OF THOSE WOMEN SHOOT *DOWN* AT HIM? BESIDES, HE WAS BEHIND THAT MIRROR!
THAT'S RIGHT! HOW, JIMMY?
AHA
AHA
ER... I HAVEN'T FIGURED THAT OUT YET.
OH...
Dressing Room

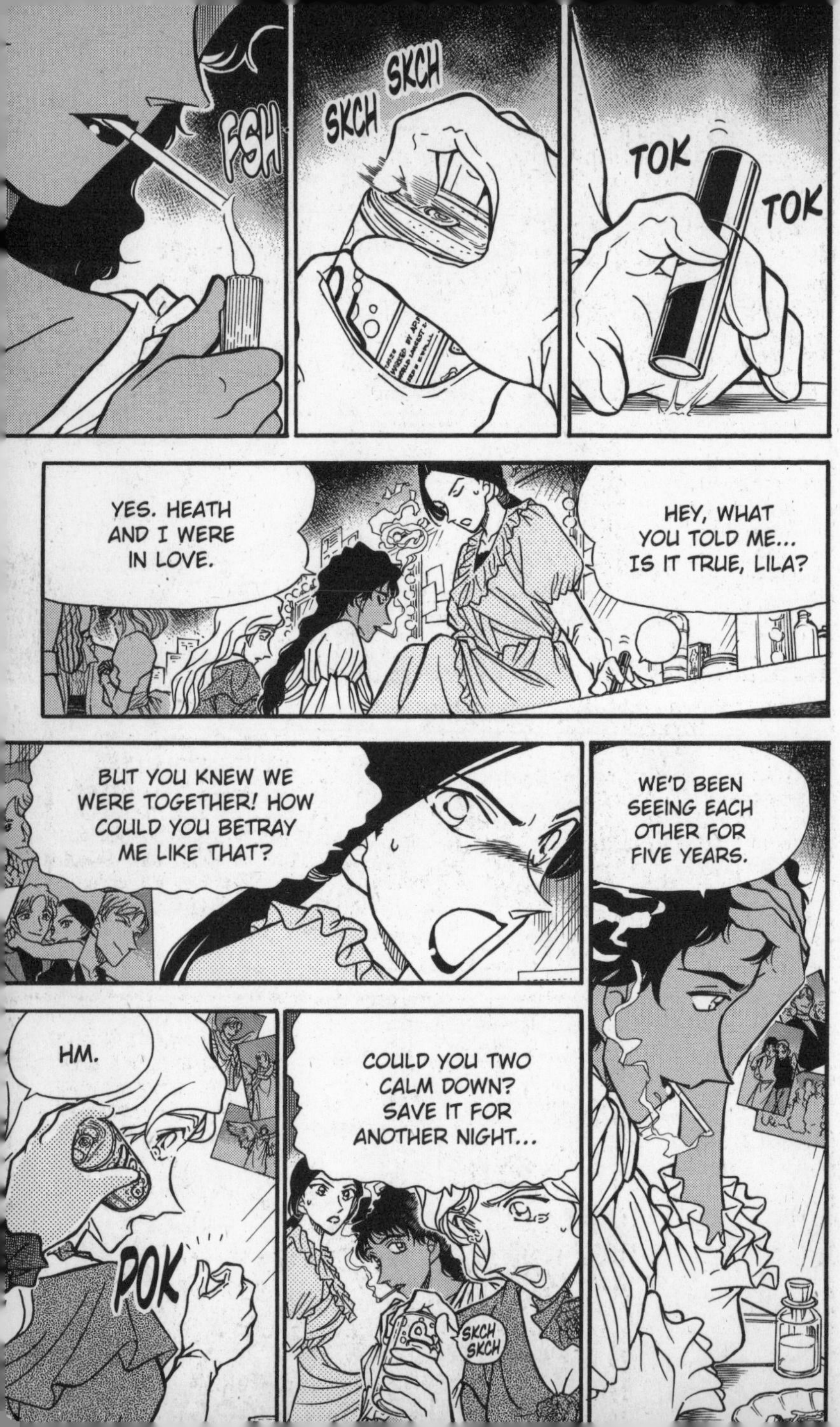
TOK
TOK
SKCH
SKCH
FSH
HEY, WHAT YOU TOLD ME... IS IT TRUE, LILA?
YES. HEATH AND I WERE IN LOVE.
WE'D BEEN SEEING EACH OTHER FOR FIVE YEARS.
BUT YOU KNEW WE WERE TOGETHER! HOW COULD YOU BETRAY ME LIKE THAT?
COULD YOU TWO CALM DOWN? SAVE IT FOR ANOTHER NIGHT...
SKCH SKCH
HM.
POK

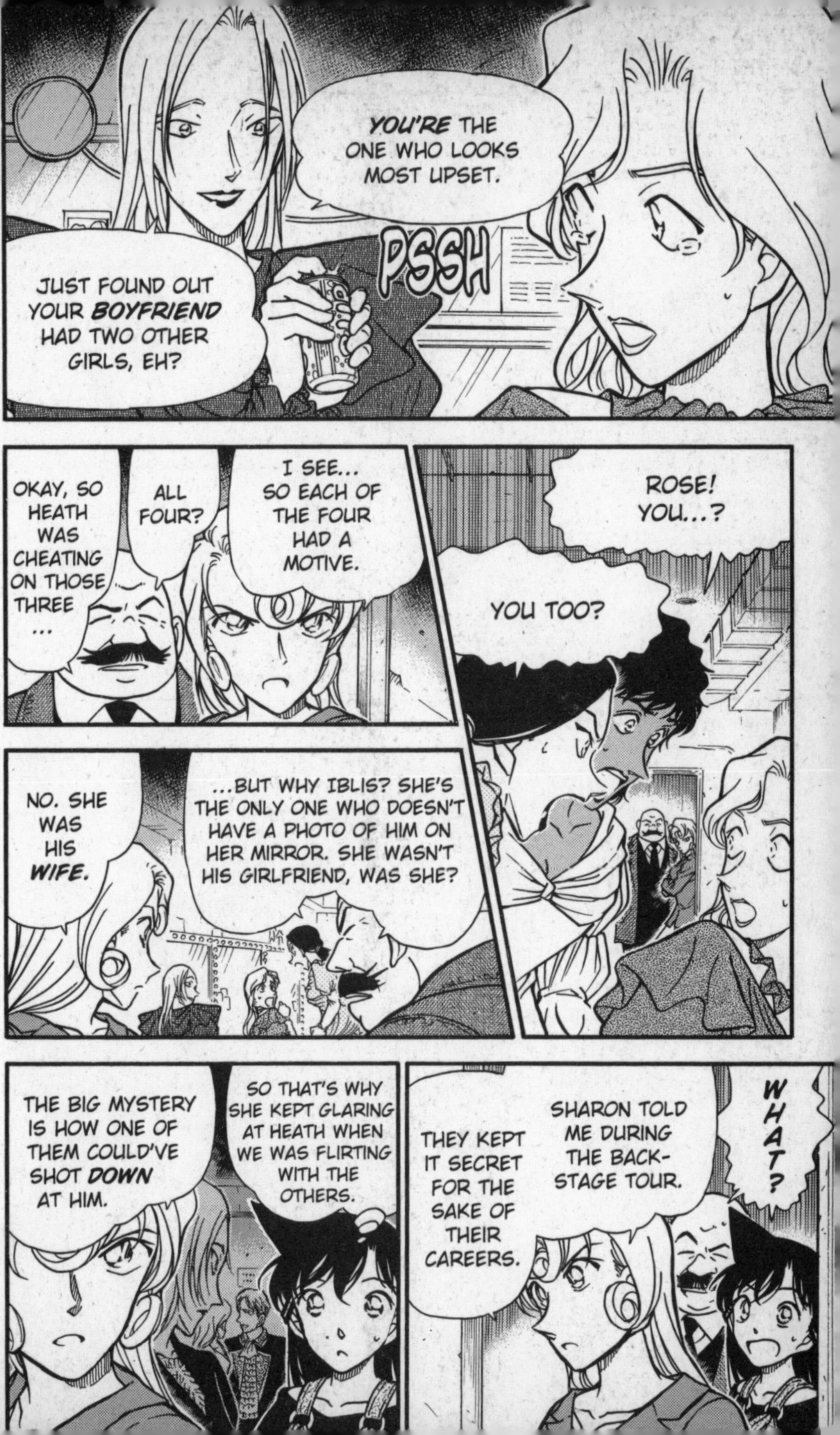
YOU'RE THE ONE WHO LOOKS MOST UPSET.
PSSH
JUST FOUND OUT YOUR BOYFRIEND HAD TWO OTHER GIRLS, EH?
ROSE! YOU...?
YOU TOO?
I SEE... SO EACH OF THE FOUR HAD A MOTIVE.
ALL FOUR?
OKAY, SO HEATH WAS CHEATING ON THOSE THREE ...
...BUT WHY IBLIS? SHE'S THE ONLY ONE WHO DOESN'T HAVE A PHOTO OF HIM ON HER MIRROR. SHE WASN'T HIS GIRLFRIEND, WAS SHE?
NO. SHE WAS HIS WIFE.
WHAT?
SHARON TOLD ME DURING THE BACK-STAGE TOUR.
THEY KEPT IT SECRET FOR THE SAKE OF THEIR CAREERS.
SO THAT'S WHY SHE KEPT GLARING AT HEATH WHEN WE WAS FLIRTING WITH THE OTHERS.
THE BIG MYSTERY IS HOW ONE OF THEM COULD'VE SHOT DOWN AT HIM.

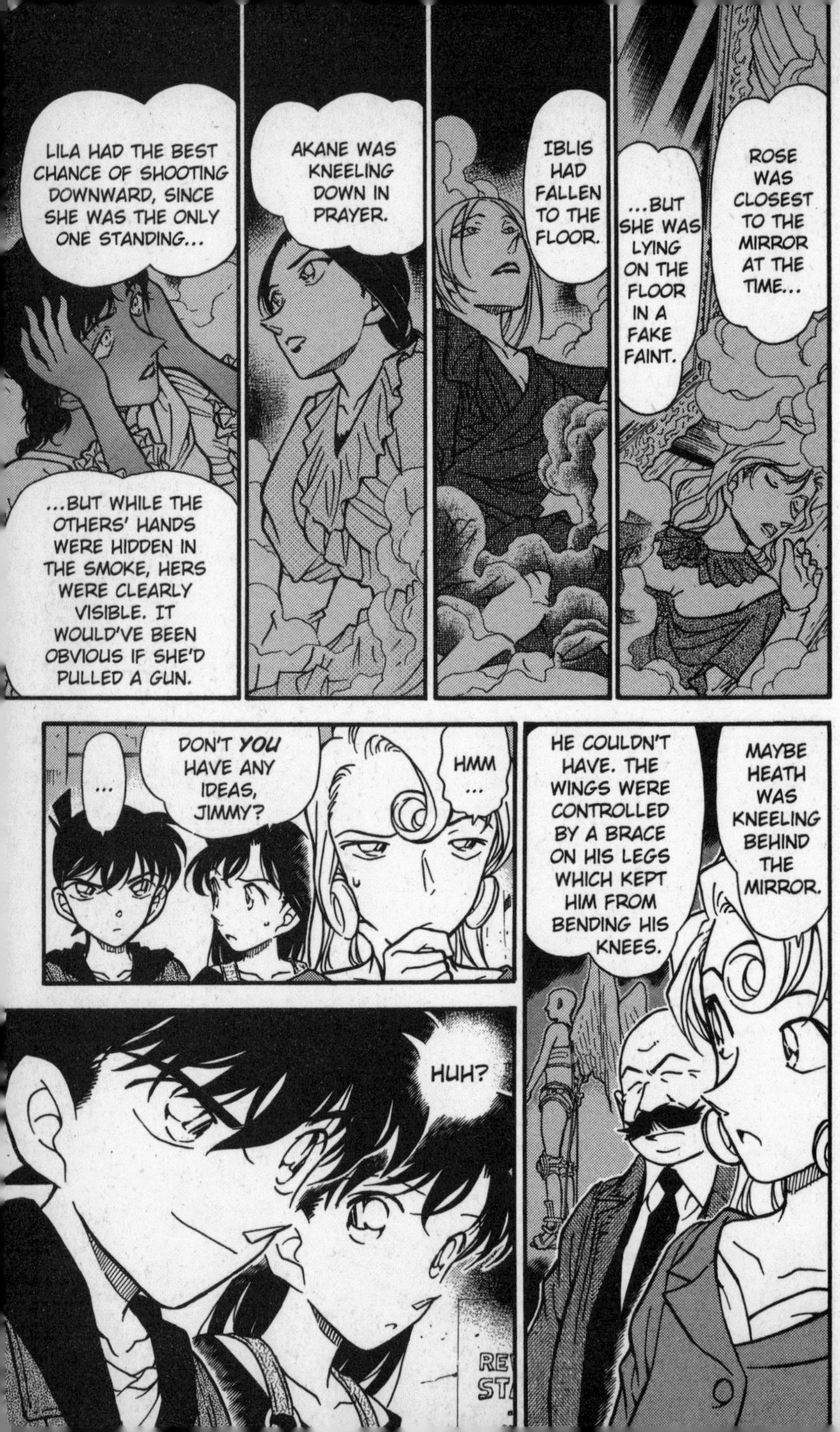
ROSE WAS CLOSEST TO THE MIRROR AT THE TIME...
...BUT SHE WAS LYING ON THE FLOOR IN A FAKE FAINT.
IBLIS HAD FALLEN TO THE FLOOR.
AKANE WAS KNEELING DOWN IN PRAYER.
LILA HAD THE BEST CHANCE OF SHOOTING DOWNWARD, SINCE SHE WAS THE ONLY ONE STANDING...
...BUT WHILE THE OTHERS' HANDS WERE HIDDEN IN THE SMOKE, HERS WERE CLEARLY VISIBLE. IT WOULD'VE BEEN OBVIOUS IF SHE'D PULLED A GUN.
MAYBE HEATH WAS KNEELING BEHIND THE MIRROR.
HE COULDN'T HAVE. THE WINGS WERE CONTROLLED BY A BRACE ON HIS LEGS WHICH KEPT HIM FROM BENDING HIS KNEES.
HMM ...
DON'T *YOU* HAVE ANY IDEAS, JIMMY?
...
HUH?

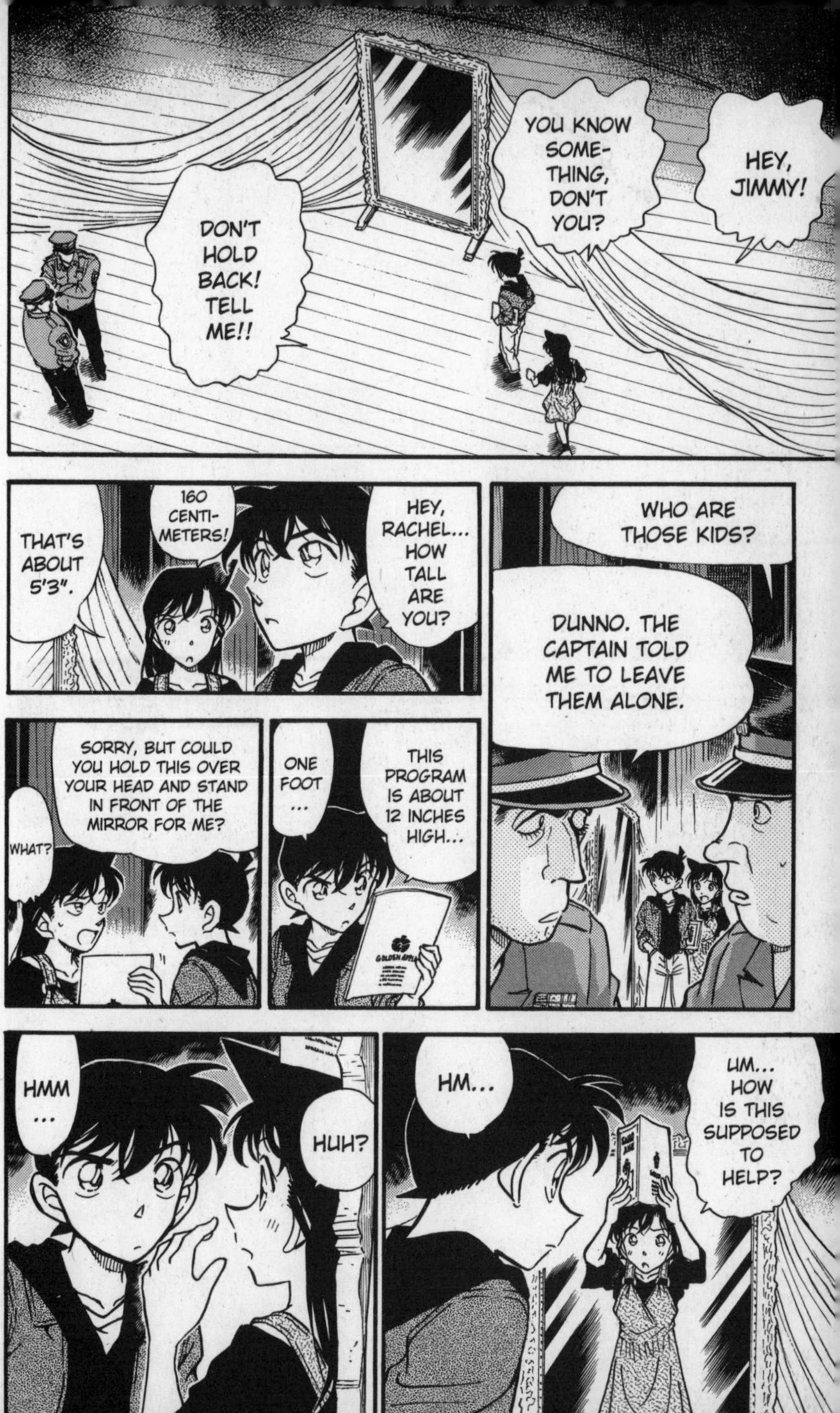
HEY, JIMMY!
YOU KNOW SOME-THING, DON'T YOU?
DON'T HOLD BACK! TELL ME!!
WHO ARE THOSE KIDS?
DUNNO. THE CAPTAIN TOLD ME TO LEAVE THEM ALONE.
HEY, RACHEL... HOW TALL ARE YOU?
160 CENTI-METERS!
THAT'S ABOUT 5'3".
THIS PROGRAM IS ABOUT 12 INCHES HIGH...
ONE FOOT ...
SORRY, BUT COULD YOU HOLD THIS OVER YOUR HEAD AND STAND IN FRONT OF THE MIRROR FOR ME?
WHAT?
UM... HOW IS THIS SUPPOSED TO HELP?
HM...
HUH?
HMM ...

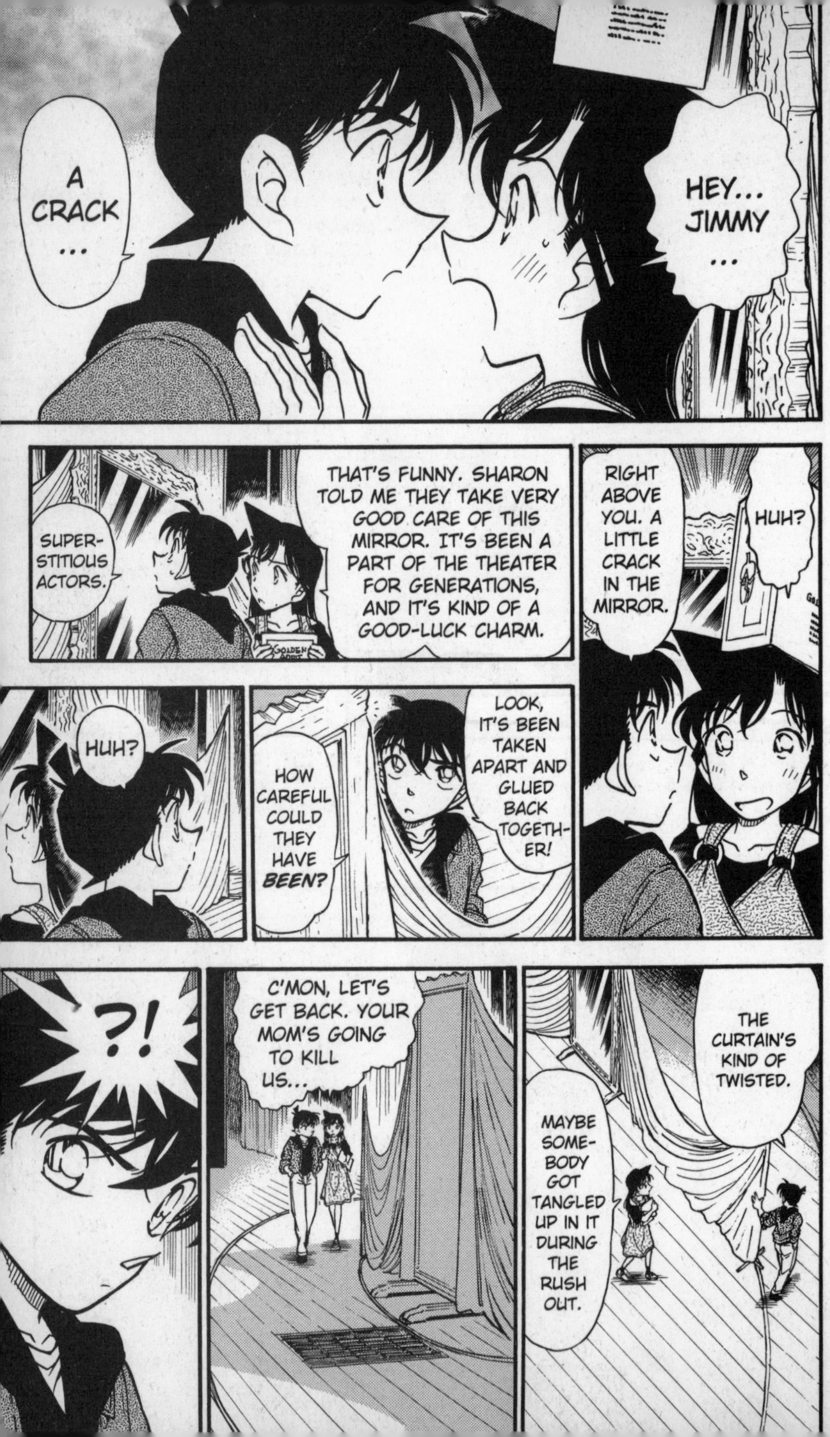
HEY... JIMMY ...
A CRACK ...
HUH?
RIGHT ABOVE YOU. A LITTLE CRACK IN THE MIRROR.
THAT'S FUNNY. SHARON TOLD ME THEY TAKE VERY GOOD CARE OF THIS MIRROR. IT'S BEEN A PART OF THE THEATER FOR GENERATIONS, AND IT'S KIND OF A GOOD-LUCK CHARM.
SUPER-STITIOUS ACTORS.
LOOK, IT'S BEEN TAKEN APART AND GLUED BACK TOGETH-ER!
HOW CAREFUL COULD THEY HAVE *BEEN?*
HUH?
THE CURTAIN'S KIND OF TWISTED.
MAYBE SOME-BODY GOT TANGLED UP IN IT DURING THE RUSH OUT.
C'MON, LET'S GET BACK. YOUR MOM'S GOING TO KILL US...
?!

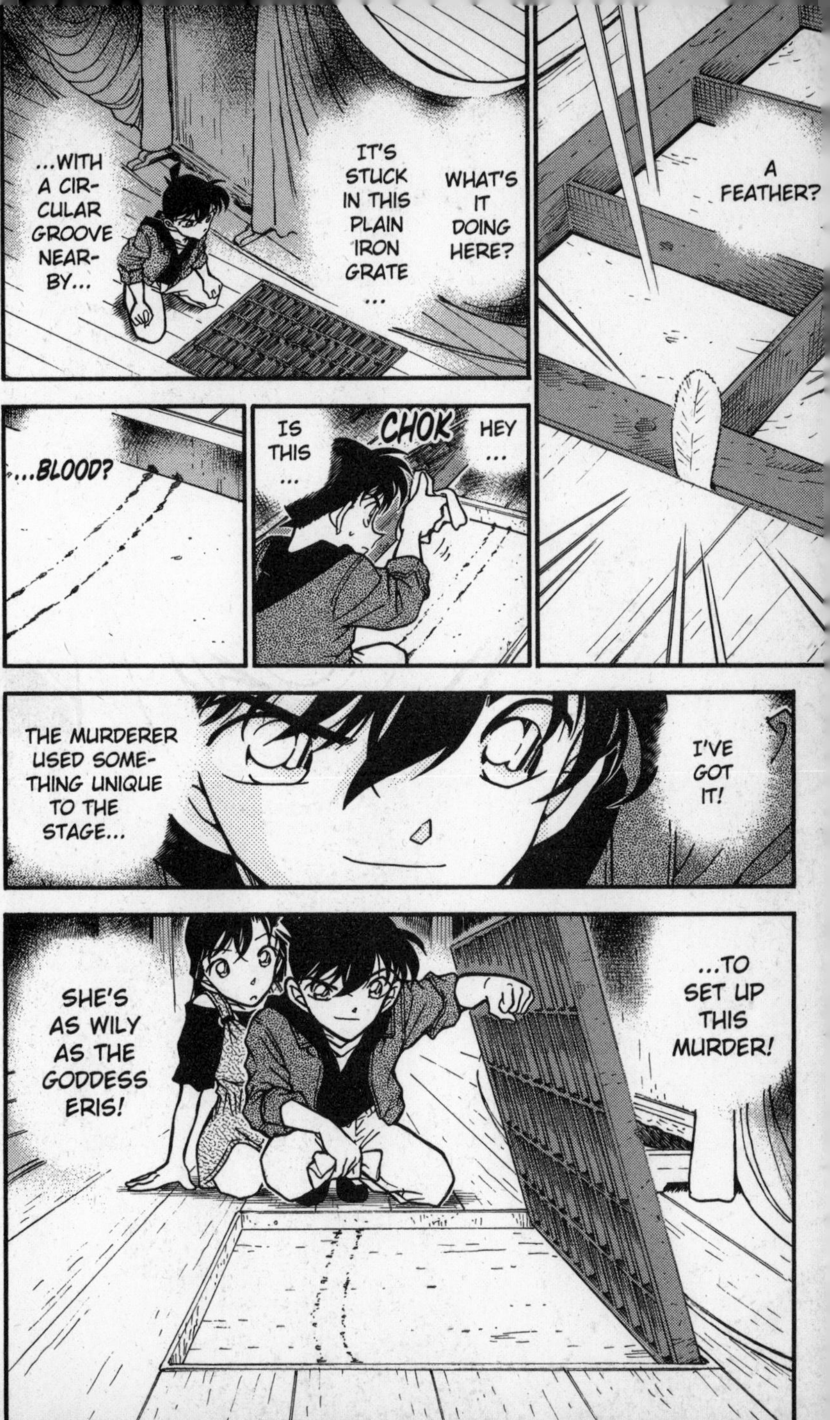
A FEATHER?
WHAT'S IT DOING HERE?
IT'S STUCK IN THIS PLAIN IRON GRATE...
...WITH A CIR-CULAR GROOVE NEAR-BY...
HEY...
CHOK
IS THIS...
...BLOOD?
I'VE GOT IT!
THE MURDERER USED SOME-THING UNIQUE TO THE STAGE...
...TO SET UP THIS MURDER!
SHE'S AS WILY AS THE GODDESS ERIS!

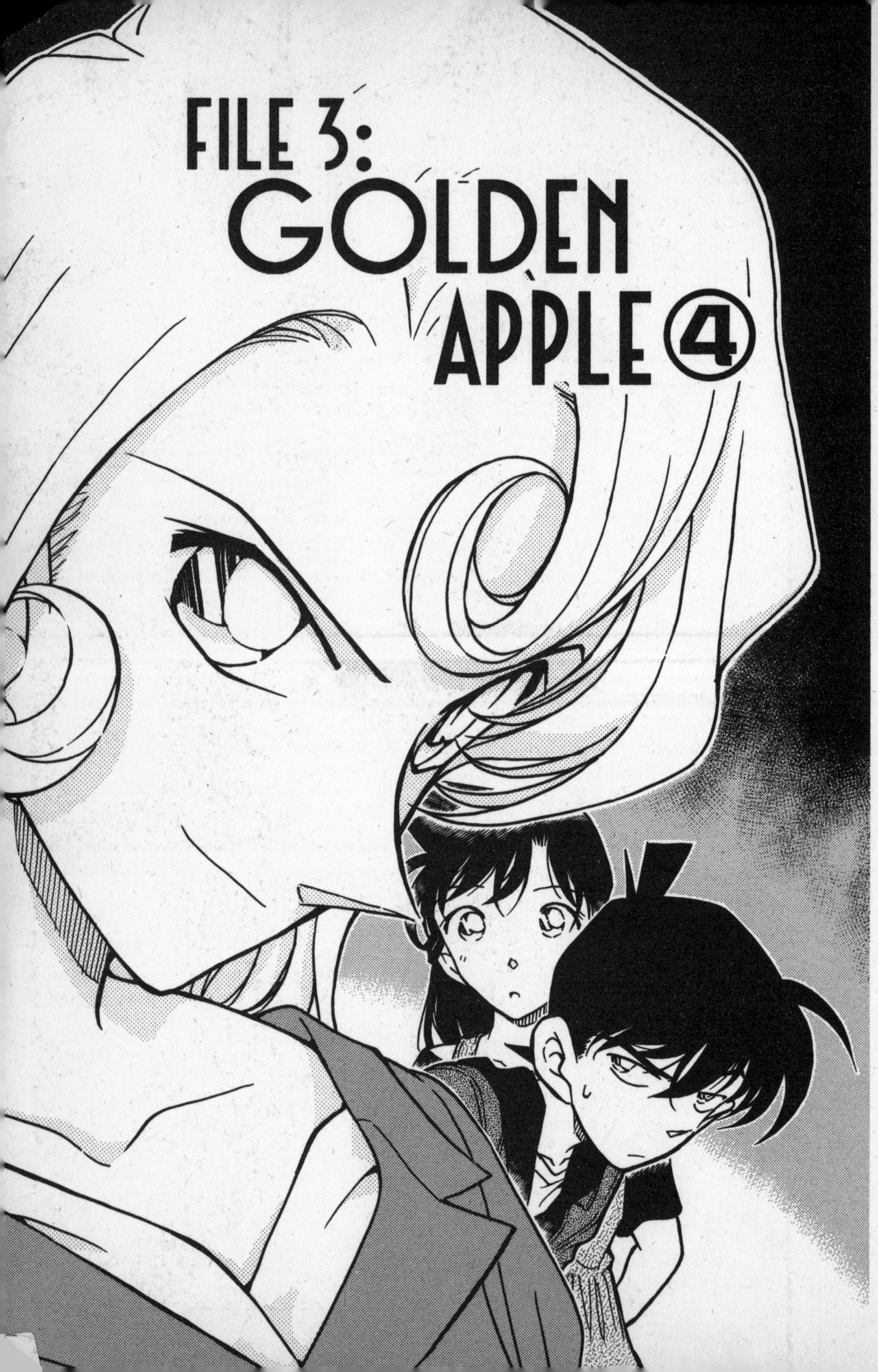
FILE 3:
GOLDEN APPLE ④

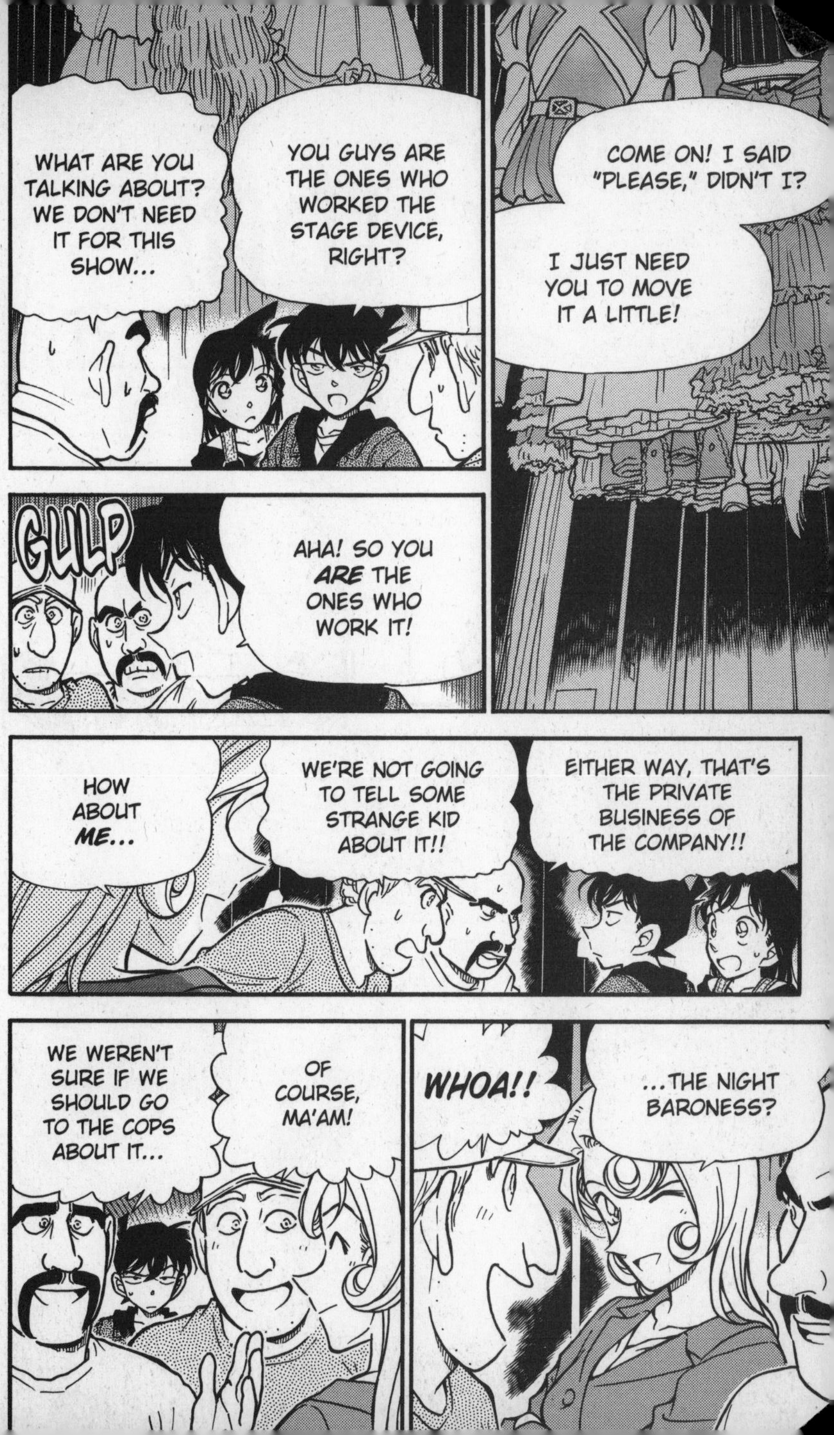
COME ON! I SAID "PLEASE," DIDN'T I?
I JUST NEED YOU TO MOVE IT A LITTLE!
YOU GUYS ARE THE ONES WHO WORKED THE STAGE DEVICE, RIGHT?
WHAT ARE YOU TALKING ABOUT? WE DON'T NEED IT FOR THIS SHOW...
AHA! SO YOU ARE THE ONES WHO WORK IT!
GULP
EITHER WAY, THAT'S THE PRIVATE BUSINESS OF THE COMPANY!!
WE'RE NOT GOING TO TELL SOME STRANGE KID ABOUT IT!!
HOW ABOUT ME...
...THE NIGHT BARONESS?
WHOA!!
OF COURSE, MA'AM!
WE WEREN'T SURE IF WE SHOULD GO TO THE COPS ABOUT IT...

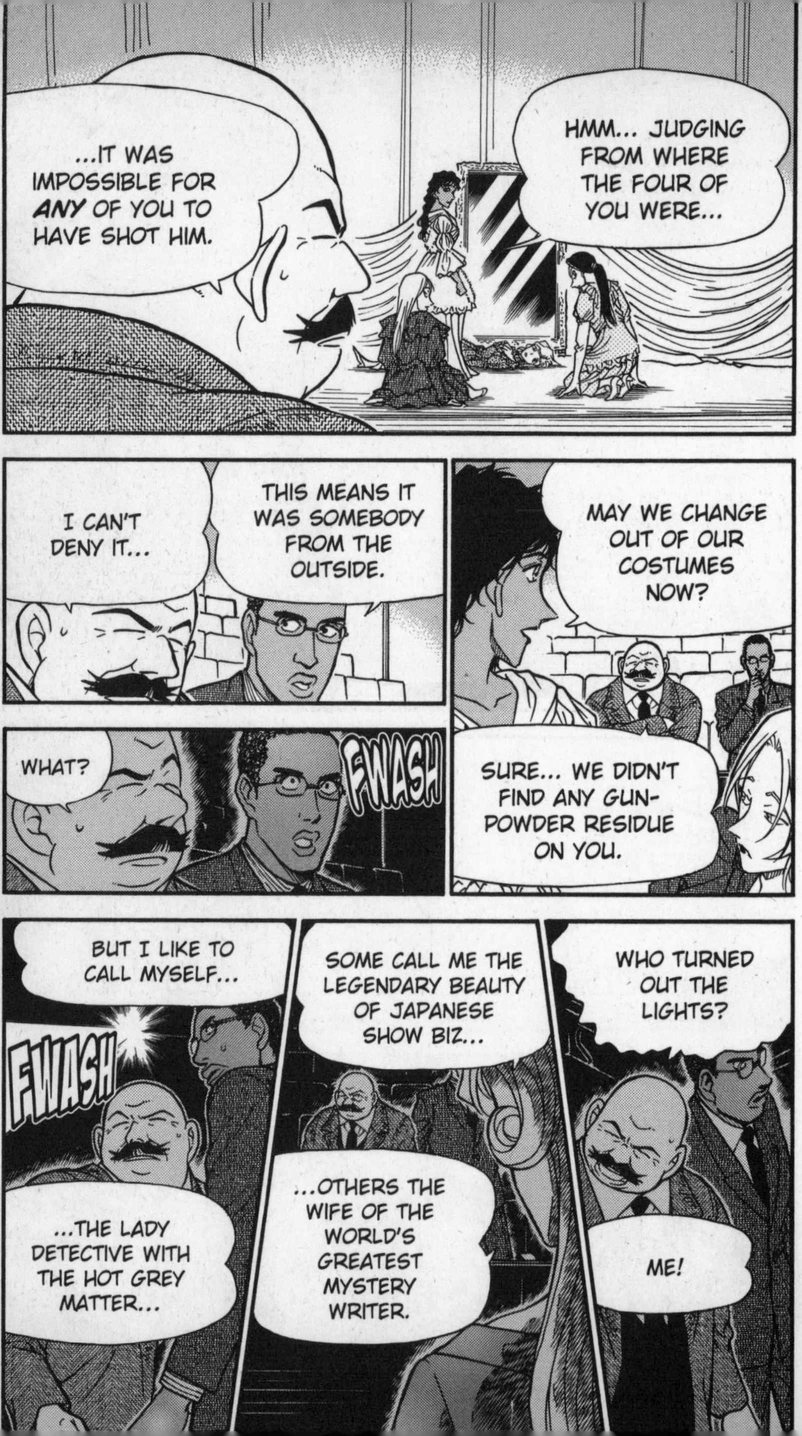
HMM... JUDGING FROM WHERE THE FOUR OF YOU WERE...
...IT WAS IMPOSSIBLE FOR ANY OF YOU TO HAVE SHOT HIM.
MAY WE CHANGE OUT OF OUR COSTUMES NOW?
SURE... WE DIDN'T FIND ANY GUN-POWDER RESIDUE ON YOU.
THIS MEANS IT WAS SOMEBODY FROM THE OUTSIDE.
I CAN'T DENY IT...
FWASH
WHAT?
WHO TURNED OUT THE LIGHTS?
ME!
SOME CALL ME THE LEGENDARY BEAUTY OF JAPANESE SHOW BIZ...
...OTHERS THE WIFE OF THE WORLD'S GREATEST MYSTERY WRITER.
FWASH
BUT I LIKE TO CALL MYSELF...
...THE LADY DETECTIVE WITH THE HOT GREY MATTER...

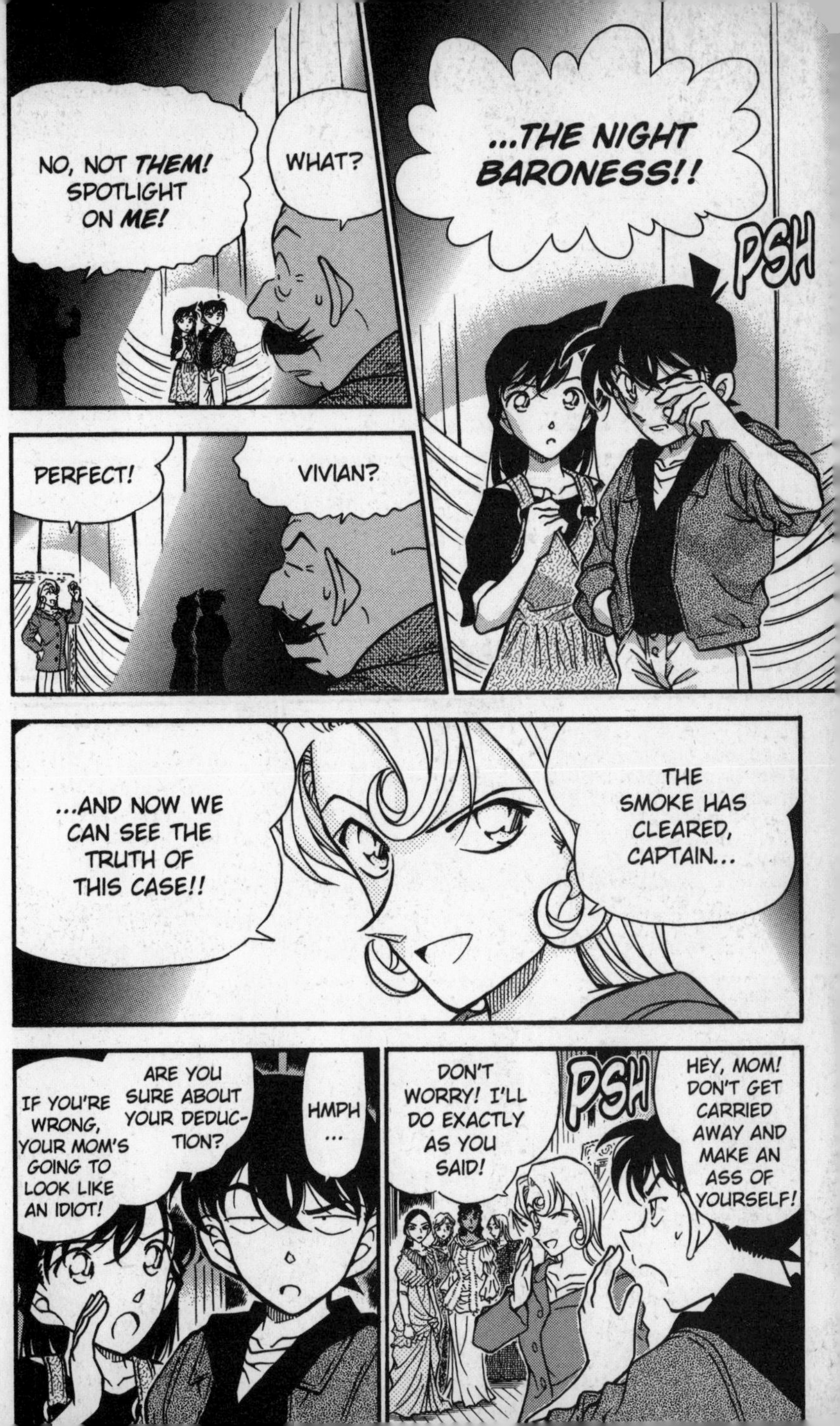
...THE NIGHT BARONESS!!
PSH
WHAT?
NO, NOT THEM! SPOTLIGHT ON ME!
VIVIAN?
PERFECT!
THE SMOKE HAS CLEARED, CAPTAIN...
...AND NOW WE CAN SEE THE TRUTH OF THIS CASE!!
HEY, MOM! DON'T GET CARRIED AWAY AND MAKE AN ASS OF YOURSELF!
PSH
DON'T WORRY! I'LL DO EXACTLY AS YOU SAID!
HMPH ...
ARE YOU SURE ABOUT YOUR DEDUCTION?
IF YOU'RE WRONG, YOUR MOM'S GOING TO LOOK LIKE AN IDIOT!

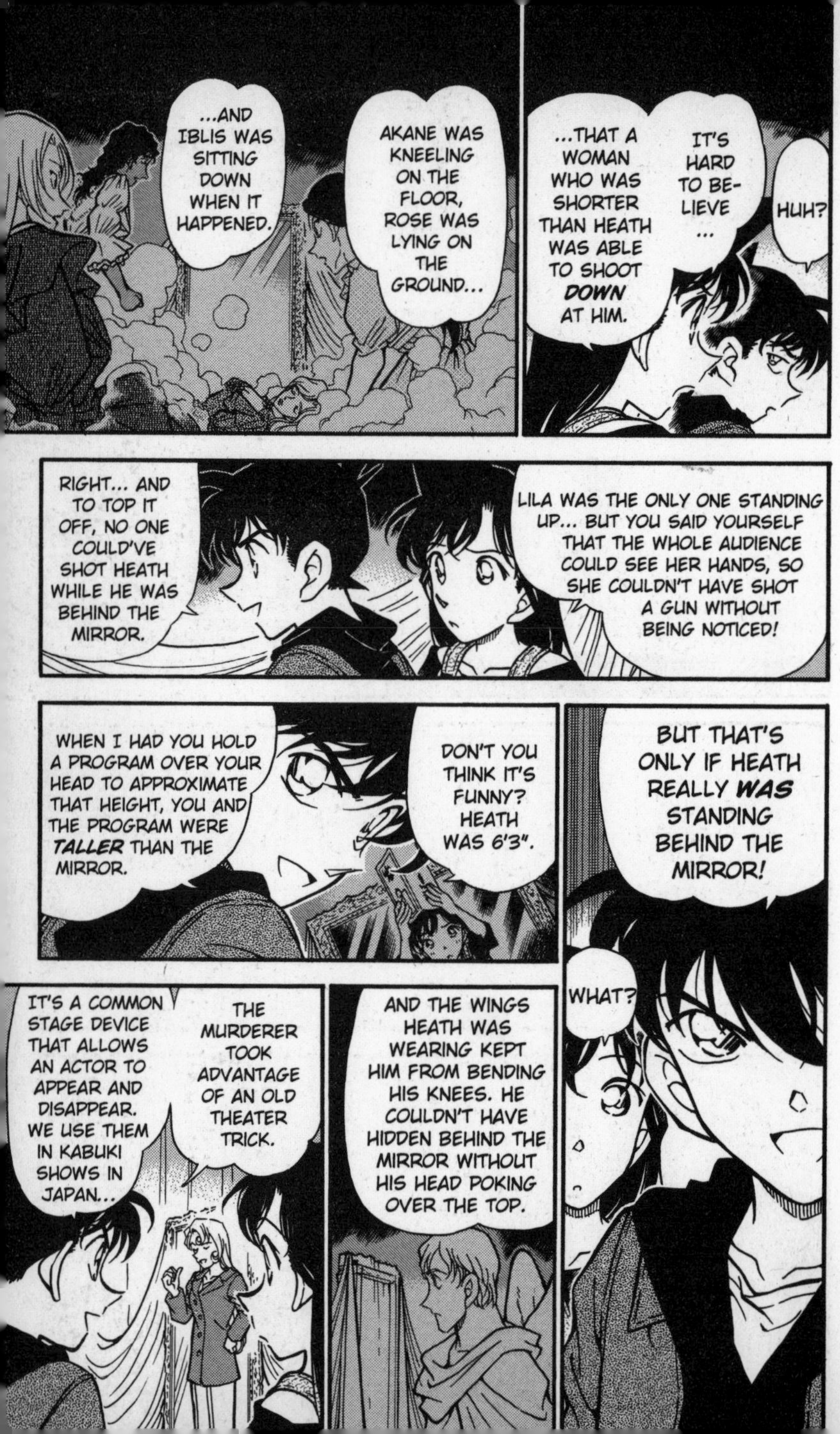
HUH?
IT'S HARD TO BE-LIEVE ...
...THAT A WOMAN WHO WAS SHORTER THAN HEATH WAS ABLE TO SHOOT DOWN AT HIM.
AKANE WAS KNEELING ON THE FLOOR, ROSE WAS LYING ON THE GROUND...
...AND IBLIS WAS SITTING DOWN WHEN IT HAPPENED.
LILA WAS THE ONLY ONE STANDING UP... BUT YOU SAID YOURSELF THAT THE WHOLE AUDIENCE COULD SEE HER HANDS, SO SHE COULDN'T HAVE SHOT A GUN WITHOUT BEING NOTICED!
RIGHT... AND TO TOP IT OFF, NO ONE COULD'VE SHOT HEATH WHILE HE WAS BEHIND THE MIRROR.
BUT THAT'S ONLY IF HEATH REALLY WAS STANDING BEHIND THE MIRROR!
WHAT?
DON'T YOU THINK IT'S FUNNY? HEATH WAS 6'3".
WHEN I HAD YOU HOLD A PROGRAM OVER YOUR HEAD TO APPROXIMATE THAT HEIGHT, YOU AND THE PROGRAM WERE TALLER THAN THE MIRROR.
AND THE WINGS HEATH WAS WEARING KEPT HIM FROM BENDING HIS KNEES. HE COULDN'T HAVE HIDDEN BEHIND THE MIRROR WITHOUT HIS HEAD POKING OVER THE TOP.
THE MURDERER TOOK ADVANTAGE OF AN OLD THEATER TRICK.
IT'S A COMMON STAGE DEVICE THAT ALLOWS AN ACTOR TO APPEAR AND DISAPPEAR. WE USE THEM IN KABUKI SHOWS IN JAPAN...

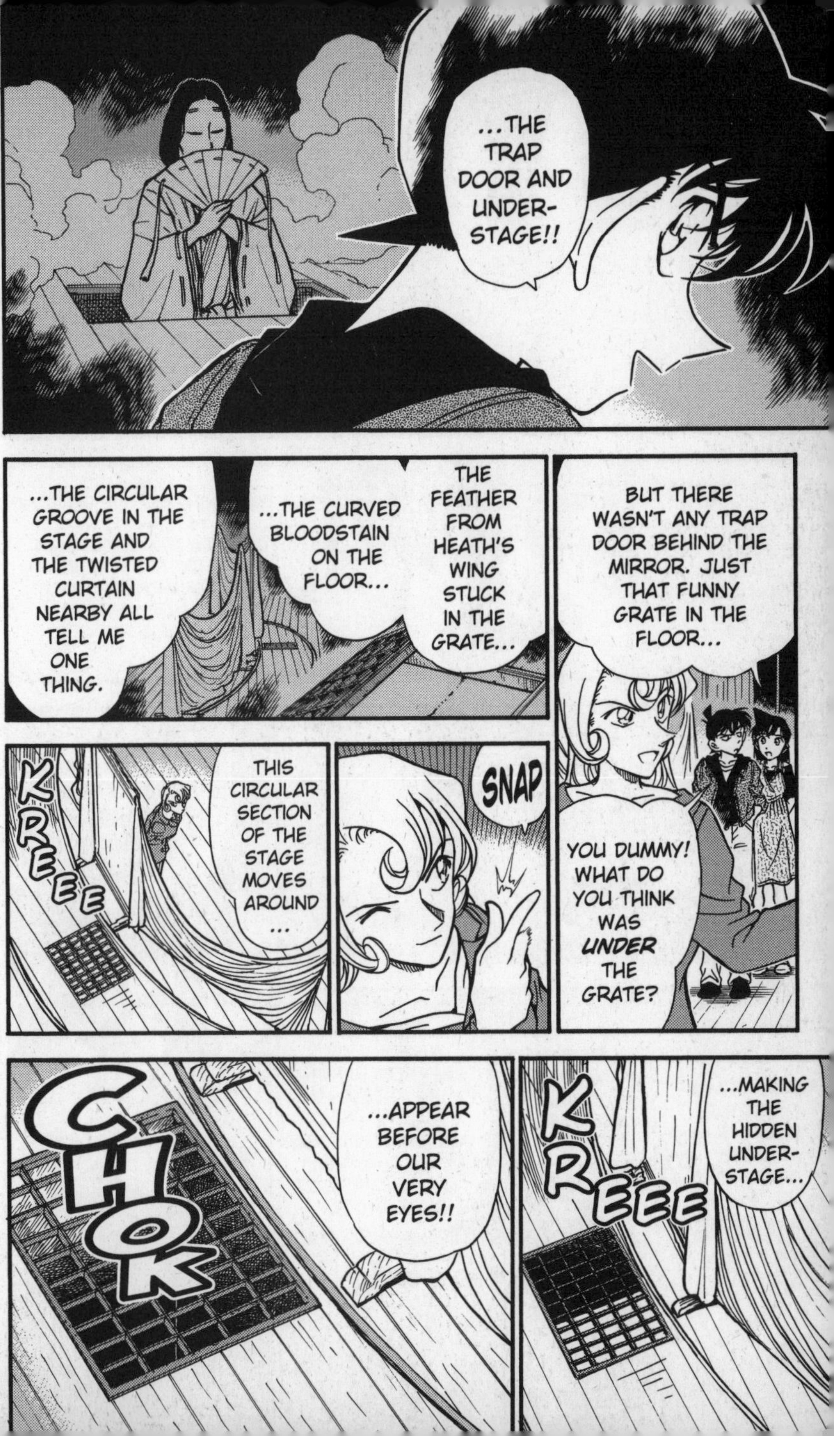
...THE TRAP DOOR AND UNDER-STAGE!!
BUT THERE WASN'T ANY TRAP DOOR BEHIND THE MIRROR. JUST THAT FUNNY GRATE IN THE FLOOR...
YOU DUMMY! WHAT DO YOU THINK WAS *UNDER* THE GRATE?
THE FEATHER FROM HEATH'S WING STUCK IN THE GRATE...
...THE CURVED BLOODSTAIN ON THE FLOOR...
...THE CIRCULAR GROOVE IN THE STAGE AND THE TWISTED CURTAIN NEARBY ALL TELL ME ONE THING.
SNAP
THIS CIRCULAR SECTION OF THE STAGE MOVES AROUND ...
KREEEE
...MAKING THE HIDDEN UNDER-STAGE...
KREEEE
...APPEAR BEFORE OUR VERY EYES!!
CHOK

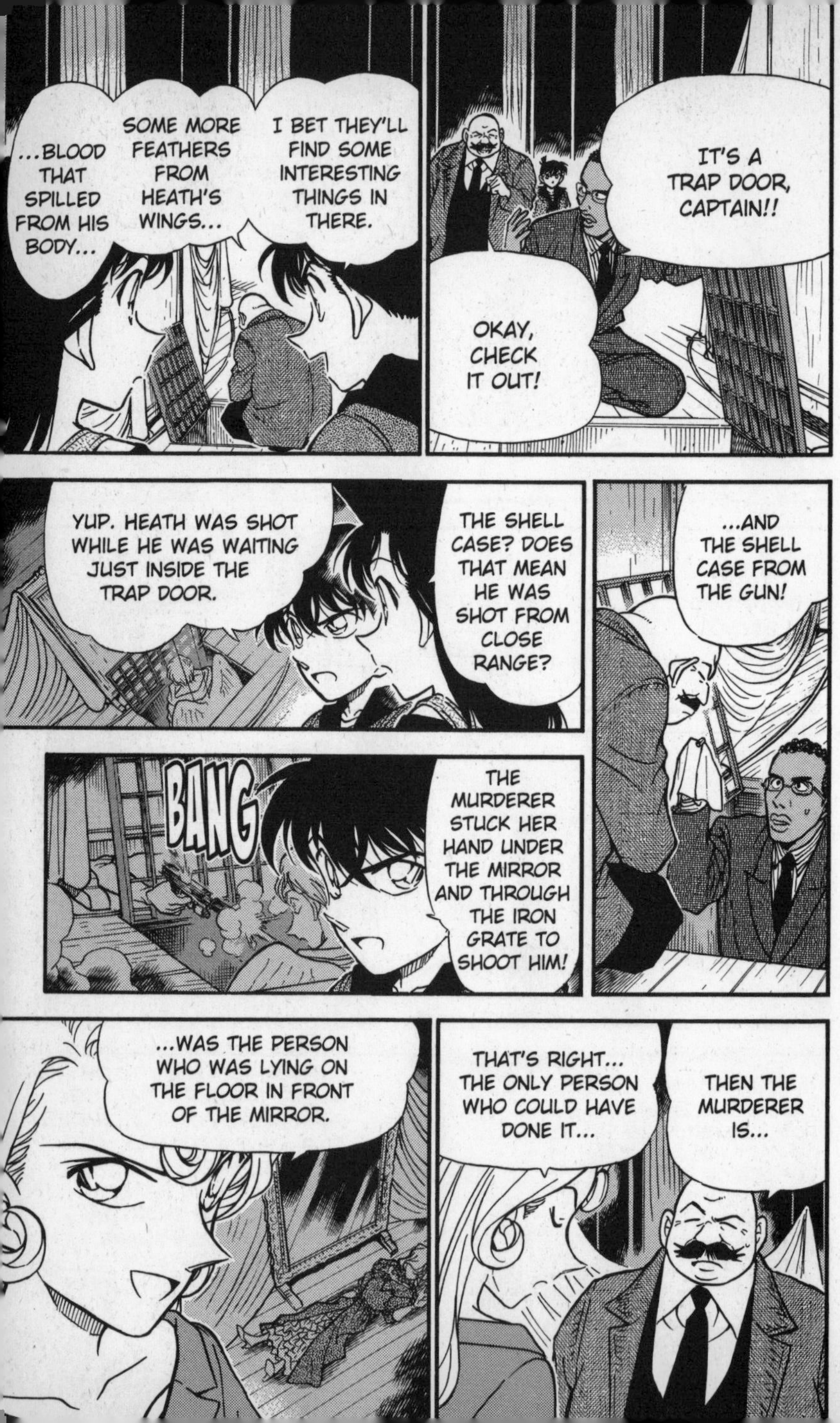
IT'S A TRAP DOOR, CAPTAIN!!
OKAY, CHECK IT OUT!
I BET THEY'LL FIND SOME INTERESTING THINGS IN THERE.
SOME MORE FEATHERS FROM HEATH'S WINGS...
...BLOOD THAT SPILLED FROM HIS BODY...
...AND THE SHELL CASE FROM THE GUN!
THE SHELL CASE? DOES THAT MEAN HE WAS SHOT FROM CLOSE RANGE?
YUP. HEATH WAS SHOT WHILE HE WAS WAITING JUST INSIDE THE TRAP DOOR.
THE MURDERER STUCK HER HAND UNDER THE MIRROR AND THROUGH THE IRON GRATE TO SHOOT HIM!
BANG
THEN THE MURDERER IS...
THAT'S RIGHT... THE ONLY PERSON WHO COULD HAVE DONE IT...
...WAS THE PERSON WHO WAS LYING ON THE FLOOR IN FRONT OF THE MIRROR.

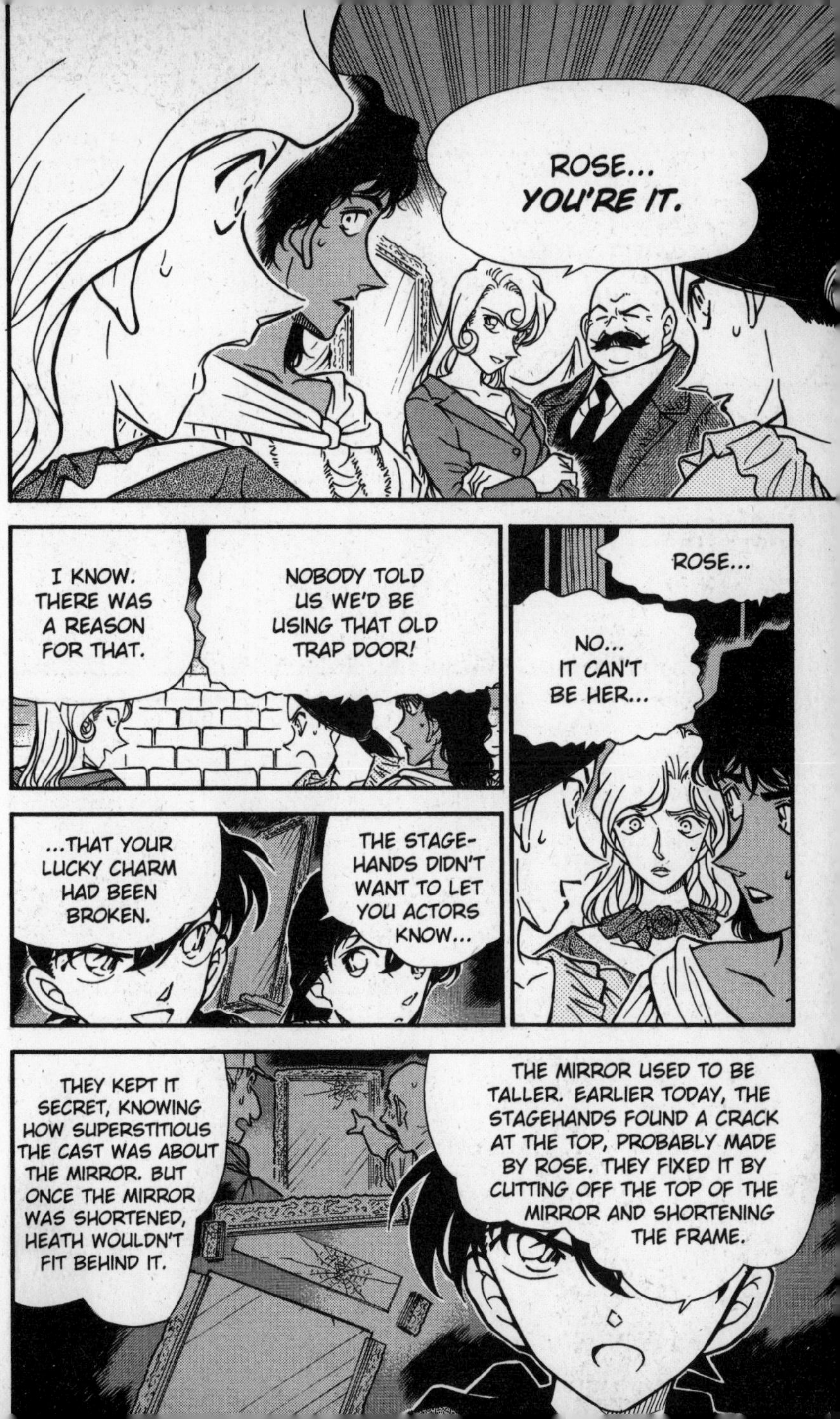
ROSE... YOU'RE IT.
ROSE...
NO... IT CAN'T BE HER...
NOBODY TOLD US WE'D BE USING THAT OLD TRAP DOOR!
I KNOW. THERE WAS A REASON FOR THAT.
THE STAGE-HANDS DIDN'T WANT TO LET YOU ACTORS KNOW...
...THAT YOUR LUCKY CHARM HAD BEEN BROKEN.
THE MIRROR USED TO BE TALLER. EARLIER TODAY, THE STAGEHANDS FOUND A CRACK AT THE TOP, PROBABLY MADE BY ROSE. THEY FIXED IT BY CUTTING OFF THE TOP OF THE MIRROR AND SHORTENING THE FRAME.
THEY KEPT IT SECRET, KNOWING HOW SUPERSTITIOUS THE CAST WAS ABOUT THE MIRROR. BUT ONCE THE MIRROR WAS SHORTENED, HEATH WOULDN'T FIT BEHIND IT.

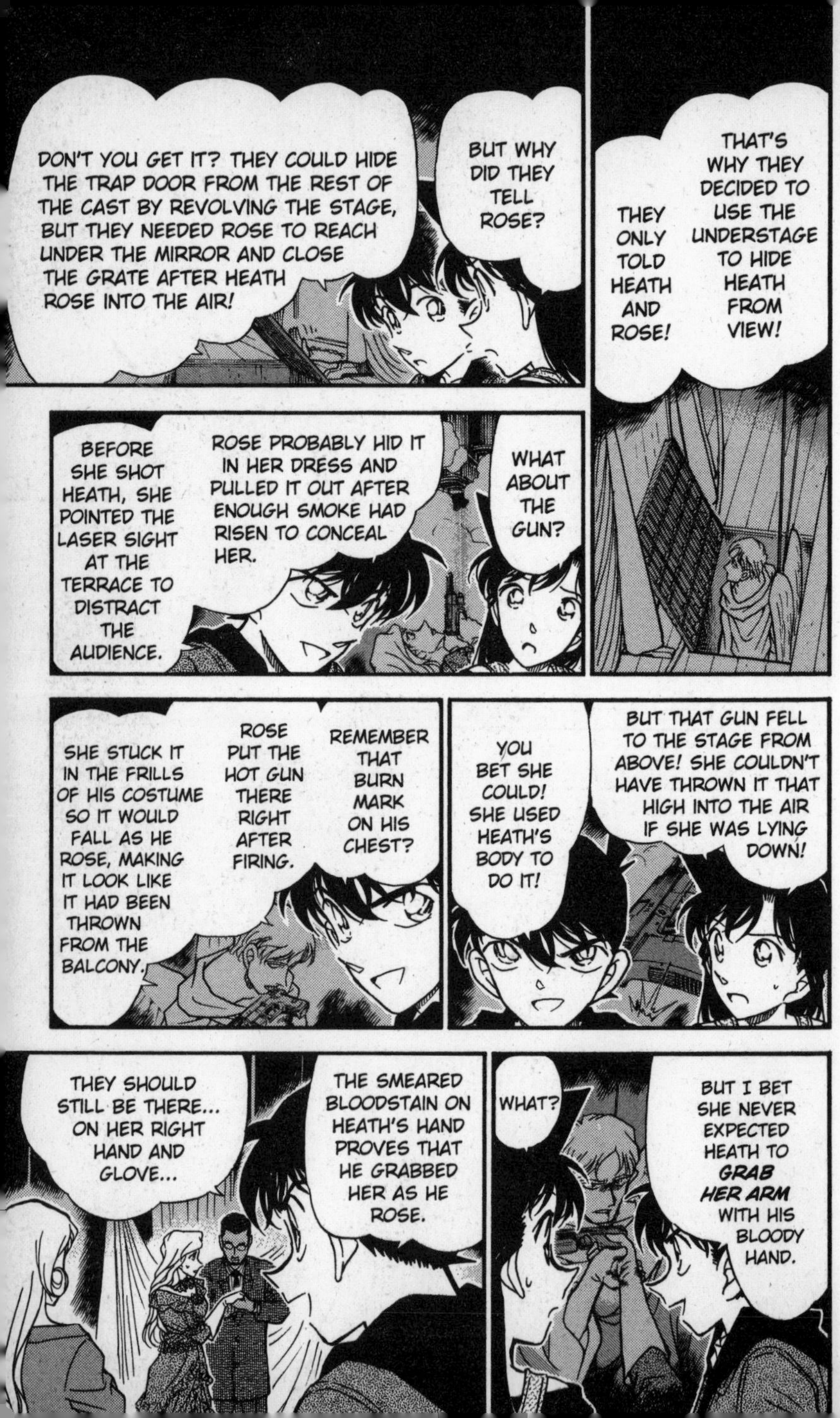
THAT'S WHY THEY DECIDED TO USE THE UNDERSTAGE TO HIDE HEATH FROM VIEW!
THEY ONLY TOLD HEATH AND ROSE!
BUT WHY DID THEY TELL ROSE?
DON'T YOU GET IT? THEY COULD HIDE THE TRAP DOOR FROM THE REST OF THE CAST BY REVOLVING THE STAGE, BUT THEY NEEDED ROSE TO REACH UNDER THE MIRROR AND CLOSE THE GRATE AFTER HEATH ROSE INTO THE AIR!
WHAT ABOUT THE GUN?
ROSE PROBABLY HID IT IN HER DRESS AND PULLED IT OUT AFTER ENOUGH SMOKE HAD RISEN TO CONCEAL HER.
BEFORE SHE SHOT HEATH, SHE POINTED THE LASER SIGHT AT THE TERRACE TO DISTRACT THE AUDIENCE.
BUT THAT GUN FELL TO THE STAGE FROM ABOVE! SHE COULDN'T HAVE THROWN IT THAT HIGH INTO THE AIR IF SHE WAS LYING DOWN!
YOU BET SHE COULD! SHE USED HEATH'S BODY TO DO IT!
REMEMBER THAT BURN MARK ON HIS CHEST?
ROSE PUT THE HOT GUN THERE RIGHT AFTER FIRING.
SHE STUCK IT IN THE FRILLS OF HIS COSTUME SO IT WOULD FALL AS HE ROSE, MAKING IT LOOK LIKE IT HAD BEEN THROWN FROM THE BALCONY.
BUT I BET SHE NEVER EXPECTED HEATH TO ***GRAB HER ARM*** WITH HIS BLOODY HAND.
WHAT?
THE SMEARED BLOODSTAIN ON HEATH'S HAND PROVES THAT HE GRABBED HER AS HE ROSE.
THEY SHOULD STILL BE THERE... ON HER RIGHT HAND AND GLOVE...

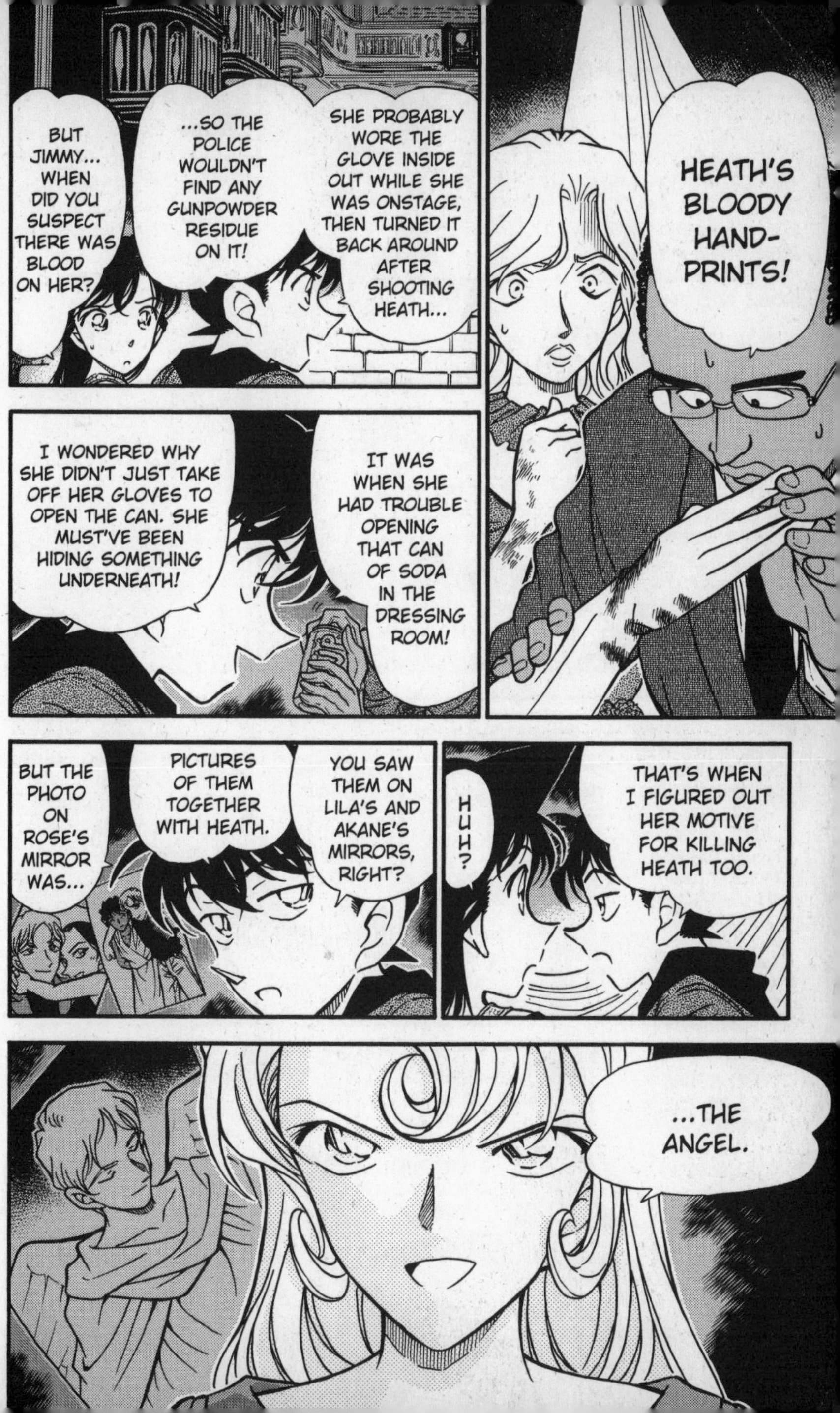
HEATH'S BLOODY HAND-PRINTS!
SHE PROBABLY WORE THE GLOVE INSIDE OUT WHILE SHE WAS ONSTAGE, THEN TURNED IT BACK AROUND AFTER SHOOTING HEATH...
...SO THE POLICE WOULDN'T FIND ANY GUNPOWDER RESIDUE ON IT!
BUT JIMMY... WHEN DID YOU SUSPECT THERE WAS BLOOD ON HER?
IT WAS WHEN SHE HAD TROUBLE OPENING THAT CAN OF SODA IN THE DRESSING ROOM!
I WONDERED WHY SHE DIDN'T JUST TAKE OFF HER GLOVES TO OPEN THE CAN. SHE MUST'VE BEEN HIDING SOMETHING UNDERNEATH!
THAT'S WHEN I FIGURED OUT HER MOTIVE FOR KILLING HEATH TOO.
HUH?
YOU SAW THEM ON LILA'S AND AKANE'S MIRRORS, RIGHT?
PICTURES OF THEM TOGETHER WITH HEATH.
BUT THE PHOTO ON ROSE'S MIRROR WAS...
...THE ANGEL.

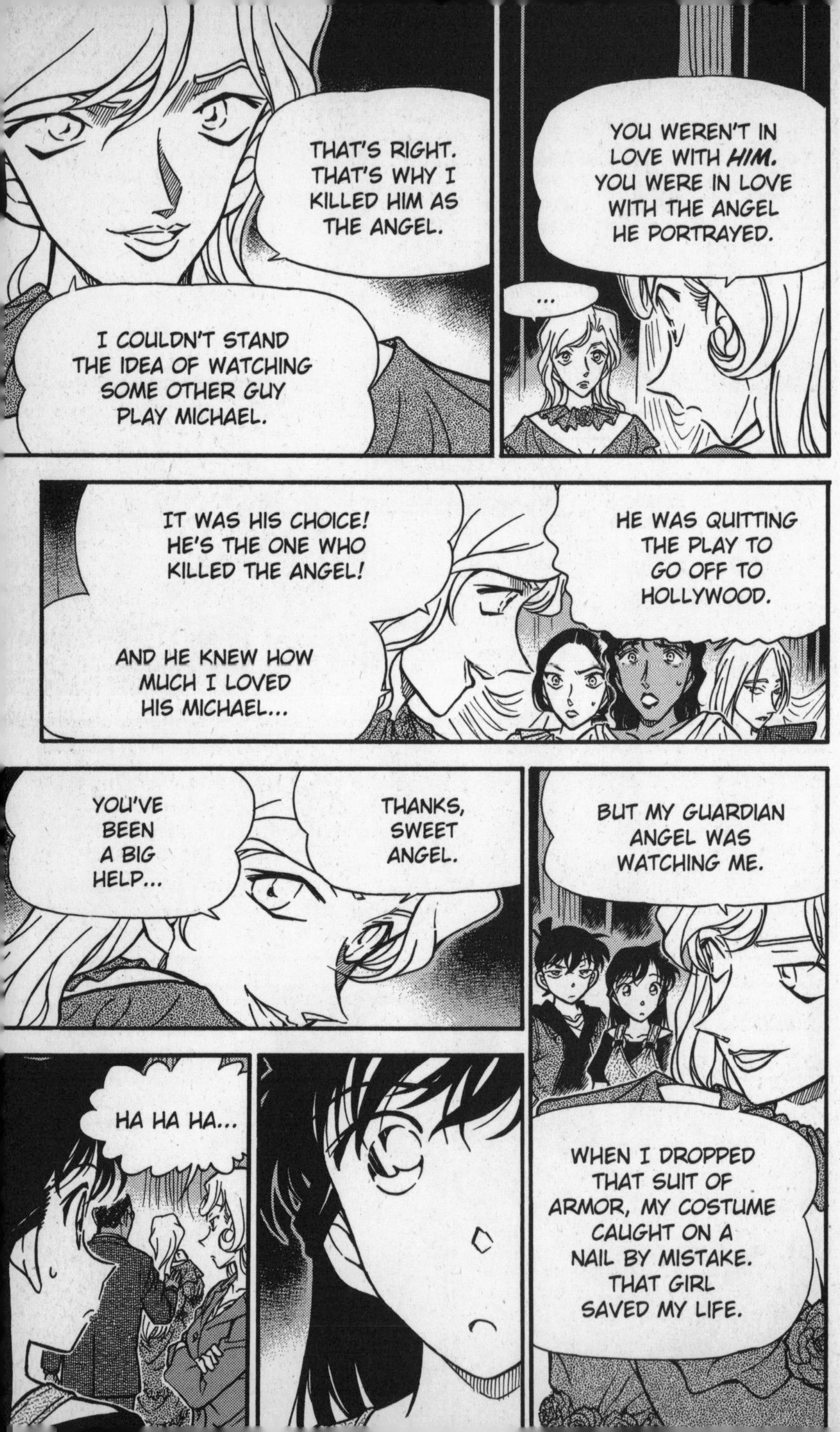
YOU WEREN'T IN LOVE WITH *HIM.* YOU WERE IN LOVE WITH THE ANGEL HE PORTRAYED.
...
THAT'S RIGHT. THAT'S WHY I KILLED HIM AS THE ANGEL.
I COULDN'T STAND THE IDEA OF WATCHING SOME OTHER GUY PLAY MICHAEL.
HE WAS QUITTING THE PLAY TO GO OFF TO HOLLYWOOD.
IT WAS HIS CHOICE! HE'S THE ONE WHO KILLED THE ANGEL!
AND HE KNEW HOW MUCH I LOVED HIS MICHAEL...
BUT MY GUARDIAN ANGEL WAS WATCHING ME.
WHEN I DROPPED THAT SUIT OF ARMOR, MY COSTUME CAUGHT ON A NAIL BY MISTAKE. THAT GIRL SAVED MY LIFE.
THANKS, SWEET ANGEL.
YOU'VE BEEN A BIG HELP...
HA HA HA...

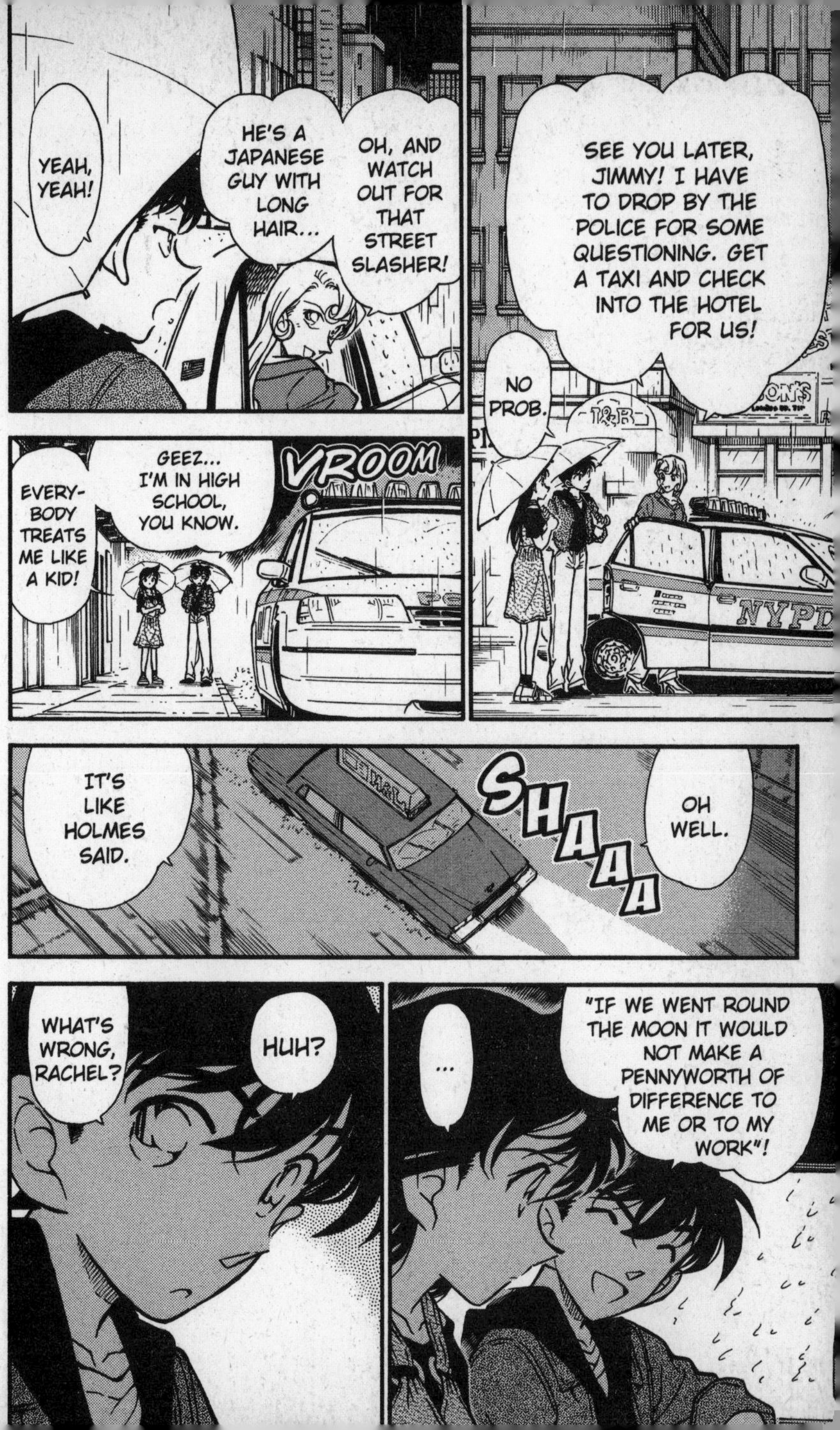
SEE YOU LATER, JIMMY! I HAVE TO DROP BY THE POLICE FOR SOME QUESTIONING. GET A TAXI AND CHECK INTO THE HOTEL FOR US!
NO PROB.
NYPD
OH, AND WATCH OUT FOR THAT STREET SLASHER!
HE'S A JAPANESE GUY WITH LONG HAIR...
YEAH, YEAH!
VROOM
GEEZ... I'M IN HIGH SCHOOL, YOU KNOW.
EVERY-BODY TREATS ME LIKE A KID!
OH WELL.
SHAAAA
IT'S LIKE HOLMES SAID.
"IF WE WENT ROUND THE MOON IT WOULD NOT MAKE A PENNYWORTH OF DIFFERENCE TO ME OR TO MY WORK"!
...
HUH?
WHAT'S WRONG, RACHEL?

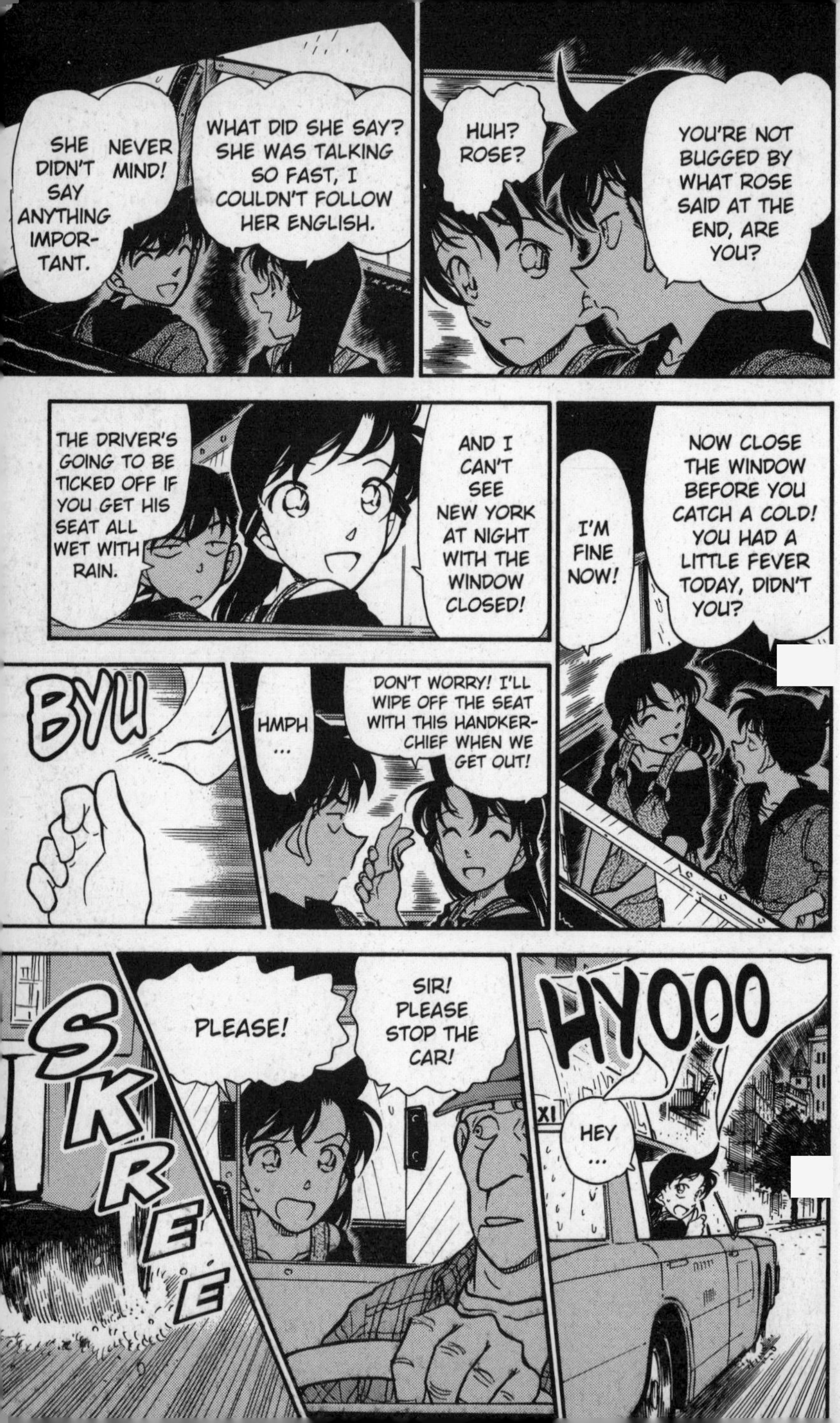
YOU'RE NOT BUGGED BY WHAT ROSE SAID AT THE END, ARE YOU?
HUH? ROSE?
WHAT DID SHE SAY? SHE WAS TALKING SO FAST, I COULDN'T FOLLOW HER ENGLISH.
NEVER MIND! SHE DIDN'T SAY ANYTHING IMPOR-TANT.
NOW CLOSE THE WINDOW BEFORE YOU CATCH A COLD! YOU HAD A LITTLE FEVER TODAY, DIDN'T YOU?
I'M FINE NOW!
AND I CAN'T SEE NEW YORK AT NIGHT WITH THE WINDOW CLOSED!
THE DRIVER'S GOING TO BE TICKED OFF IF YOU GET HIS SEAT ALL WET WITH RAIN.
DON'T WORRY! I'LL WIPE OFF THE SEAT WITH THIS HANDKER-CHIEF WHEN WE GET OUT!
HMPH ...
BYU
HYOOO
HEY ...
SIR! PLEASE STOP THE CAR!
PLEASE!
SKREE

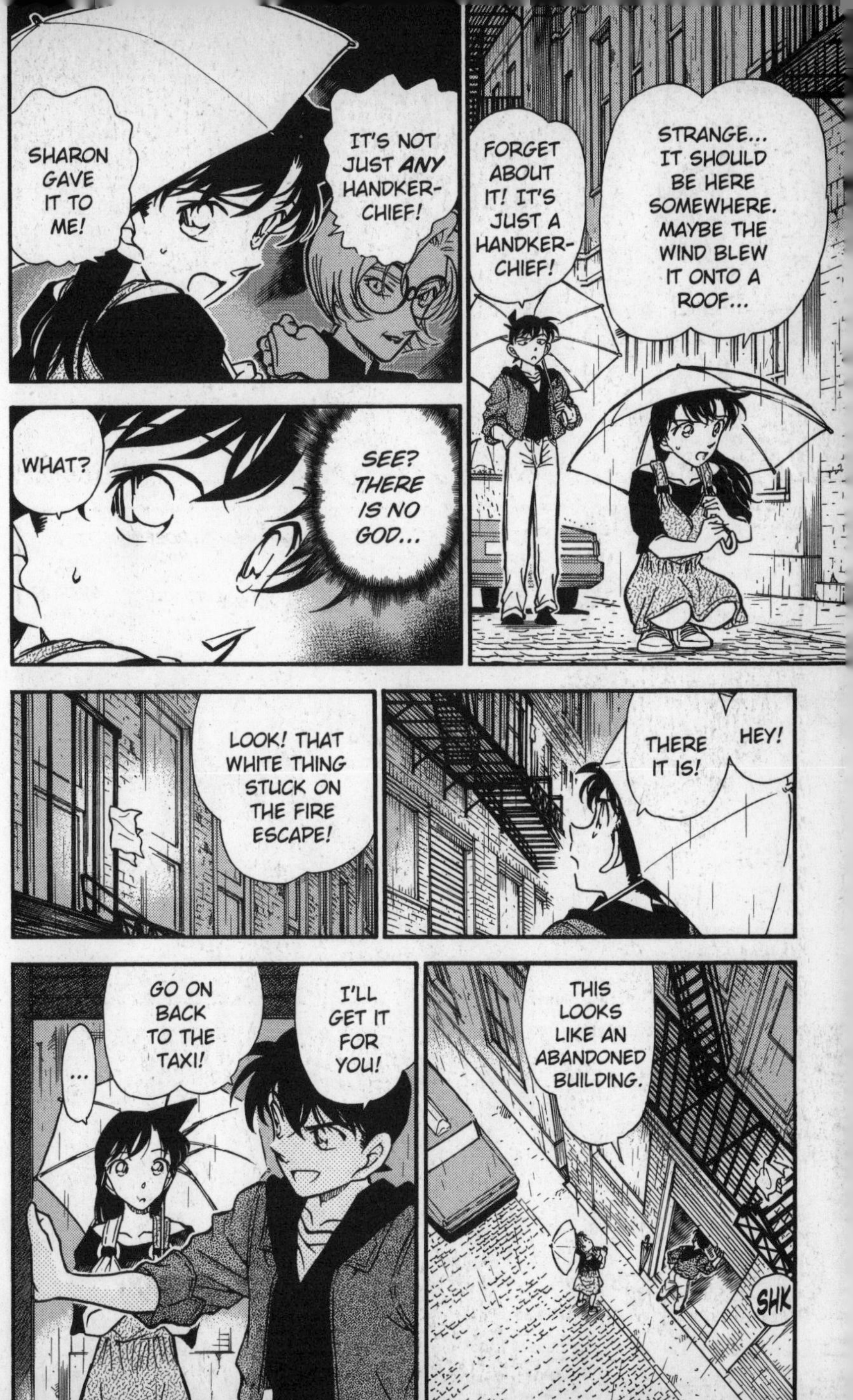
STRANGE... IT SHOULD BE HERE SOMEWHERE. MAYBE THE WIND BLEW IT ONTO A ROOF...
FORGET ABOUT IT! IT'S JUST A HANDKER-CHIEF!
IT'S NOT JUST *ANY* HANDKER-CHIEF!
SHARON GAVE IT TO ME!
SEE? THERE IS NO GOD...
WHAT?
HEY!
THERE IT IS!
LOOK! THAT WHITE THING STUCK ON THE FIRE ESCAPE!
THIS LOOKS LIKE AN ABANDONED BUILDING.
SHK
I'LL GET IT FOR YOU!
GO ON BACK TO THE TAXI!
...

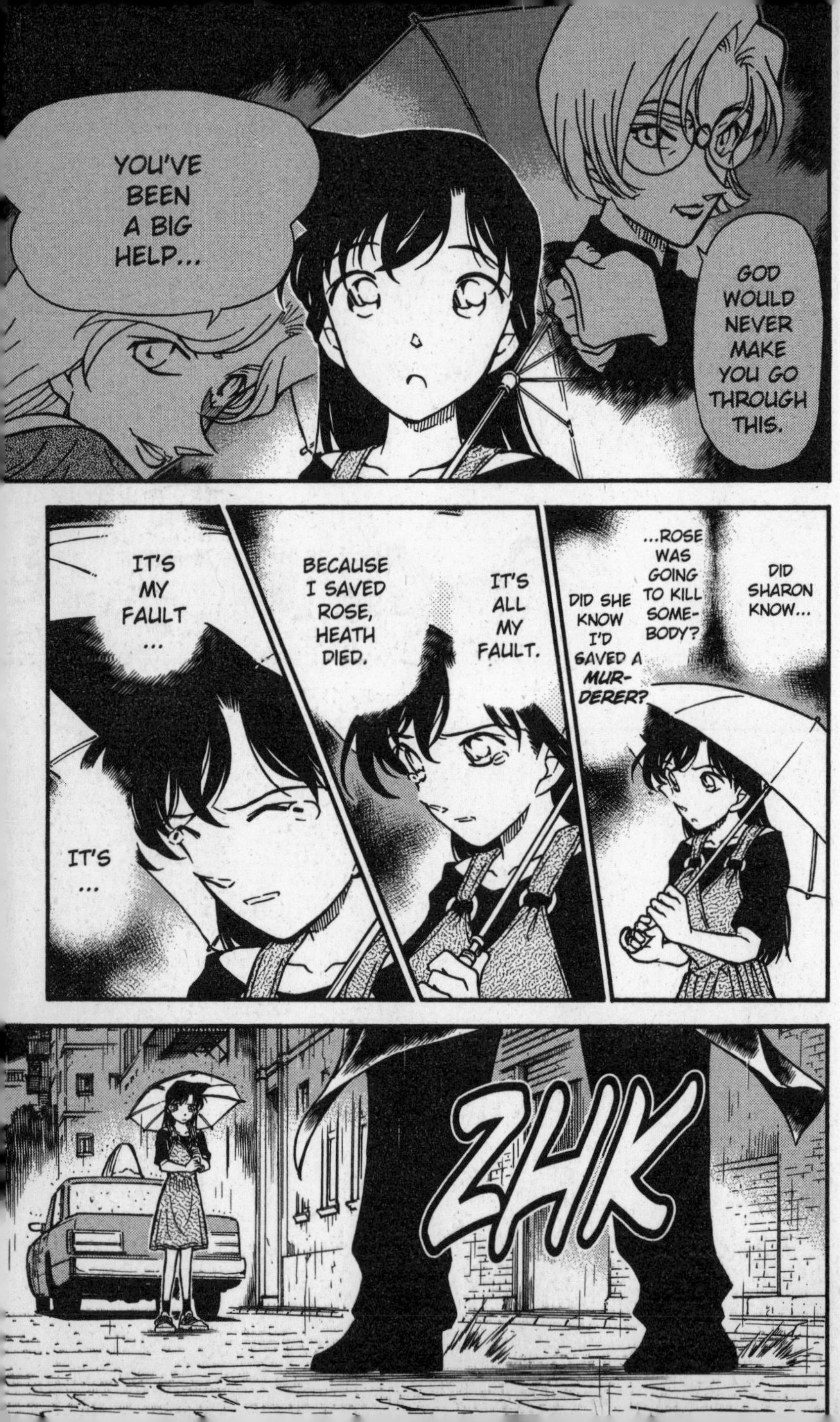
GOD WOULD NEVER MAKE YOU GO THROUGH THIS.
YOU'VE BEEN A BIG HELP...
DID SHARON KNOW...
...ROSE WAS GOING TO KILL SOMEBODY?
DID SHE KNOW I'D SAVED A *MURDERER?*
IT'S ALL MY FAULT.
BECAUSE I SAVED ROSE, HEATH DIED.
IT'S MY FAULT ...
IT'S ...
ZHK

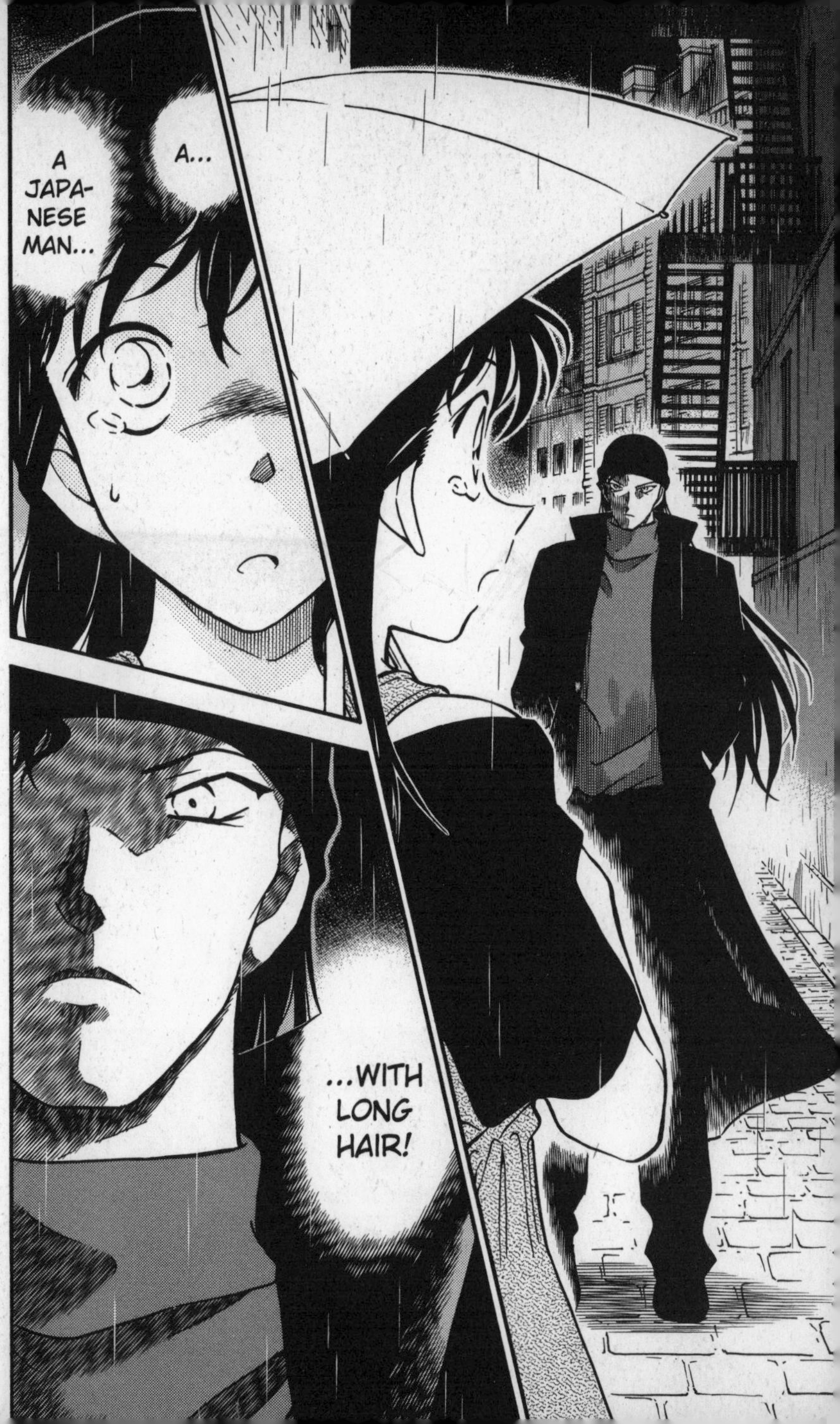
A...
A JAPANESE MAN...
...WITH LONG HAIR!

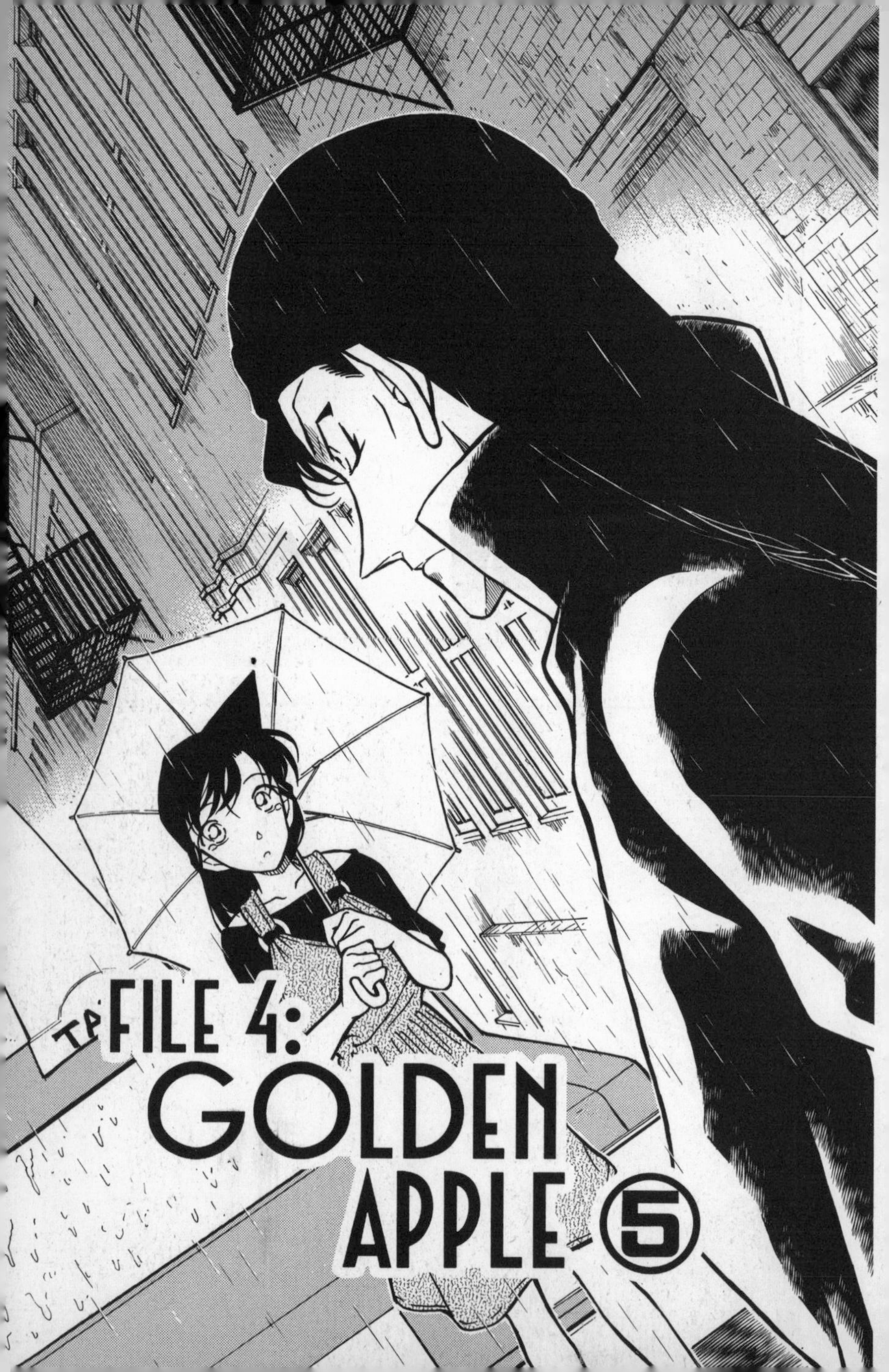
FILE 4:
GOLDEN
APPLE ⑤

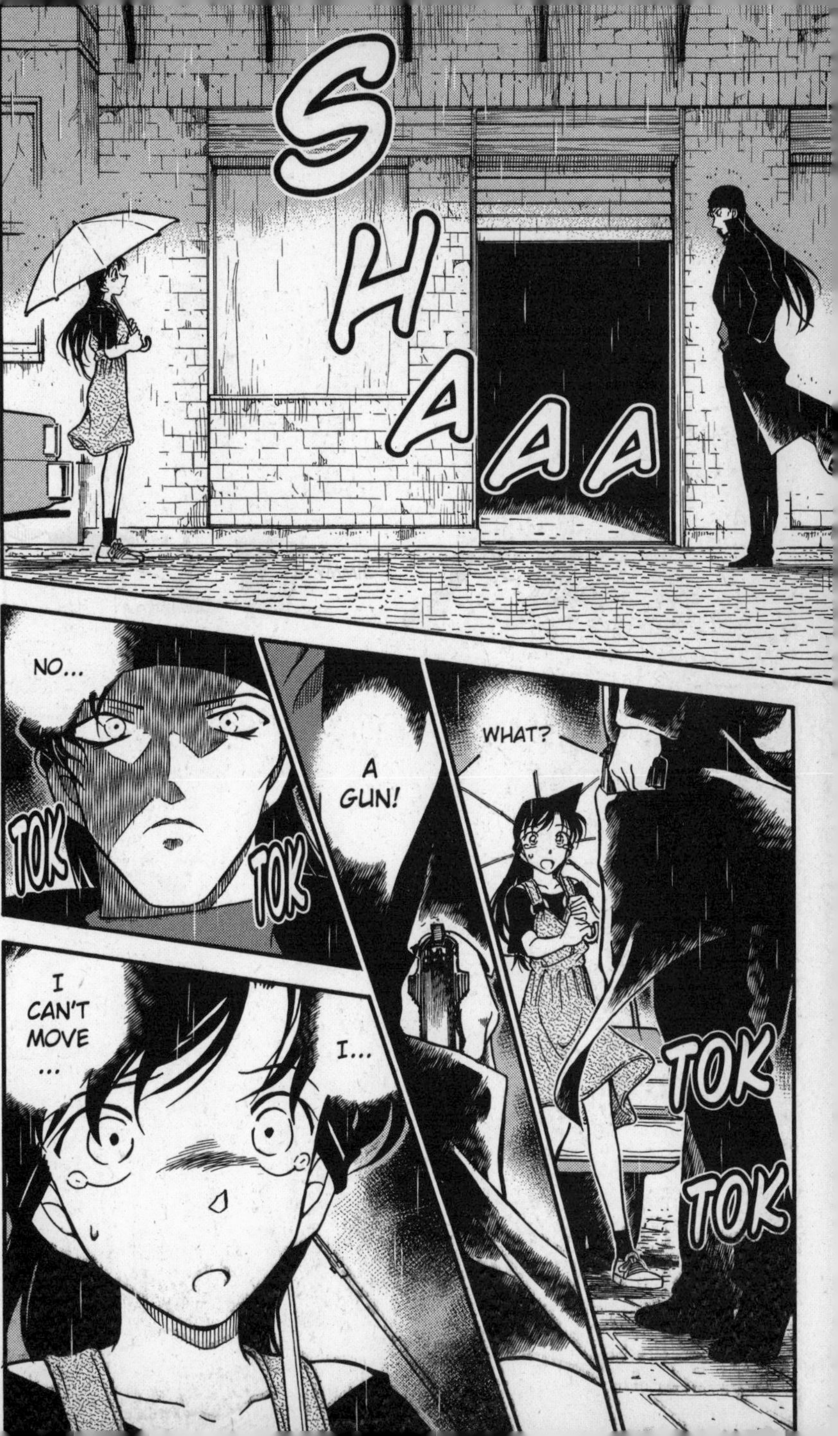
SHAAAA
WHAT?
TOK
TOK
A GUN!
NO...
TOK
TOK
I...
I CAN'T MOVE ...

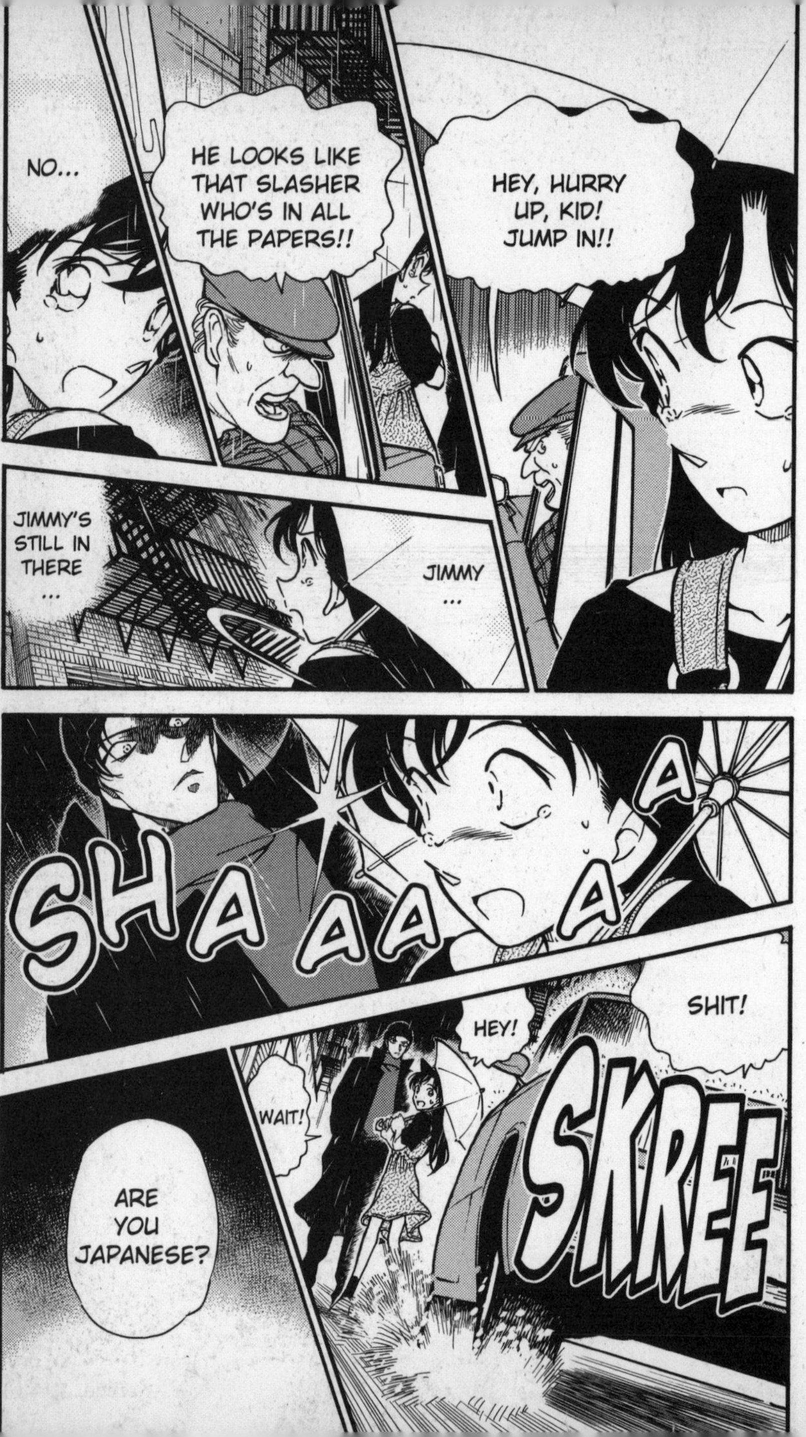
HEY, HURRY UP, KID! JUMP IN!!
HE LOOKS LIKE THAT SLASHER WHO'S IN ALL THE PAPERS!!
NO...
JIMMY ...
JIMMY'S STILL IN THERE ...
SHAAAAA
SHIT!
HEY!
SKREE
WAIT!
ARE YOU JAPANESE?

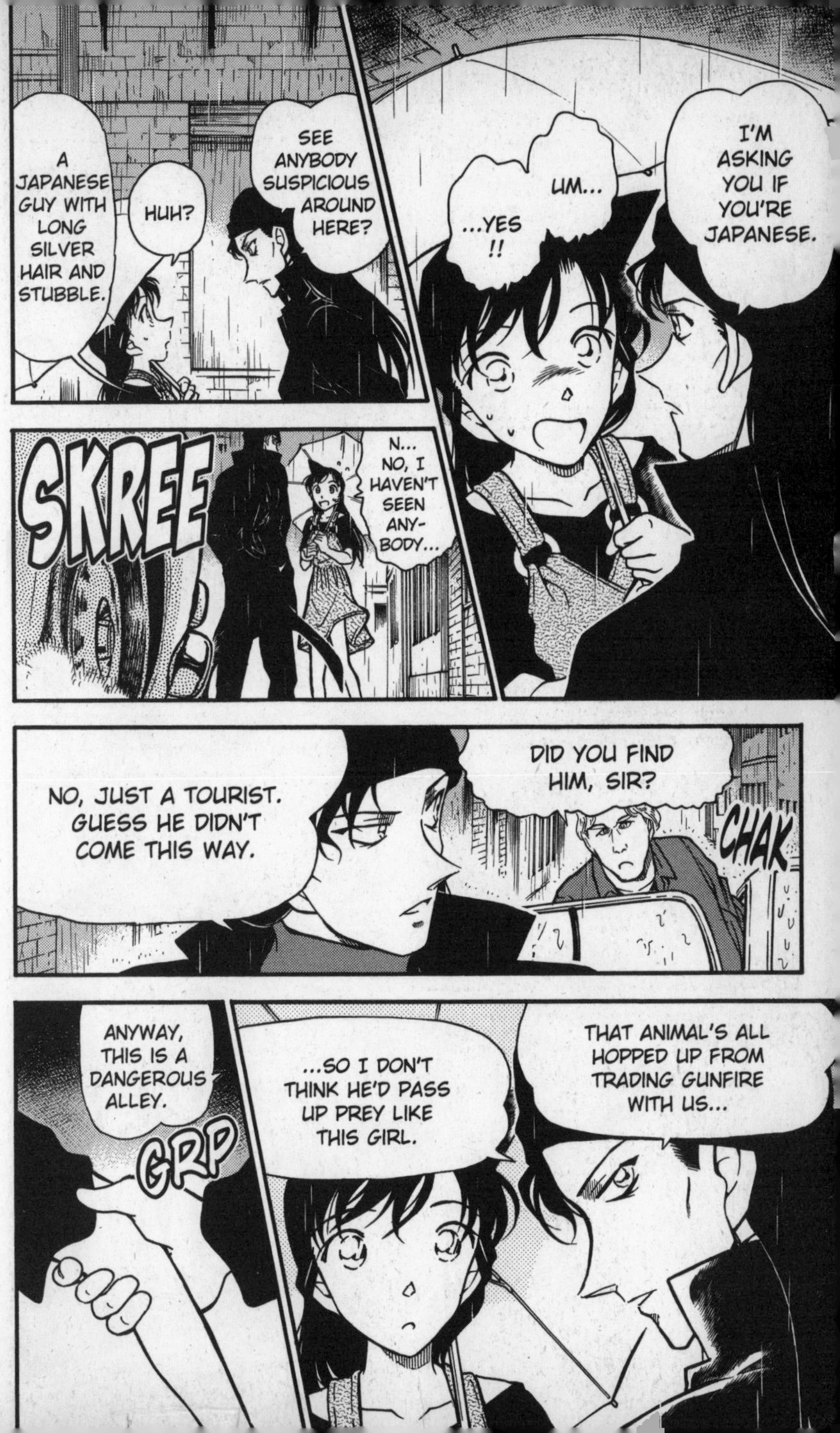
I'M ASKING YOU IF YOU'RE JAPANESE.
UM... ...YES !!
SEE ANYBODY SUSPICIOUS AROUND HERE?
HUH?
A JAPANESE GUY WITH LONG SILVER HAIR AND STUBBLE.
N... NO, I HAVEN'T SEEN ANY-BODY...
SKREE
CHAK
DID YOU FIND HIM, SIR?
NO, JUST A TOURIST. GUESS HE DIDN'T COME THIS WAY.
THAT ANIMAL'S ALL HOPPED UP FROM TRADING GUNFIRE WITH US...
...SO I DON'T THINK HE'D PASS UP PREY LIKE THIS GIRL.
ANYWAY, THIS IS A DANGEROUS ALLEY.
GRP

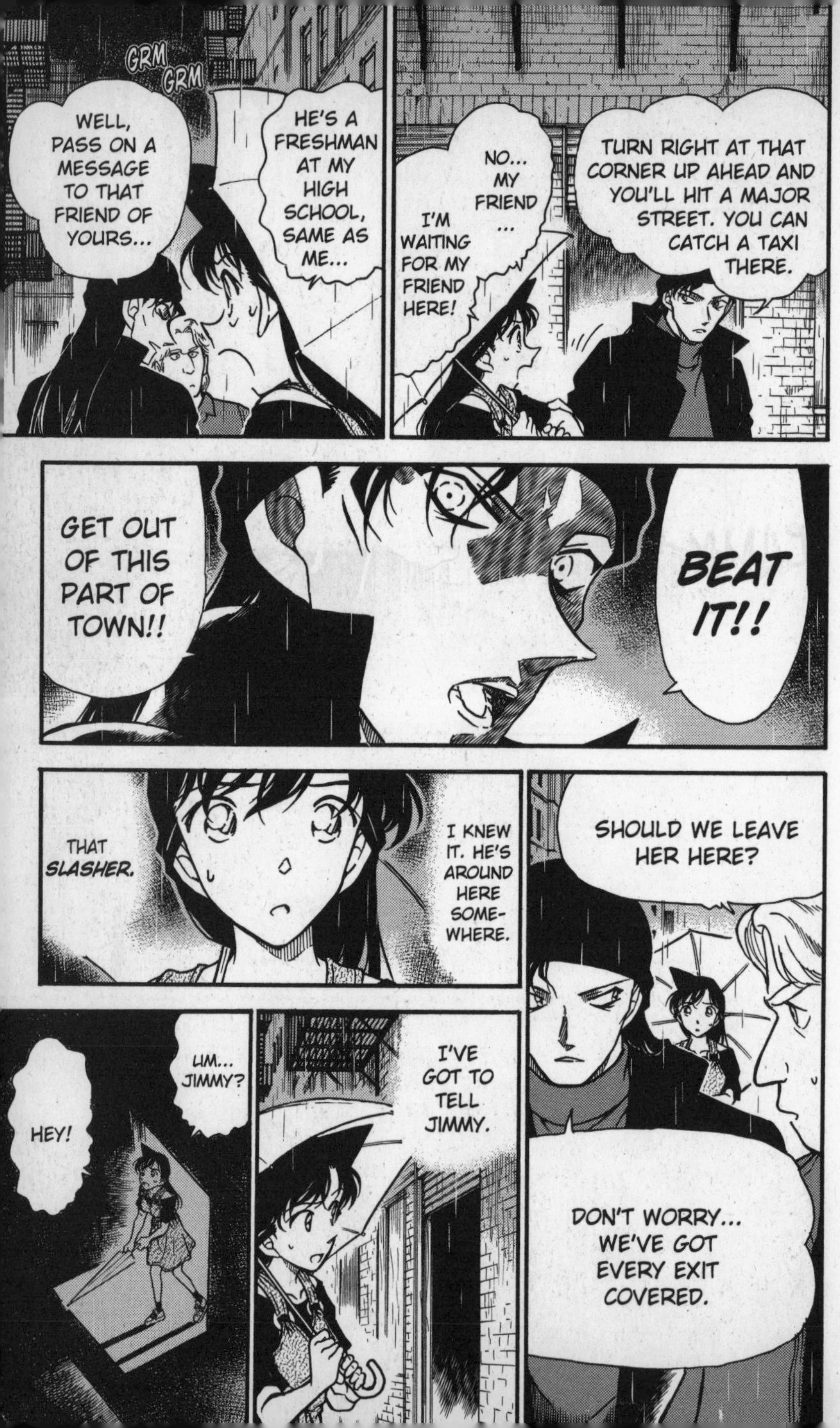
TURN RIGHT AT THAT CORNER UP AHEAD AND YOU'LL HIT A MAJOR STREET. YOU CAN CATCH A TAXI THERE.
NO... MY FRIEND ...
I'M WAITING FOR MY FRIEND HERE!
GRM GRM
HE'S A FRESHMAN AT MY HIGH SCHOOL, SAME AS ME...
WELL, PASS ON A MESSAGE TO THAT FRIEND OF YOURS...
BEAT IT!!
GET OUT OF THIS PART OF TOWN!!
SHOULD WE LEAVE HER HERE?
DON'T WORRY... WE'VE GOT EVERY EXIT COVERED.
I KNEW IT. HE'S AROUND HERE SOME-WHERE.
THAT *SLASHER.*
I'VE GOT TO TELL JIMMY.
UM... JIMMY?
HEY!

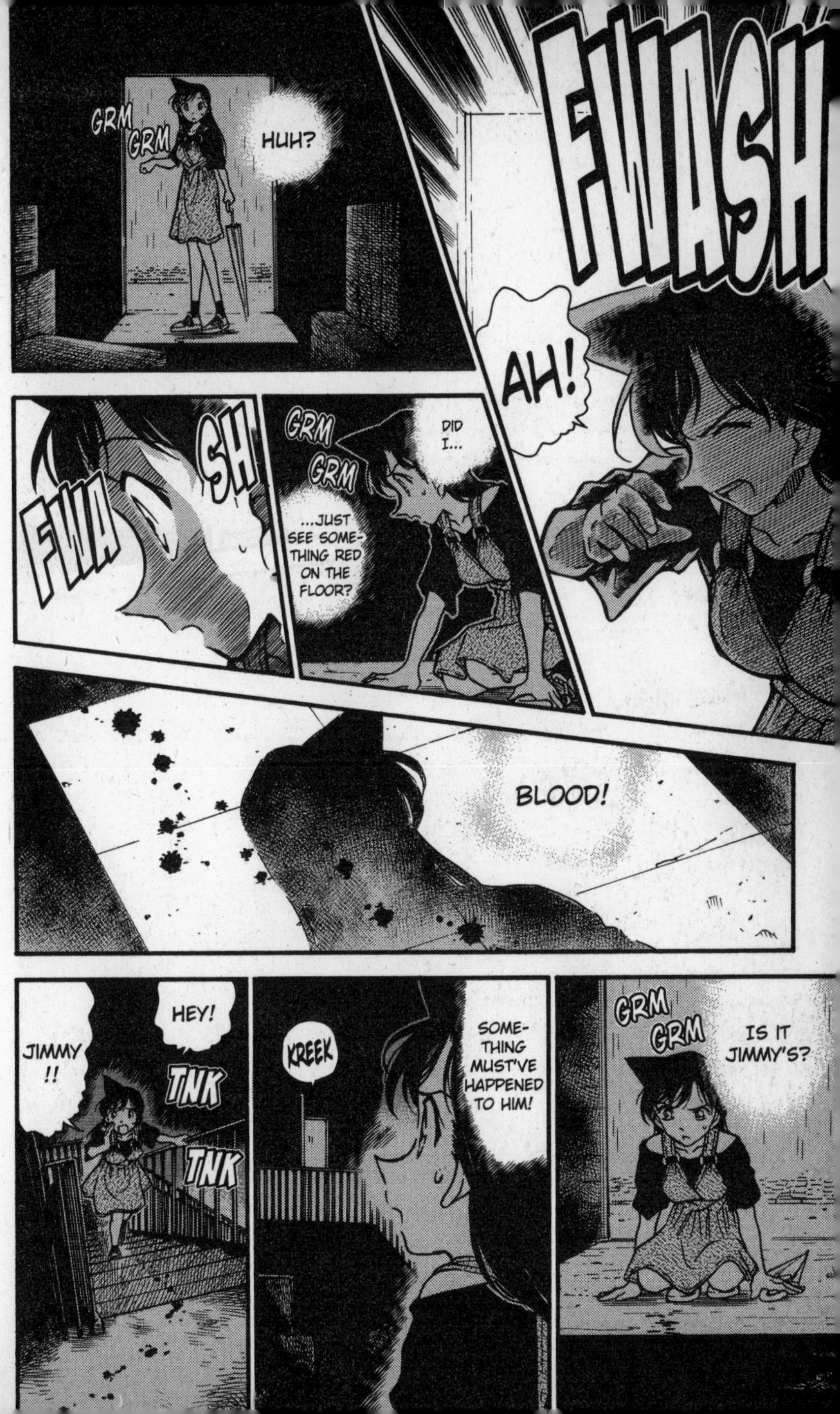
FWASH
AH!
GRM GRM
HUH?
GRM GRM
DID I...
...JUST SEE SOME-THING RED ON THE FLOOR?
FWASH
BLOOD!
GRM GRM
IS IT JIMMY'S?
KREEK
SOME-THING MUST'VE HAPPENED TO HIM!
HEY!
JIMMY !!
TNK
TNK

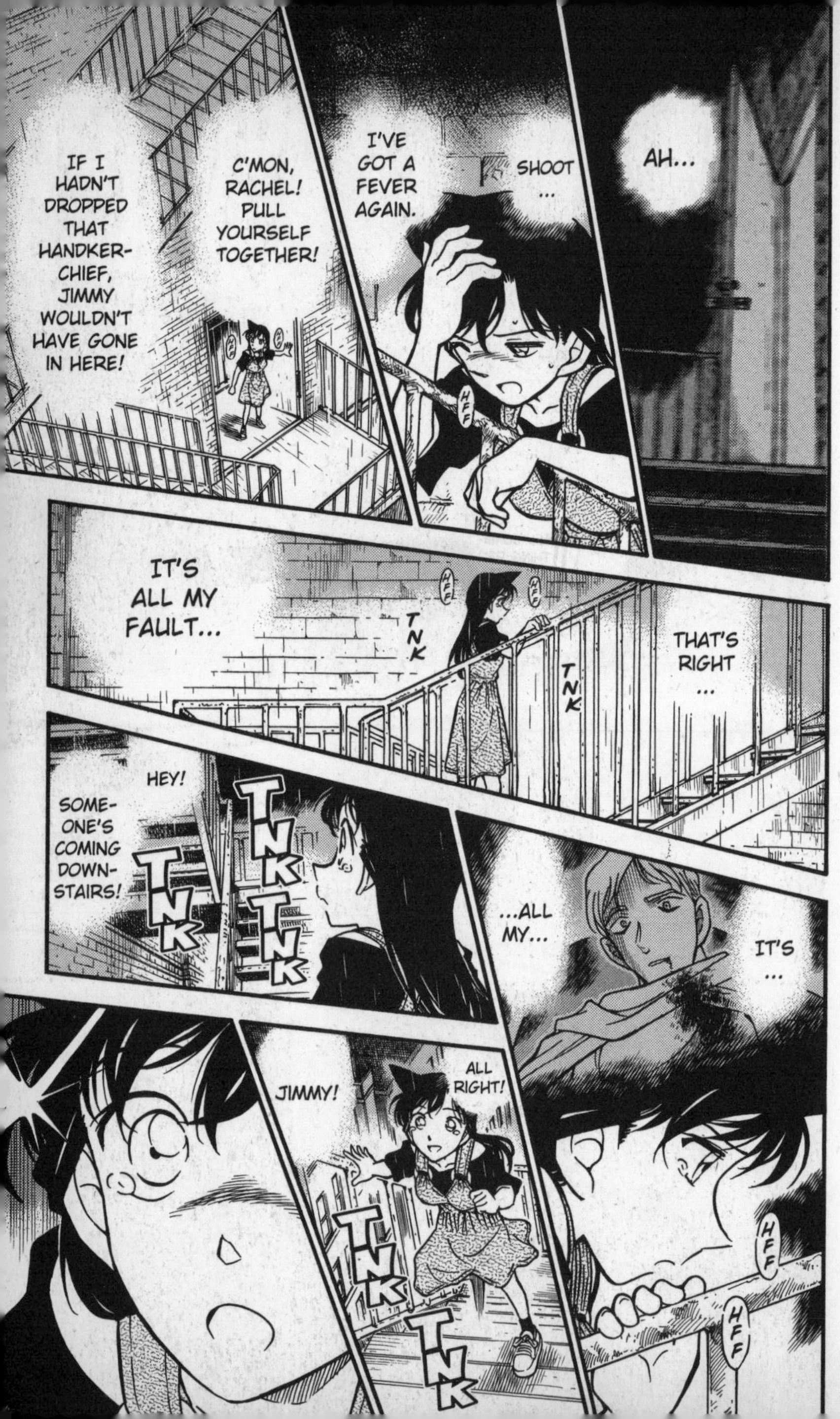
AH...
SHOOT ...
I'VE GOT A FEVER AGAIN.
HFF
C'MON, RACHEL! PULL YOURSELF TOGETHER!
IF I HADN'T DROPPED THAT HANDKER-CHIEF, JIMMY WOULDN'T HAVE GONE IN HERE!
THAT'S RIGHT ...
TNK
TNK
HFF
HFF
IT'S ALL MY FAULT...
IT'S ...
...ALL MY...
TNK TNK
TNK
HEY!
SOME-ONE'S COMING DOWN-STAIRS!
HFF
HFF
ALL RIGHT!
JIMMY!
TNK
TNK

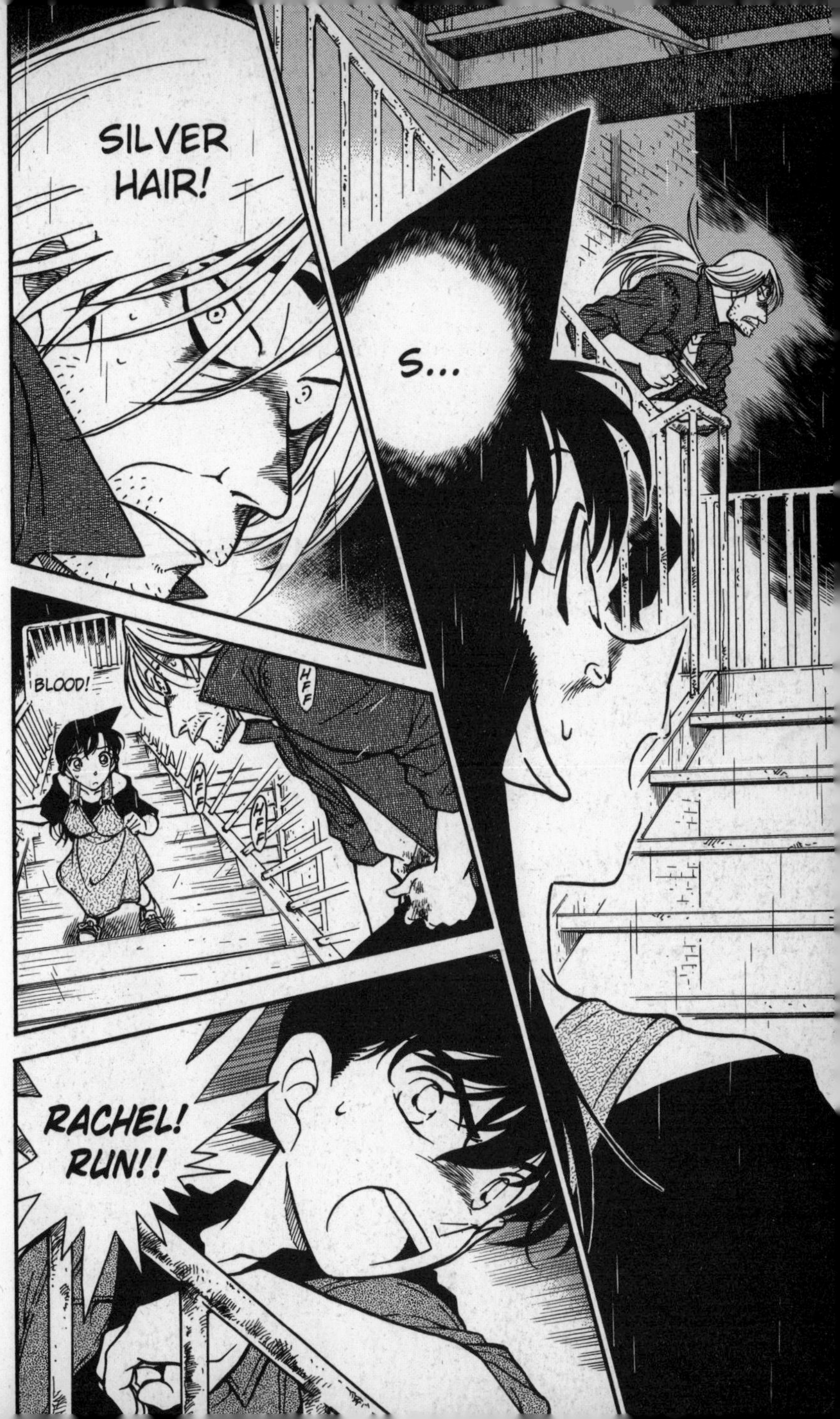
S...
SILVER HAIR!
HFF
HFF
HFF
BLOOD!
RACHEL! RUN!!

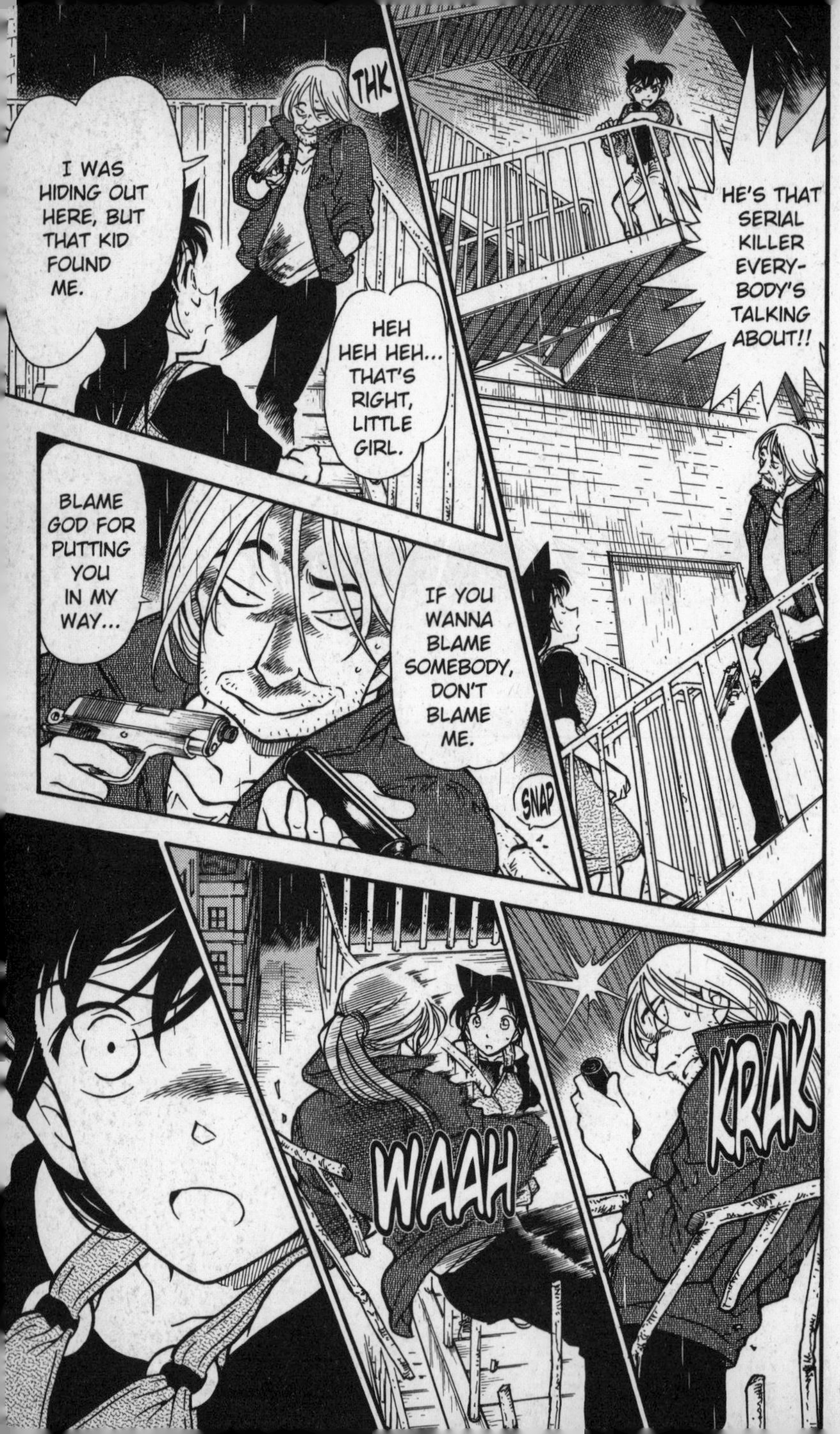
HE'S THAT SERIAL KILLER EVERY-BODY'S TALKING ABOUT!!
SNAP
THK
I WAS HIDING OUT HERE, BUT THAT KID FOUND ME.
HEH HEH HEH... THAT'S RIGHT, LITTLE GIRL.
IF YOU WANNA BLAME SOMEBODY, DON'T BLAME ME.
BLAME GOD FOR PUTTING YOU IN MY WAY...
KRAK
WAAH

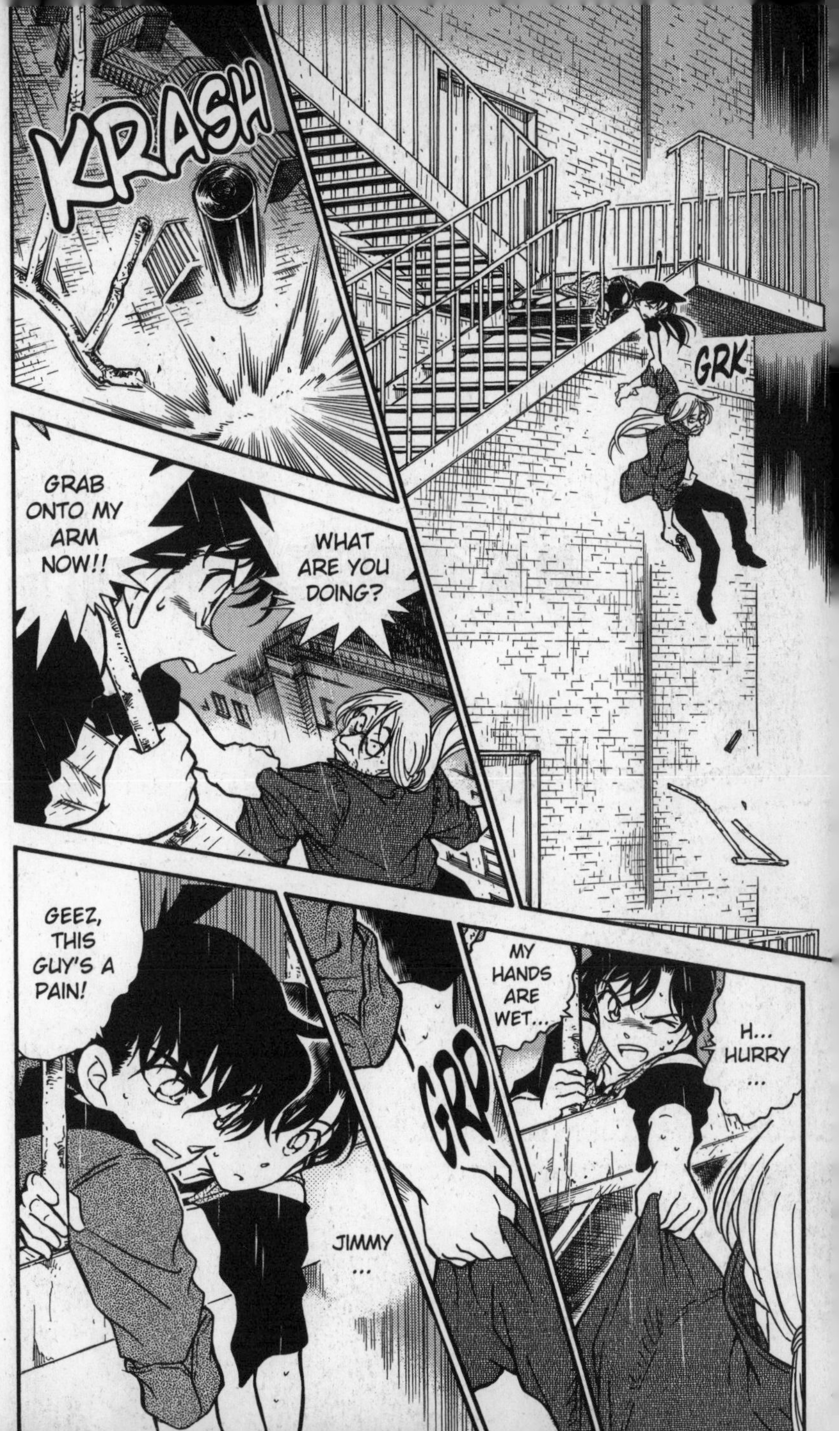
GRK
KRASH
WHAT ARE YOU DOING?
GRAB ONTO MY ARM NOW!!
H... HURRY ...
MY HANDS ARE WET...
GRP
JIMMY ...
GEEZ, THIS GUY'S A PAIN!

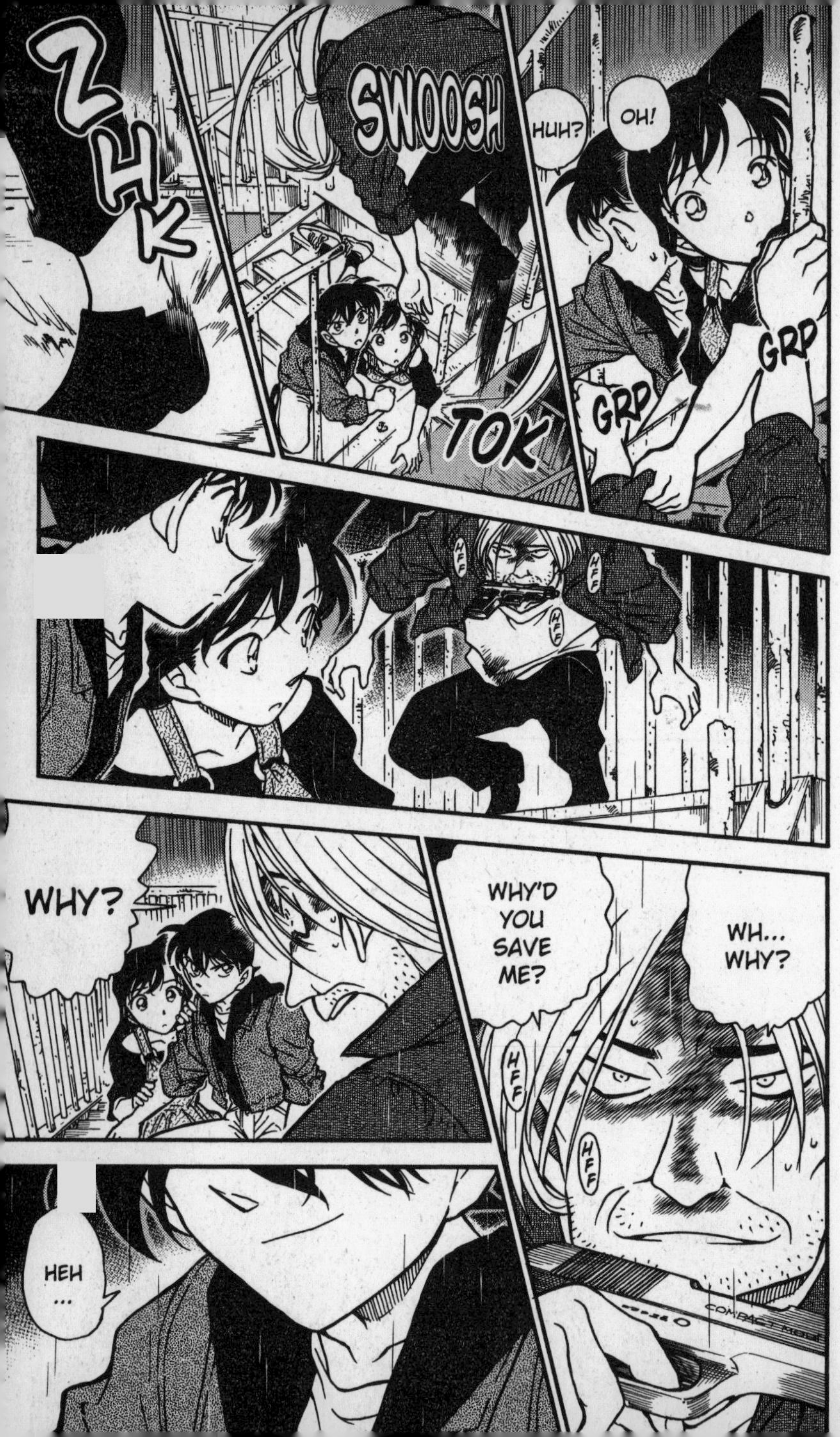
OH!
HUH?
GRP
GRP
SWOOSH
TOK
ZHK
HFF
HFF
HFF
WH... WHY?
WHY'D YOU SAVE ME?
HFF
HFF
WHY?
HEH ...

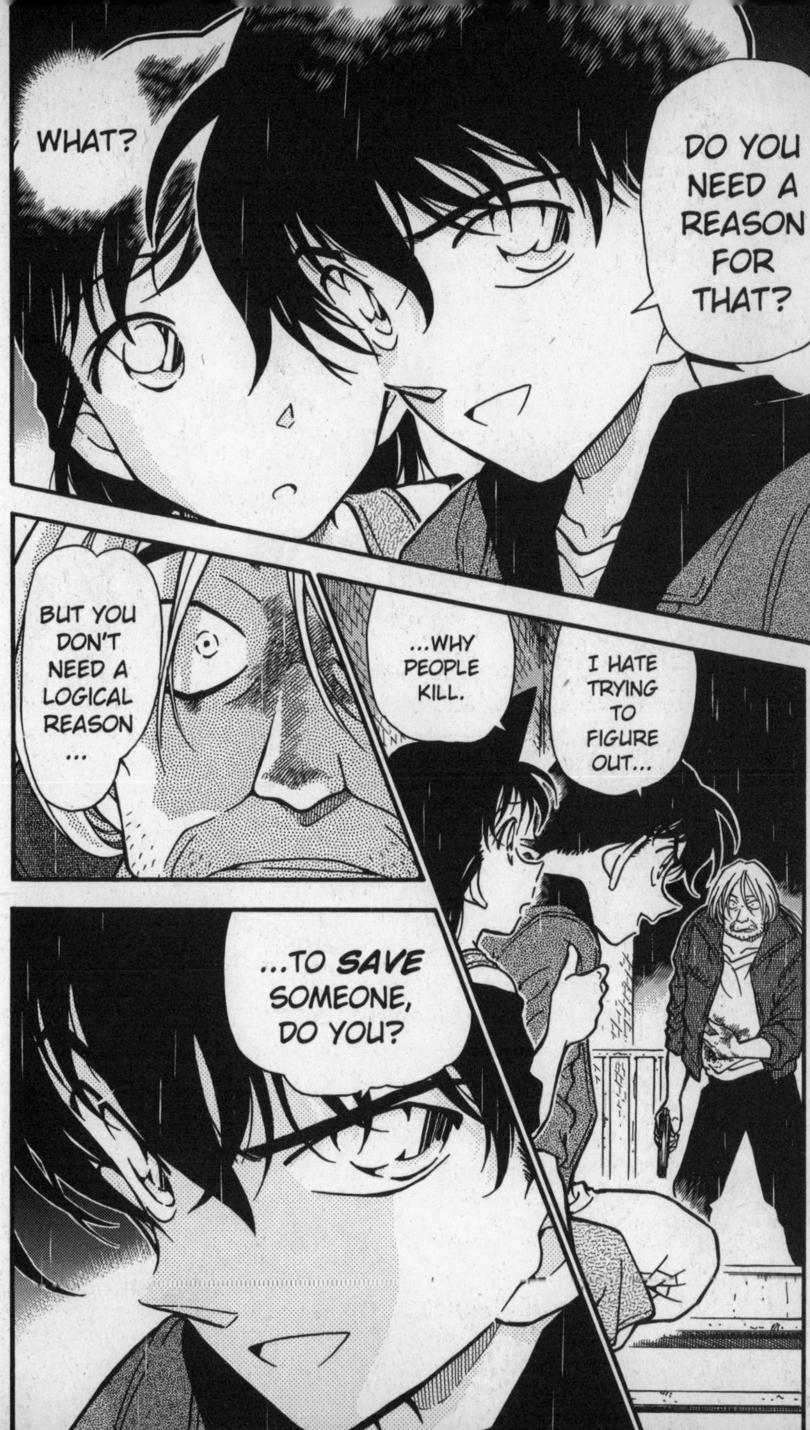
DO YOU NEED A REASON FOR THAT?
WHAT?
I HATE TRYING TO FIGURE OUT...
...WHY PEOPLE KILL.
BUT YOU DON'T NEED A LOGICAL REASON ...
...TO *SAVE* SOMEONE, DO YOU?

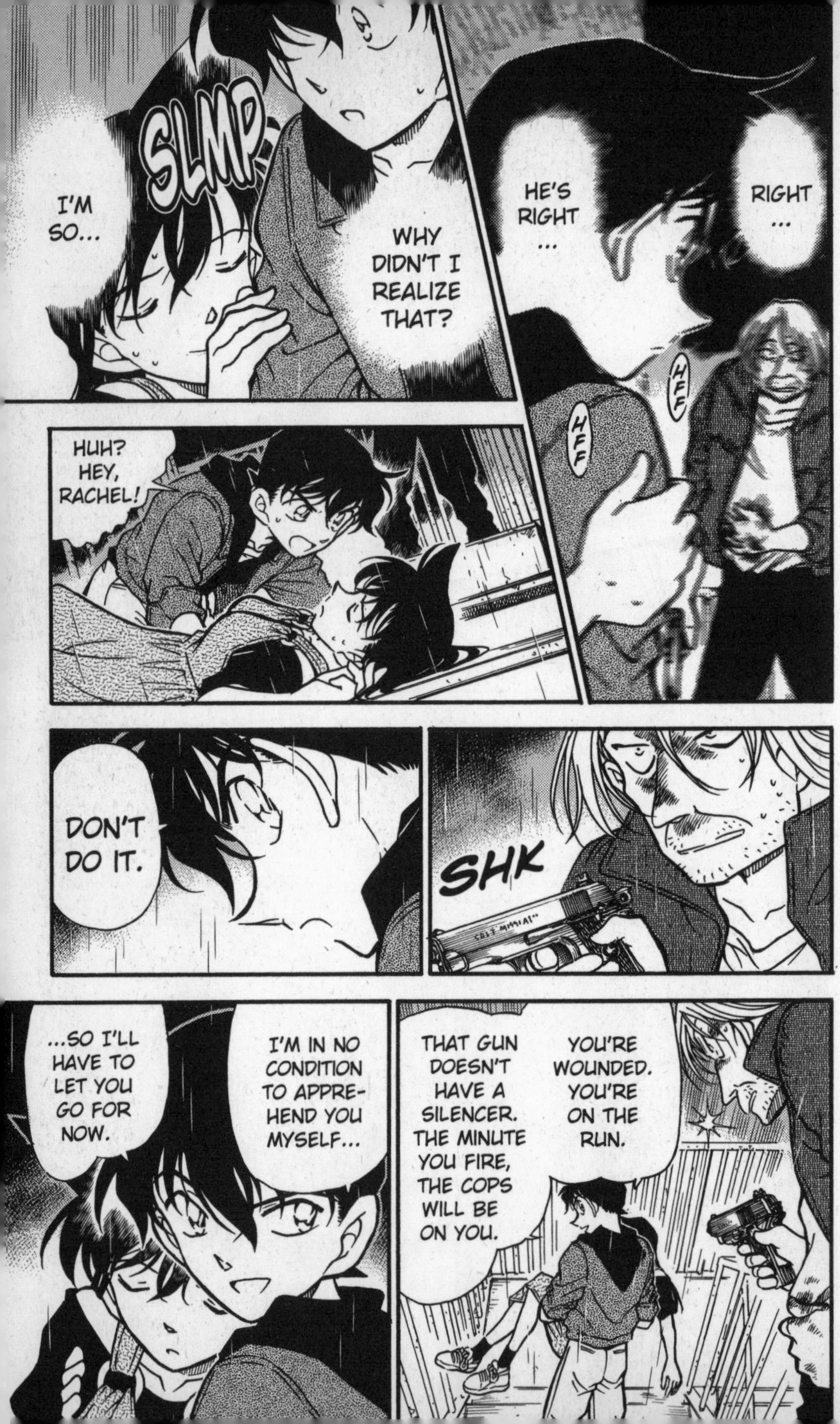
RIGHT...
HE'S RIGHT...
HFF
HFF
WHY DIDN'T I REALIZE THAT?
SLMP
I'M SO...
HUH? HEY, RACHEL!
SHK
DON'T DO IT.
YOU'RE WOUNDED. YOU'RE ON THE RUN.
THAT GUN DOESN'T HAVE A SILENCER. THE MINUTE YOU FIRE, THE COPS WILL BE ON YOU.
I'M IN NO CONDITION TO APPRE-HEND YOU MYSELF...
...SO I'LL HAVE TO LET YOU GO FOR NOW.

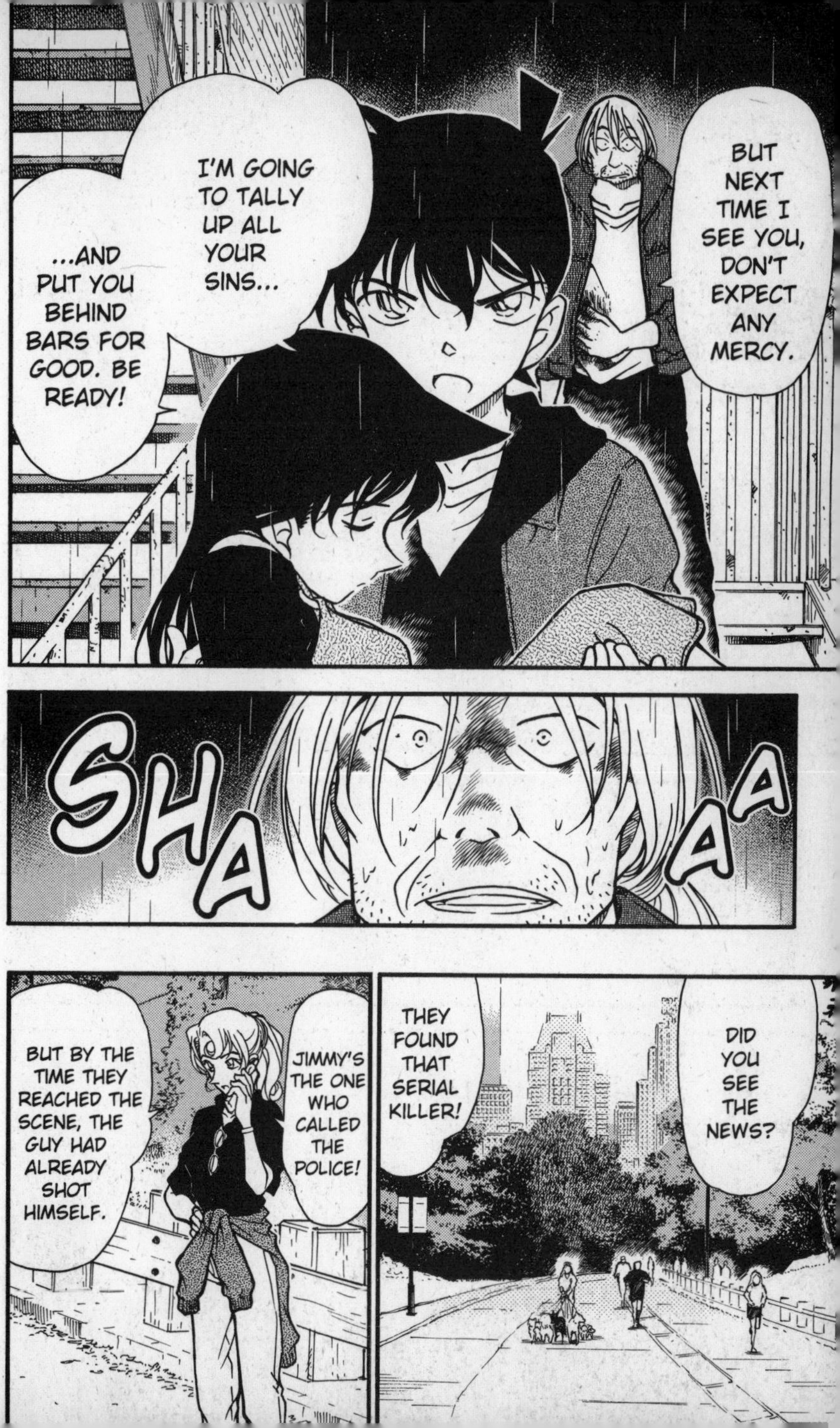
BUT NEXT TIME I SEE YOU, DON'T EXPECT ANY MERCY.
I'M GOING TO TALLY UP ALL YOUR SINS...
...AND PUT YOU BEHIND BARS FOR GOOD. BE READY!
SHAAAA
DID YOU SEE THE NEWS?
THEY FOUND THAT SERIAL KILLER!
JIMMY'S THE ONE WHO CALLED THE POLICE!
BUT BY THE TIME THEY REACHED THE SCENE, THE GUY HAD ALREADY SHOT HIMSELF.

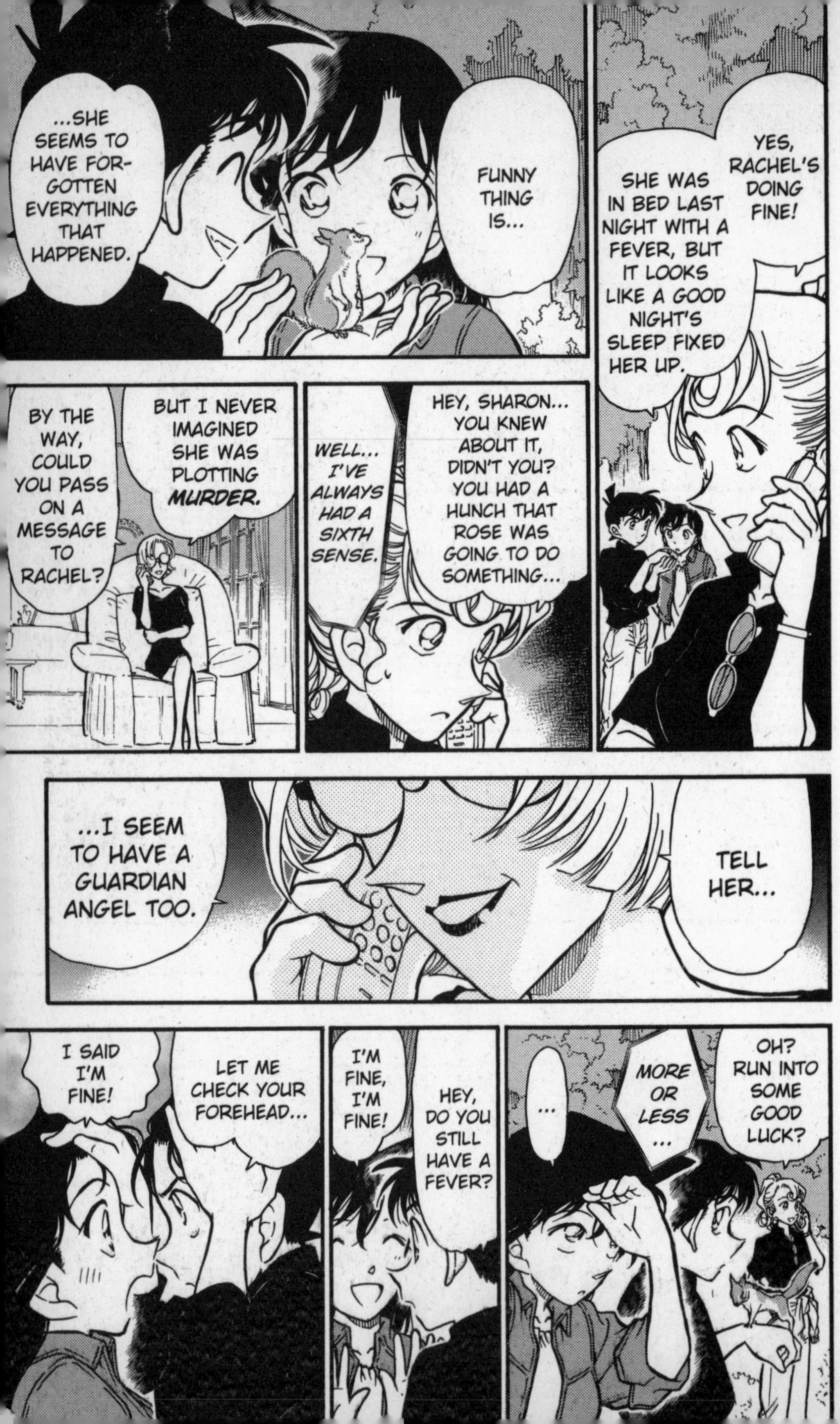
YES, RACHEL'S DOING FINE!
SHE WAS IN BED LAST NIGHT WITH A FEVER, BUT IT LOOKS LIKE A GOOD NIGHT'S SLEEP FIXED HER UP.
FUNNY THING IS...
...SHE SEEMS TO HAVE FOR-GOTTEN EVERYTHING THAT HAPPENED.
HEY, SHARON... YOU KNEW ABOUT IT, DIDN'T YOU? YOU HAD A HUNCH THAT ROSE WAS GOING TO DO SOMETHING...
WELL... I'VE ALWAYS HAD A SIXTH SENSE.
BUT I NEVER IMAGINED SHE WAS PLOTTING MURDER.
BY THE WAY, COULD YOU PASS ON A MESSAGE TO RACHEL?
TELL HER...
...I SEEM TO HAVE A GUARDIAN ANGEL TOO.
OH? RUN INTO SOME GOOD LUCK?
MORE OR LESS...
...
HEY, DO YOU STILL HAVE A FEVER?
I'M FINE, I'M FINE!
LET ME CHECK YOUR FOREHEAD...
I SAID I'M FINE!

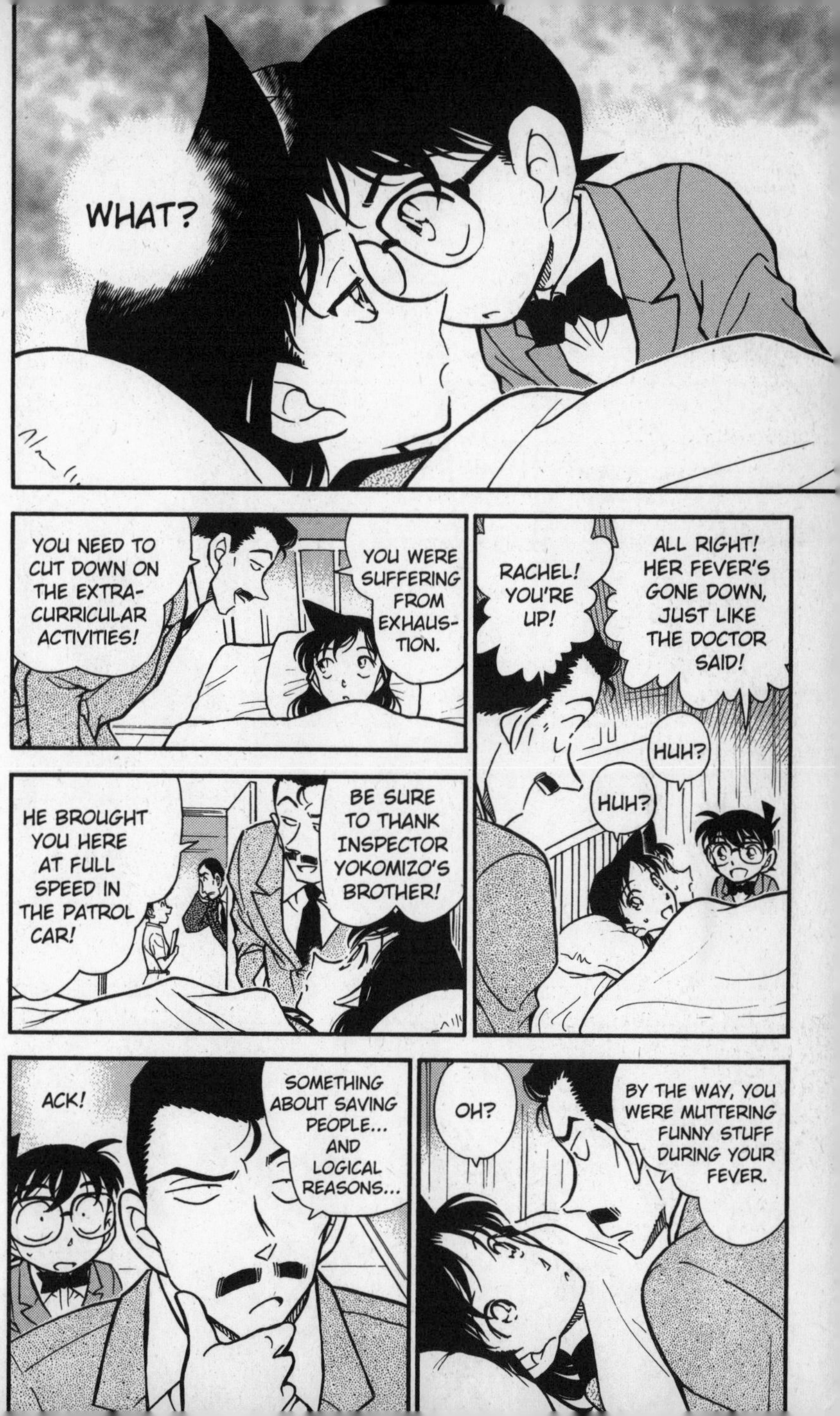
WHAT?
ALL RIGHT! HER FEVER'S GONE DOWN, JUST LIKE THE DOCTOR SAID!
RACHEL! YOU'RE UP!
HUH?
HUH?
YOU WERE SUFFERING FROM EXHAUS-TION.
YOU NEED TO CUT DOWN ON THE EXTRA-CURRICULAR ACTIVITIES!
BE SURE TO THANK INSPECTOR YOKOMIZO'S BROTHER!
HE BROUGHT YOU HERE AT FULL SPEED IN THE PATROL CAR!
BY THE WAY, YOU WERE MUTTERING FUNNY STUFF DURING YOUR FEVER.
OH?
SOMETHING ABOUT SAVING PEOPLE... AND LOGICAL REASONS...
ACK!

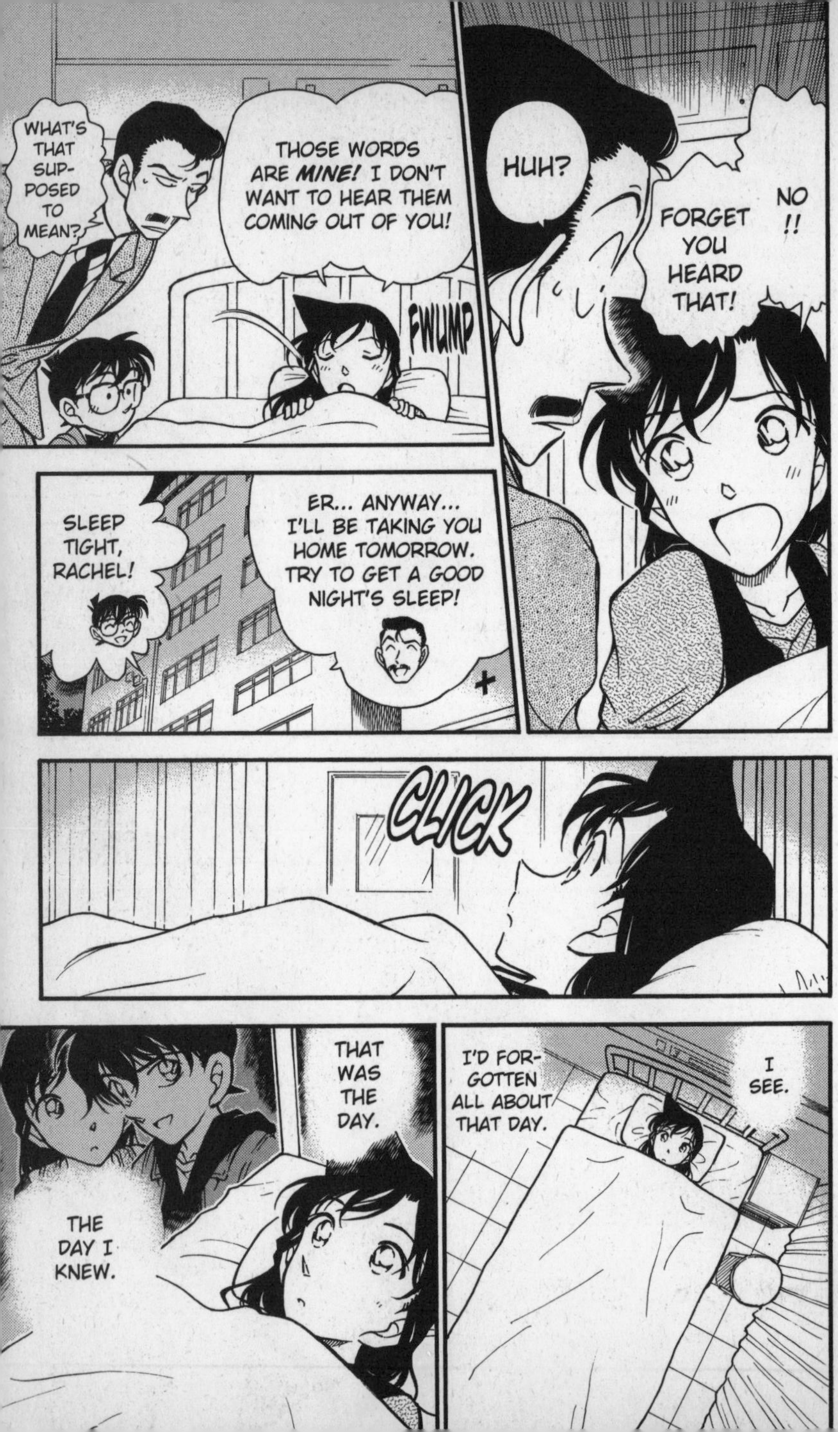
HUH?
NO !!
FORGET YOU HEARD THAT!
THOSE WORDS ARE *MINE!* I DON'T WANT TO HEAR THEM COMING OUT OF YOU!
WHAT'S THAT SUP-POSED TO MEAN?
FWUMP
ER... ANYWAY... I'LL BE TAKING YOU HOME TOMORROW. TRY TO GET A GOOD NIGHT'S SLEEP!
SLEEP TIGHT, RACHEL!
CLICK
I SEE.
I'D FOR-GOTTEN ALL ABOUT THAT DAY.
THAT WAS THE DAY.
THE DAY I KNEW.

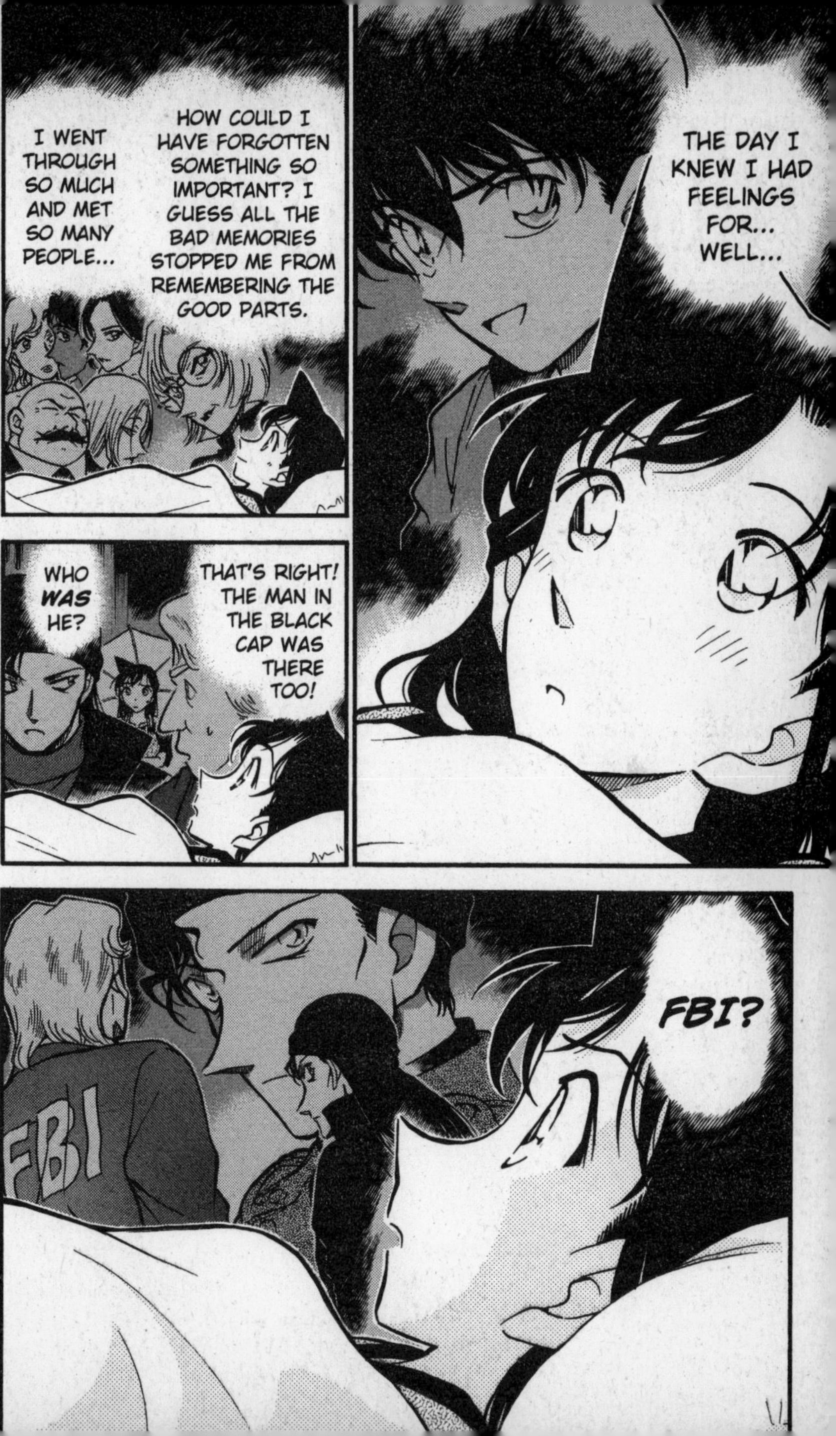
THE DAY I KNEW I HAD FEELINGS FOR... WELL...
HOW COULD I HAVE FORGOTTEN SOMETHING SO IMPORTANT? I GUESS ALL THE BAD MEMORIES STOPPED ME FROM REMEMBERING THE GOOD PARTS.
I WENT THROUGH SO MUCH AND MET SO MANY PEOPLE...
THAT'S RIGHT! THE MAN IN THE BLACK CAP WAS THERE TOO!
WHO *WAS* HE?
FBI?
FBI

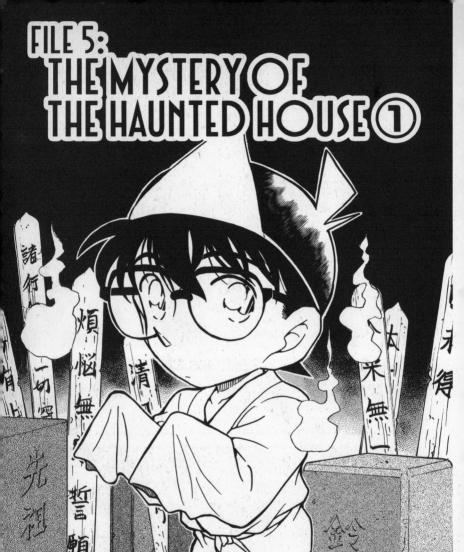

FILE 5: THE MYSTERY OF THE HAUNTED HOUSE ①

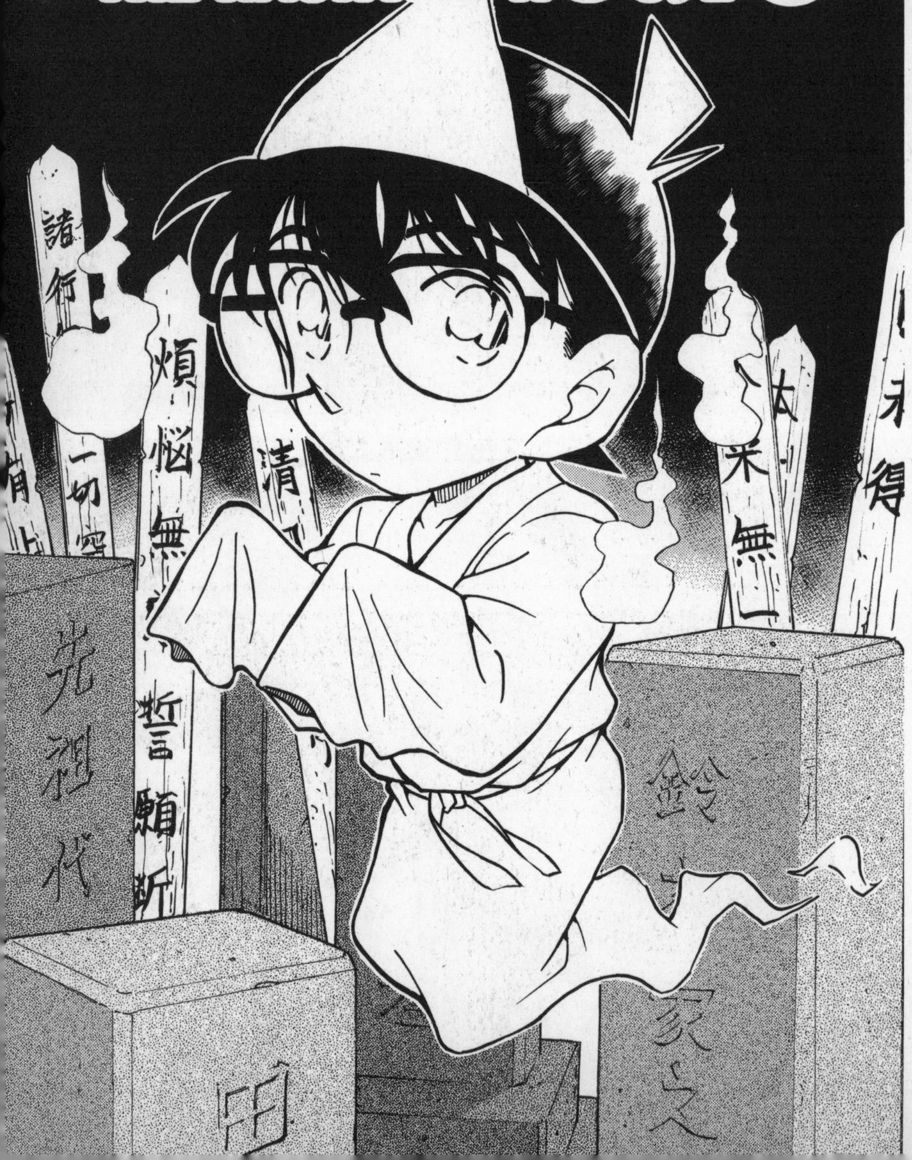

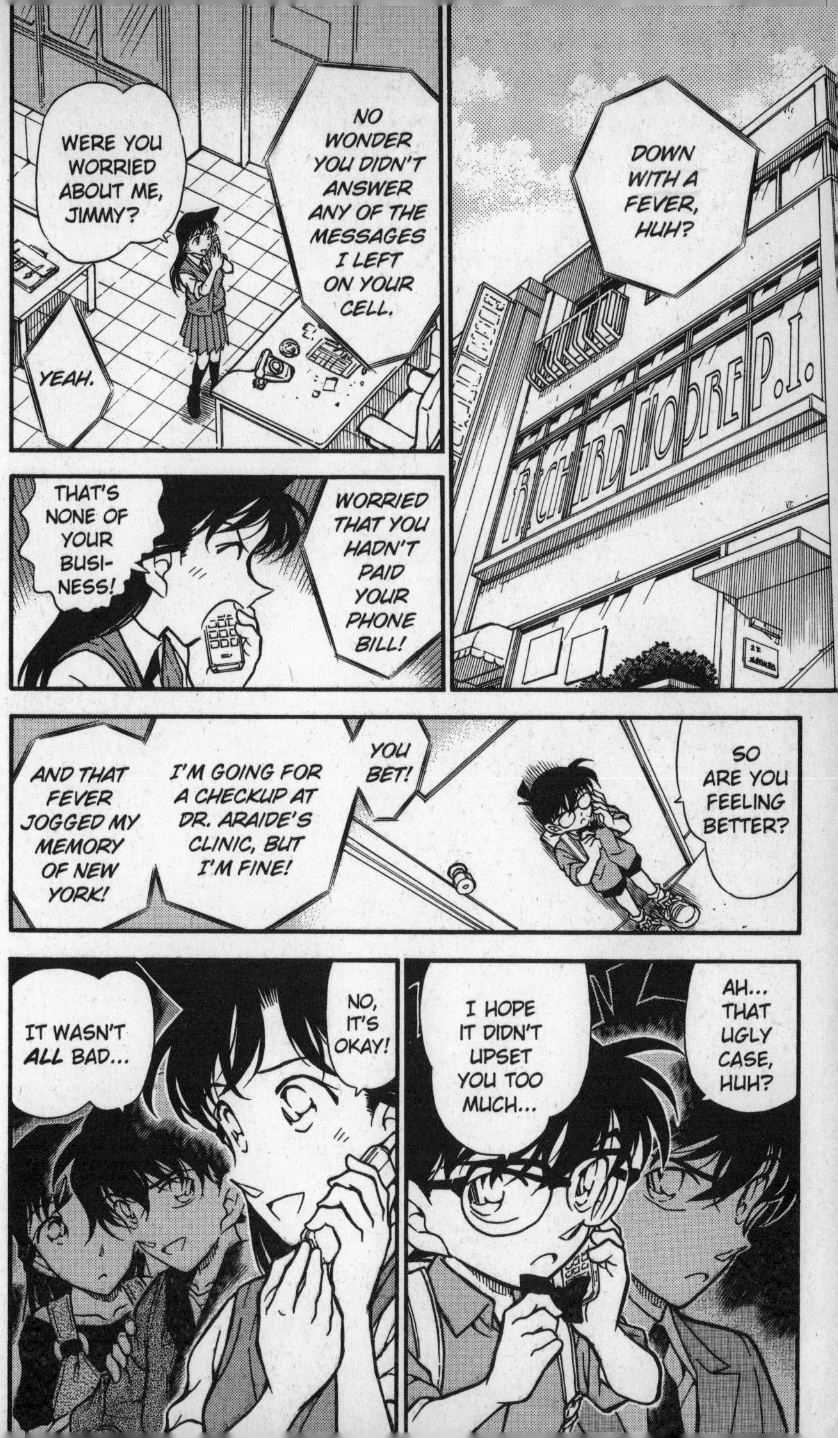
DOWN WITH A FEVER, HUH?
RICHARD MOORE P.I.
NO WONDER YOU DIDN'T ANSWER ANY OF THE MESSAGES I LEFT ON YOUR CELL.
WERE YOU WORRIED ABOUT ME, JIMMY?
YEAH.
WORRIED THAT YOU HADN'T PAID YOUR PHONE BILL!
THAT'S NONE OF YOUR BUSI-NESS!
SO ARE YOU FEELING BETTER?
YOU BET!
I'M GOING FOR A CHECKUP AT DR. ARAIDE'S CLINIC, BUT I'M FINE!
AND THAT FEVER JOGGED MY MEMORY OF NEW YORK!
AH... THAT UGLY CASE, HUH?
I HOPE IT DIDN'T UPSET YOU TOO MUCH...
NO, IT'S OKAY!
IT WASN'T **ALL** BAD...

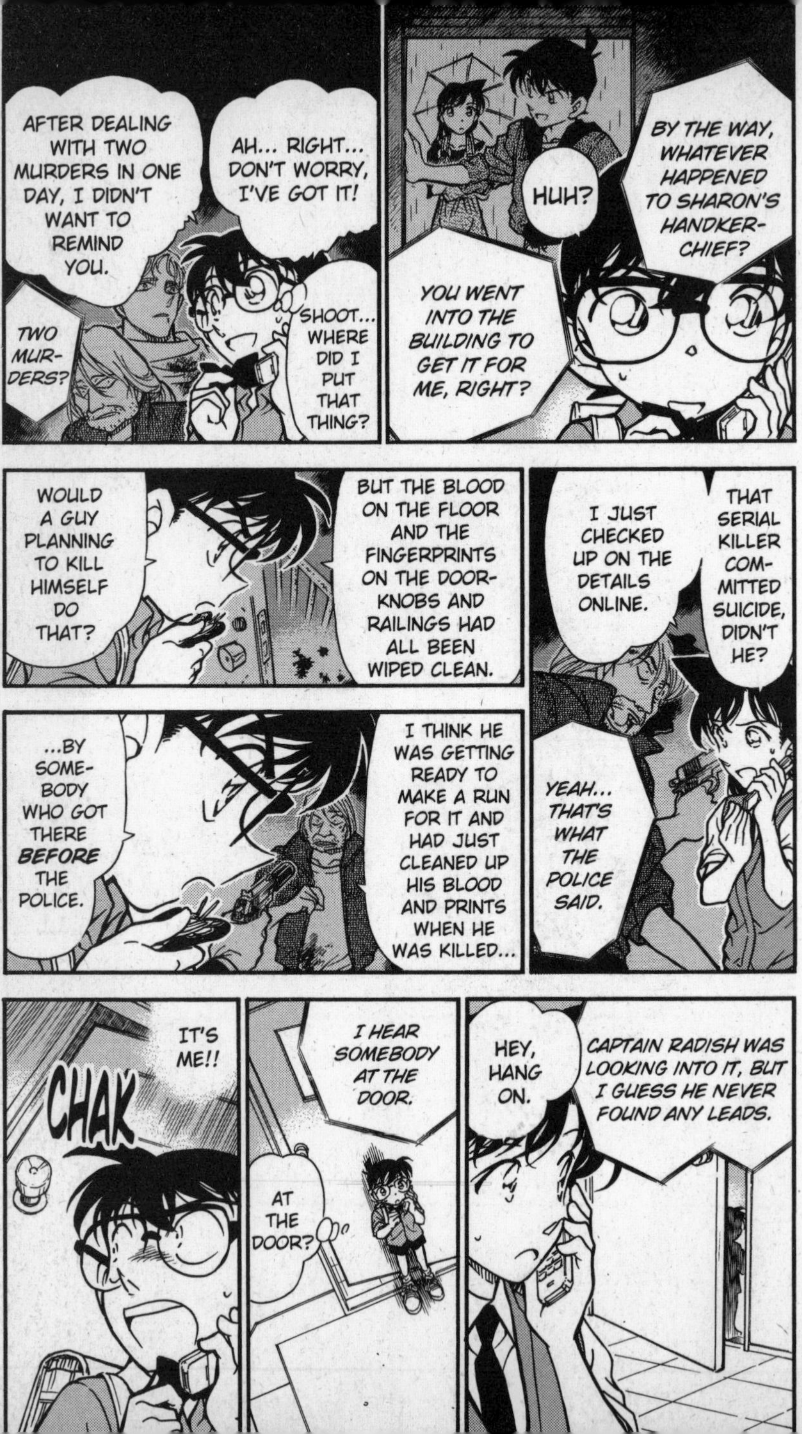

BY THE WAY, WHATEVER HAPPENED TO SHARON'S HANDKERCHIEF?
HUH?
YOU WENT INTO THE BUILDING TO GET IT FOR ME, RIGHT?
AH... RIGHT... DON'T WORRY, I'VE GOT IT!
AFTER DEALING WITH TWO MURDERS IN ONE DAY, I DIDN'T WANT TO REMIND YOU.
SHOOT... WHERE DID I PUT THAT THING?
TWO MURDERS?
THAT SERIAL KILLER COMMITTED SUICIDE, DIDN'T HE?
I JUST CHECKED UP ON THE DETAILS ONLINE.
YEAH... THAT'S WHAT THE POLICE SAID.
BUT THE BLOOD ON THE FLOOR AND THE FINGERPRINTS ON THE DOORKNOBS AND RAILINGS HAD ALL BEEN WIPED CLEAN.
WOULD A GUY PLANNING TO KILL HIMSELF DO THAT?
I THINK HE WAS GETTING READY TO MAKE A RUN FOR IT AND HAD JUST CLEANED UP HIS BLOOD AND PRINTS WHEN HE WAS KILLED...
...BY SOMEBODY WHO GOT THERE **BEFORE** THE POLICE.
CAPTAIN RADISH WAS LOOKING INTO IT, BUT I GUESS HE NEVER FOUND ANY LEADS.
HEY, HANG ON.
I HEAR SOMEBODY AT THE DOOR.
AT THE DOOR?
IT'S ME!!
CHAK

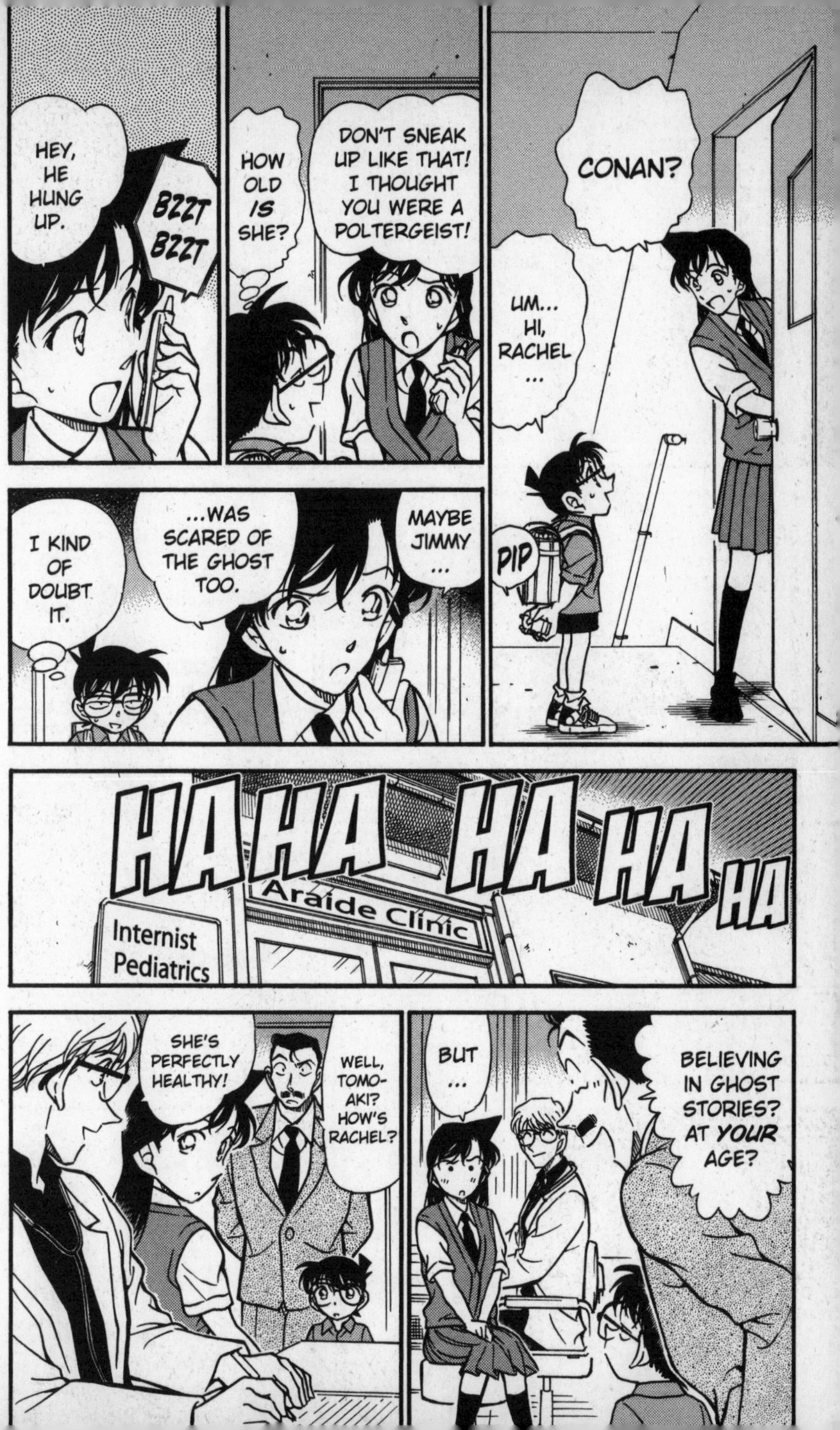
CONAN?
UM... HI, RACHEL ...
PIP
DON'T SNEAK UP LIKE THAT! I THOUGHT YOU WERE A POLTERGEIST!
HOW OLD IS SHE?
BZZT BZZT
HEY, HE HUNG UP.
MAYBE JIMMY ...
...WAS SCARED OF THE GHOST TOO.
I KIND OF DOUBT IT.
HAHA HA HA HA
Araide Clinic
Internist
Pediatrics
BELIEVING IN GHOST STORIES? AT YOUR AGE?
BUT ...
WELL, TOMO-AKI? HOW'S RACHEL?
SHE'S PERFECTLY HEALTHY!

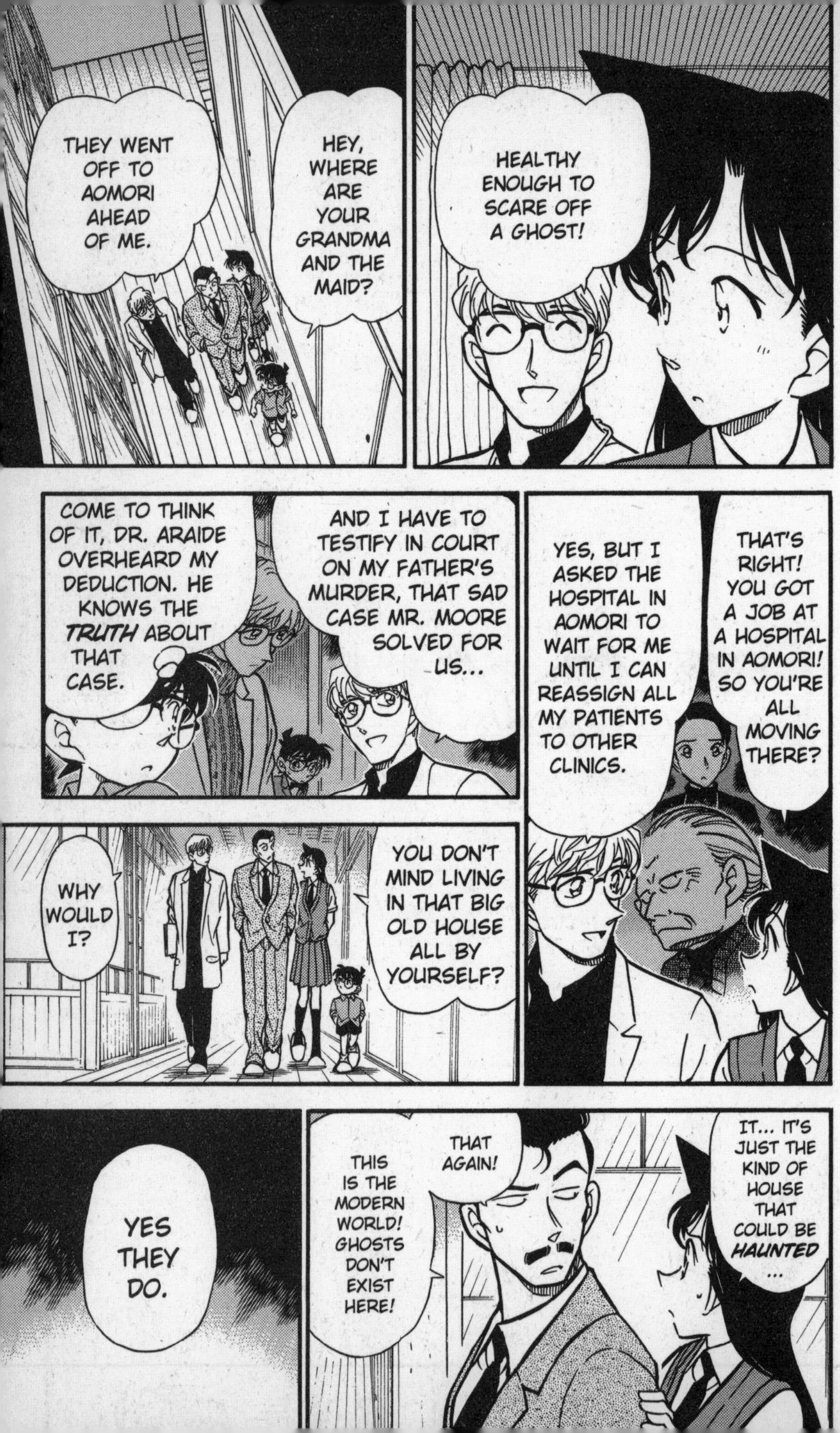
HEALTHY ENOUGH TO SCARE OFF A GHOST!
HEY, WHERE ARE YOUR GRANDMA AND THE MAID?
THEY WENT OFF TO AOMORI AHEAD OF ME.
THAT'S RIGHT! YOU GOT A JOB AT A HOSPITAL IN AOMORI! SO YOU'RE ALL MOVING THERE?
YES, BUT I ASKED THE HOSPITAL IN AOMORI TO WAIT FOR ME UNTIL I CAN REASSIGN ALL MY PATIENTS TO OTHER CLINICS.
AND I HAVE TO TESTIFY IN COURT ON MY FATHER'S MURDER, THAT SAD CASE MR. MOORE SOLVED FOR US...
COME TO THINK OF IT, DR. ARAIDE OVERHEARD MY DEDUCTION. HE KNOWS THE *TRUTH* ABOUT THAT CASE.
YOU DON'T MIND LIVING IN THAT BIG OLD HOUSE ALL BY YOURSELF?
WHY WOULD I?
IT... IT'S JUST THE KIND OF HOUSE THAT COULD BE *HAUNTED*...
THAT AGAIN!
THIS IS THE MODERN WORLD! GHOSTS DON'T EXIST HERE!
YES THEY DO.

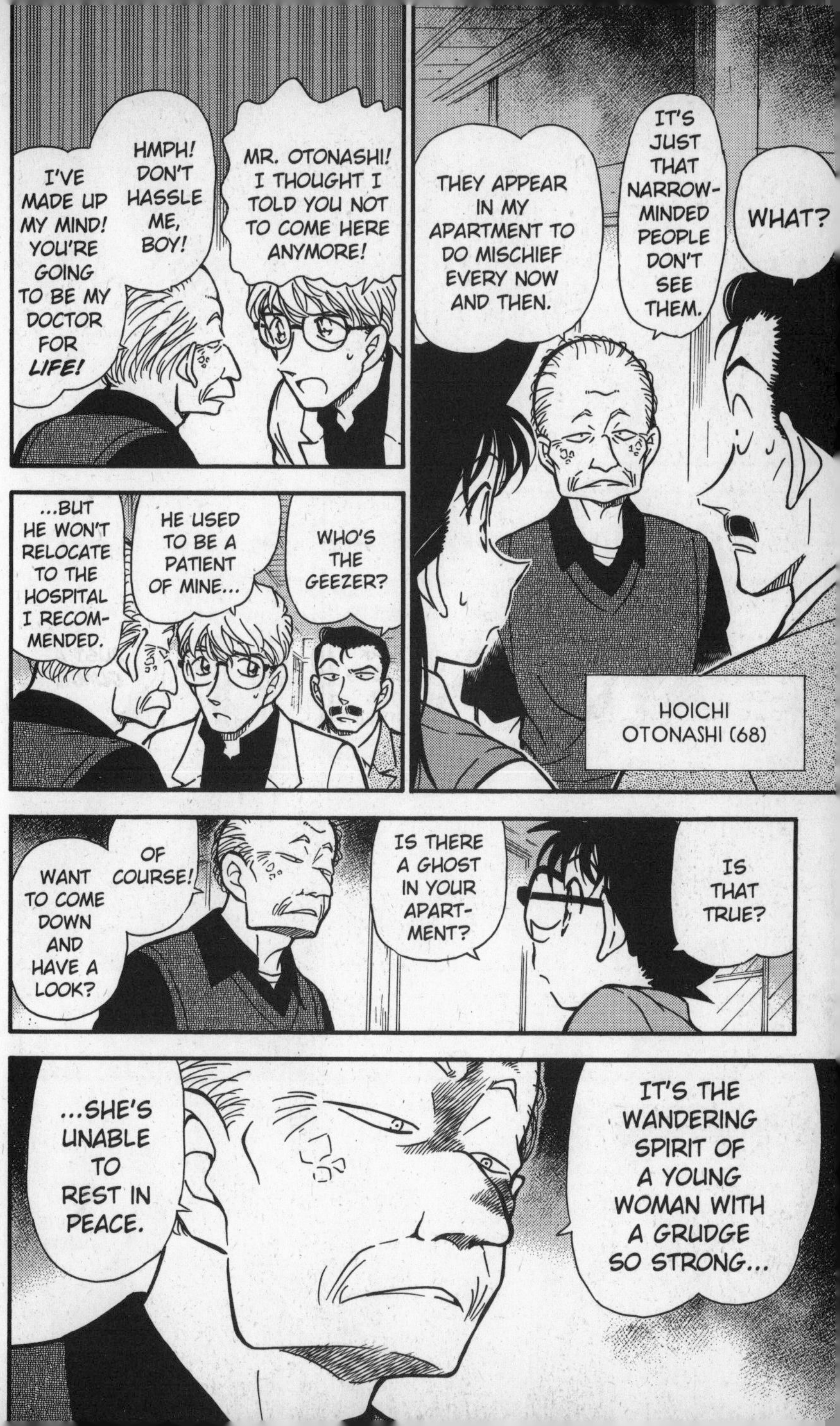
WHAT?
IT'S JUST THAT NARROW-MINDED PEOPLE DON'T SEE THEM.
THEY APPEAR IN MY APARTMENT TO DO MISCHIEF EVERY NOW AND THEN.
HOICHI OTONASHI (68)
MR. OTONASHI! I THOUGHT I TOLD YOU NOT TO COME HERE ANYMORE!
HMPH! DON'T HASSLE ME, BOY!
I'VE MADE UP MY MIND! YOU'RE GOING TO BE MY DOCTOR FOR *LIFE!*
WHO'S THE GEEZER?
HE USED TO BE A PATIENT OF MINE...
...BUT HE WON'T RELOCATE TO THE HOSPITAL I RECOMMENDED.
IS THAT TRUE?
IS THERE A GHOST IN YOUR APARTMENT?
OF COURSE!
WANT TO COME DOWN AND HAVE A LOOK?
IT'S THE WANDERING SPIRIT OF A YOUNG WOMAN WITH A GRUDGE SO STRONG...
...SHE'S UNABLE TO REST IN PEACE.

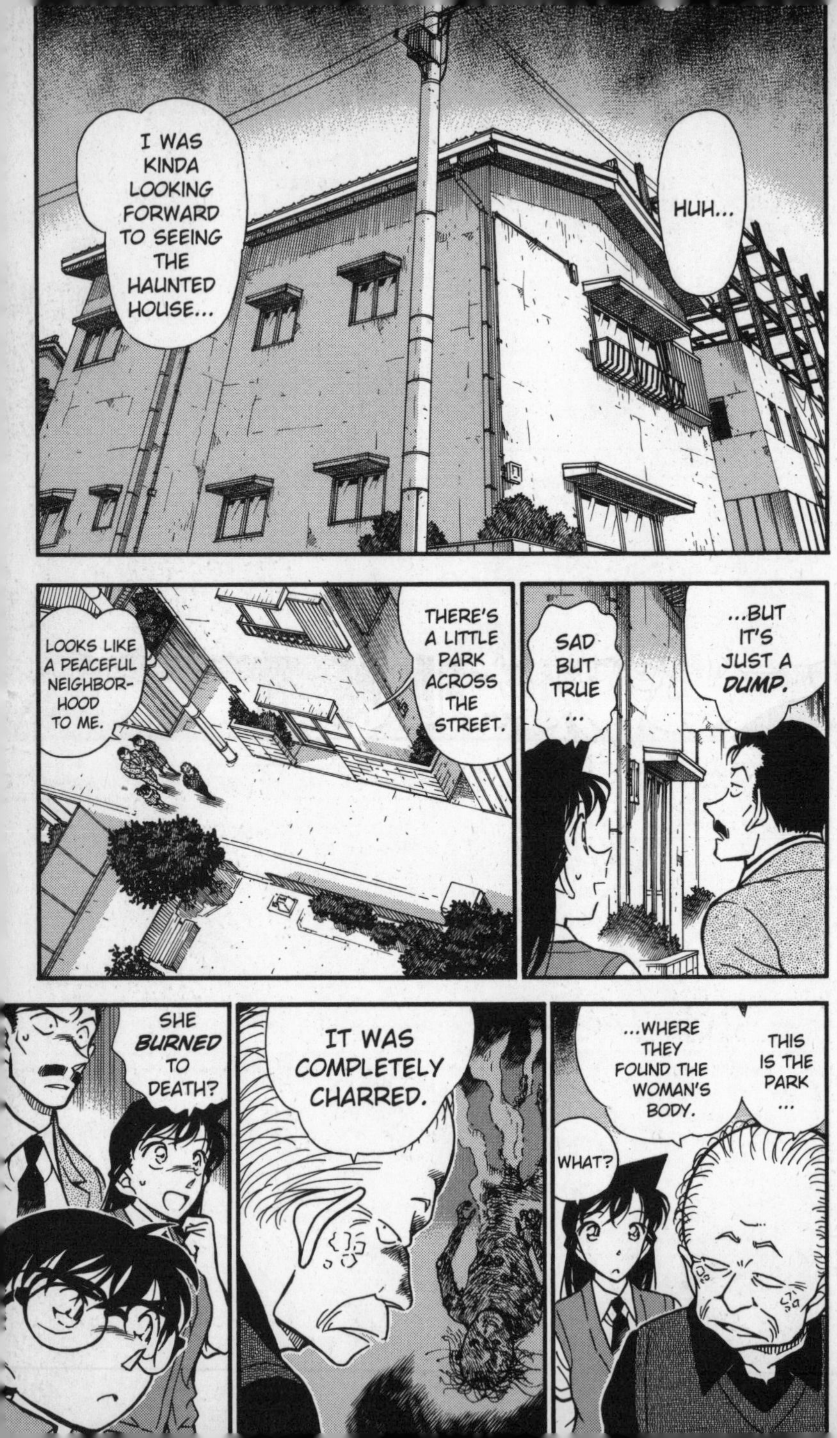
HUH...
I WAS KINDA LOOKING FORWARD TO SEEING THE HAUNTED HOUSE...
...BUT IT'S JUST A **DUMP.**
SAD BUT TRUE...
THERE'S A LITTLE PARK ACROSS THE STREET.
LOOKS LIKE A PEACEFUL NEIGHBORHOOD TO ME.
THIS IS THE PARK...
...WHERE THEY FOUND THE WOMAN'S BODY.
...
WHAT?
IT WAS COMPLETELY CHARRED.
SHE **BURNED** TO DEATH?

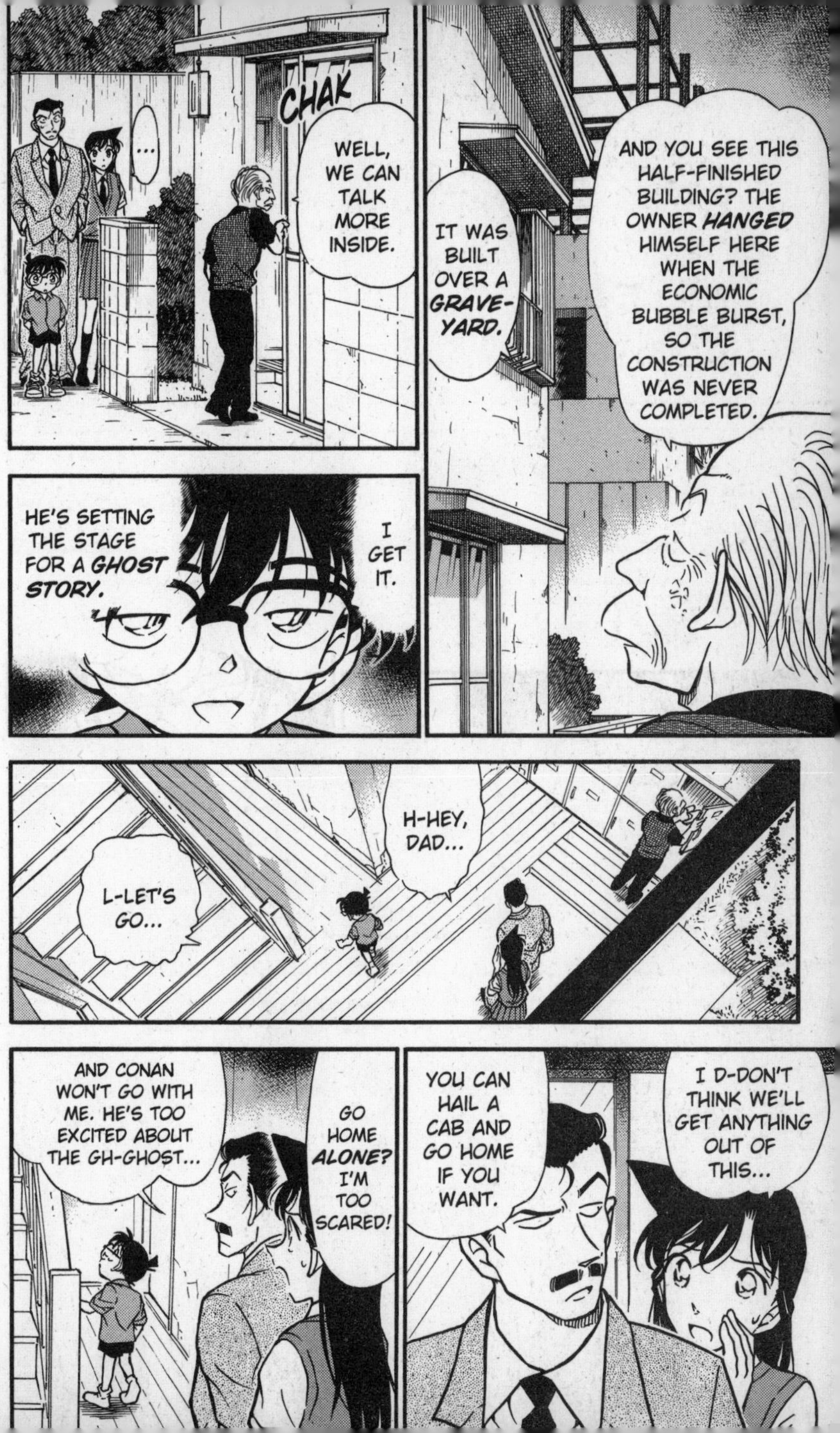
AND YOU SEE THIS HALF-FINISHED BUILDING? THE OWNER HANGED HIMSELF HERE WHEN THE ECONOMIC BUBBLE BURST, SO THE CONSTRUCTION WAS NEVER COMPLETED.
IT WAS BUILT OVER A GRAVEYARD.
CHAK
WELL, WE CAN TALK MORE INSIDE.
...
I GET IT.
HE'S SETTING THE STAGE FOR A GHOST STORY.
H-HEY, DAD...
L-LET'S GO...
I D-DON'T THINK WE'LL GET ANYTHING OUT OF THIS...
YOU CAN HAIL A CAB AND GO HOME IF YOU WANT.
GO HOME ALONE? I'M TOO SCARED!
AND CONAN WON'T GO WITH ME. HE'S TOO EXCITED ABOUT THE GH-GHOST...

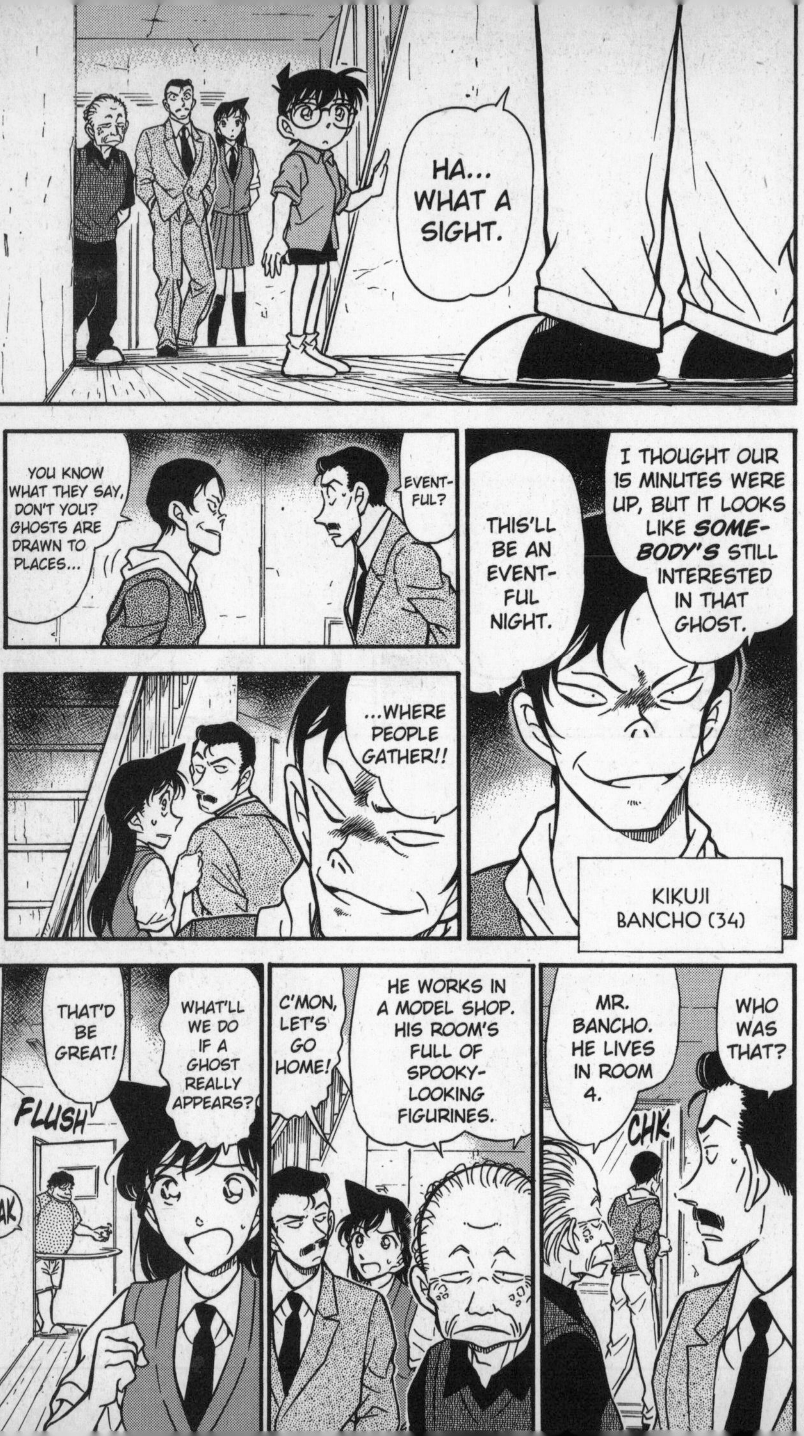
HA... WHAT A SIGHT.
I THOUGHT OUR 15 MINUTES WERE UP, BUT IT LOOKS LIKE SOMEBODY'S STILL INTERESTED IN THAT GHOST.
THIS'LL BE AN EVENTFUL NIGHT.
KIKUJI BANCHO (34)
EVENTFUL?
YOU KNOW WHAT THEY SAY, DON'T YOU? GHOSTS ARE DRAWN TO PLACES...
...WHERE PEOPLE GATHER!!
WHO WAS THAT?
MR. BANCHO. HE LIVES IN ROOM 4.
CHK
HE WORKS IN A MODEL SHOP. HIS ROOM'S FULL OF SPOOKY-LOOKING FIGURINES.
C'MON, LET'S GO HOME!
WHAT'LL WE DO IF A GHOST REALLY APPEARS?
THAT'D BE GREAT!
FLUSH
CHAK

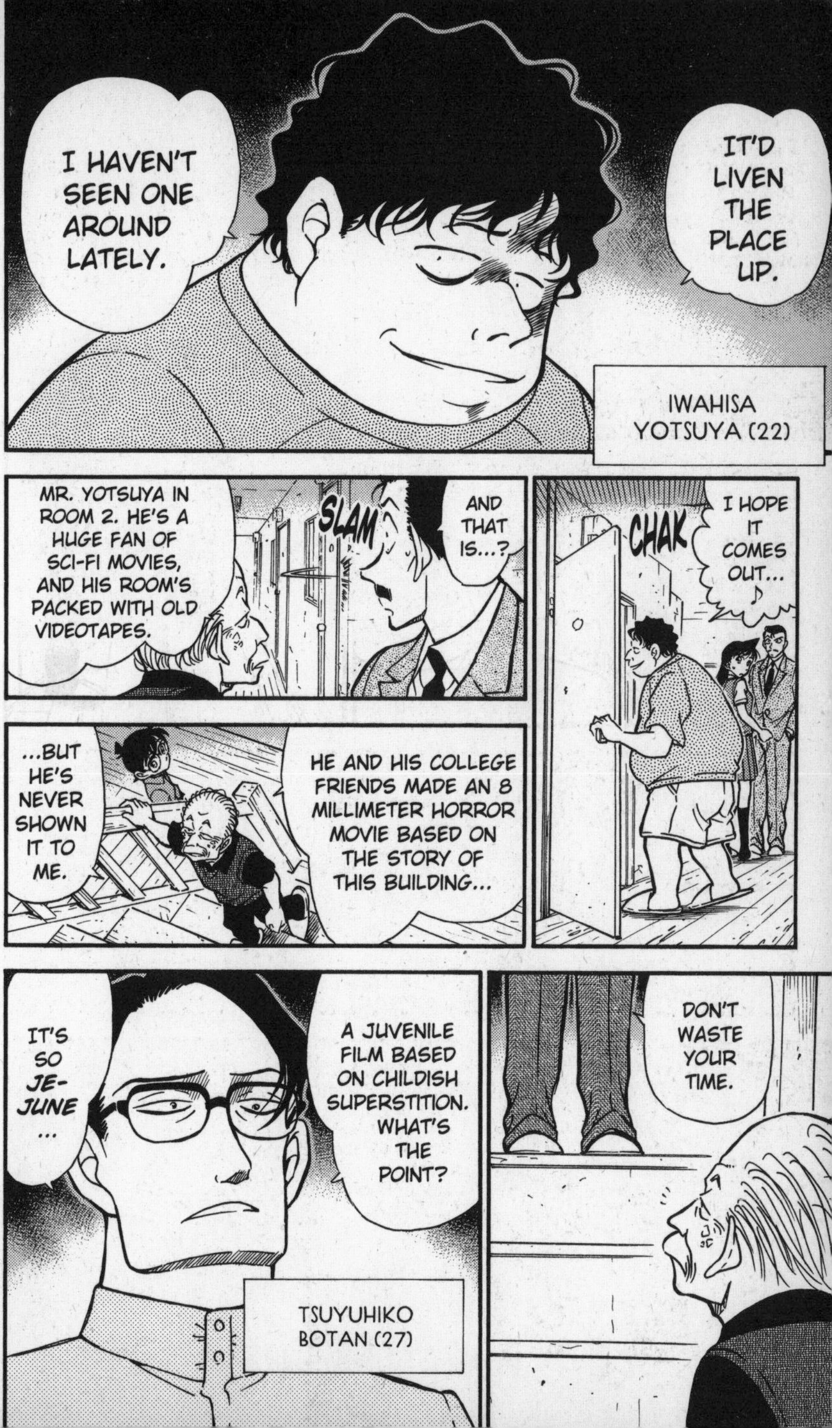
IT'D LIVEN THE PLACE UP.
I HAVEN'T SEEN ONE AROUND LATELY.
IWAHISA YOTSUYA (22)
CHAK
I HOPE IT COMES OUT... ♪
AND THAT IS...?
SLAM
MR. YOTSUYA IN ROOM 2. HE'S A HUGE FAN OF SCI-FI MOVIES, AND HIS ROOM'S PACKED WITH OLD VIDEOTAPES.
HE AND HIS COLLEGE FRIENDS MADE AN 8 MILLIMETER HORROR MOVIE BASED ON THE STORY OF THIS BUILDING...
...BUT HE'S NEVER SHOWN IT TO ME.
DON'T WASTE YOUR TIME.
A JUVENILE FILM BASED ON CHILDISH SUPERSTITION. WHAT'S THE POINT?
IT'S SO JE-JUNE...
TSUYUHIKO BOTAN (27)

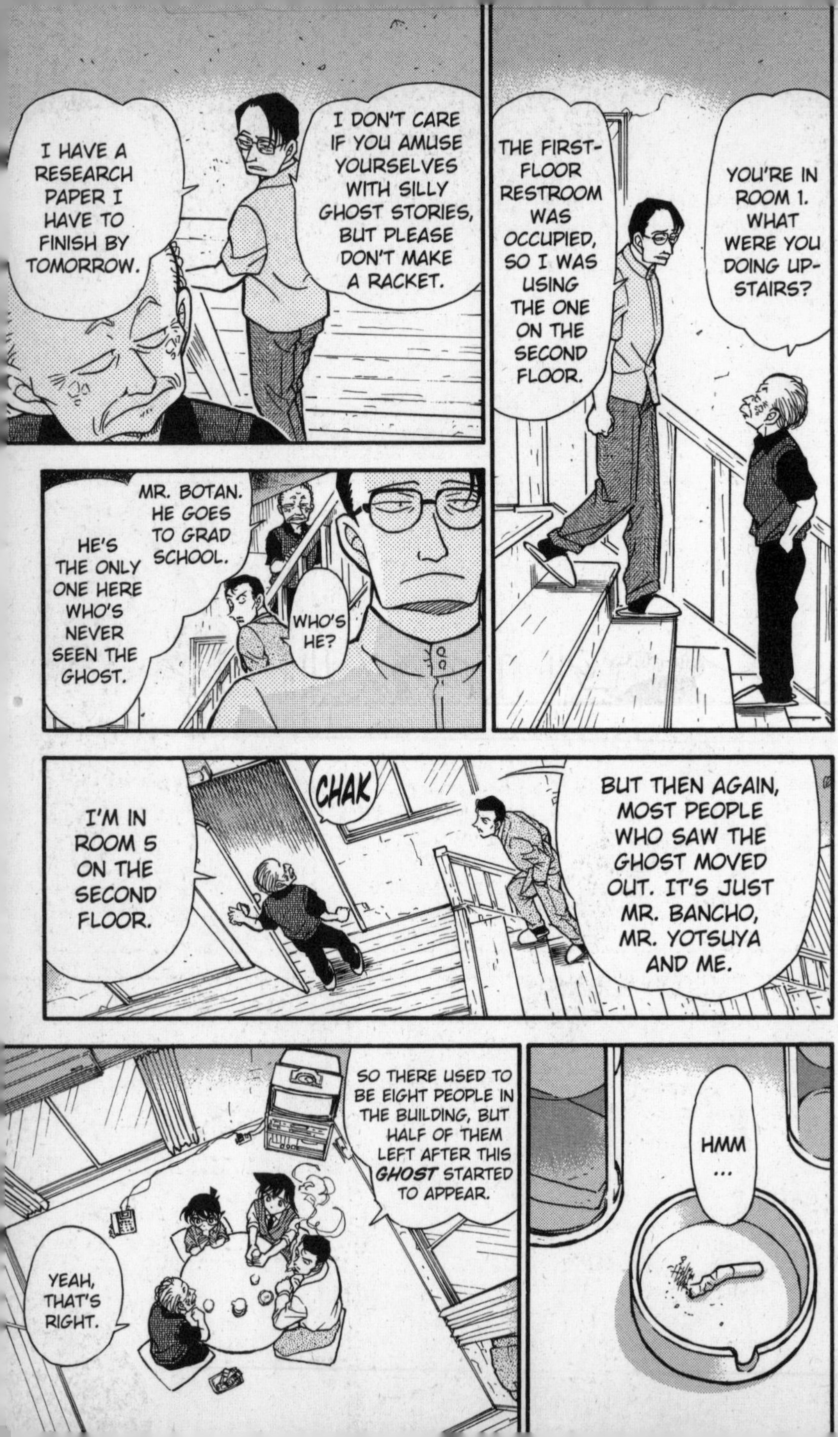
YOU'RE IN ROOM 1. WHAT WERE YOU DOING UP-STAIRS?
THE FIRST-FLOOR RESTROOM WAS OCCUPIED, SO I WAS USING THE ONE ON THE SECOND FLOOR.
I DON'T CARE IF YOU AMUSE YOURSELVES WITH SILLY GHOST STORIES, BUT PLEASE DON'T MAKE A RACKET.
I HAVE A RESEARCH PAPER I HAVE TO FINISH BY TOMORROW.
WHO'S HE?
MR. BOTAN. HE GOES TO GRAD SCHOOL.
HE'S THE ONLY ONE HERE WHO'S NEVER SEEN THE GHOST.
BUT THEN AGAIN, MOST PEOPLE WHO SAW THE GHOST MOVED OUT. IT'S JUST MR. BANCHO, MR. YOTSUYA AND ME.
CHAK
I'M IN ROOM 5 ON THE SECOND FLOOR.
HMM ...
SO THERE USED TO BE EIGHT PEOPLE IN THE BUILDING, BUT HALF OF THEM LEFT AFTER THIS GHOST STARTED TO APPEAR.
YEAH, THAT'S RIGHT.

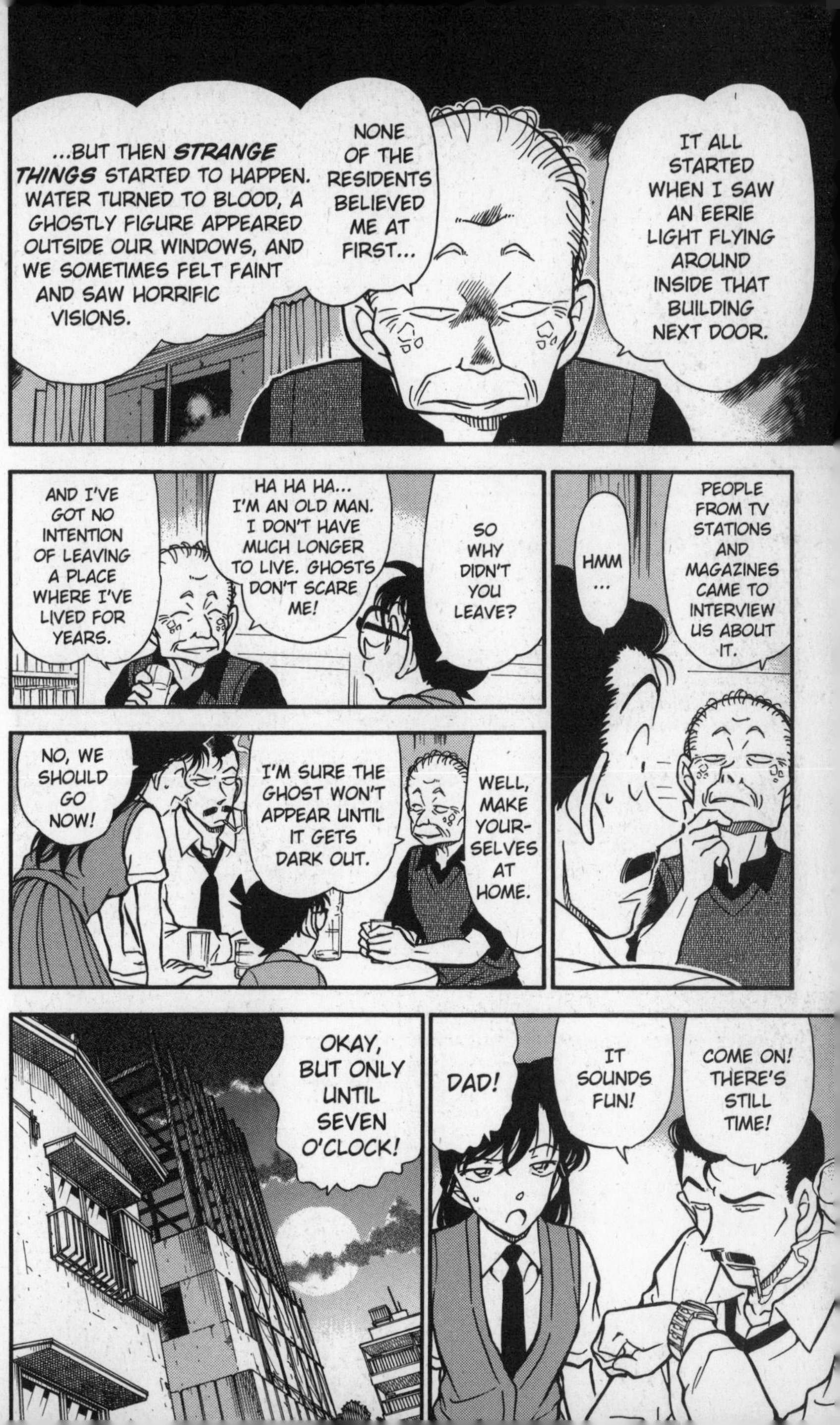
IT ALL STARTED WHEN I SAW AN EERIE LIGHT FLYING AROUND INSIDE THAT BUILDING NEXT DOOR.
NONE OF THE RESIDENTS BELIEVED ME AT FIRST...
...BUT THEN *STRANGE THINGS* STARTED TO HAPPEN. WATER TURNED TO BLOOD, A GHOSTLY FIGURE APPEARED OUTSIDE OUR WINDOWS, AND WE SOMETIMES FELT FAINT AND SAW HORRIFIC VISIONS.
PEOPLE FROM TV STATIONS AND MAGAZINES CAME TO INTERVIEW US ABOUT IT.
HMM...
SO WHY DIDN'T YOU LEAVE?
HA HA HA... I'M AN OLD MAN. I DON'T HAVE MUCH LONGER TO LIVE. GHOSTS DON'T SCARE ME!
AND I'VE GOT NO INTENTION OF LEAVING A PLACE WHERE I'VE LIVED FOR YEARS.
WELL, MAKE YOURSELVES AT HOME.
I'M SURE THE GHOST WON'T APPEAR UNTIL IT GETS DARK OUT.
NO, WE SHOULD GO NOW!
COME ON! THERE'S STILL TIME!
IT SOUNDS FUN!
DAD!
OKAY, BUT ONLY UNTIL SEVEN O'CLOCK!

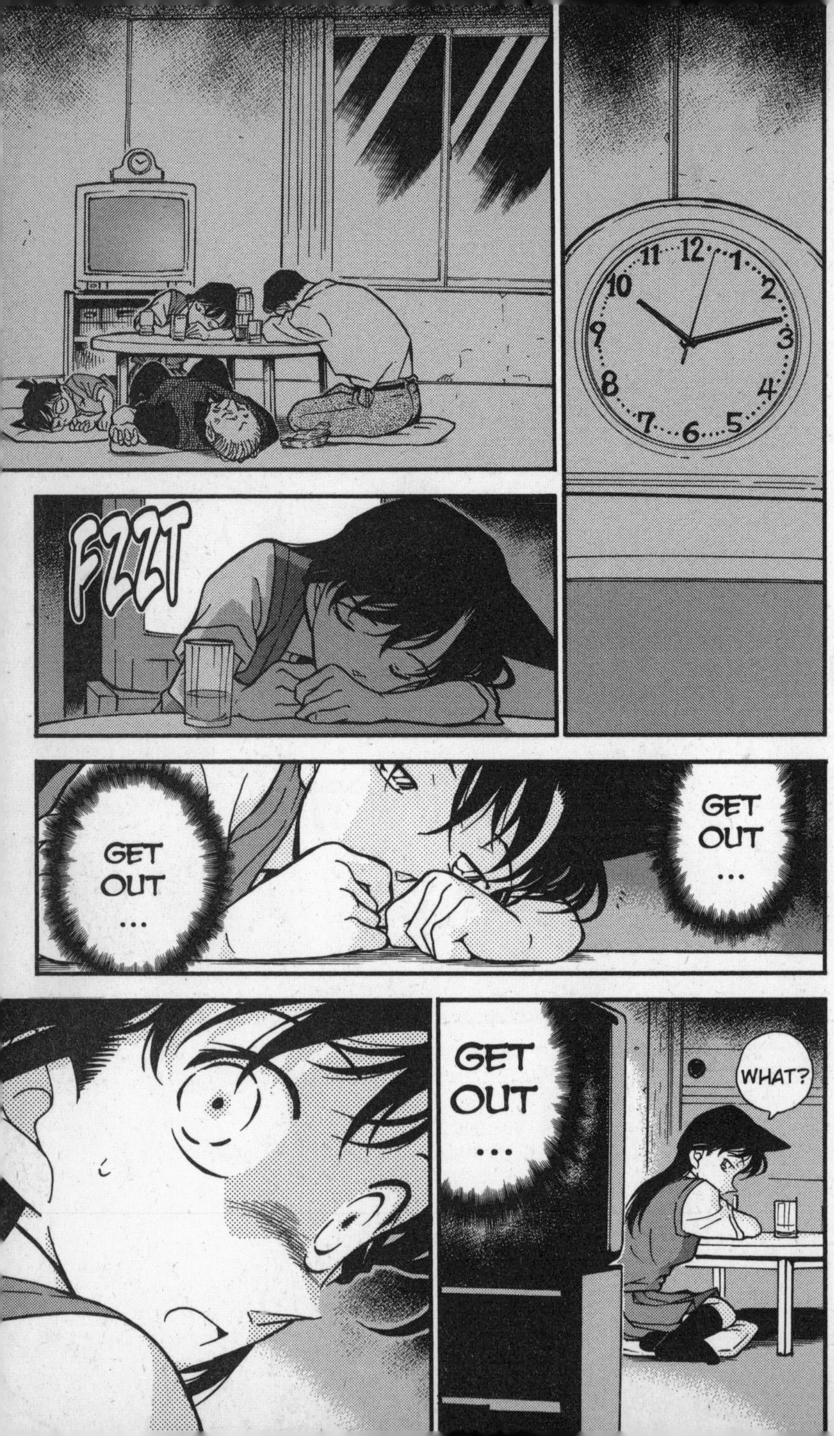
FZZT
GET OUT ...
GET OUT ...
WHAT?
GET OUT ...

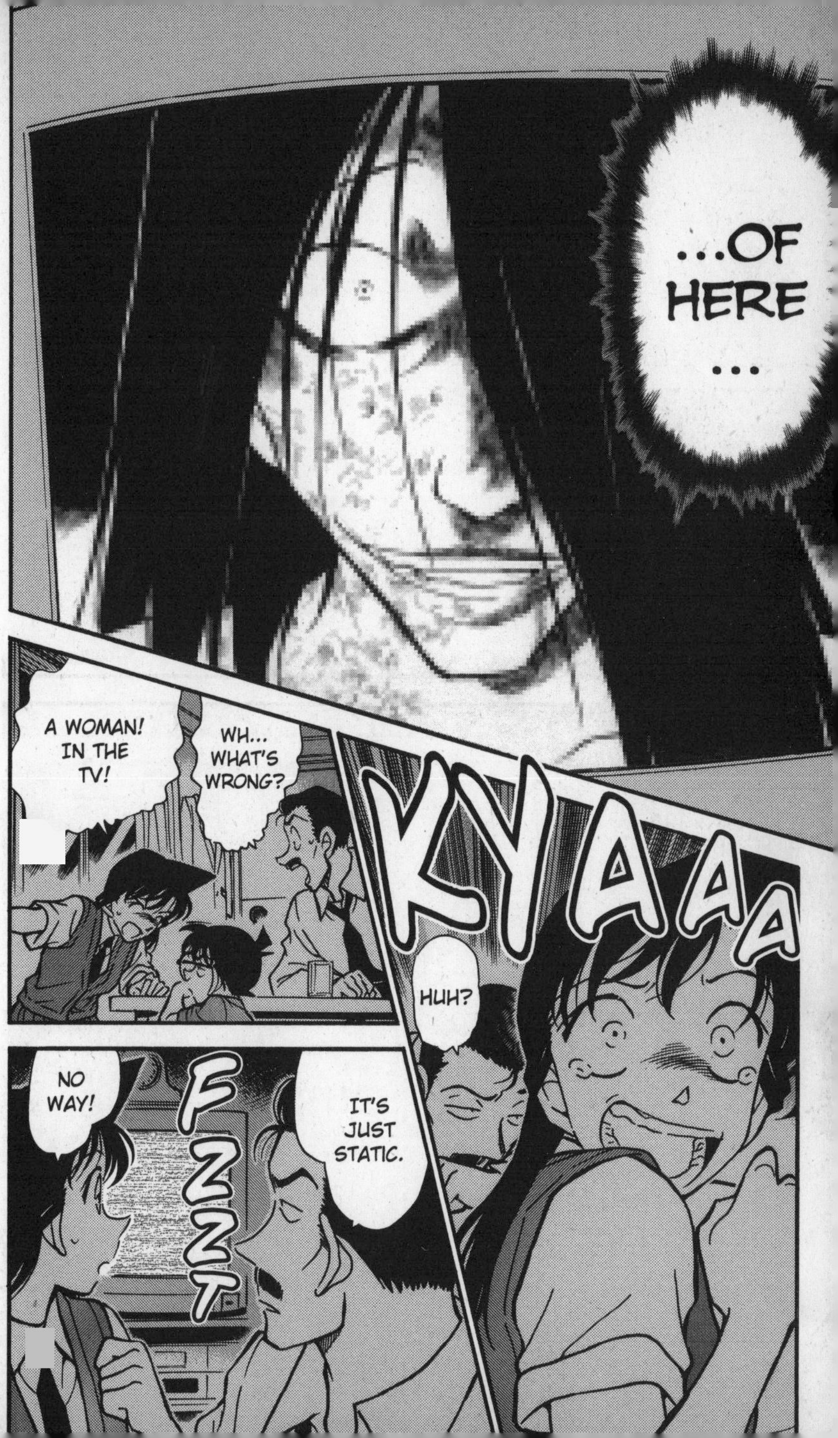
...OF HERE ...
KYAAAA
HUH?
WH... WHAT'S WRONG?
A WOMAN! IN THE TV!
IT'S JUST STATIC.
FZZT
NO WAY!

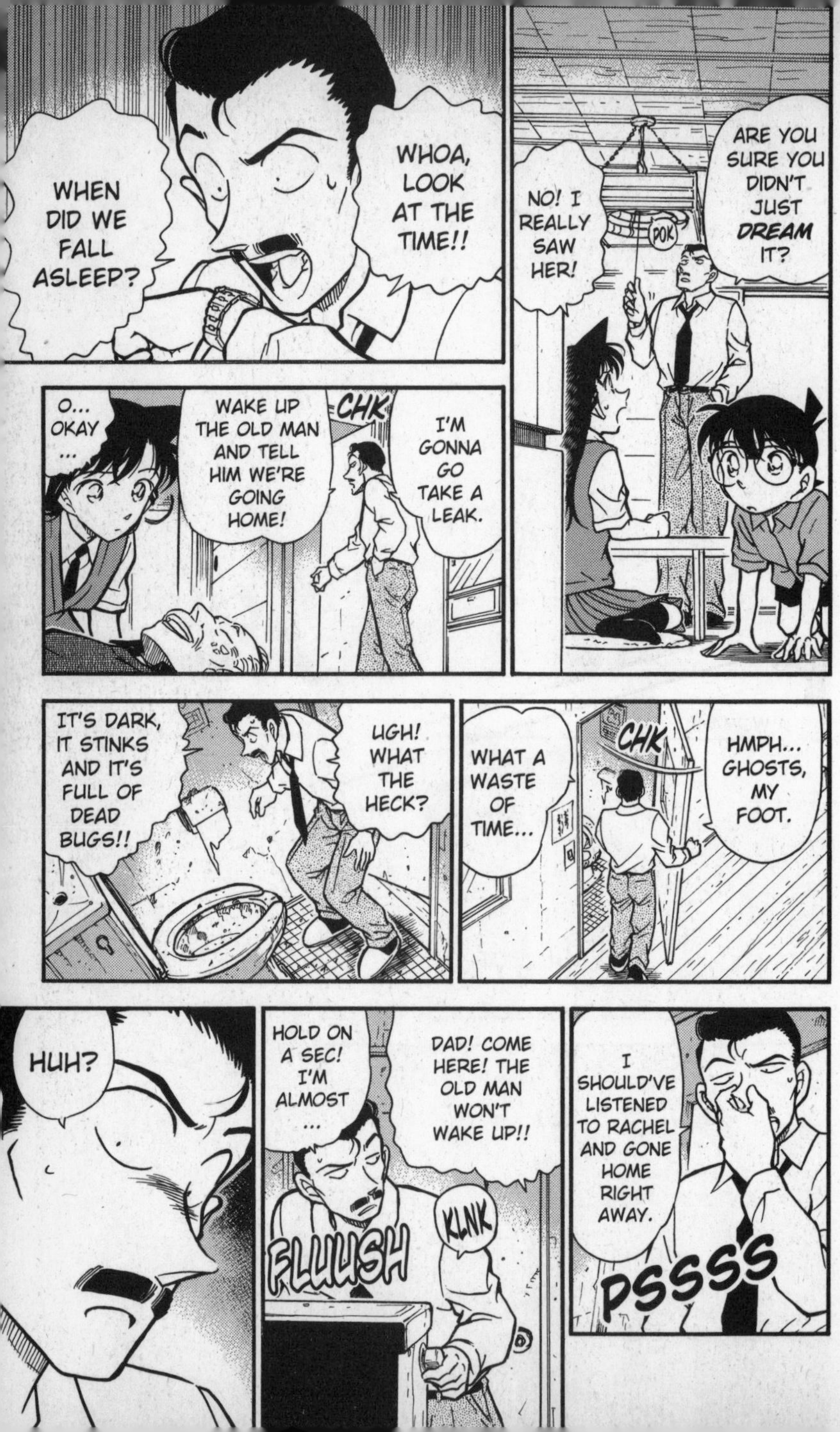
ARE YOU SURE YOU DIDN'T JUST DREAM IT?
NO! I REALLY SAW HER!
POK
WHOA, LOOK AT THE TIME!!
WHEN DID WE FALL ASLEEP?
CHK
I'M GONNA GO TAKE A LEAK.
WAKE UP THE OLD MAN AND TELL HIM WE'RE GOING HOME!
O... OKAY ...
CHK
HMPH... GHOSTS, MY FOOT.
WHAT A WASTE OF TIME...
UGH! WHAT THE HECK?
IT'S DARK, IT STINKS AND IT'S FULL OF DEAD BUGS!!
I SHOULD'VE LISTENED TO RACHEL AND GONE HOME RIGHT AWAY.
PSSSS
DAD! COME HERE! THE OLD MAN WON'T WAKE UP!!
HOLD ON A SEC! I'M ALMOST ...
KLNK
FLUUSH
HUH?

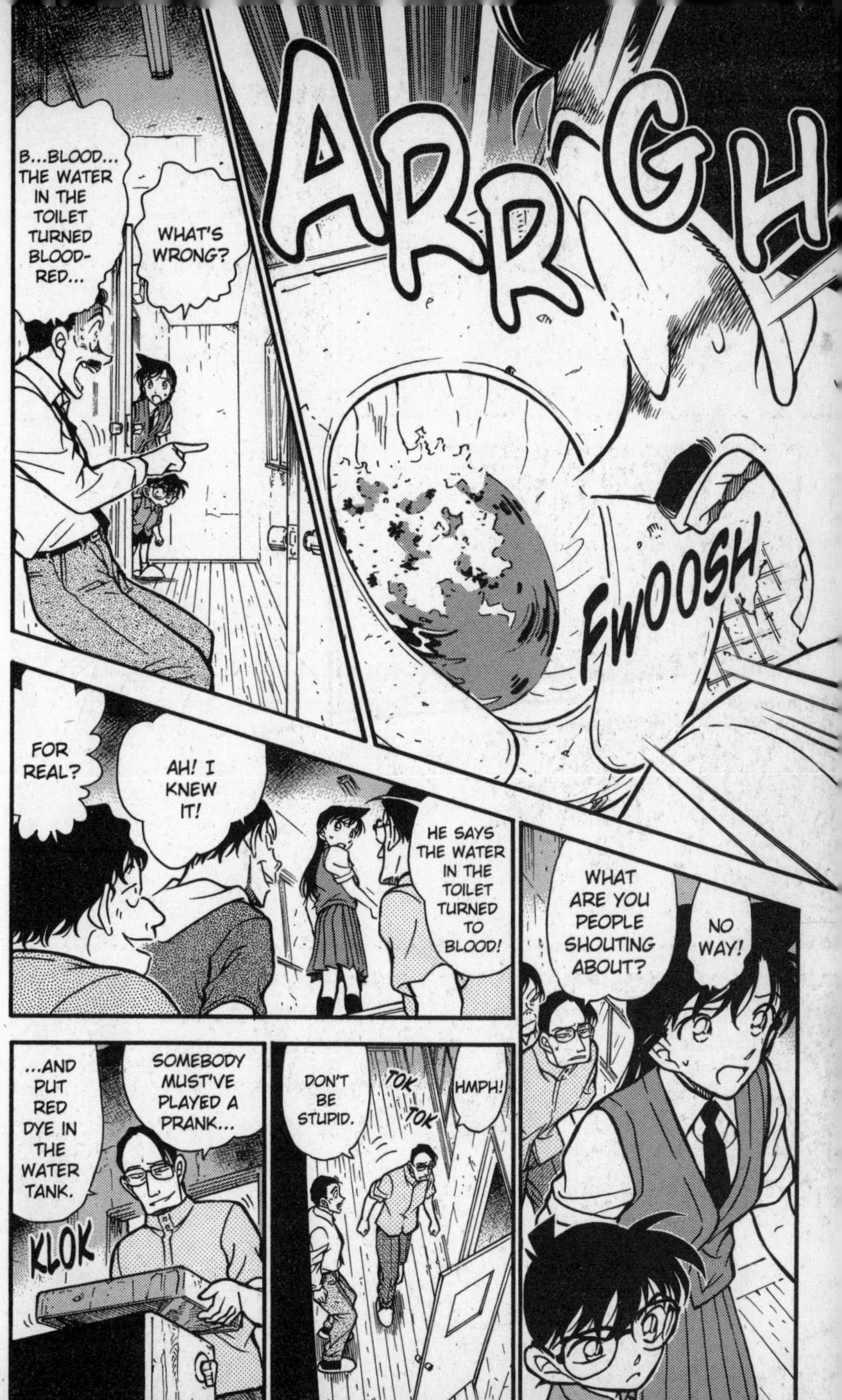
ARRGH
FWOOSH
B...BLOOD... THE WATER IN THE TOILET TURNED BLOOD-RED...
WHAT'S WRONG?
WHAT ARE YOU PEOPLE SHOUTING ABOUT?
NO WAY!
HE SAYS THE WATER IN THE TOILET TURNED TO BLOOD!
AH! I KNEW IT!
FOR REAL?
HMPH!
TOK TOK
DON'T BE STUPID.
SOMEBODY MUST'VE PLAYED A PRANK...
...AND PUT RED DYE IN THE WATER TANK.
KLOK

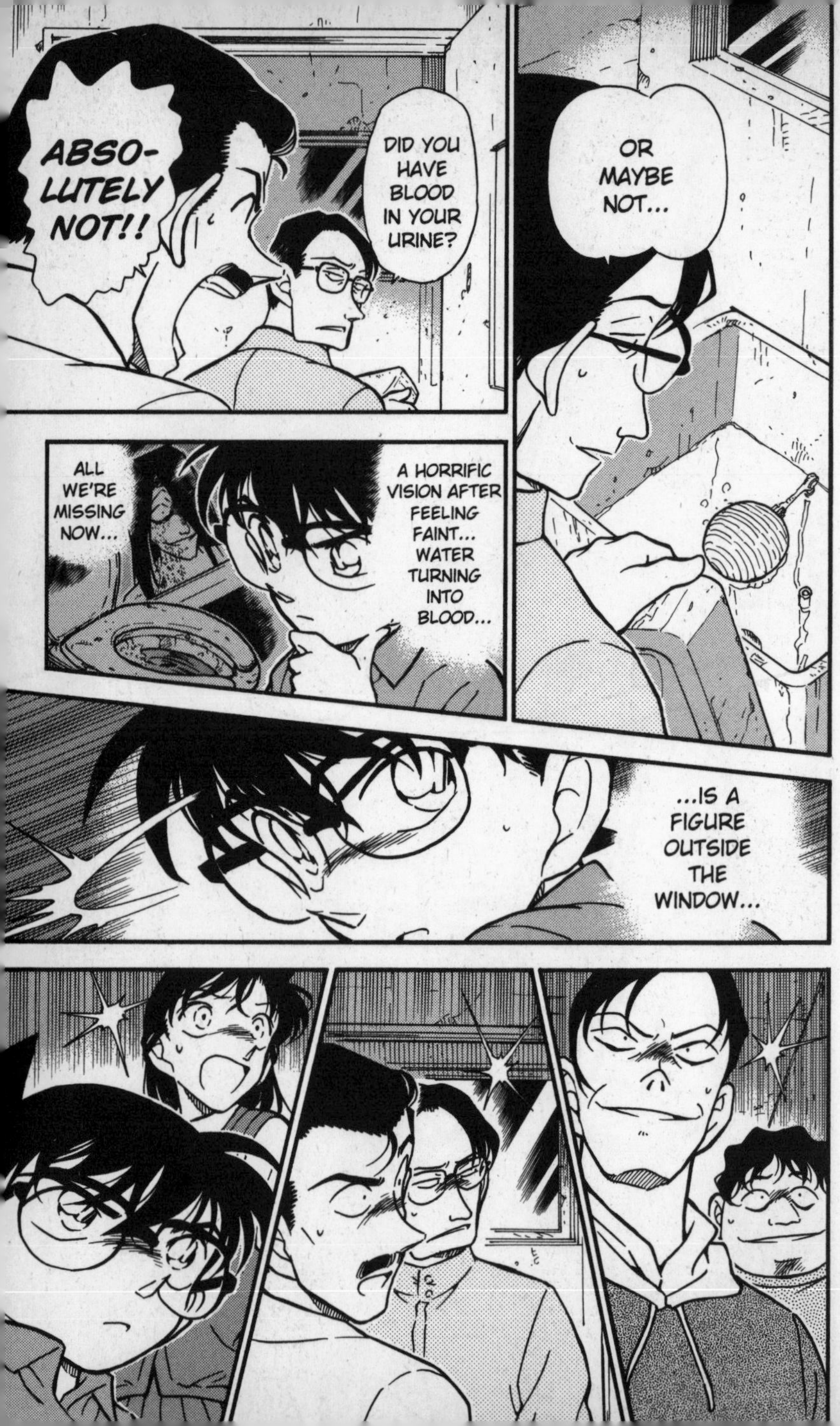
OR MAYBE NOT...
DID YOU HAVE BLOOD IN YOUR URINE?
ABSO-LUTELY NOT!!
A HORRIFIC VISION AFTER FEELING FAINT... WATER TURNING INTO BLOOD...
ALL WE'RE MISSING NOW...
...IS A FIGURE OUTSIDE THE WINDOW...

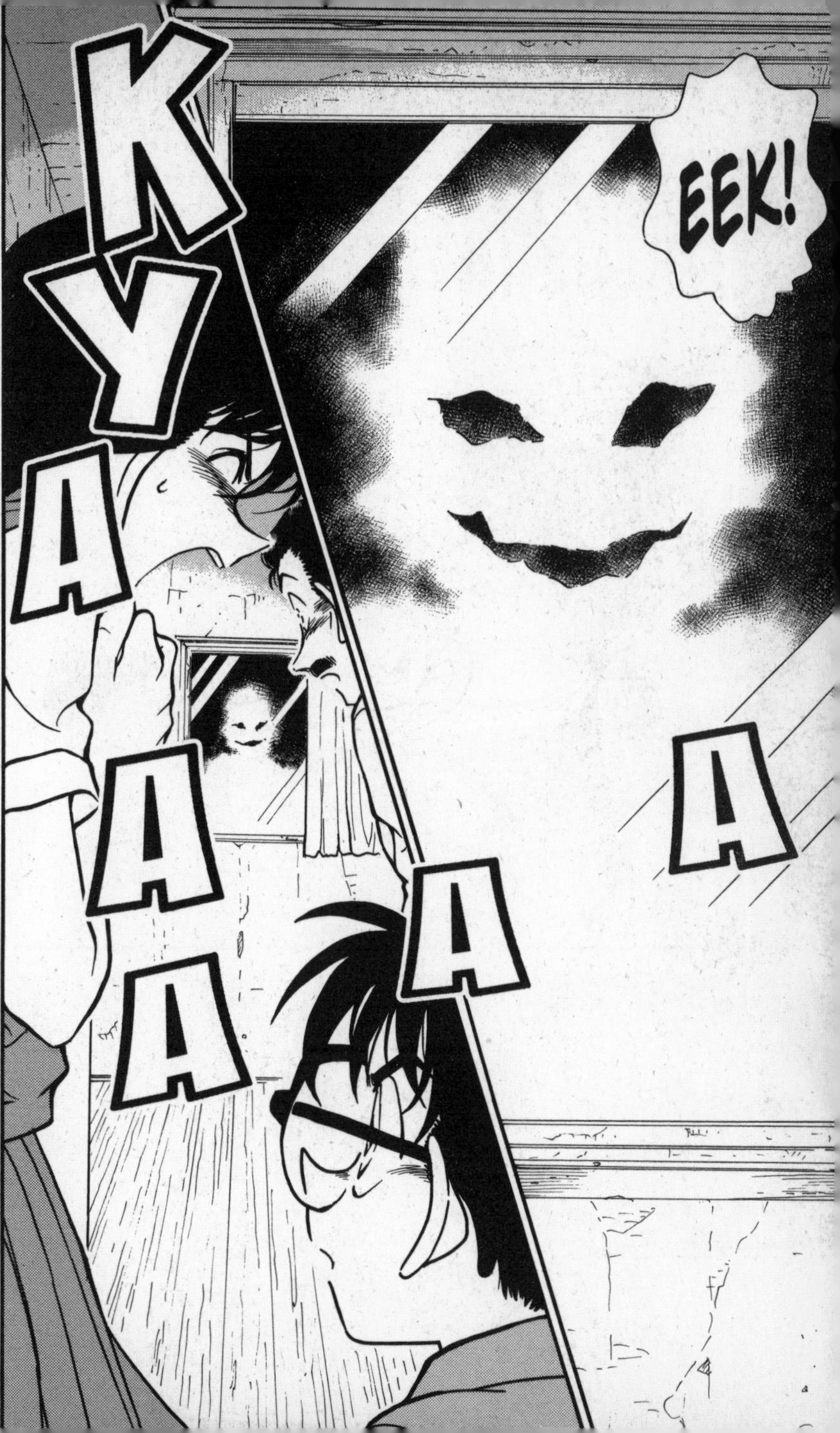
EEK!
KYAAAAA

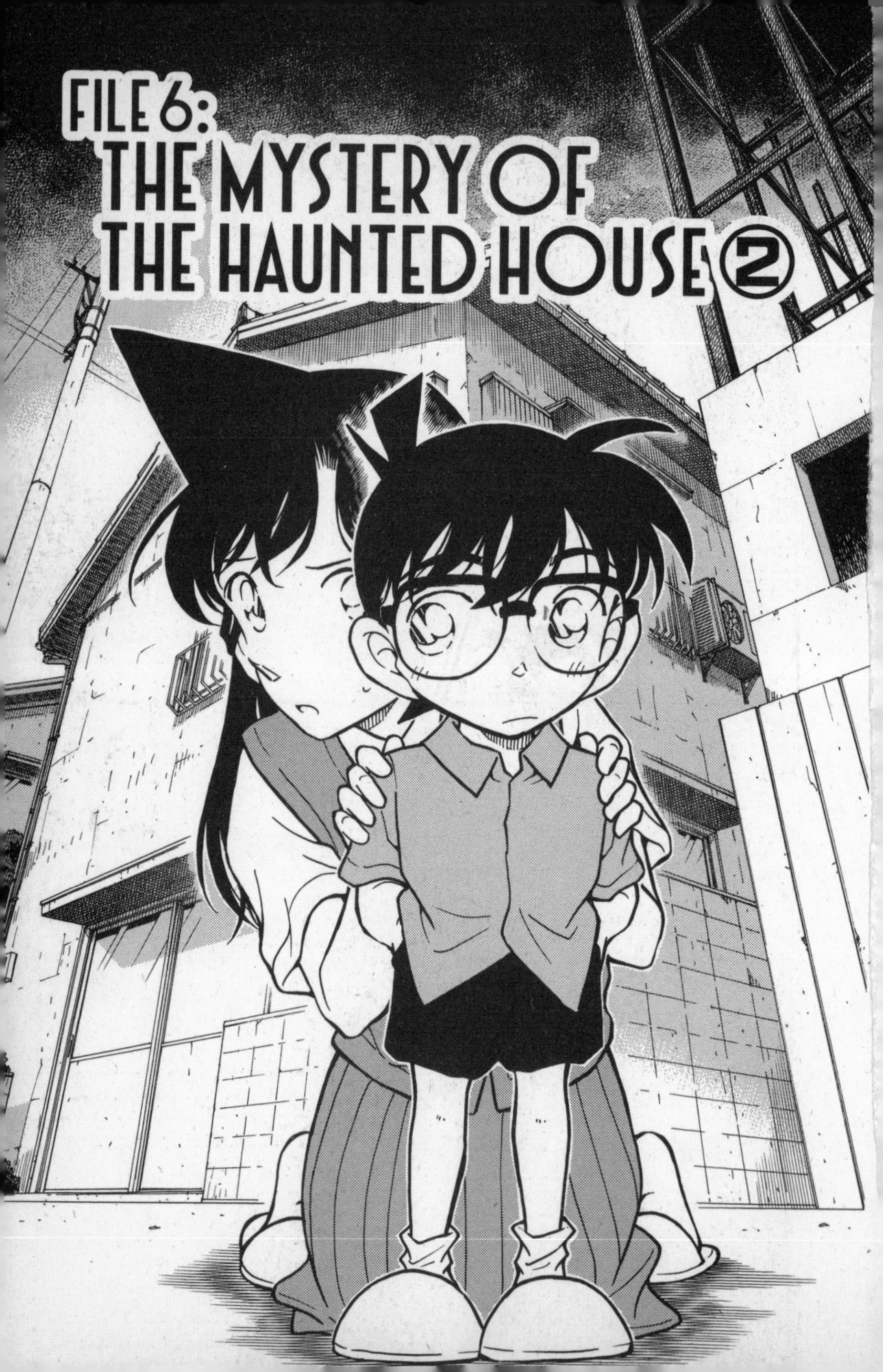
FILE 6:
THE MYSTERY OF
THE HAUNTED HOUSE ②

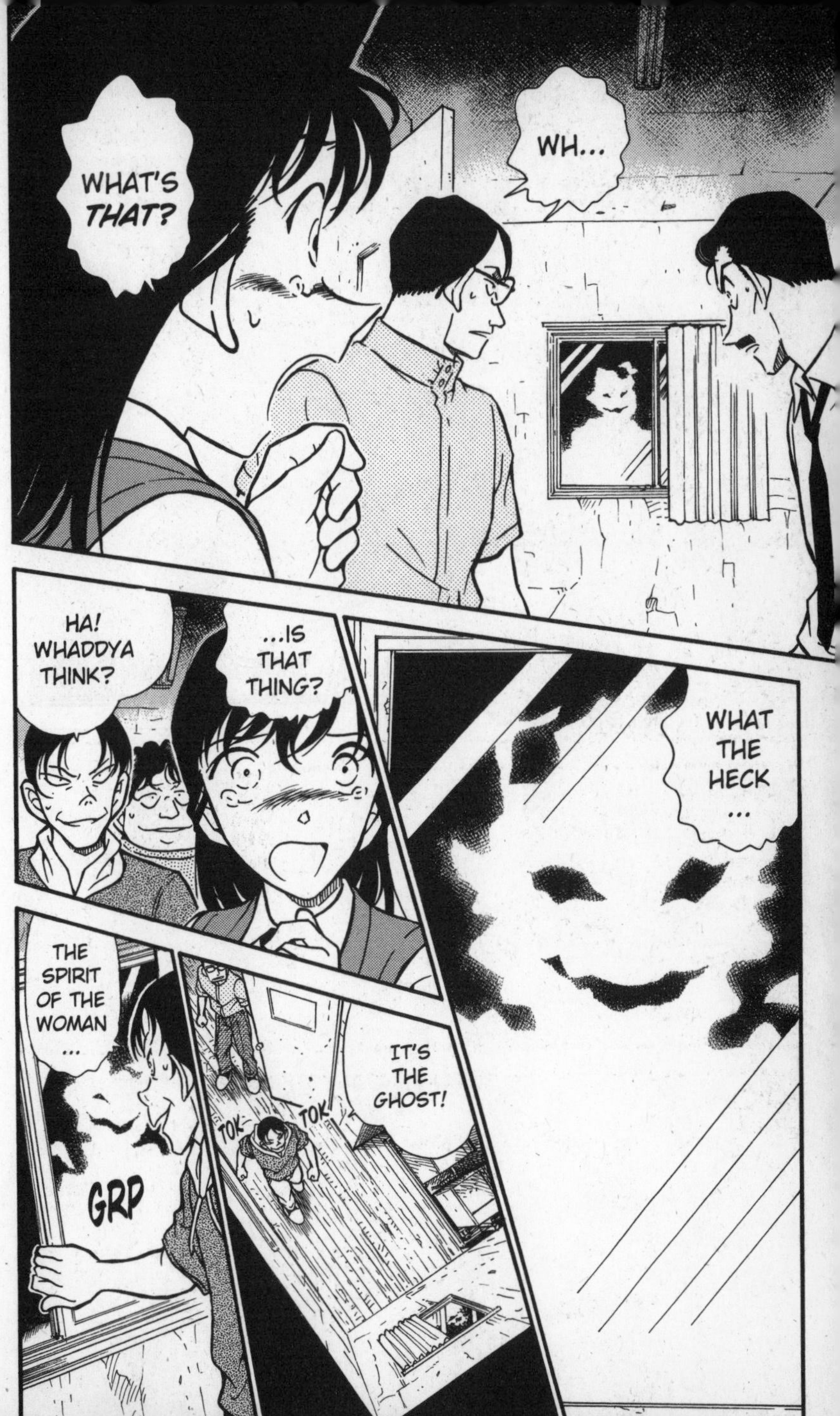
WH...
WHAT'S *THAT?*
WHAT THE HECK ...
...IS THAT THING?
HA! WHADDYA THINK?
IT'S THE GHOST!
TOK TOK
THE SPIRIT OF THE WOMAN ...
GRP

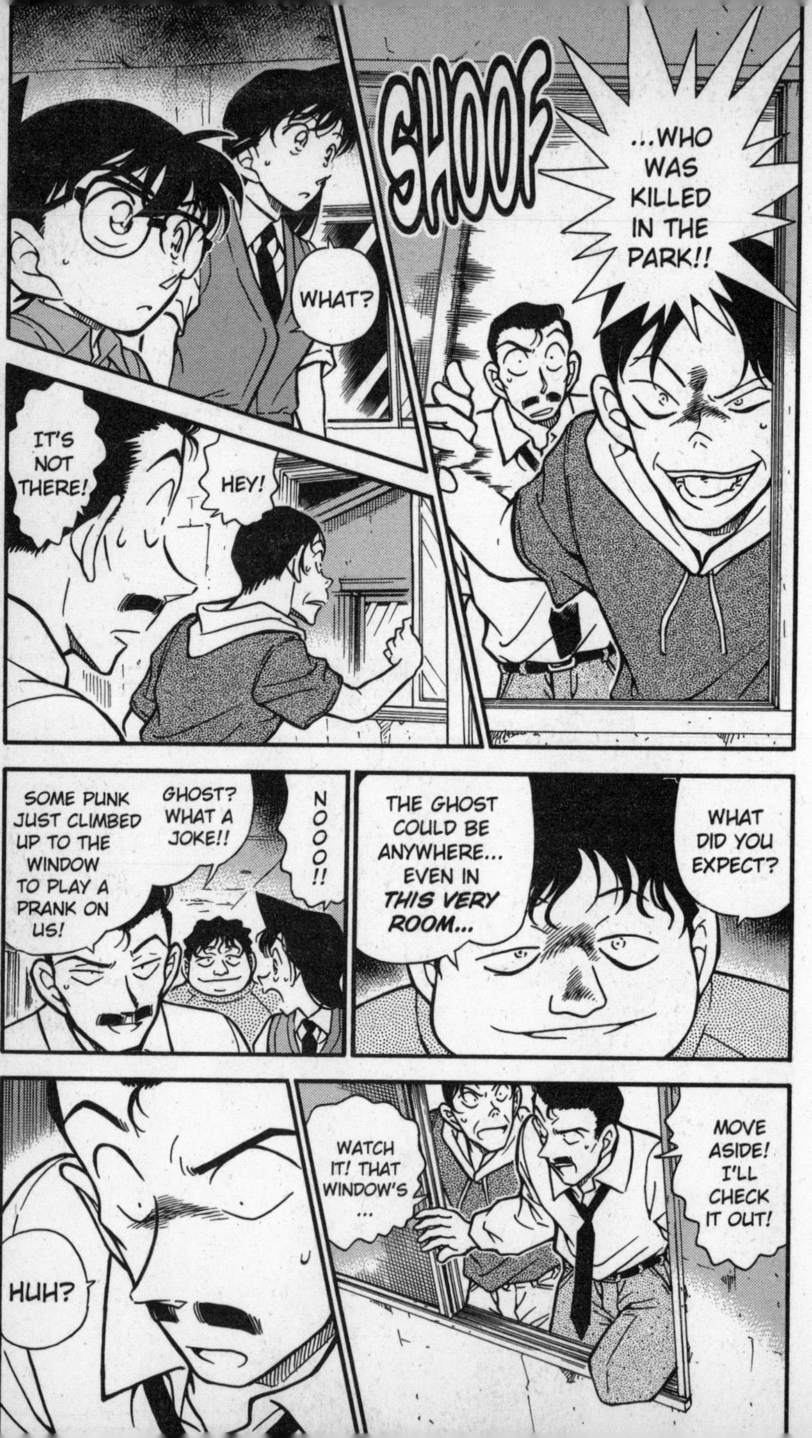
SHOOF
...WHO WAS KILLED IN THE PARK!!
WHAT?
HEY!
IT'S NOT THERE!
WHAT DID YOU EXPECT?
THE GHOST COULD BE ANYWHERE... EVEN IN *THIS VERY ROOM...*
NOOOO!!
GHOST? WHAT A JOKE!!
SOME PUNK JUST CLIMBED UP TO THE WINDOW TO PLAY A PRANK ON US!
MOVE ASIDE! I'LL CHECK IT OUT!
WATCH IT! THAT WINDOW'S ...
HUH?

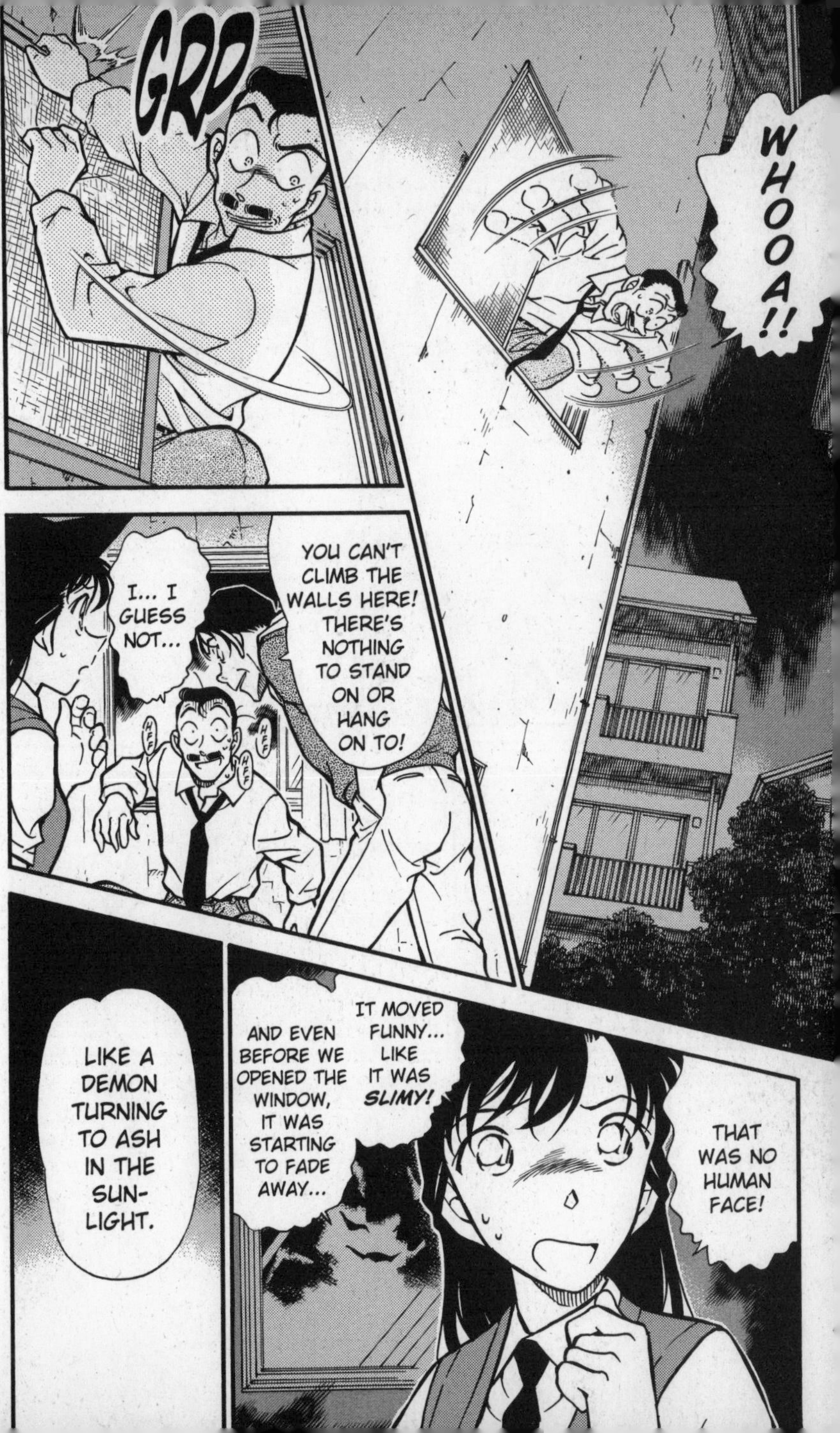
WHOOA!!
GRP
YOU CAN'T CLIMB THE WALLS HERE! THERE'S NOTHING TO STAND ON OR HANG ON TO!
HFF
HFF
HFF
I... I GUESS NOT...
THAT WAS NO HUMAN FACE!
IT MOVED FUNNY... LIKE IT WAS *SLIMY!*
AND EVEN BEFORE WE OPENED THE WINDOW, IT WAS STARTING TO FADE AWAY...
LIKE A DEMON TURNING TO ASH IN THE SUN-LIGHT.

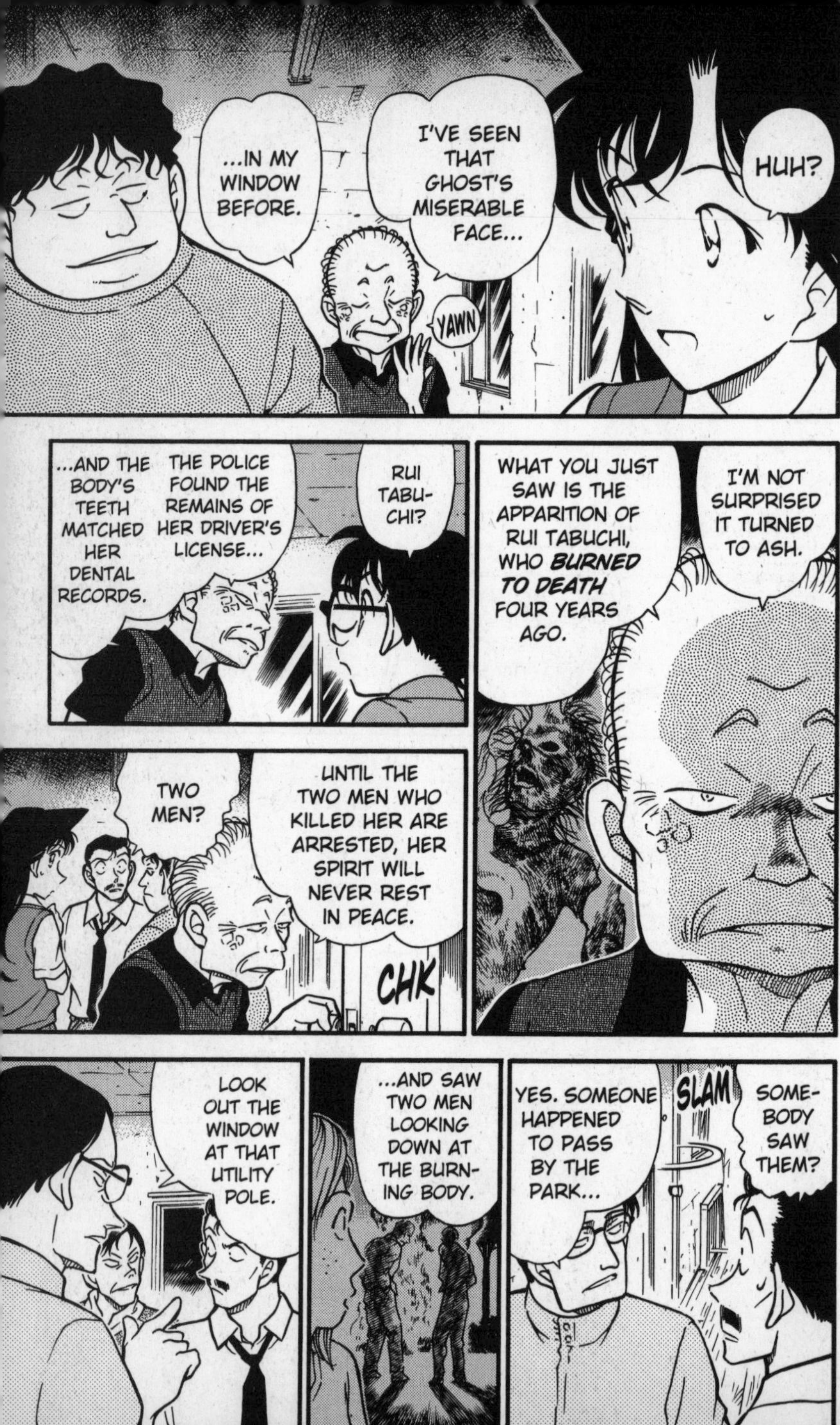
HUH?
I'VE SEEN THAT GHOST'S MISERABLE FACE...
YAWN
...IN MY WINDOW BEFORE.
I'M NOT SURPRISED IT TURNED TO ASH.
WHAT YOU JUST SAW IS THE APPARITION OF RUI TABUCHI, WHO ***BURNED TO DEATH*** FOUR YEARS AGO.
RUI TABU-CHI?
THE POLICE FOUND THE REMAINS OF HER DRIVER'S LICENSE...
...AND THE BODY'S TEETH MATCHED HER DENTAL RECORDS.
UNTIL THE TWO MEN WHO KILLED HER ARE ARRESTED, HER SPIRIT WILL NEVER REST IN PEACE.
CHK
TWO MEN?
SOME-BODY SAW THEM?
SLAM
YES. SOMEONE HAPPENED TO PASS BY THE PARK...
...AND SAW TWO MEN LOOKING DOWN AT THE BURN-ING BODY.
LOOK OUT THE WINDOW AT THAT UTILITY POLE.

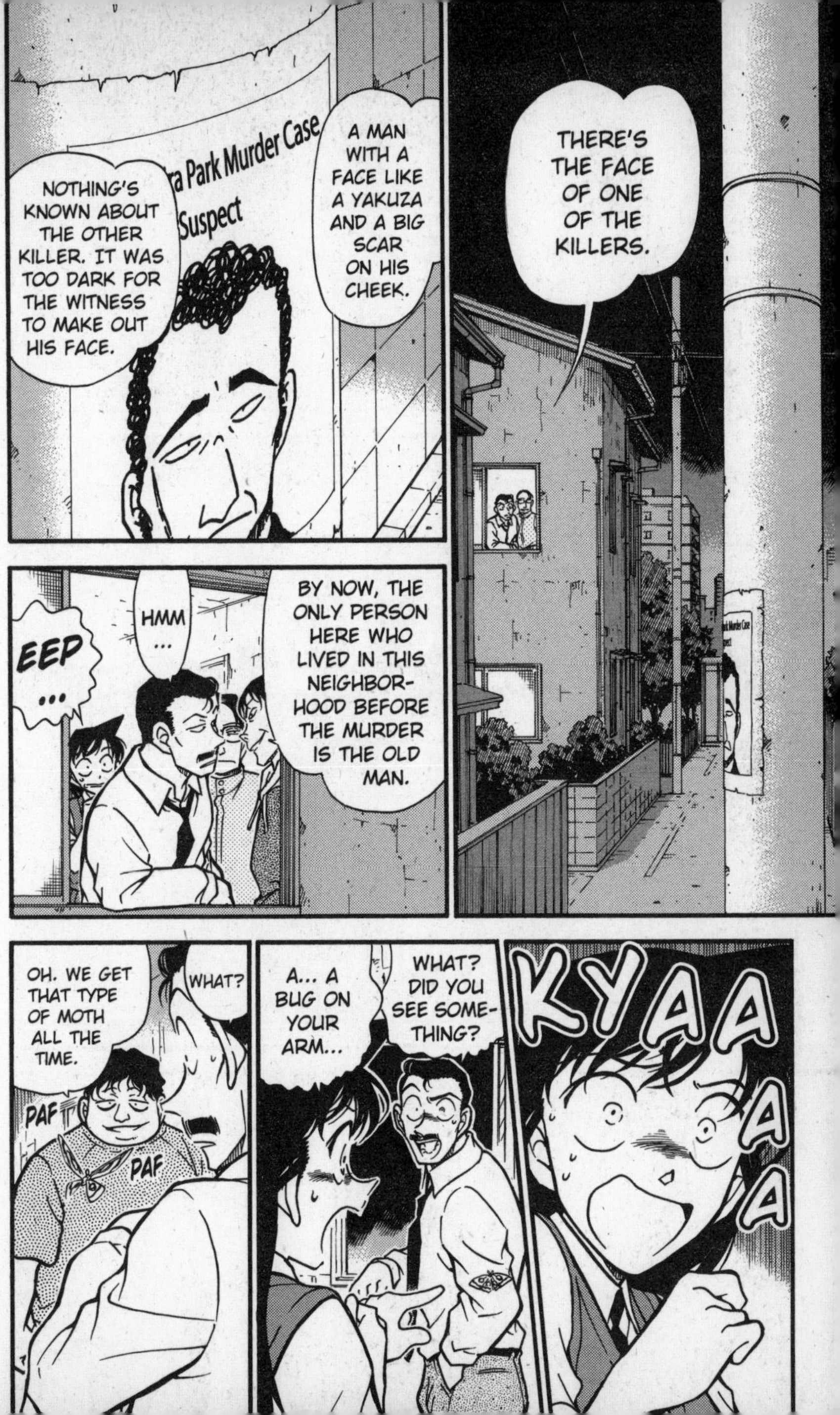
THERE'S THE FACE OF ONE OF THE KILLERS.
Park Murder Case
Suspect
A MAN WITH A FACE LIKE A YAKUZA AND A BIG SCAR ON HIS CHEEK.
NOTHING'S KNOWN ABOUT THE OTHER KILLER. IT WAS TOO DARK FOR THE WITNESS TO MAKE OUT HIS FACE.
BY NOW, THE ONLY PERSON HERE WHO LIVED IN THIS NEIGHBOR-HOOD BEFORE THE MURDER IS THE OLD MAN.
HMM...
EEP...
KYAAAA
WHAT? DID YOU SEE SOME-THING?
A... A BUG ON YOUR ARM...
WHAT?
OH. WE GET THAT TYPE OF MOTH ALL THE TIME.
PAF
PAF

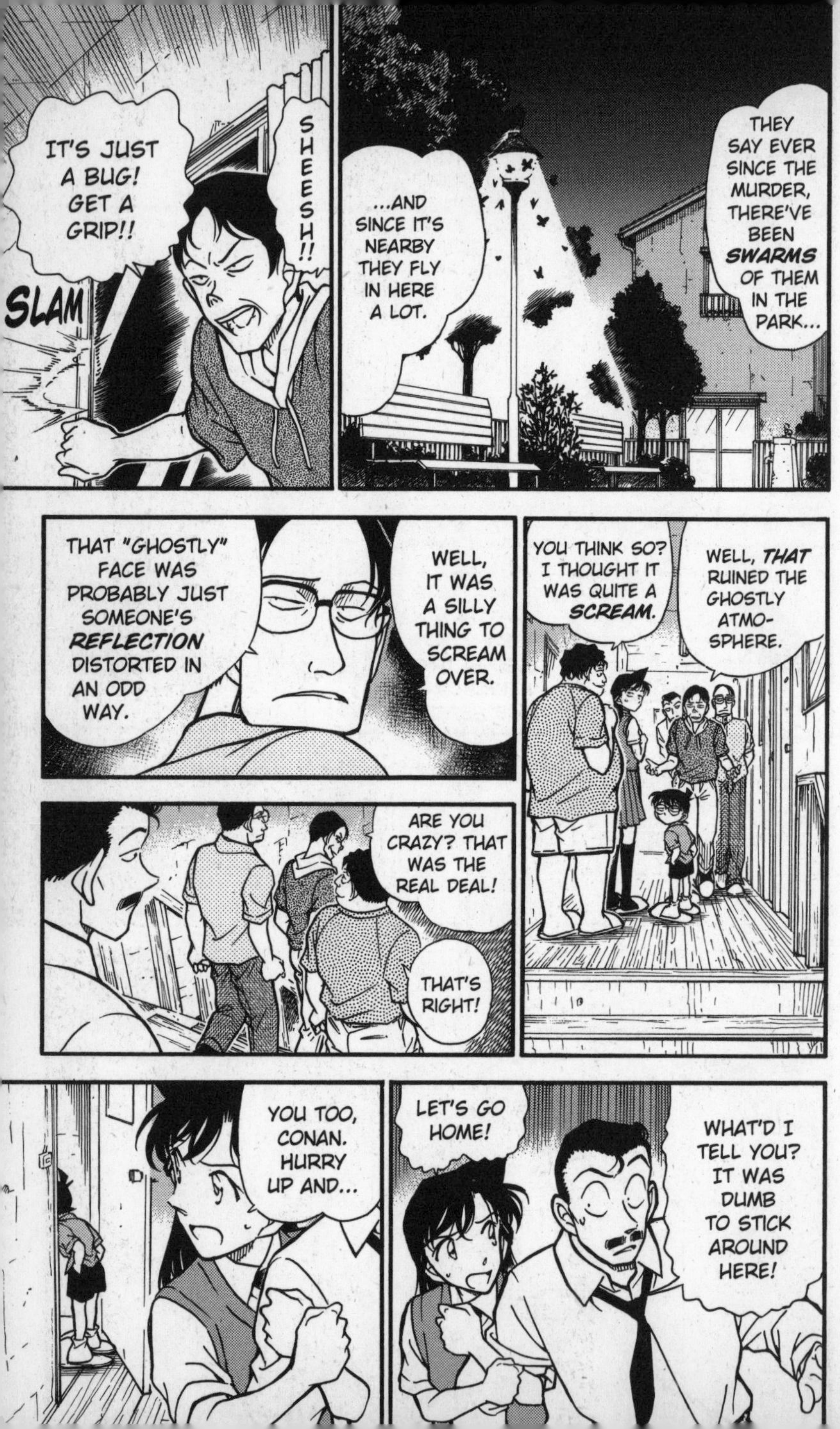
THEY SAY EVER SINCE THE MURDER, THERE'VE BEEN SWARMS OF THEM IN THE PARK...
...AND SINCE IT'S NEARBY THEY FLY IN HERE A LOT.
SHEESH!!
IT'S JUST A BUG! GET A GRIP!!
SLAM
WELL, THAT RUINED THE GHOSTLY ATMOSPHERE.
YOU THINK SO? I THOUGHT IT WAS QUITE A SCREAM.
WELL, IT WAS A SILLY THING TO SCREAM OVER.
THAT "GHOSTLY" FACE WAS PROBABLY JUST SOMEONE'S REFLECTION DISTORTED IN AN ODD WAY.
ARE YOU CRAZY? THAT WAS THE REAL DEAL!
THAT'S RIGHT!
WHAT'D I TELL YOU? IT WAS DUMB TO STICK AROUND HERE!
LET'S GO HOME!
YOU TOO, CONAN. HURRY UP AND...

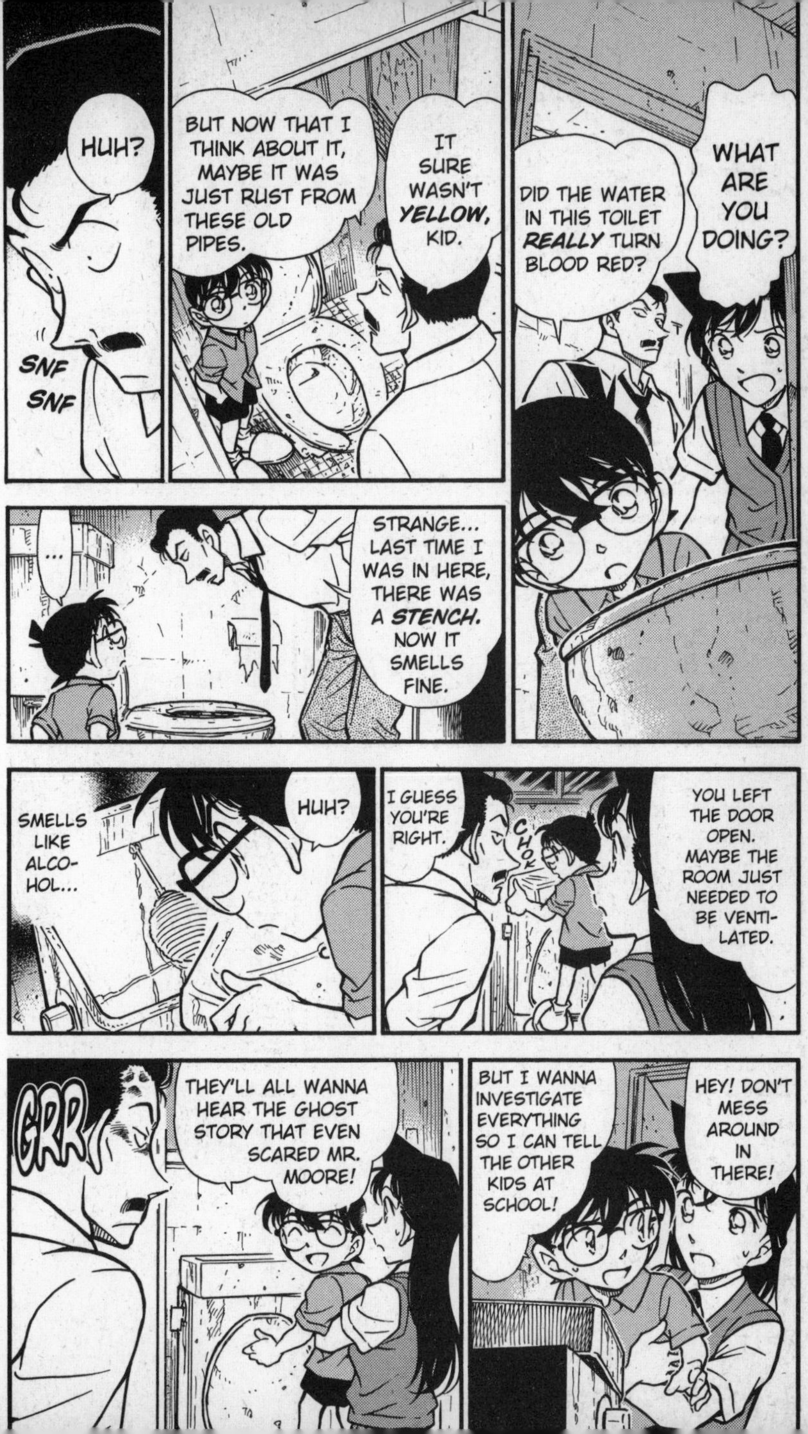
WHAT ARE YOU DOING?
DID THE WATER IN THIS TOILET REALLY TURN BLOOD RED?
IT SURE WASN'T YELLOW, KID.
BUT NOW THAT I THINK ABOUT IT, MAYBE IT WAS JUST RUST FROM THESE OLD PIPES.
HUH?
SNF SNF
STRANGE... LAST TIME I WAS IN HERE, THERE WAS A STENCH. NOW IT SMELLS FINE.
...
YOU LEFT THE DOOR OPEN. MAYBE THE ROOM JUST NEEDED TO BE VENTI- LATED.
I GUESS YOU'RE RIGHT.
CHOK
HUH?
SMELLS LIKE ALCO- HOL...
HEY! DON'T MESS AROUND IN THERE!
BUT I WANNA INVESTIGATE EVERYTHING SO I CAN TELL THE OTHER KIDS AT SCHOOL!
THEY'LL ALL WANNA HEAR THE GHOST STORY THAT EVEN SCARED MR. MOORE!
GRR

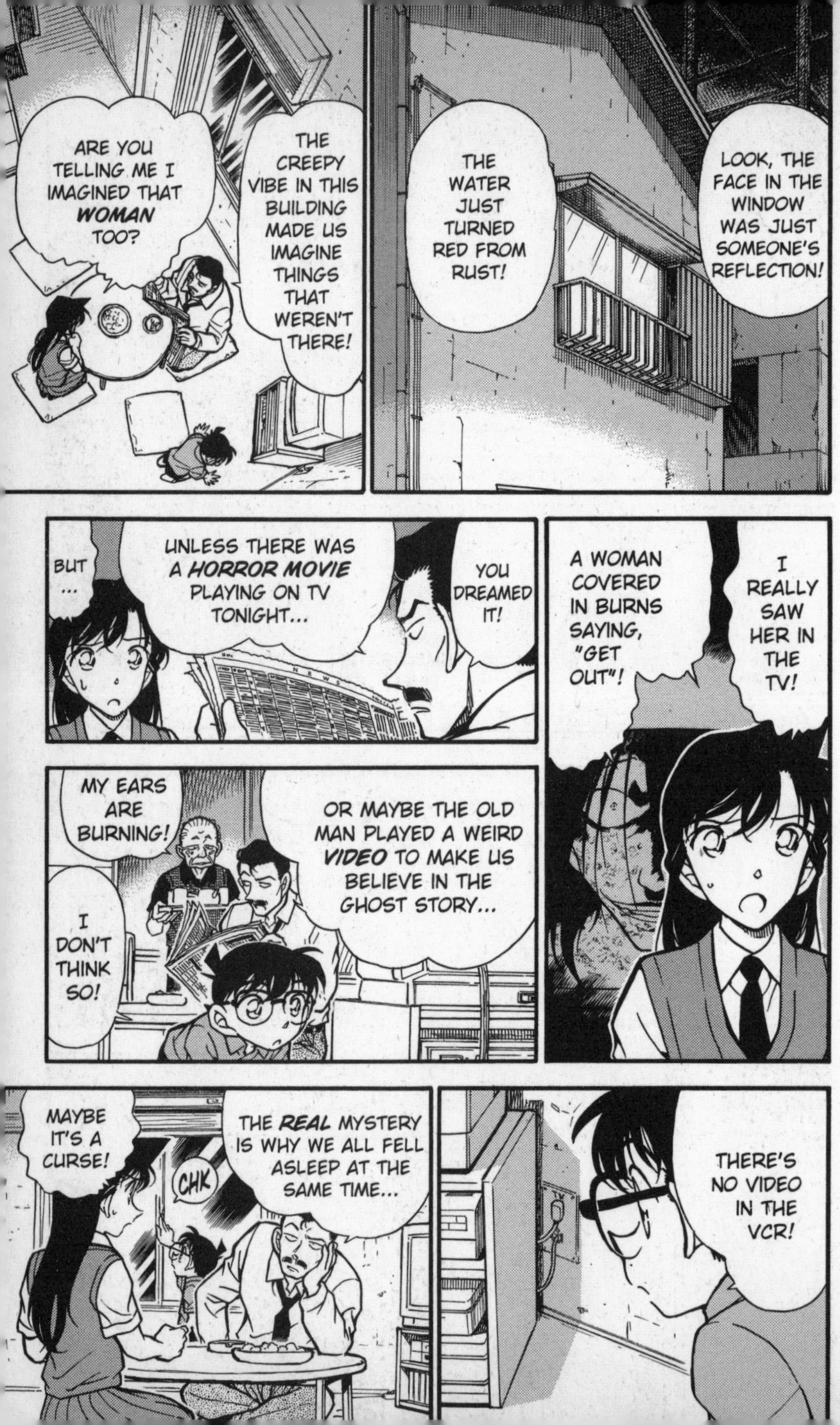
LOOK, THE FACE IN THE WINDOW WAS JUST SOMEONE'S REFLECTION!
THE WATER JUST TURNED RED FROM RUST!
THE CREEPY VIBE IN THIS BUILDING MADE US IMAGINE THINGS THAT WEREN'T THERE!
ARE YOU TELLING ME I IMAGINED THAT **WOMAN** TOO?
I REALLY SAW HER IN THE TV!
A WOMAN COVERED IN BURNS SAYING, "GET OUT"!
YOU DREAMED IT!
UNLESS THERE WAS A ***HORROR MOVIE*** PLAYING ON TV TONIGHT...
BUT ...
OR MAYBE THE OLD MAN PLAYED A WEIRD ***VIDEO*** TO MAKE US BELIEVE IN THE GHOST STORY...
MY EARS ARE BURNING!
I DON'T THINK SO!
THERE'S NO VIDEO IN THE VCR!
THE ***REAL*** MYSTERY IS WHY WE ALL FELL ASLEEP AT THE SAME TIME...
CHK
MAYBE IT'S A CURSE!

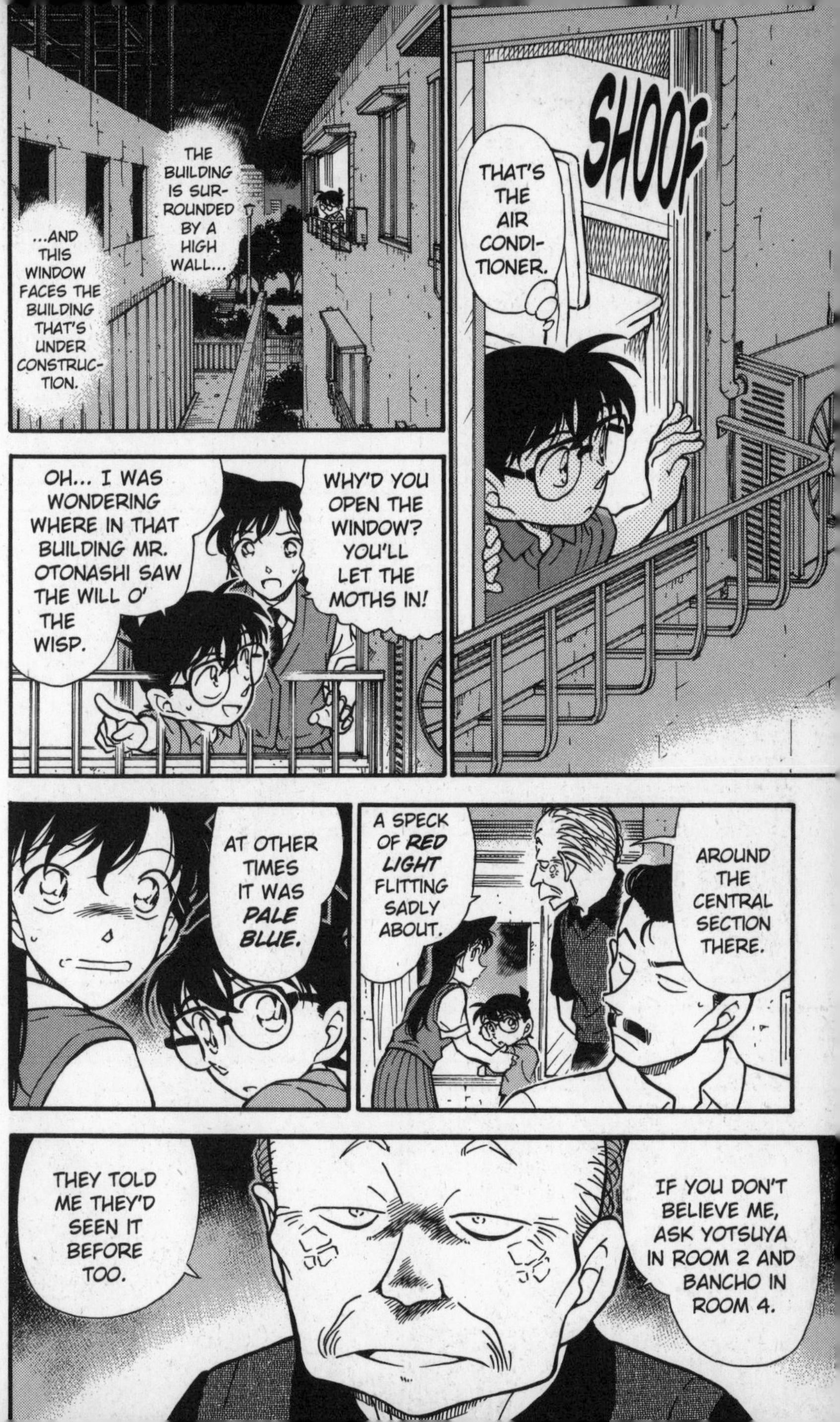
SHOOF
THAT'S THE AIR CONDITIONER.
THE BUILDING IS SURROUNDED BY A HIGH WALL...
...AND THIS WINDOW FACES THE BUILDING THAT'S UNDER CONSTRUCTION.
WHY'D YOU OPEN THE WINDOW? YOU'LL LET THE MOTHS IN!
OH... I WAS WONDERING WHERE IN THAT BUILDING MR. OTONASHI SAW THE WILL O' THE WISP.
AROUND THE CENTRAL SECTION THERE.
A SPECK OF *RED LIGHT* FLITTING SADLY ABOUT.
AT OTHER TIMES IT WAS *PALE BLUE.*
IF YOU DON'T BELIEVE ME, ASK YOTSUYA IN ROOM 2 AND BANCHO IN ROOM 4.
THEY TOLD ME THEY'D SEEN IT BEFORE TOO.

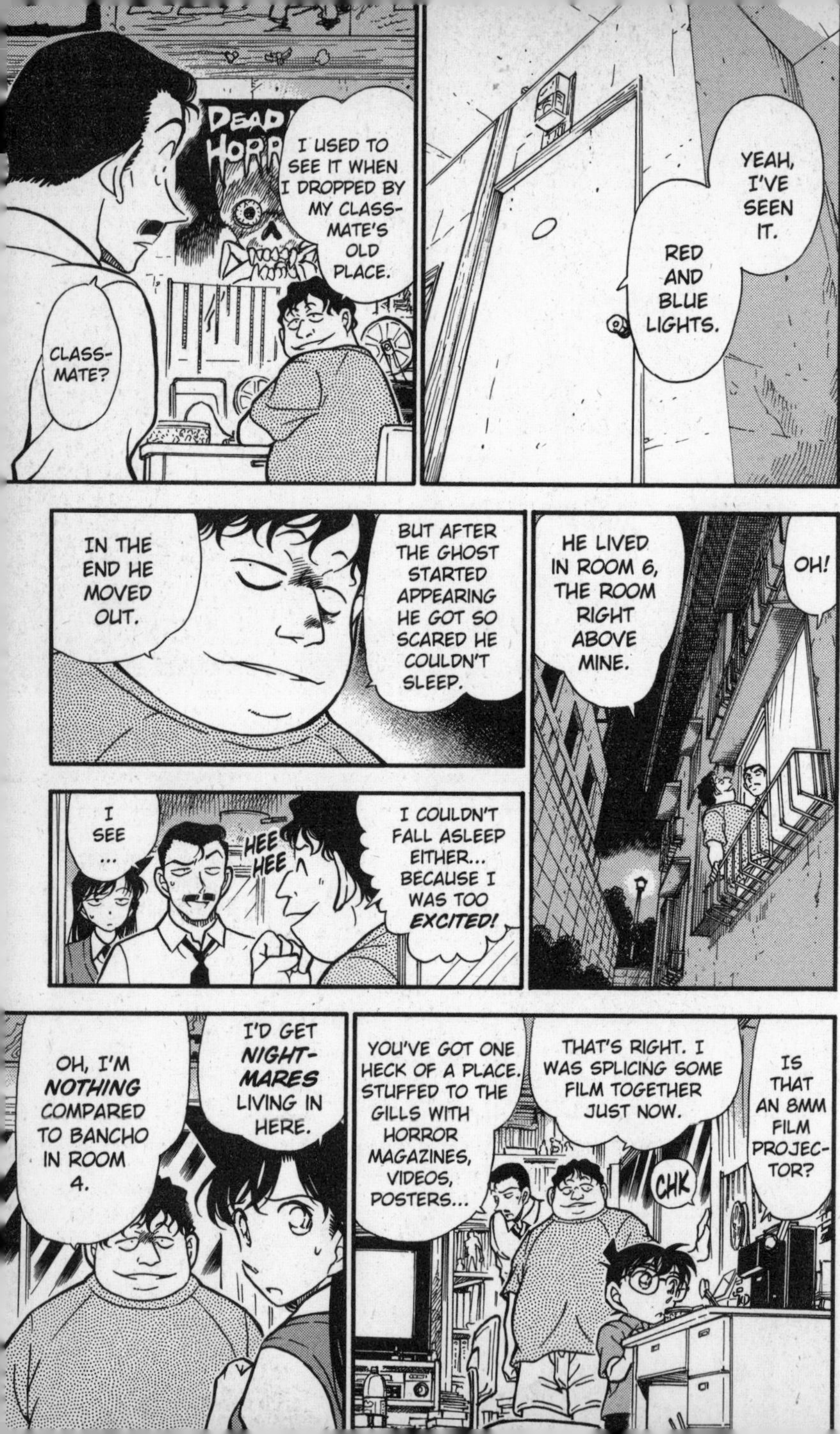
YEAH, I'VE SEEN IT.
RED AND BLUE LIGHTS.
I USED TO SEE IT WHEN I DROPPED BY MY CLASSMATE'S OLD PLACE.
DEAD HORR
CLASSMATE?
OH!
HE LIVED IN ROOM 6, THE ROOM RIGHT ABOVE MINE.
BUT AFTER THE GHOST STARTED APPEARING HE GOT SO SCARED HE COULDN'T SLEEP.
IN THE END HE MOVED OUT.
I COULDN'T FALL ASLEEP EITHER... BECAUSE I WAS TOO *EXCITED!*
HEE HEE
I SEE ...
IS THAT AN 8MM FILM PROJECTOR?
THAT'S RIGHT. I WAS SPLICING SOME FILM TOGETHER JUST NOW.
CHK
YOU'VE GOT ONE HECK OF A PLACE. STUFFED TO THE GILLS WITH HORROR MAGAZINES, VIDEOS, POSTERS...
I'D GET *NIGHTMARES* LIVING IN HERE.
OH, I'M *NOTHING* COMPARED TO BANCHO IN ROOM 4.

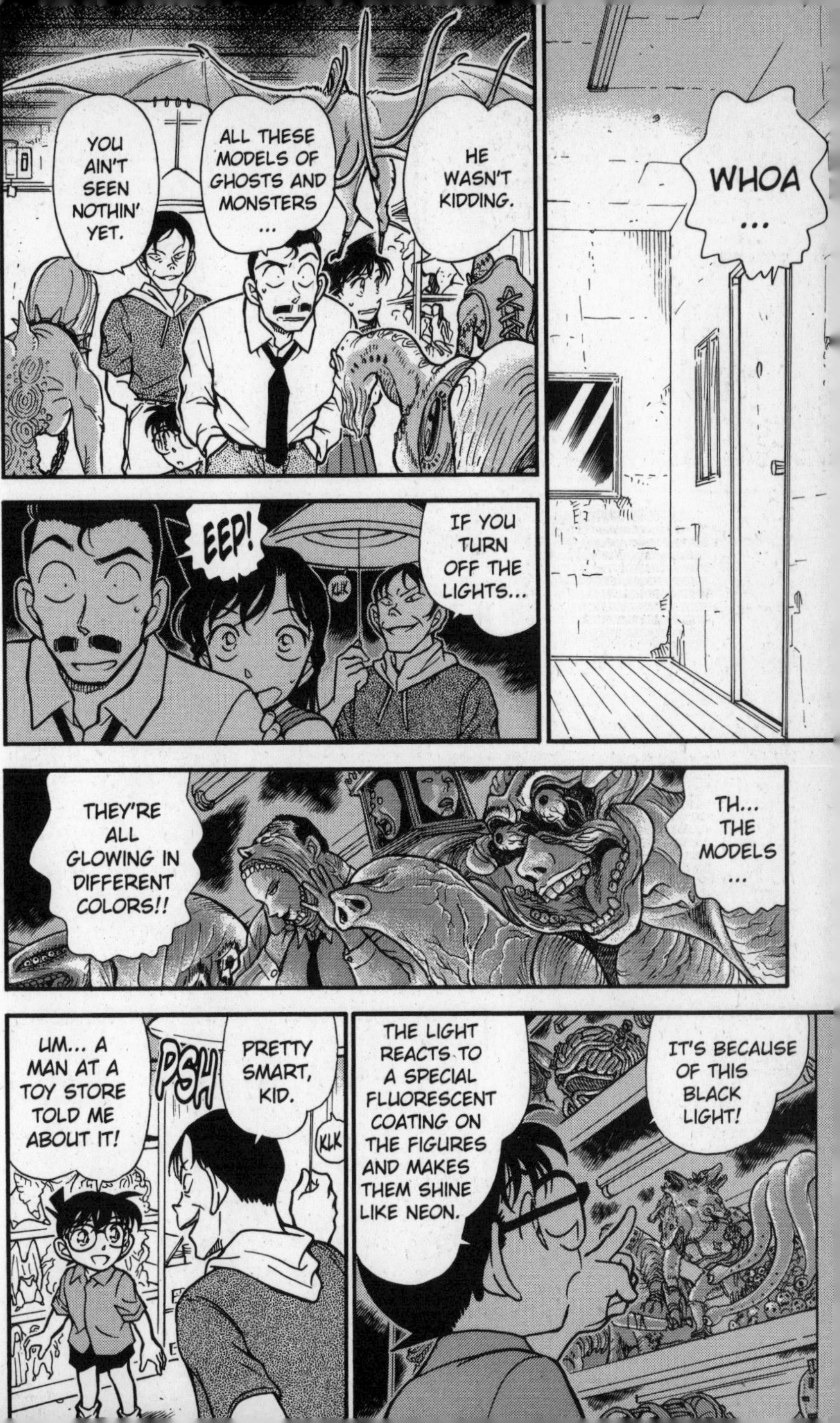
WHOA ...
HE WASN'T KIDDING.
ALL THESE MODELS OF GHOSTS AND MONSTERS ...
YOU AIN'T SEEN NOTHIN' YET.
IF YOU TURN OFF THE LIGHTS...
KLK
EEP!
TH... THE MODELS ...
THEY'RE ALL GLOWING IN DIFFERENT COLORS!!
IT'S BECAUSE OF THIS BLACK LIGHT!
THE LIGHT REACTS TO A SPECIAL FLUORESCENT COATING ON THE FIGURES AND MAKES THEM SHINE LIKE NEON.
KLK
PRETTY SMART, KID.
PSH
UM... A MAN AT A TOY STORE TOLD ME ABOUT IT!

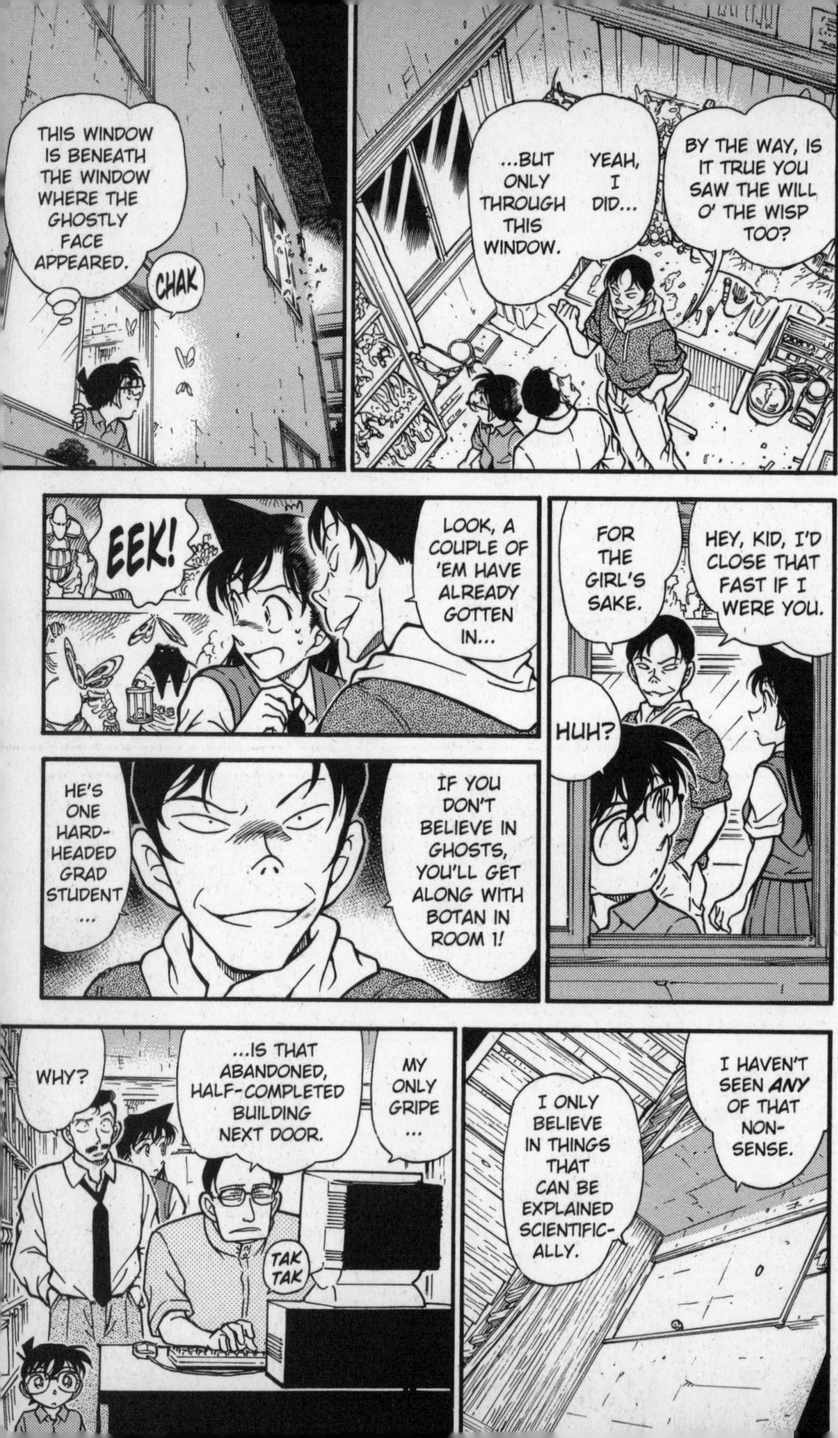

BY THE WAY, IS IT TRUE YOU SAW THE WILL O' THE WISP TOO?
YEAH, I DID...
...BUT ONLY THROUGH THIS WINDOW.
THIS WINDOW IS BENEATH THE WINDOW WHERE THE GHOSTLY FACE APPEARED.
CHAK
HEY, KID, I'D CLOSE THAT FAST IF I WERE YOU.
FOR THE GIRL'S SAKE.
HUH?
LOOK, A COUPLE OF 'EM HAVE ALREADY GOTTEN IN...
EEK!
IF YOU DON'T BELIEVE IN GHOSTS, YOU'LL GET ALONG WITH BOTAN IN ROOM 1!
HE'S ONE HARD-HEADED GRAD STUDENT ...
I HAVEN'T SEEN *ANY* OF THAT NON-SENSE.
I ONLY BELIEVE IN THINGS THAT CAN BE EXPLAINED SCIENTIFIC-ALLY.
MY ONLY GRIPE ...
...IS THAT ABANDONED, HALF-COMPLETED BUILDING NEXT DOOR.
WHY?
TAK TAK

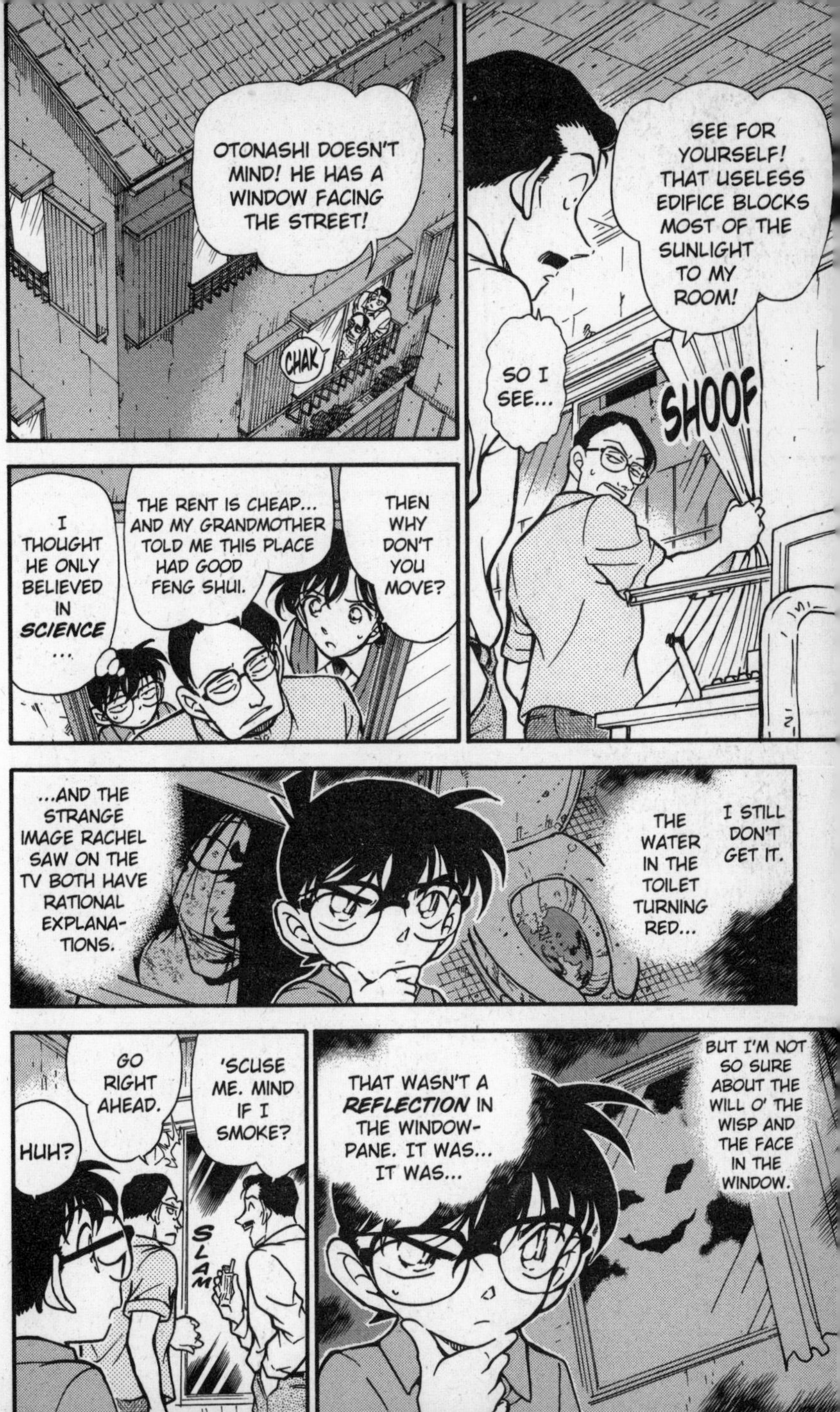
SEE FOR YOURSELF! THAT USELESS EDIFICE BLOCKS MOST OF THE SUNLIGHT TO MY ROOM!
SHOOF
SO I SEE...
OTONASHI DOESN'T MIND! HE HAS A WINDOW FACING THE STREET!
CHAK
THEN WHY DON'T YOU MOVE?
THE RENT IS CHEAP... AND MY GRANDMOTHER TOLD ME THIS PLACE HAD GOOD FENG SHUI.
I THOUGHT HE ONLY BELIEVED IN *SCIENCE*...
I STILL DON'T GET IT.
THE WATER IN THE TOILET TURNING RED...
...AND THE STRANGE IMAGE RACHEL SAW ON THE TV BOTH HAVE RATIONAL EXPLANATIONS.
BUT I'M NOT SO SURE ABOUT THE WILL O' THE WISP AND THE FACE IN THE WINDOW.
THAT WASN'T A *REFLECTION* IN THE WINDOW-PANE. IT WAS... IT WAS...
'SCUSE ME. MIND IF I SMOKE?
SLAM
GO RIGHT AHEAD.
HUH?

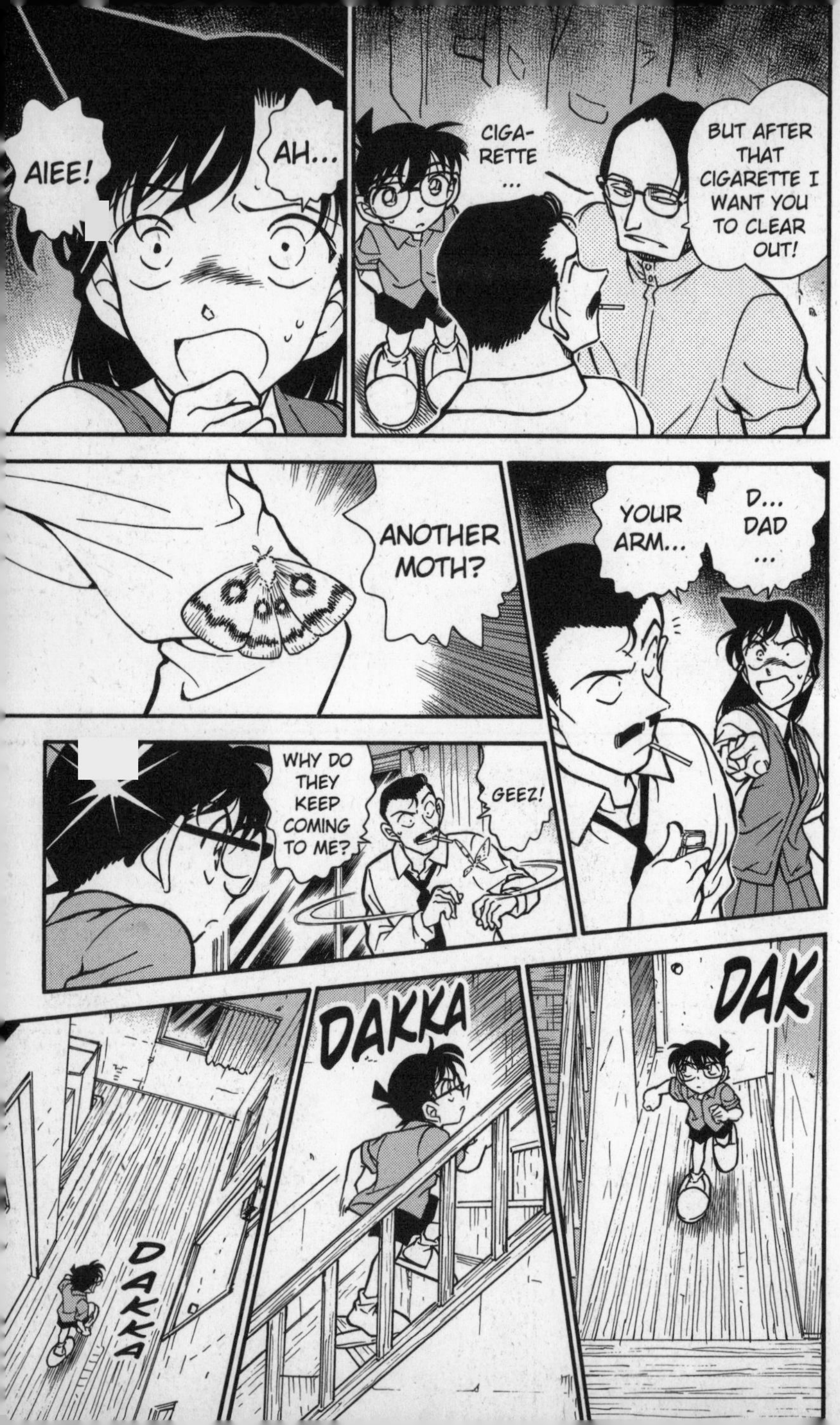
BUT AFTER THAT CIGARETTE I WANT YOU TO CLEAR OUT!
CIGA-RETTE ...
AH...
AIEE!
D... DAD ...
YOUR ARM...
ANOTHER MOTH?
GEEZ!
WHY DO THEY KEEP COMING TO ME?
DAK
DAKKA
DAKKA

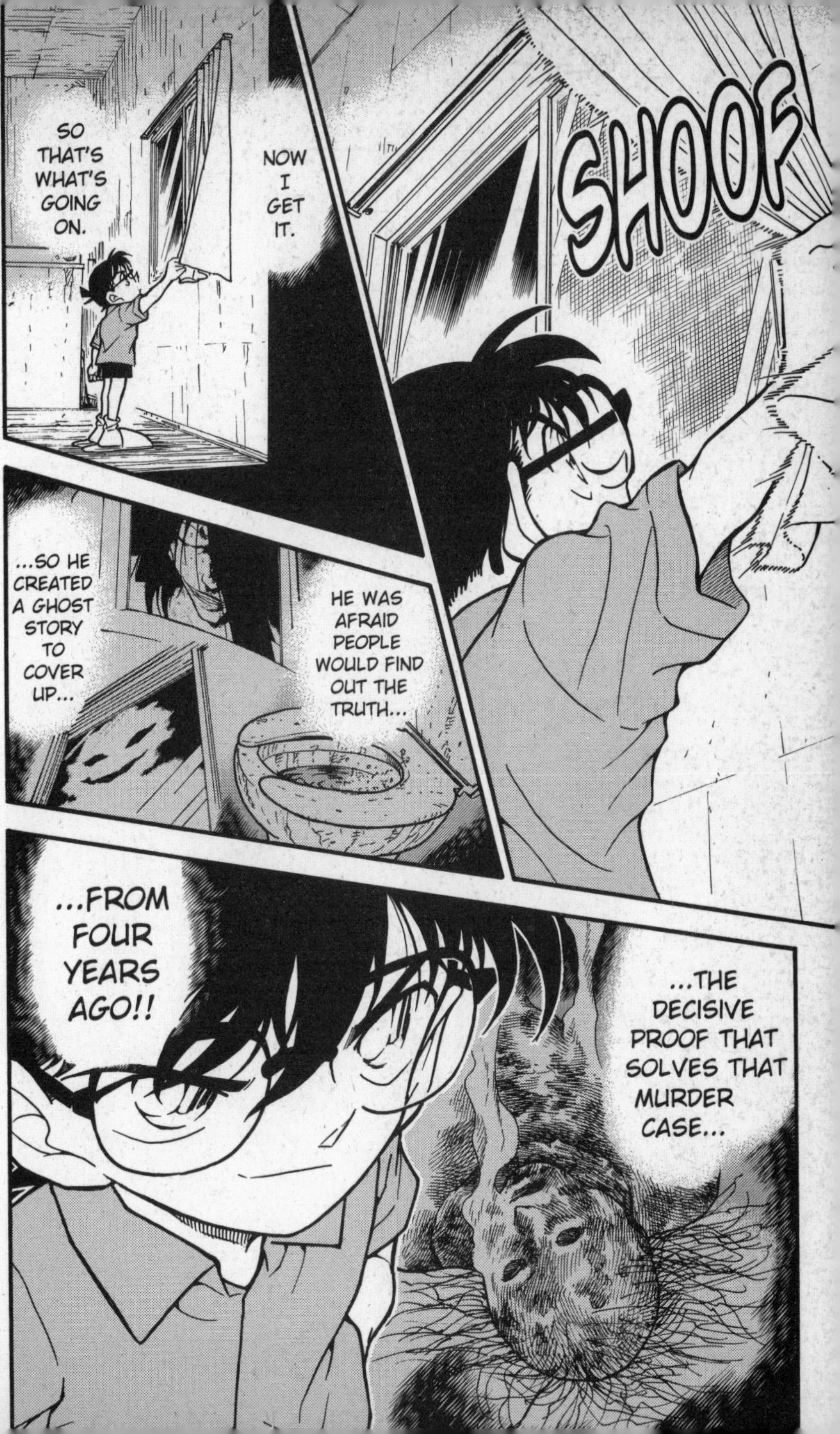
SHOOF
NOW I GET IT.
SO THAT'S WHAT'S GOING ON.
HE WAS AFRAID PEOPLE WOULD FIND OUT THE TRUTH...
...SO HE CREATED A GHOST STORY TO COVER UP...
...THE DECISIVE PROOF THAT SOLVES THAT MURDER CASE...
...FROM FOUR YEARS AGO!!

FILE 7: THE MYSTERY OF THE HAUNTED HOUSE ③

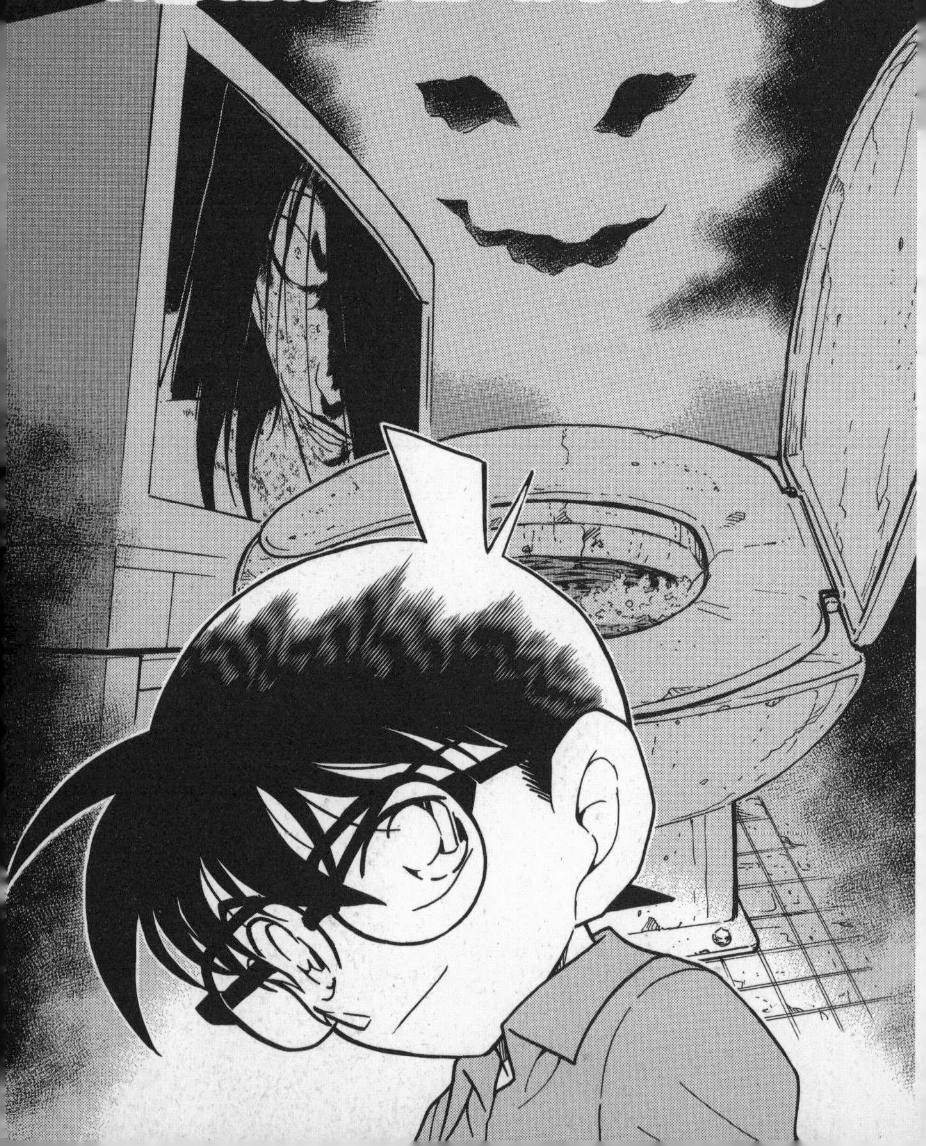

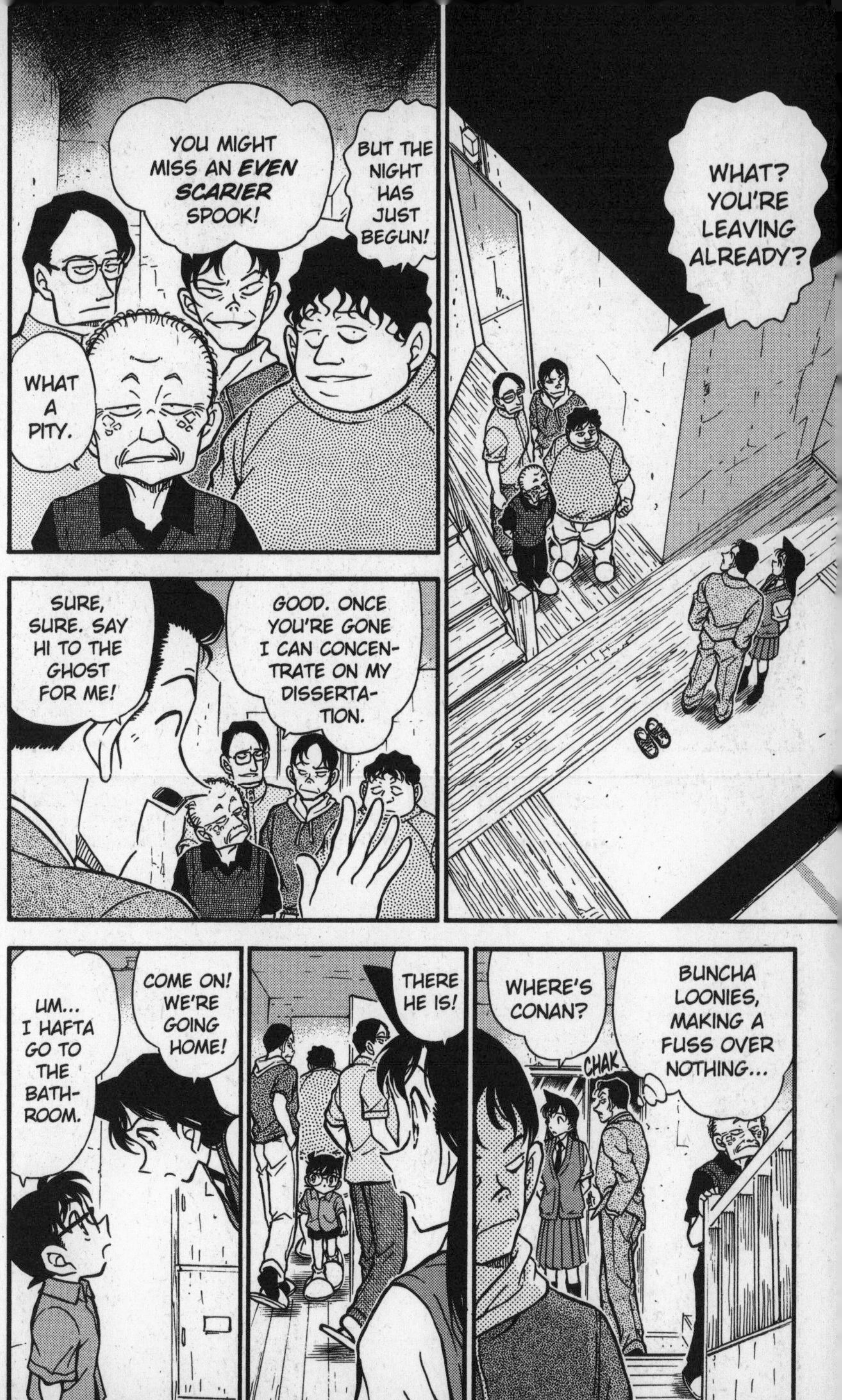
WHAT? YOU'RE LEAVING ALREADY?
BUT THE NIGHT HAS JUST BEGUN!
YOU MIGHT MISS AN *EVEN SCARIER* SPOOK!
WHAT A PITY.
GOOD. ONCE YOU'RE GONE I CAN CONCENTRATE ON MY DISSERTATION.
SURE, SURE. SAY HI TO THE GHOST FOR ME!
BUNCHA LOONIES, MAKING A FUSS OVER NOTHING...
CHAK
WHERE'S CONAN?
THERE HE IS!
COME ON! WE'RE GOING HOME!
UM... I HAFTA GO TO THE BATHROOM.

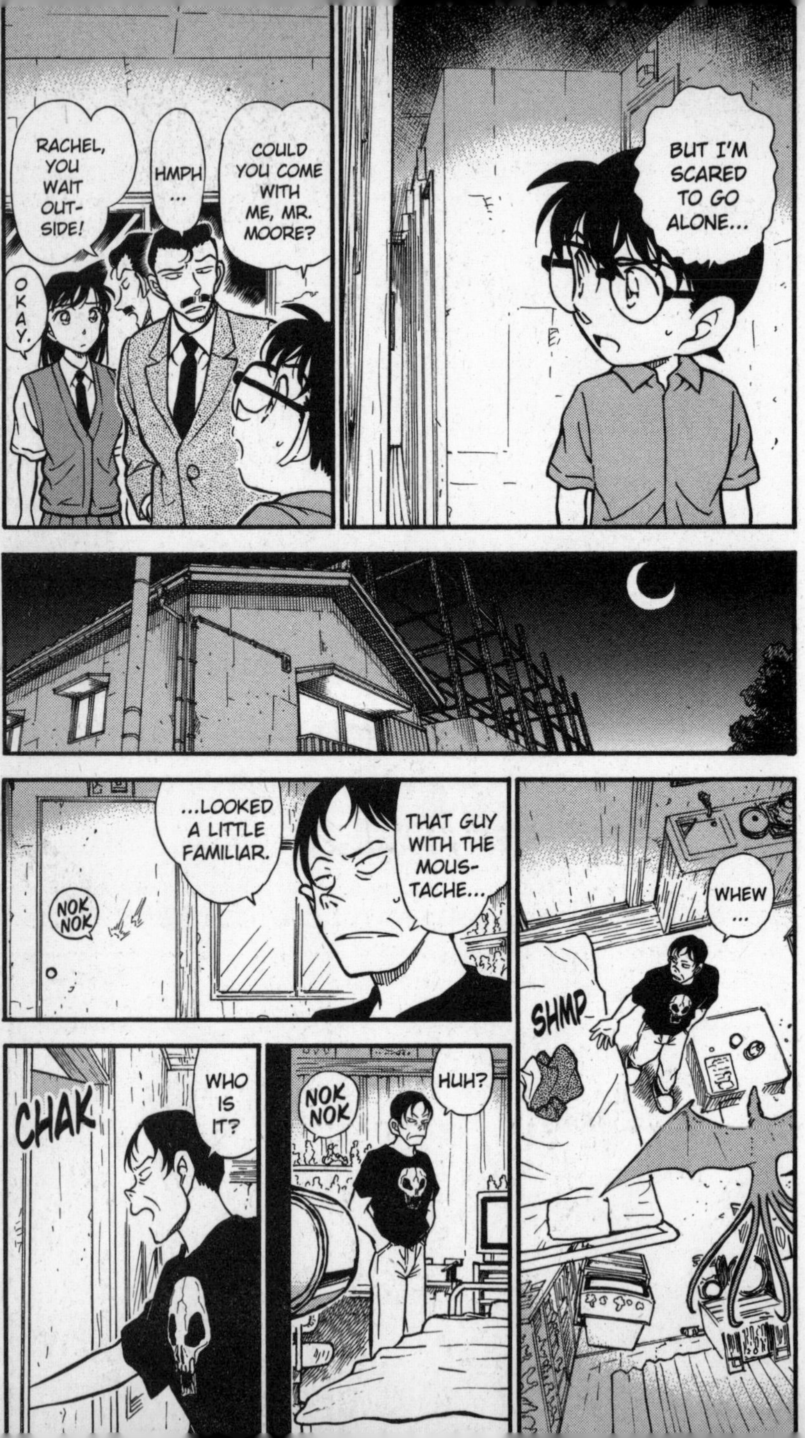
BUT I'M SCARED TO GO ALONE...
COULD YOU COME WITH ME, MR. MOORE?
HMPH ...
RACHEL, YOU WAIT OUT-SIDE!
OKAY.
WHEW ...
SHMP
THAT GUY WITH THE MOUS-TACHE...
...LOOKED A LITTLE FAMILIAR.
NOK NOK
HUH?
NOK NOK
WHO IS IT?
CHAK

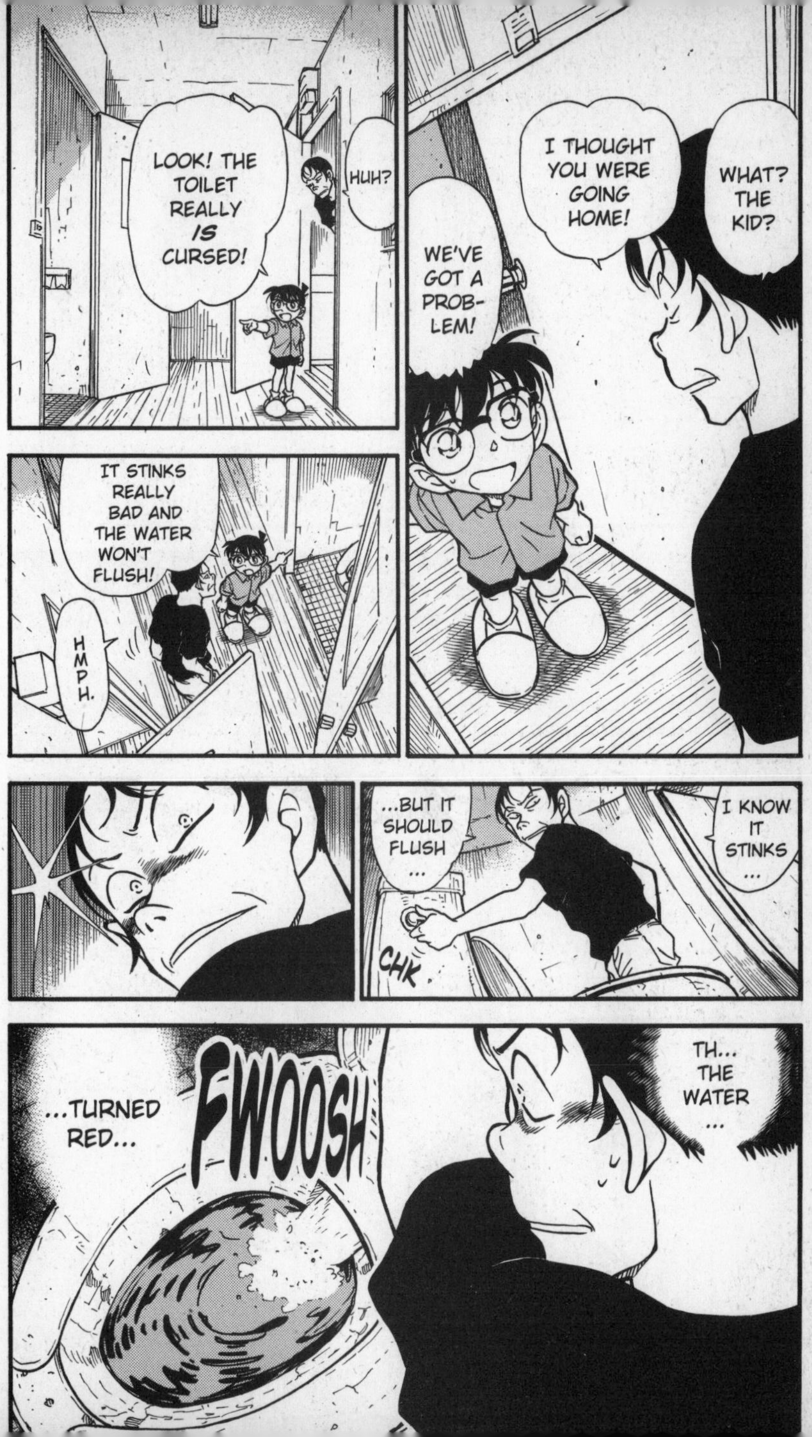
WHAT? THE KID?
I THOUGHT YOU WERE GOING HOME!
WE'VE GOT A PROB-LEM!
HUH?
LOOK! THE TOILET REALLY *IS* CURSED!
IT STINKS REALLY BAD AND THE WATER WON'T FLUSH!
HMPH.
I KNOW IT STINKS...
...BUT IT SHOULD FLUSH...
CHK
TH... THE WATER...
FWOOSH
...TURNED RED...

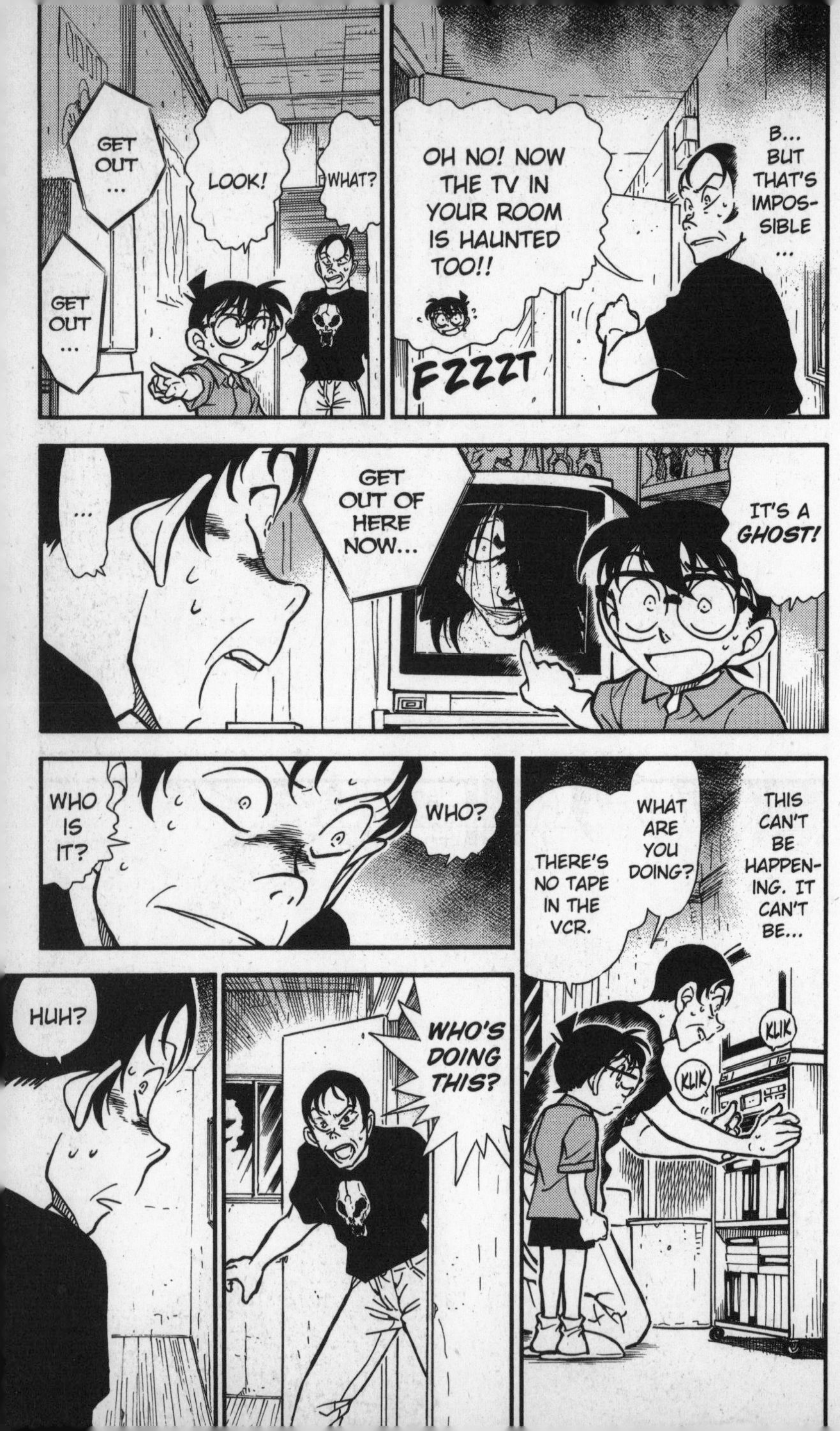
B... BUT THAT'S IMPOS-SIBLE...
OH NO! NOW THE TV IN YOUR ROOM IS HAUNTED TOO!!
FZZZT
WHAT?
LOOK!
GET OUT...
GET OUT...
IT'S A *GHOST!*
GET OUT OF HERE NOW...
...
THIS CAN'T BE HAPPEN-ING. IT CAN'T BE...
WHAT ARE YOU DOING?
THERE'S NO TAPE IN THE VCR.
KLIK
KLIK
WHO?
WHO IS IT?
WHO'S DOING THIS?
HUH?

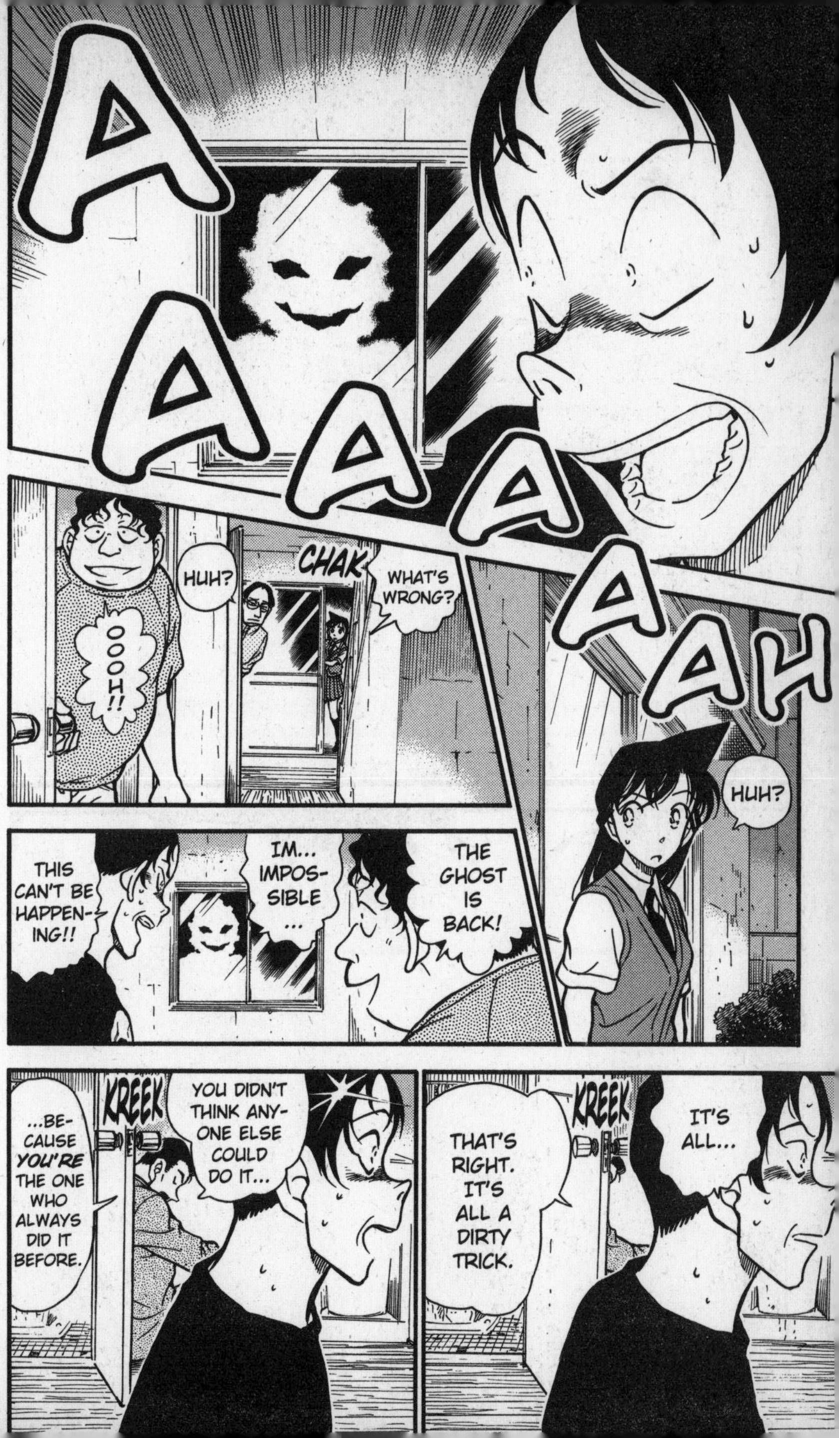
AAAAAAAH
HUH?
WHAT'S WRONG?
CHAK
HUH?
OOOOH!!
THE GHOST IS BACK!
IM... IMPOSSIBLE...
THIS CAN'T BE HAPPENING!!
IT'S ALL...
KREEK
THAT'S RIGHT. IT'S ALL A DIRTY TRICK.
YOU DIDN'T THINK ANYONE ELSE COULD DO IT...
KREEK
...BECAUSE *YOU'RE* THE ONE WHO ALWAYS DID IT BEFORE.

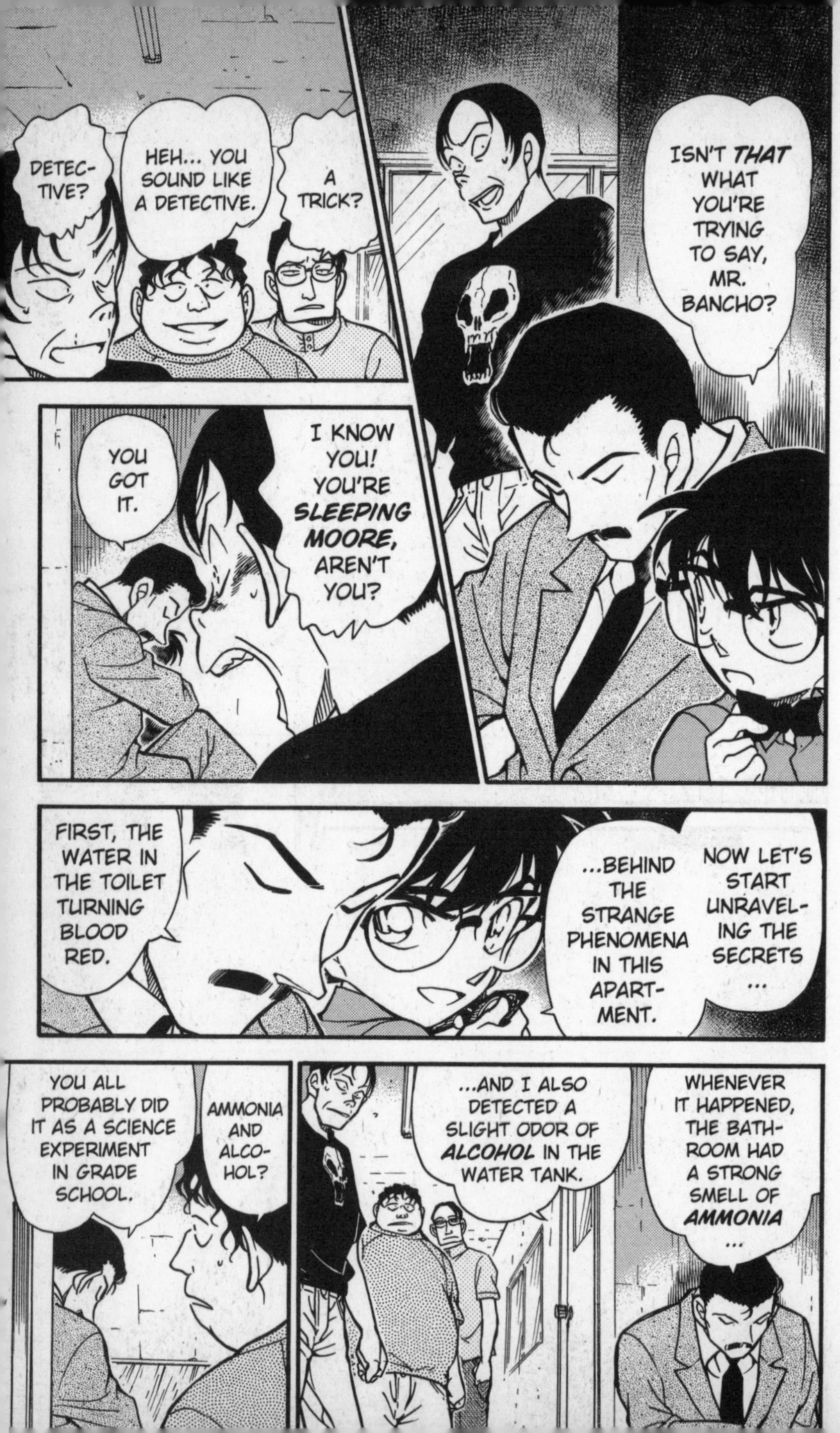
ISN'T *THAT* WHAT YOU'RE TRYING TO SAY, MR. BANCHO?
A TRICK?
HEH... YOU SOUND LIKE A DETECTIVE.
DETECTIVE?
I KNOW YOU! YOU'RE *SLEEPING MOORE,* AREN'T YOU?
YOU GOT IT.
NOW LET'S START UNRAVELING THE SECRETS ...
...BEHIND THE STRANGE PHENOMENA IN THIS APARTMENT.
FIRST, THE WATER IN THE TOILET TURNING BLOOD RED.
WHENEVER IT HAPPENED, THE BATHROOM HAD A STRONG SMELL OF *AMMONIA* ...
...AND I ALSO DETECTED A SLIGHT ODOR OF *ALCOHOL* IN THE WATER TANK.
AMMONIA AND ALCOHOL?
YOU ALL PROBABLY DID IT AS A SCIENCE EXPERIMENT IN GRADE SCHOOL.

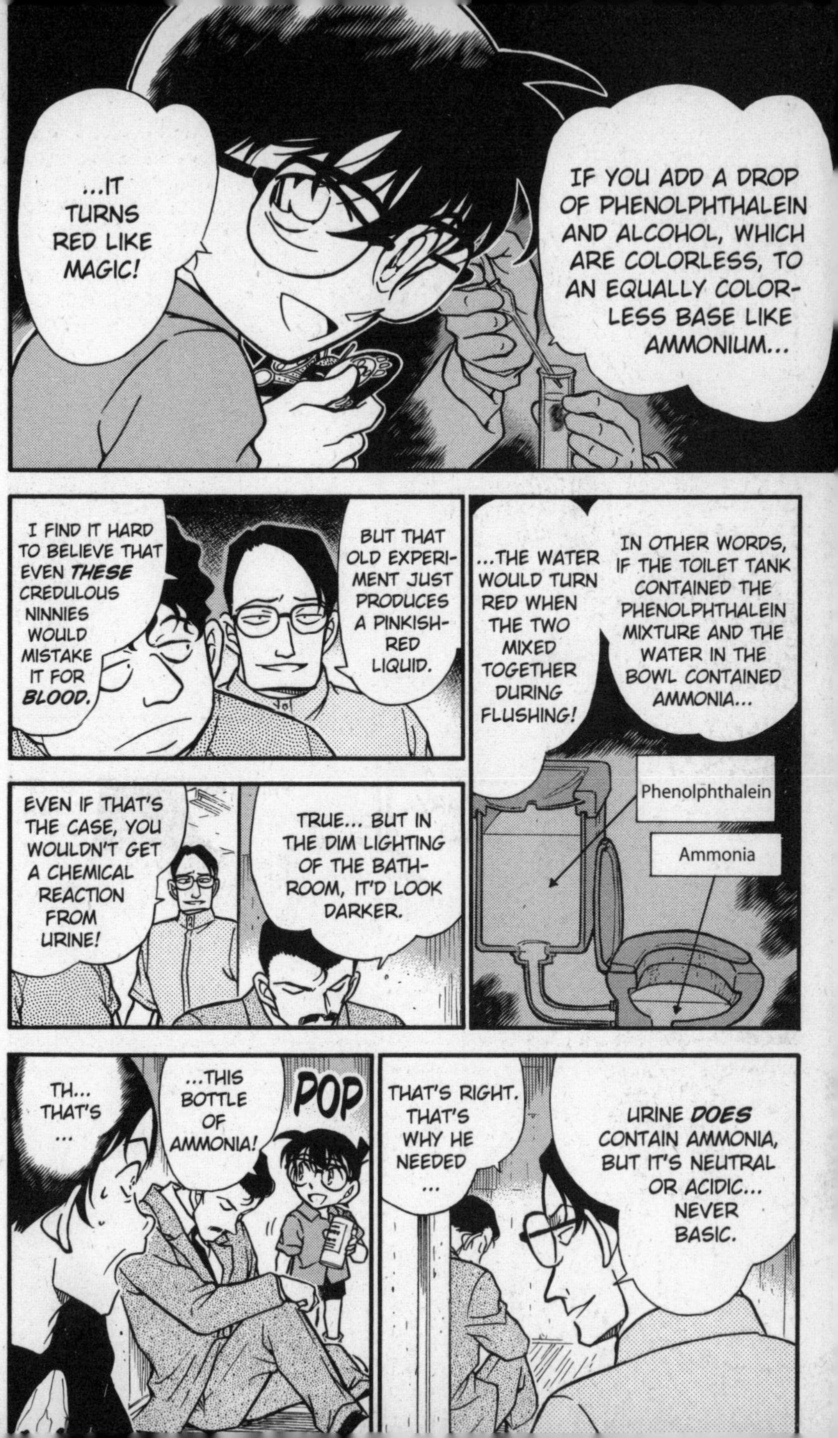
IF YOU ADD A DROP OF PHENOLPHTHALEIN AND ALCOHOL, WHICH ARE COLORLESS, TO AN EQUALLY COLOR-LESS BASE LIKE AMMONIUM...
...IT TURNS RED LIKE MAGIC!
IN OTHER WORDS, IF THE TOILET TANK CONTAINED THE PHENOLPHTHALEIN MIXTURE AND THE WATER IN THE BOWL CONTAINED AMMONIA...
...THE WATER WOULD TURN RED WHEN THE TWO MIXED TOGETHER DURING FLUSHING!
Phenolphthalein
Ammonia
BUT THAT OLD EXPERI-MENT JUST PRODUCES A PINKISH-RED LIQUID.
I FIND IT HARD TO BELIEVE THAT EVEN *THESE* CREDULOUS NINNIES WOULD MISTAKE IT FOR ***BLOOD.***
TRUE... BUT IN THE DIM LIGHTING OF THE BATH-ROOM, IT'D LOOK DARKER.
EVEN IF THAT'S THE CASE, YOU WOULDN'T GET A CHEMICAL REACTION FROM URINE!
URINE ***DOES*** CONTAIN AMMONIA, BUT IT'S NEUTRAL OR ACIDIC... NEVER BASIC.
THAT'S RIGHT. THAT'S WHY HE NEEDED ...
POP
...THIS BOTTLE OF AMMONIA!
TH... THAT'S ...

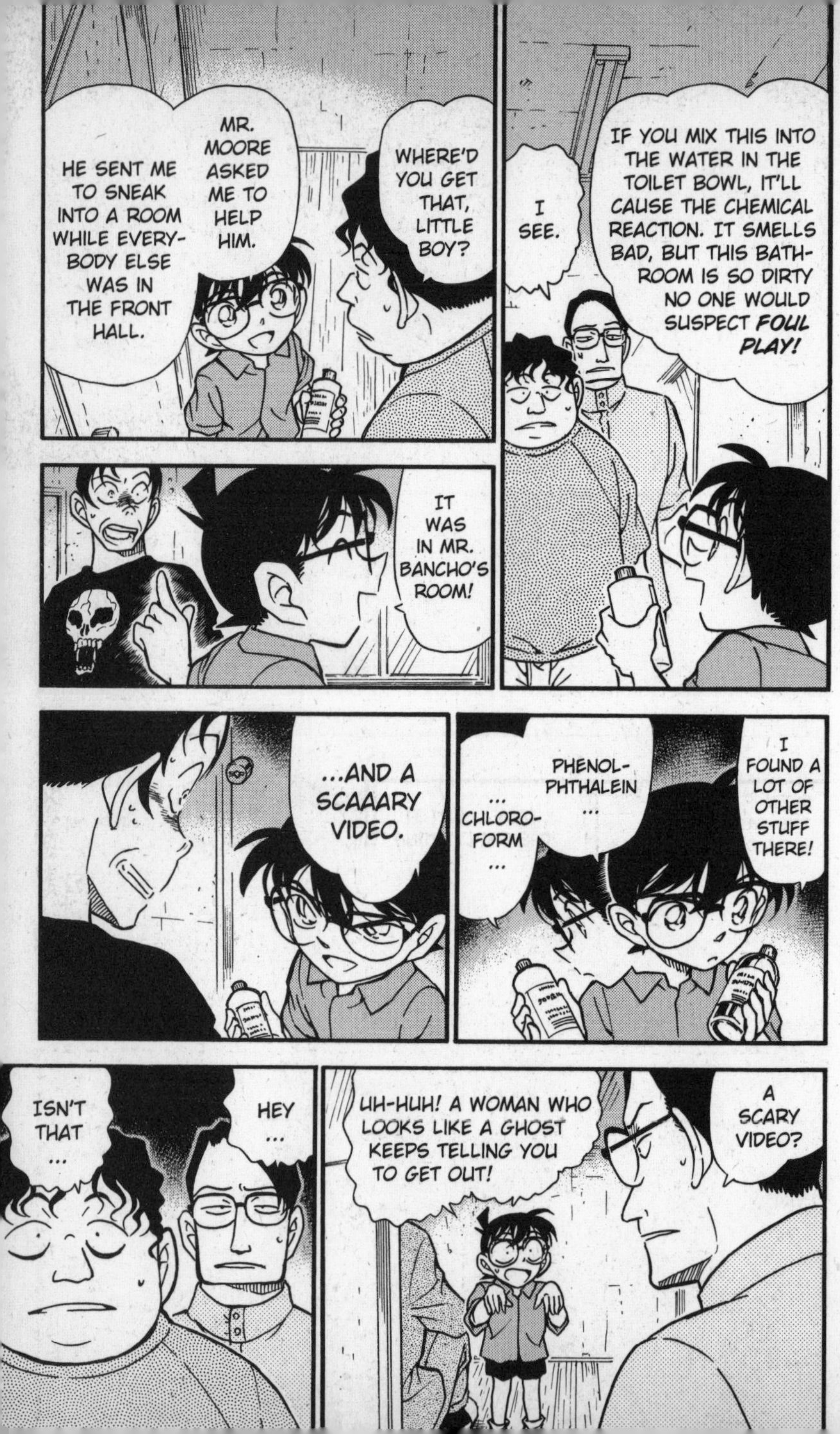
IF YOU MIX THIS INTO THE WATER IN THE TOILET BOWL, IT'LL CAUSE THE CHEMICAL REACTION. IT SMELLS BAD, BUT THIS BATHROOM IS SO DIRTY NO ONE WOULD SUSPECT FOUL PLAY!
I SEE.
WHERE'D YOU GET THAT, LITTLE BOY?
MR. MOORE ASKED ME TO HELP HIM.
HE SENT ME TO SNEAK INTO A ROOM WHILE EVERYBODY ELSE WAS IN THE FRONT HALL.
IT WAS IN MR. BANCHO'S ROOM!
I FOUND A LOT OF OTHER STUFF THERE!
PHENOLPHTHALEIN ...
... CHLOROFORM ...
...AND A SCAAARY VIDEO.
A SCARY VIDEO?
UH-HUH! A WOMAN WHO LOOKS LIKE A GHOST KEEPS TELLING YOU TO GET OUT!
HEY ...
ISN'T THAT ...

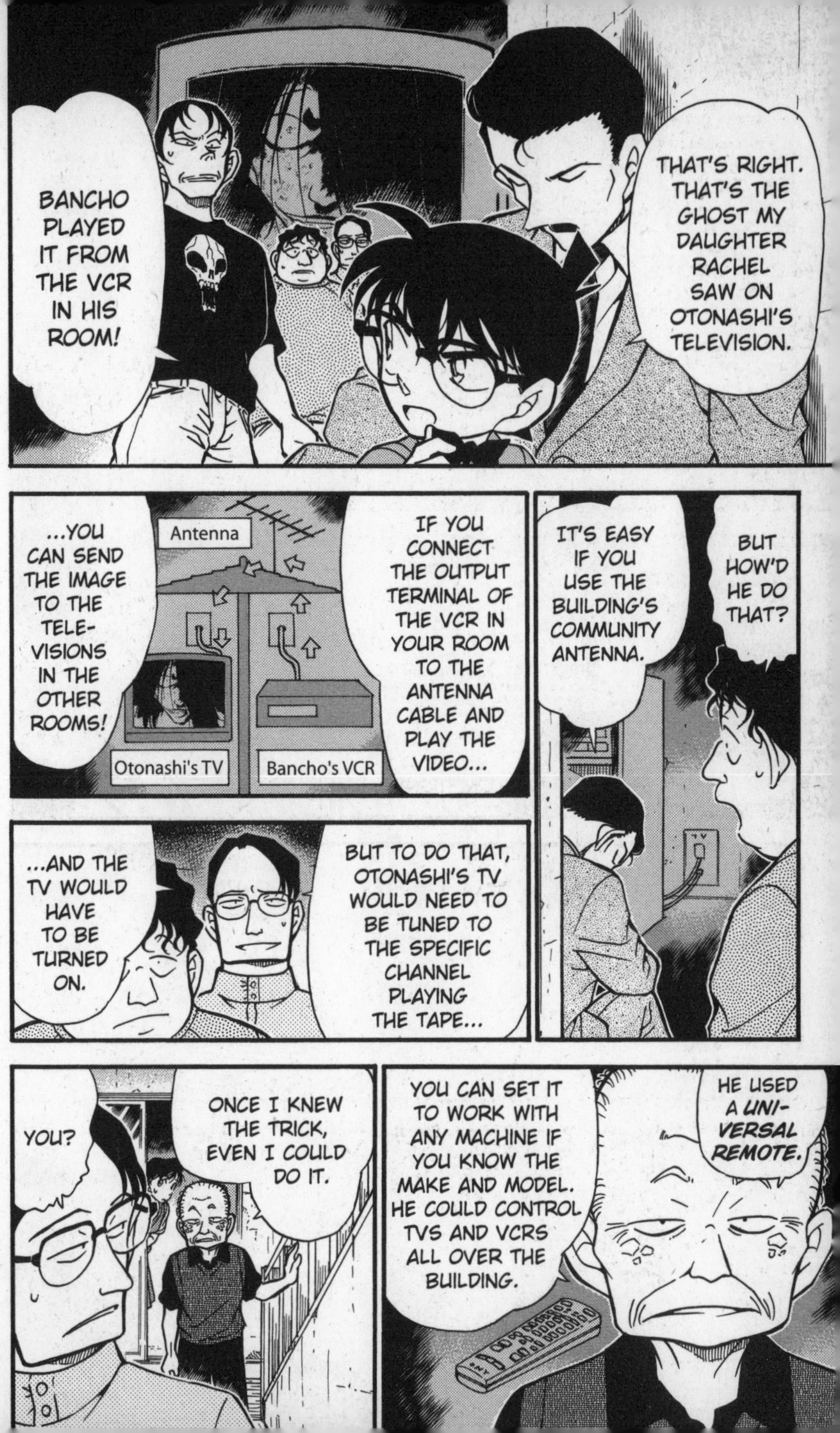
THAT'S RIGHT. THAT'S THE GHOST MY DAUGHTER RACHEL SAW ON OTONASHI'S TELEVISION.
BANCHO PLAYED IT FROM THE VCR IN HIS ROOM!
BUT HOW'D HE DO THAT?
IT'S EASY IF YOU USE THE BUILDING'S COMMUNITY ANTENNA.
IF YOU CONNECT THE OUTPUT TERMINAL OF THE VCR IN YOUR ROOM TO THE ANTENNA CABLE AND PLAY THE VIDEO...
Antenna
Otonashi's TV
Bancho's VCR
...YOU CAN SEND THE IMAGE TO THE TELE-VISIONS IN THE OTHER ROOMS!
BUT TO DO THAT, OTONASHI'S TV WOULD NEED TO BE TUNED TO THE SPECIFIC CHANNEL PLAYING THE TAPE...
...AND THE TV WOULD HAVE TO BE TURNED ON.
HE USED A UNI-VERSAL REMOTE.
YOU CAN SET IT TO WORK WITH ANY MACHINE IF YOU KNOW THE MAKE AND MODEL. HE COULD CONTROL TVS AND VCRS ALL OVER THE BUILDING.
ONCE I KNEW THE TRICK, EVEN I COULD DO IT.
YOU?

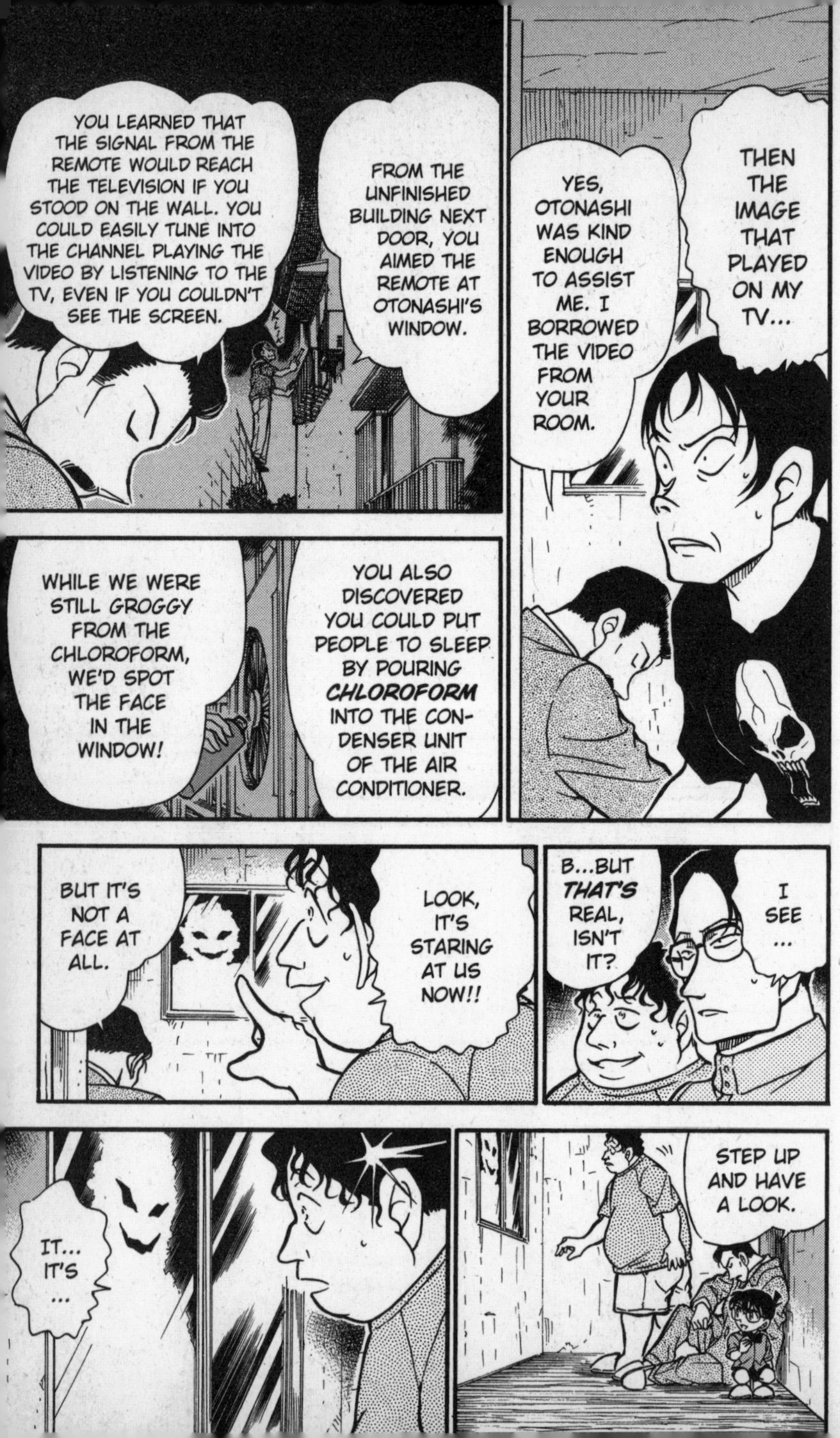
THEN THE IMAGE THAT PLAYED ON MY TV...
YES, OTONASHI WAS KIND ENOUGH TO ASSIST ME. I BORROWED THE VIDEO FROM YOUR ROOM.
FROM THE UNFINISHED BUILDING NEXT DOOR, YOU AIMED THE REMOTE AT OTONASHI'S WINDOW.
YOU LEARNED THAT THE SIGNAL FROM THE REMOTE WOULD REACH THE TELEVISION IF YOU STOOD ON THE WALL. YOU COULD EASILY TUNE INTO THE CHANNEL PLAYING THE VIDEO BY LISTENING TO THE TV, EVEN IF YOU COULDN'T SEE THE SCREEN.
YOU ALSO DISCOVERED YOU COULD PUT PEOPLE TO SLEEP BY POURING ***CHLOROFORM*** INTO THE CONDENSER UNIT OF THE AIR CONDITIONER.
WHILE WE WERE STILL GROGGY FROM THE CHLOROFORM, WE'D SPOT THE FACE IN THE WINDOW!
I SEE...
B...BUT ***THAT'S*** REAL, ISN'T IT?
LOOK, IT'S STARING AT US NOW!!
BUT IT'S NOT A FACE AT ALL.
STEP UP AND HAVE A LOOK.
IT... IT'S...

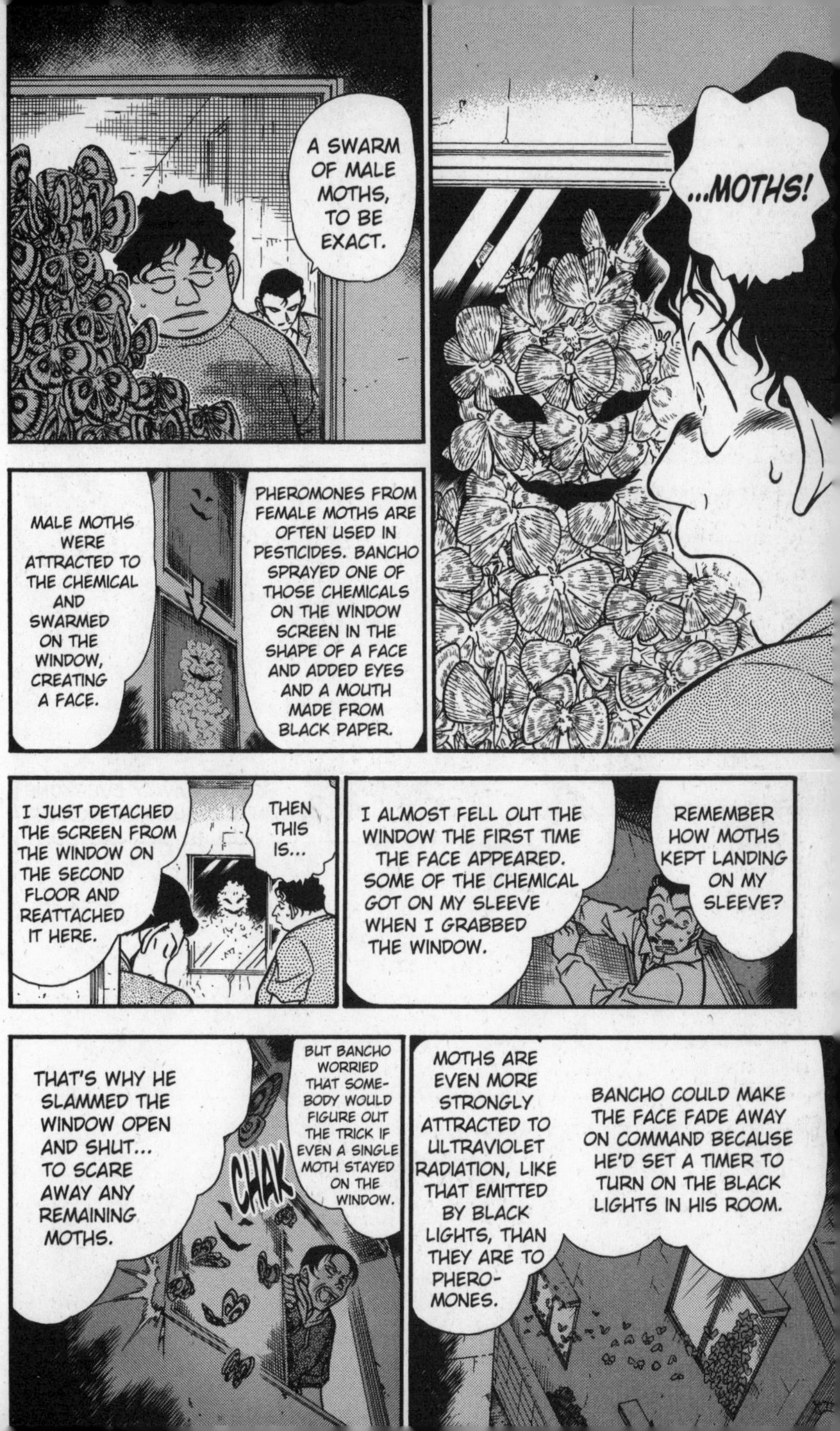
...MOTHS!
A SWARM OF MALE MOTHS, TO BE EXACT.
PHEROMONES FROM FEMALE MOTHS ARE OFTEN USED IN PESTICIDES. BANCHO SPRAYED ONE OF THOSE CHEMICALS ON THE WINDOW SCREEN IN THE SHAPE OF A FACE AND ADDED EYES AND A MOUTH MADE FROM BLACK PAPER.
MALE MOTHS WERE ATTRACTED TO THE CHEMICAL AND SWARMED ON THE WINDOW, CREATING A FACE.
REMEMBER HOW MOTHS KEPT LANDING ON MY SLEEVE?
I ALMOST FELL OUT THE WINDOW THE FIRST TIME THE FACE APPEARED. SOME OF THE CHEMICAL GOT ON MY SLEEVE WHEN I GRABBED THE WINDOW.
THEN THIS IS...
I JUST DETACHED THE SCREEN FROM THE WINDOW ON THE SECOND FLOOR AND REATTACHED IT HERE.
BANCHO COULD MAKE THE FACE FADE AWAY ON COMMAND BECAUSE HE'D SET A TIMER TO TURN ON THE BLACK LIGHTS IN HIS ROOM.
MOTHS ARE EVEN MORE STRONGLY ATTRACTED TO ULTRAVIOLET RADIATION, LIKE THAT EMITTED BY BLACK LIGHTS, THAN THEY ARE TO PHERO-MONES.
BUT BANCHO WORRIED THAT SOME-BODY WOULD FIGURE OUT THE TRICK IF EVEN A SINGLE MOTH STAYED ON THE WINDOW.
CHAK
THAT'S WHY HE SLAMMED THE WINDOW OPEN AND SHUT... TO SCARE AWAY ANY REMAINING MOTHS.

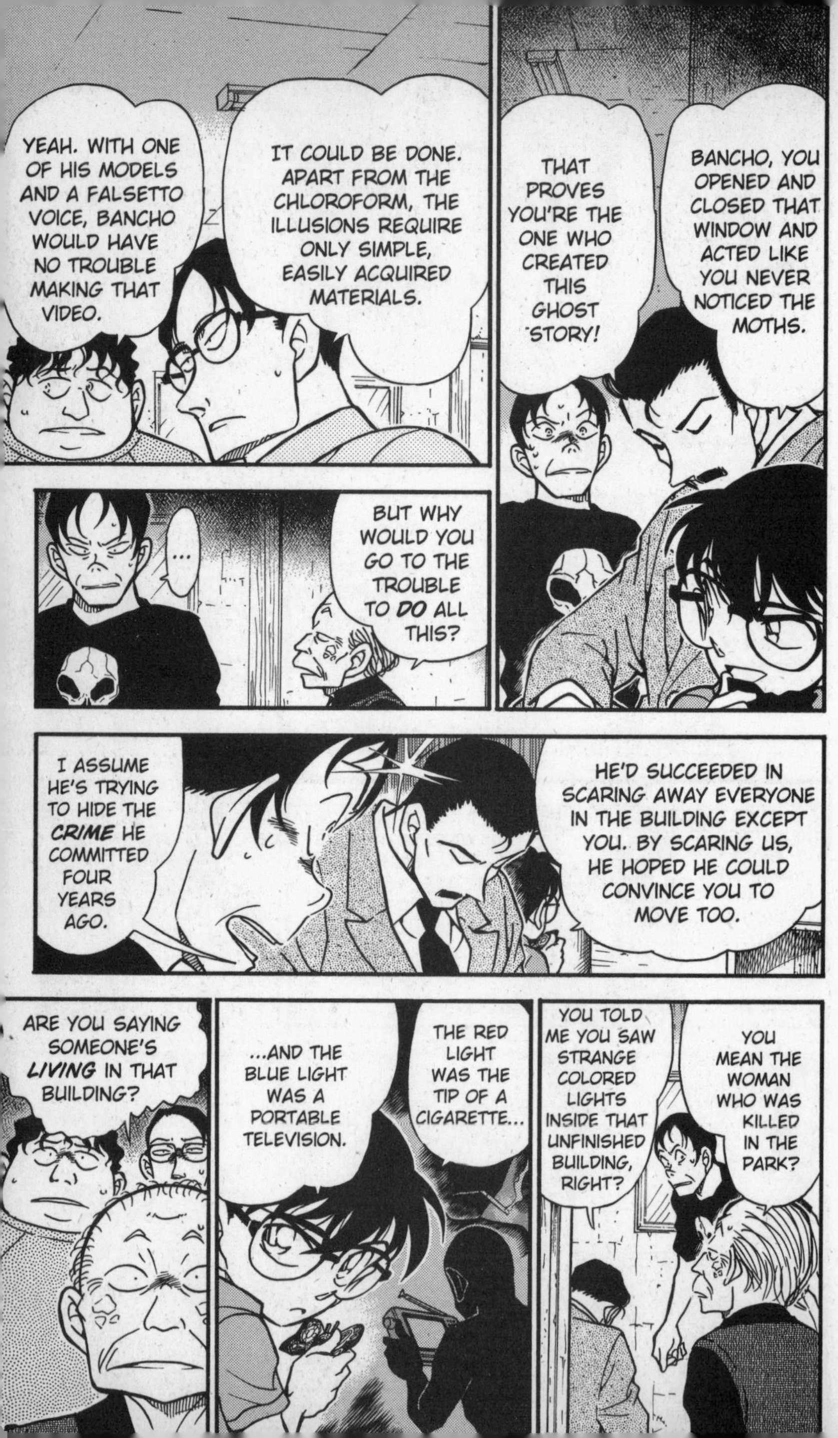
BANCHO, YOU OPENED AND CLOSED THAT WINDOW AND ACTED LIKE YOU NEVER NOTICED THE MOTHS.
THAT PROVES YOU'RE THE ONE WHO CREATED THIS GHOST STORY!
IT COULD BE DONE. APART FROM THE CHLOROFORM, THE ILLUSIONS REQUIRE ONLY SIMPLE, EASILY ACQUIRED MATERIALS.
YEAH. WITH ONE OF HIS MODELS AND A FALSETTO VOICE, BANCHO WOULD HAVE NO TROUBLE MAKING THAT VIDEO.
BUT WHY WOULD YOU GO TO THE TROUBLE TO DO ALL THIS?
...
HE'D SUCCEEDED IN SCARING AWAY EVERYONE IN THE BUILDING EXCEPT YOU. BY SCARING US, HE HOPED HE COULD CONVINCE YOU TO MOVE TOO.
I ASSUME HE'S TRYING TO HIDE THE CRIME HE COMMITTED FOUR YEARS AGO.
YOU MEAN THE WOMAN WHO WAS KILLED IN THE PARK?
YOU TOLD ME YOU SAW STRANGE COLORED LIGHTS INSIDE THAT UNFINISHED BUILDING, RIGHT?
THE RED LIGHT WAS THE TIP OF A CIGARETTE...
...AND THE BLUE LIGHT WAS A PORTABLE TELEVISION.
ARE YOU SAYING SOMEONE'S LIVING IN THAT BUILDING?

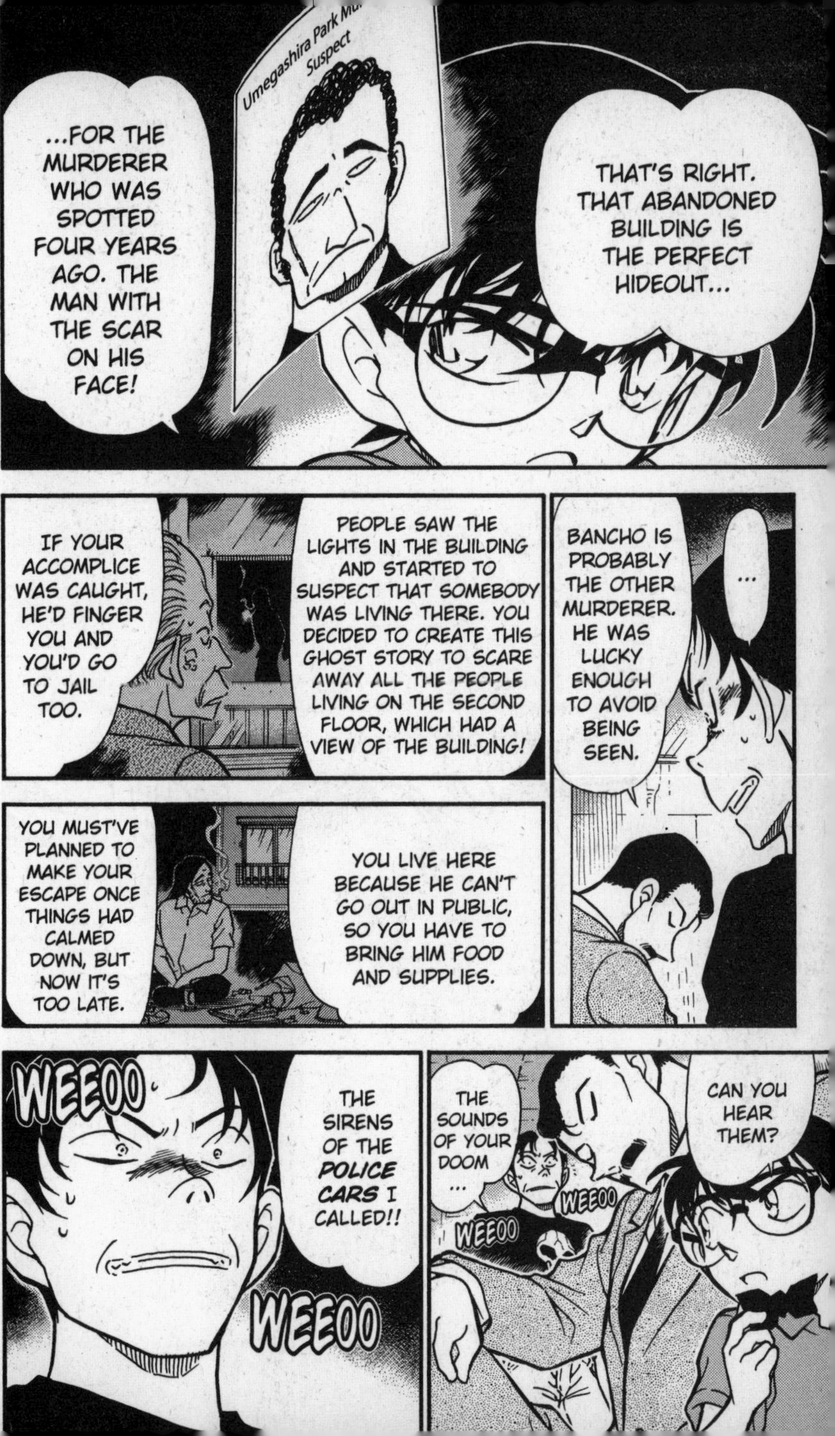
THAT'S RIGHT. THAT ABANDONED BUILDING IS THE PERFECT HIDEOUT...
Umegashira Park Mu
Suspect
...FOR THE MURDERER WHO WAS SPOTTED FOUR YEARS AGO. THE MAN WITH THE SCAR ON HIS FACE!
...
BANCHO IS PROBABLY THE OTHER MURDERER. HE WAS LUCKY ENOUGH TO AVOID BEING SEEN.
PEOPLE SAW THE LIGHTS IN THE BUILDING AND STARTED TO SUSPECT THAT SOMEBODY WAS LIVING THERE. YOU DECIDED TO CREATE THIS GHOST STORY TO SCARE AWAY ALL THE PEOPLE LIVING ON THE SECOND FLOOR, WHICH HAD A VIEW OF THE BUILDING!
IF YOUR ACCOMPLICE WAS CAUGHT, HE'D FINGER YOU AND YOU'D GO TO JAIL TOO.
YOU LIVE HERE BECAUSE HE CAN'T GO OUT IN PUBLIC, SO YOU HAVE TO BRING HIM FOOD AND SUPPLIES.
YOU MUST'VE PLANNED TO MAKE YOUR ESCAPE ONCE THINGS HAD CALMED DOWN, BUT NOW IT'S TOO LATE.
CAN YOU HEAR THEM?
WEEOO
WEEOO
THE SOUNDS OF YOUR DOOM ...
THE SIRENS OF THE *POLICE CARS* I CALLED!!
WEEOO
WEEOO

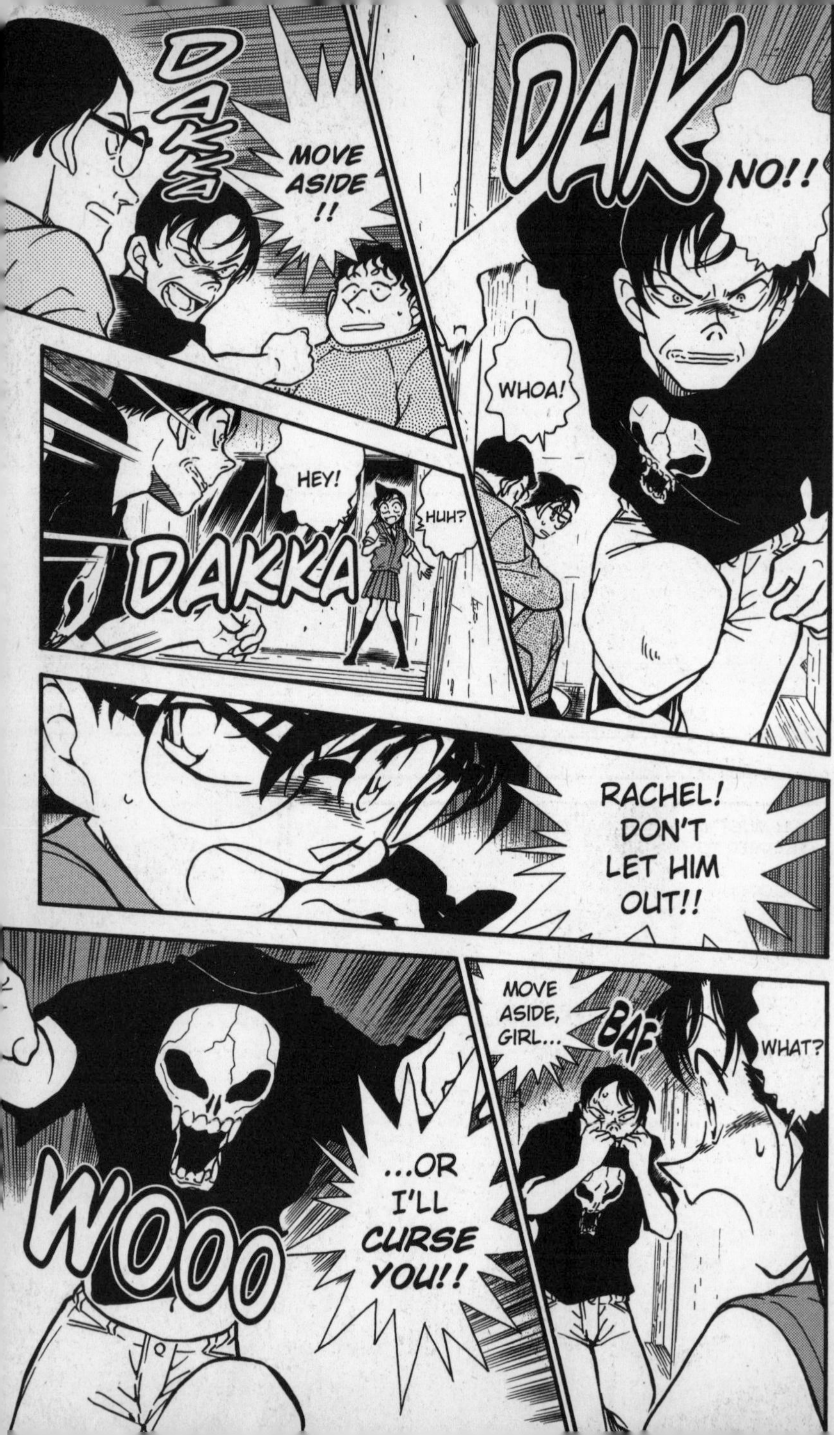
DAK
NO!!
WHOA!
DAKKA
MOVE ASIDE !!
HUH?
HEY!
DAKKA
RACHEL! DON'T LET HIM OUT!!
MOVE ASIDE, GIRL...
BAF
WHAT?
WOOO
...OR I'LL CURSE YOU!!

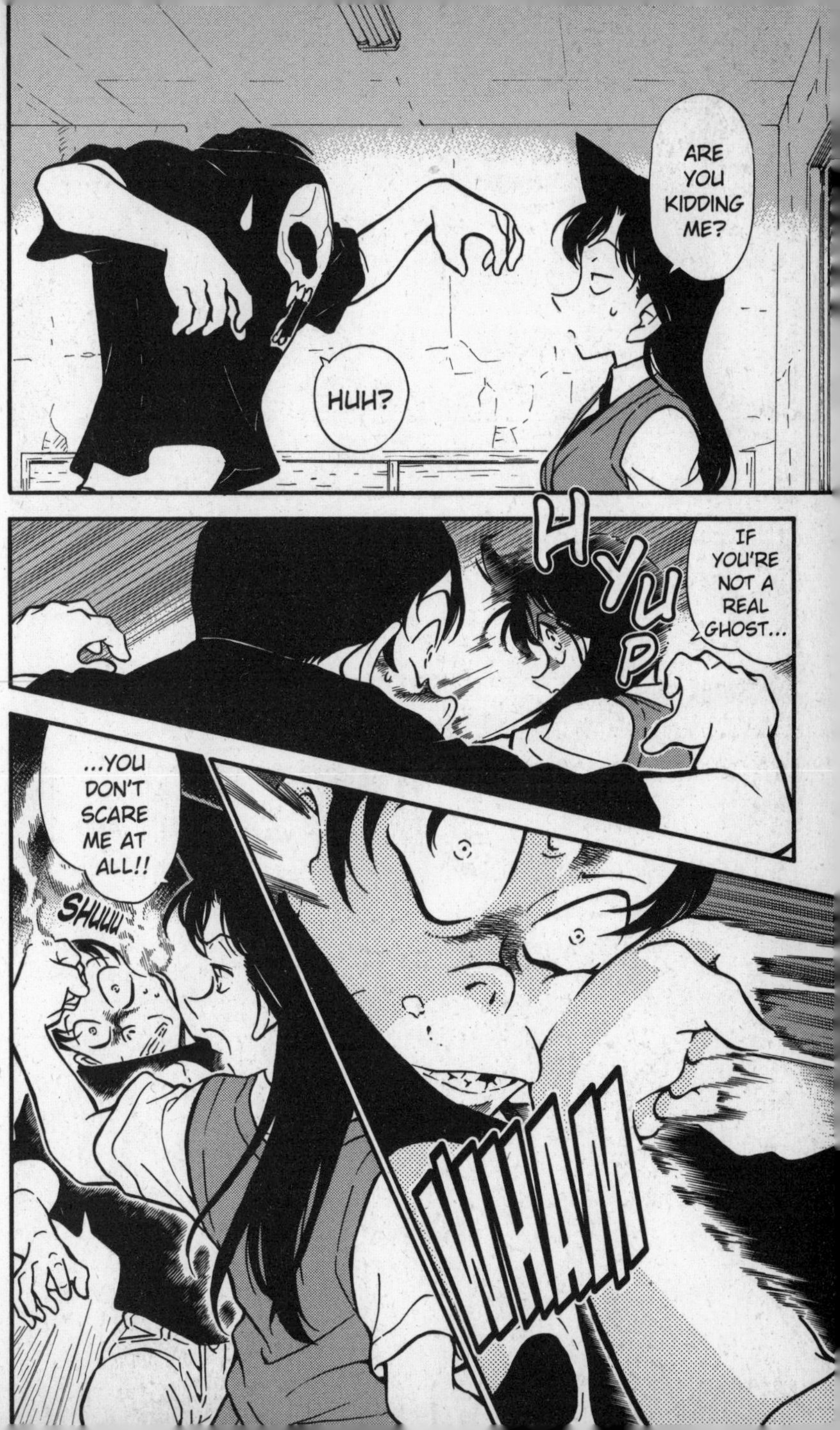
ARE YOU KIDDING ME?
HUH?
HYUP
IF YOU'RE NOT A REAL GHOST...
...YOU DON'T SCARE ME AT ALL!!
SHUUU
WHAM

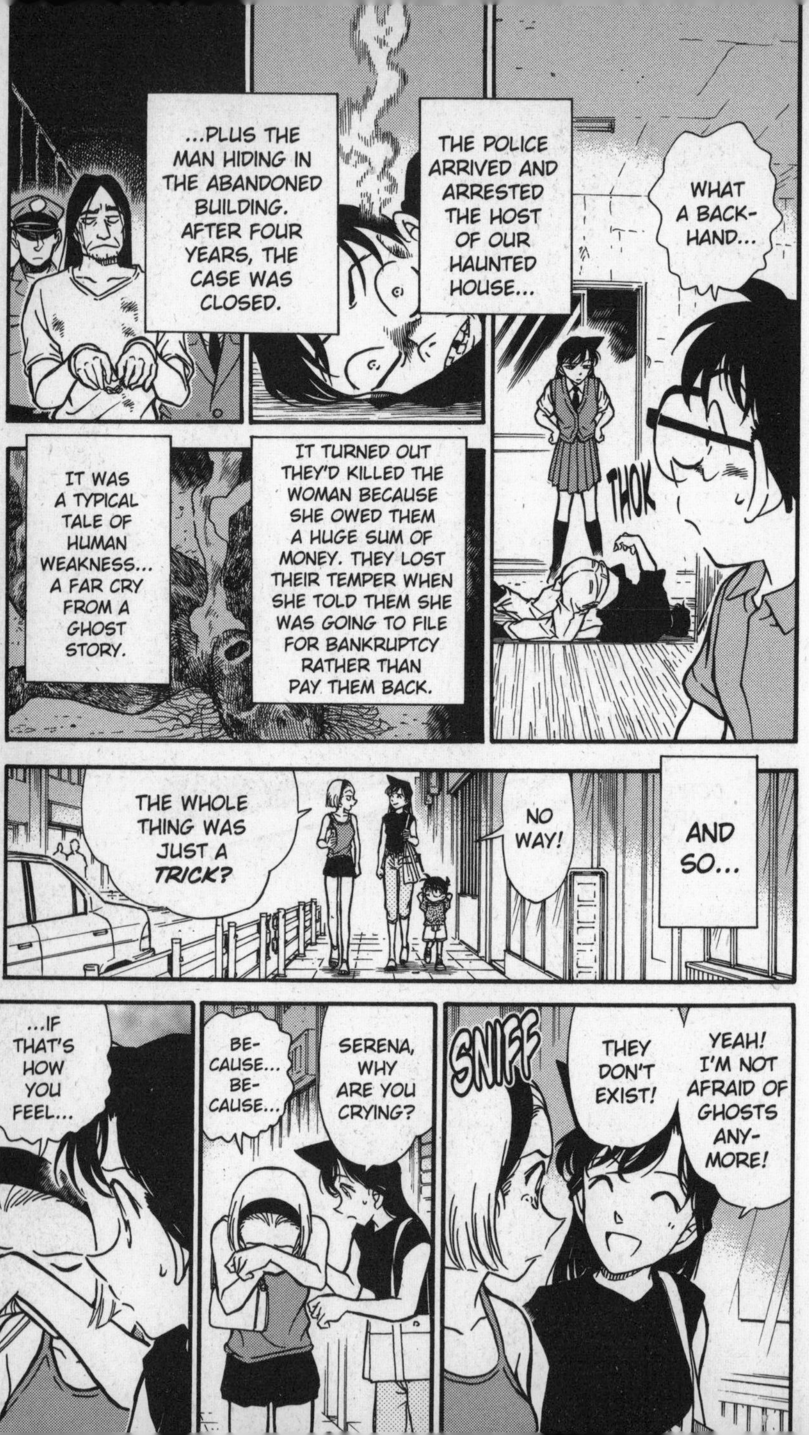
WHAT A BACK-HAND...
THOK
THE POLICE ARRIVED AND ARRESTED THE HOST OF OUR HAUNTED HOUSE...
...PLUS THE MAN HIDING IN THE ABANDONED BUILDING. AFTER FOUR YEARS, THE CASE WAS CLOSED.
IT TURNED OUT THEY'D KILLED THE WOMAN BECAUSE SHE OWED THEM A HUGE SUM OF MONEY. THEY LOST THEIR TEMPER WHEN SHE TOLD THEM SHE WAS GOING TO FILE FOR BANKRUPTCY RATHER THAN PAY THEM BACK.
IT WAS A TYPICAL TALE OF HUMAN WEAKNESS... A FAR CRY FROM A GHOST STORY.
AND SO...
NO WAY!
THE WHOLE THING WAS JUST A *TRICK?*
YEAH! I'M NOT AFRAID OF GHOSTS ANY-MORE!
THEY DON'T EXIST!
SNIFF
SERENA, WHY ARE YOU CRYING?
BE-CAUSE... BE-CAUSE...
...IF THAT'S HOW YOU FEEL...

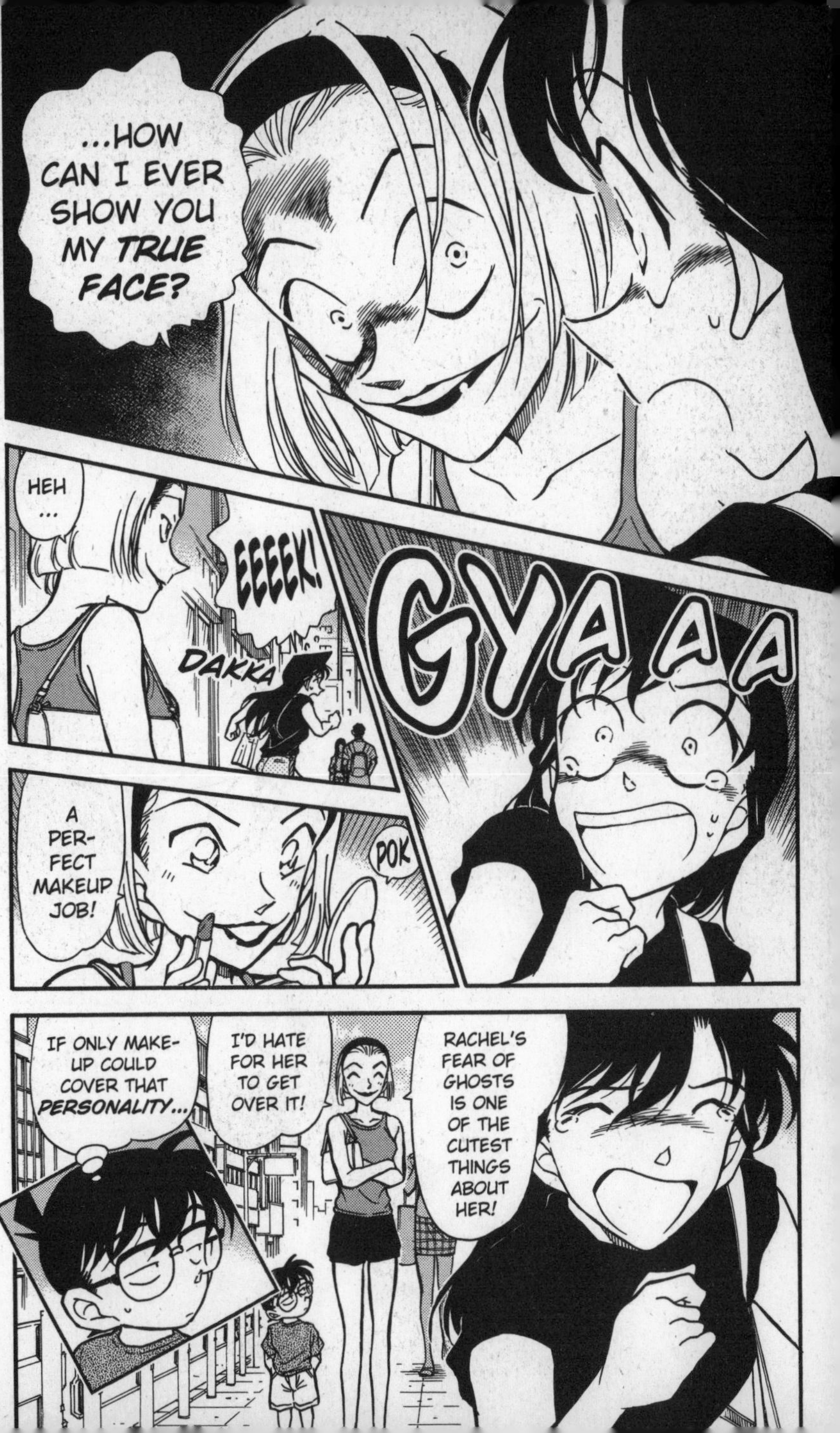
...HOW CAN I EVER SHOW YOU MY TRUE FACE?
GYAAAA
EEEEK!
HEH ...
DAKKA
POK
A PER-FECT MAKEUP JOB!
RACHEL'S FEAR OF GHOSTS IS ONE OF THE CUTEST THINGS ABOUT HER!
I'D HATE FOR HER TO GET OVER IT!
IF ONLY MAKE-UP COULD COVER THAT PERSONALITY...

FILE 8:
MISSING MITCH ①

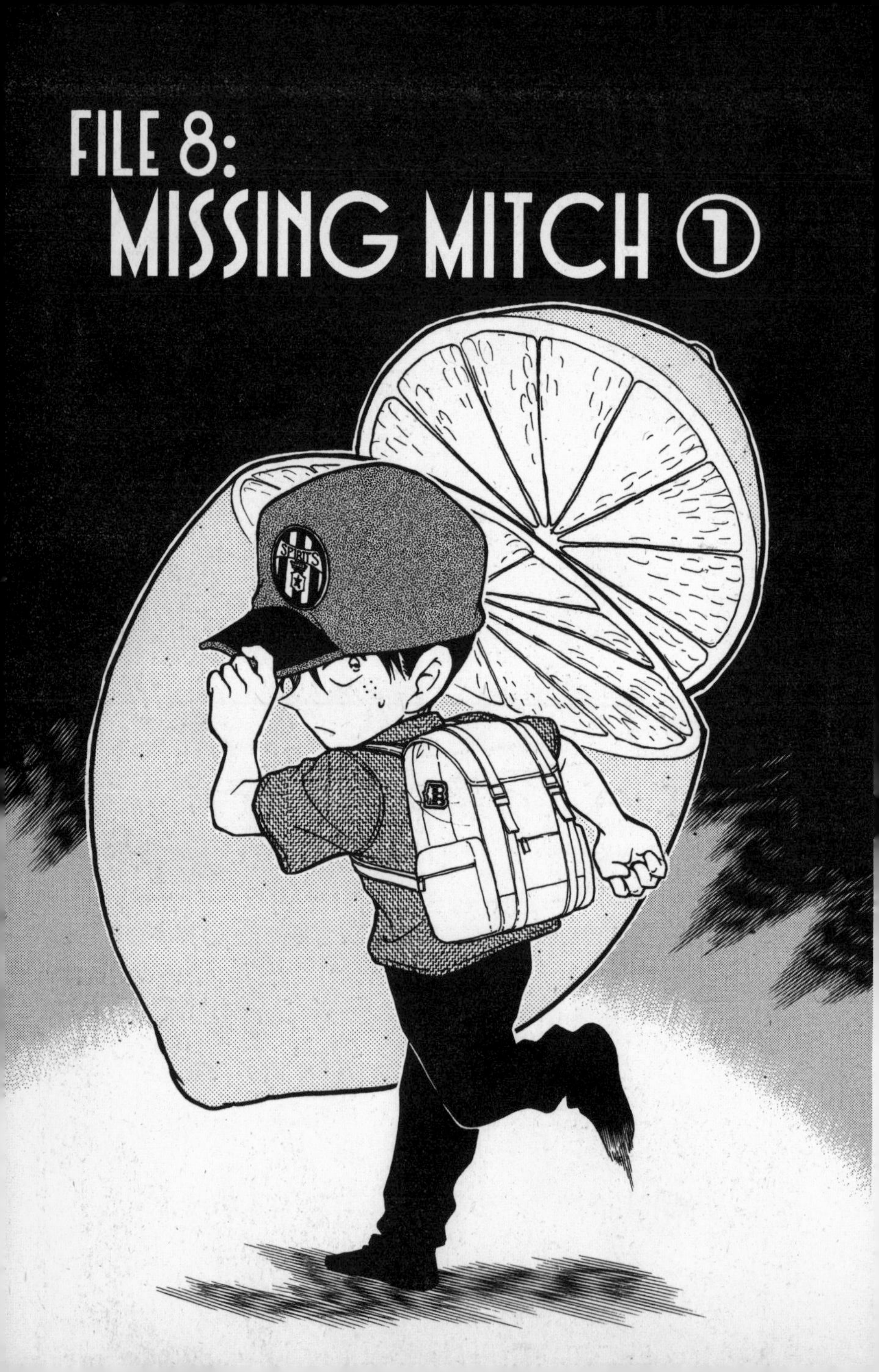
SPIRITS

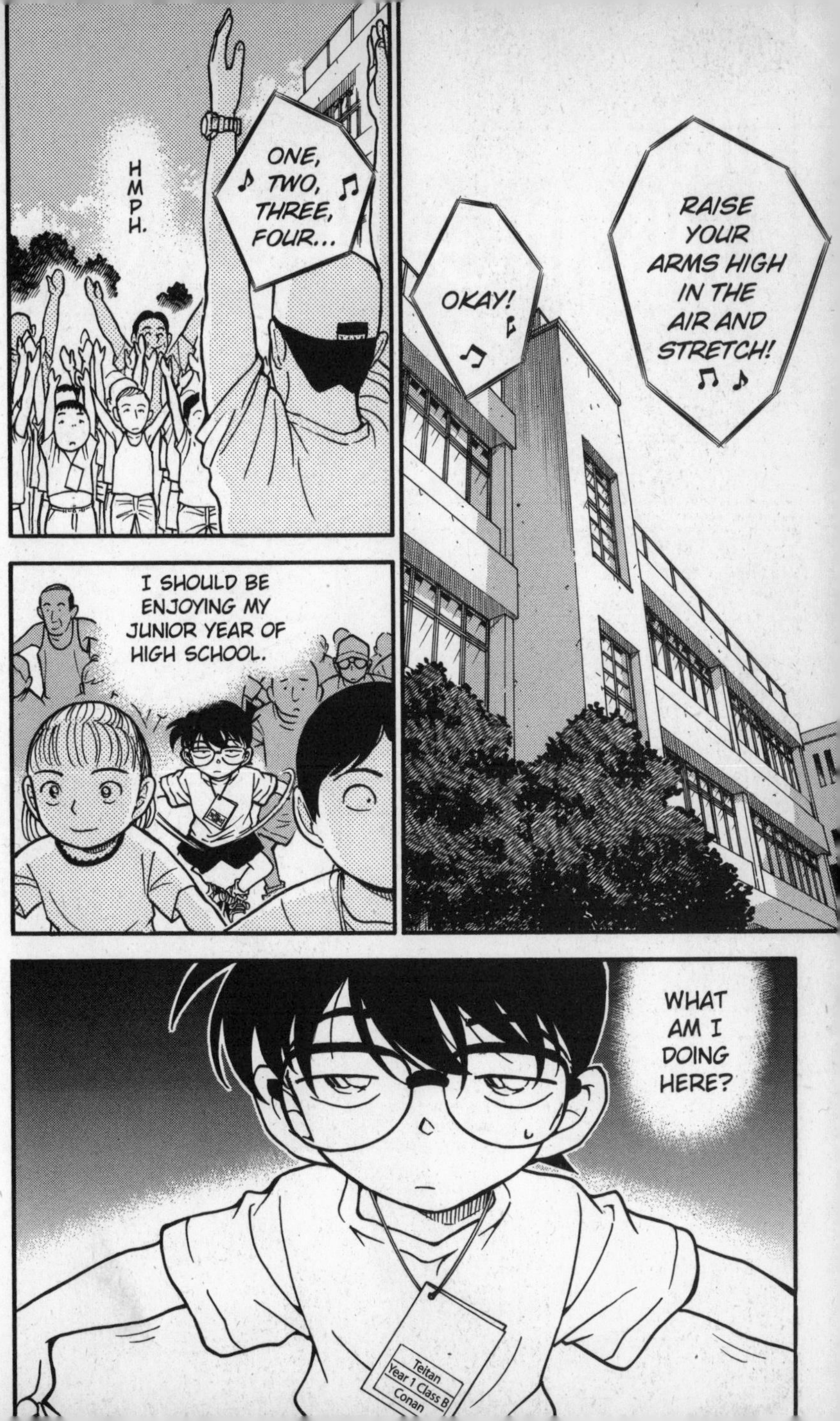
RAISE YOUR ARMS HIGH IN THE AIR AND STRETCH! ♫ ♪
♪ OKAY! ♫
♪ ONE, TWO, THREE, FOUR... ♫
HMPH.
I SHOULD BE ENJOYING MY JUNIOR YEAR OF HIGH SCHOOL.
WHAT AM I DOING HERE?
Teitan
Year 1 Class B
Conan

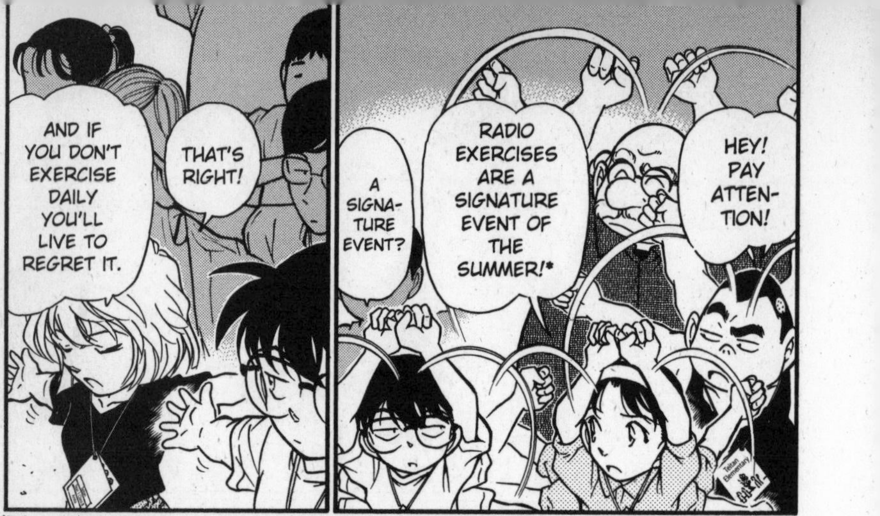
HEY! PAY ATTEN-TION!
RADIO EXERCISES ARE A SIGNATURE EVENT OF THE SUMMER!*
A SIGNA-TURE EVENT?
THAT'S RIGHT!
AND IF YOU DON'T EXERCISE DAILY YOU'LL LIVE TO REGRET IT.

*During summer break, many Japanese elementary schools organize morning exercises. They're still called *rajio taiso*, "radio exercises," but nowadays the lessons are usually on CD.

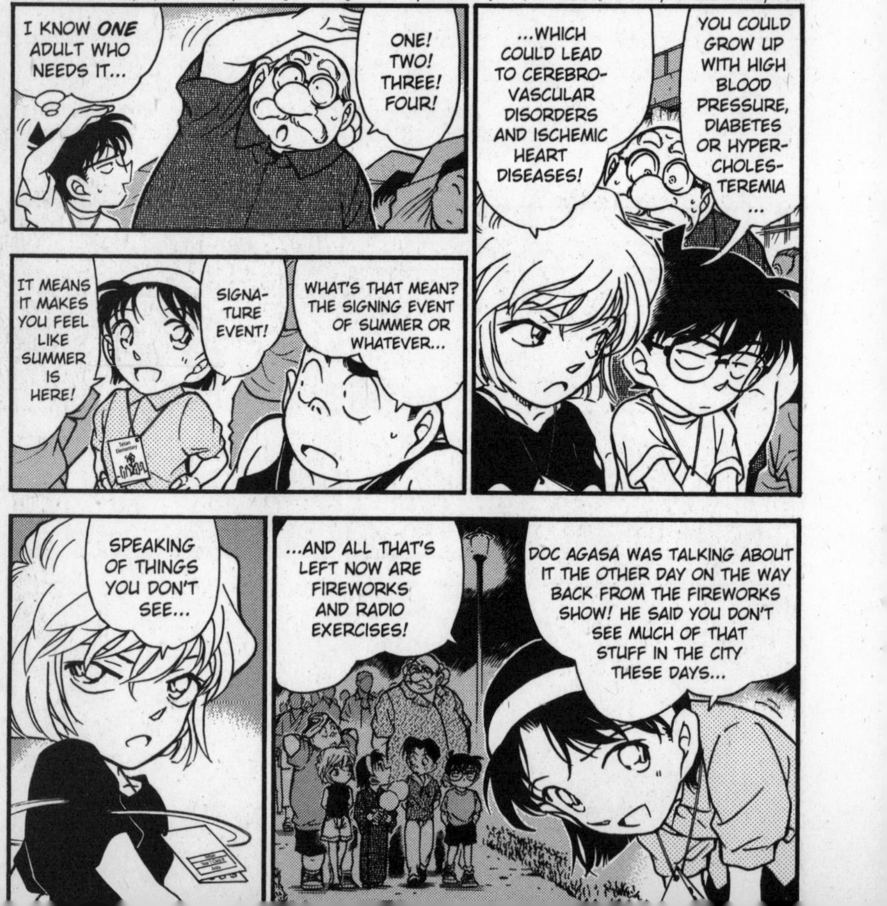
YOU COULD GROW UP WITH HIGH BLOOD PRESSURE, DIABETES OR HYPER-CHOLES-TEREMIA...
...WHICH COULD LEAD TO CEREBRO-VASCULAR DISORDERS AND ISCHEMIC HEART DISEASES!
ONE! TWO! THREE! FOUR!
I KNOW *ONE* ADULT WHO NEEDS IT...
WHAT'S THAT MEAN? THE SIGNING EVENT OF SUMMER OR WHATEVER...
SIGNA-TURE EVENT!
IT MEANS IT MAKES YOU FEEL LIKE SUMMER IS HERE!
DOC AGASA WAS TALKING ABOUT IT THE OTHER DAY ON THE WAY BACK FROM THE FIREWORKS SHOW! HE SAID YOU DON'T SEE MUCH OF THAT STUFF IN THE CITY THESE DAYS...
...AND ALL THAT'S LEFT NOW ARE FIREWORKS AND RADIO EXERCISES!
SPEAKING OF THINGS YOU DON'T SEE...

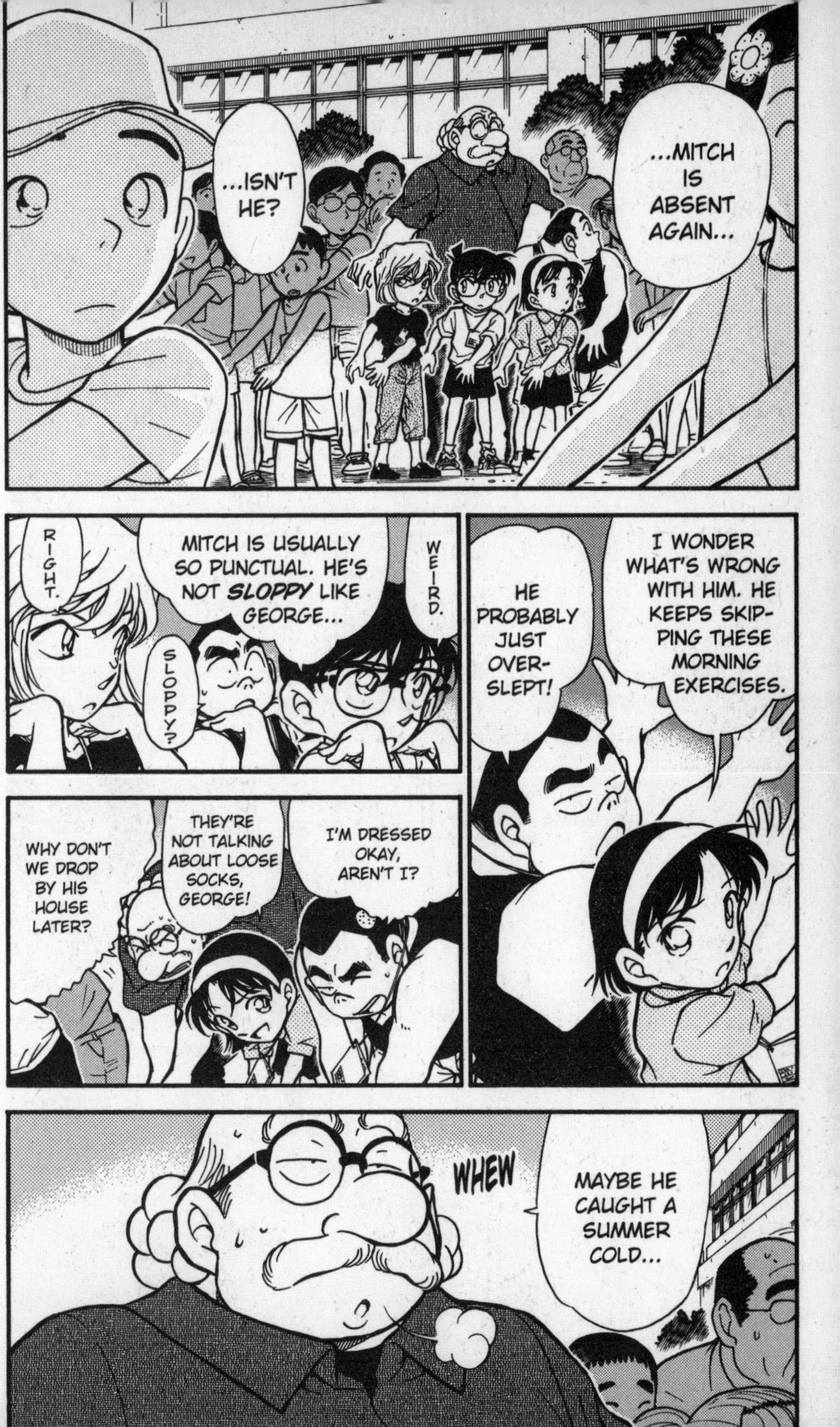
...MITCH IS ABSENT AGAIN...
...ISN'T HE?
I WONDER WHAT'S WRONG WITH HIM. HE KEEPS SKIPPING THESE MORNING EXERCISES.
HE PROBABLY JUST OVERSLEPT!
WEIRD.
MITCH IS USUALLY SO PUNCTUAL. HE'S NOT *SLOPPY* LIKE GEORGE...
RIGHT.
SLOPPY?
I'M DRESSED OKAY, AREN'T I?
THEY'RE NOT TALKING ABOUT LOOSE SOCKS, GEORGE!
WHY DON'T WE DROP BY HIS HOUSE LATER?
MAYBE HE CAUGHT A SUMMER COLD...
WHEW

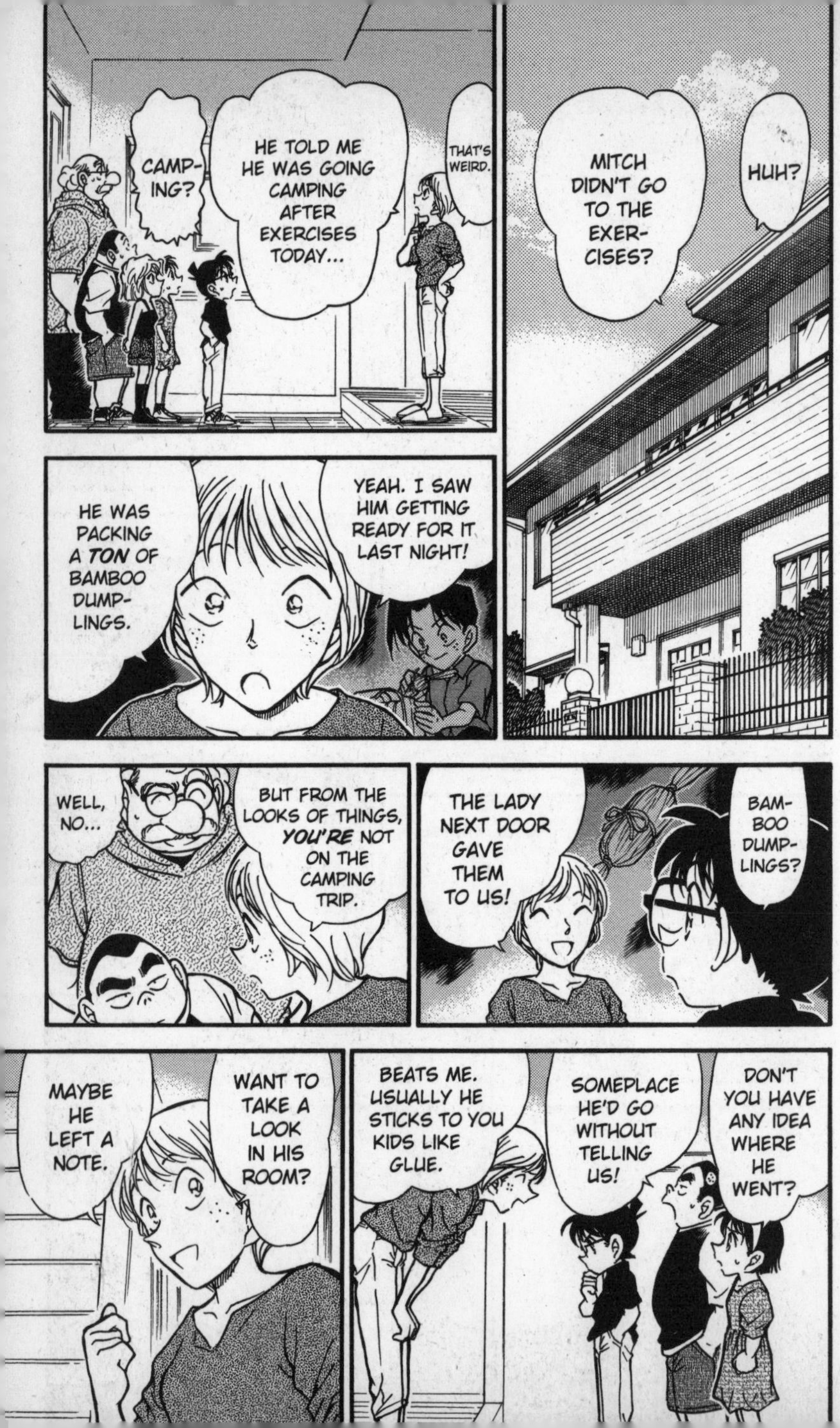
HUH?
MITCH DIDN'T GO TO THE EXERCISES?
THAT'S WEIRD.
HE TOLD ME HE WAS GOING CAMPING AFTER EXERCISES TODAY...
CAMPING?
YEAH. I SAW HIM GETTING READY FOR IT LAST NIGHT!
HE WAS PACKING A *TON* OF BAMBOO DUMPLINGS.
BAMBOO DUMPLINGS?
THE LADY NEXT DOOR GAVE THEM TO US!
BUT FROM THE LOOKS OF THINGS, *YOU'RE* NOT ON THE CAMPING TRIP.
WELL, NO...
DON'T YOU HAVE ANY IDEA WHERE HE WENT?
SOMEPLACE HE'D GO WITHOUT TELLING US!
BEATS ME. USUALLY HE STICKS TO YOU KIDS LIKE GLUE.
WANT TO TAKE A LOOK IN HIS ROOM?
MAYBE HE LEFT A NOTE.

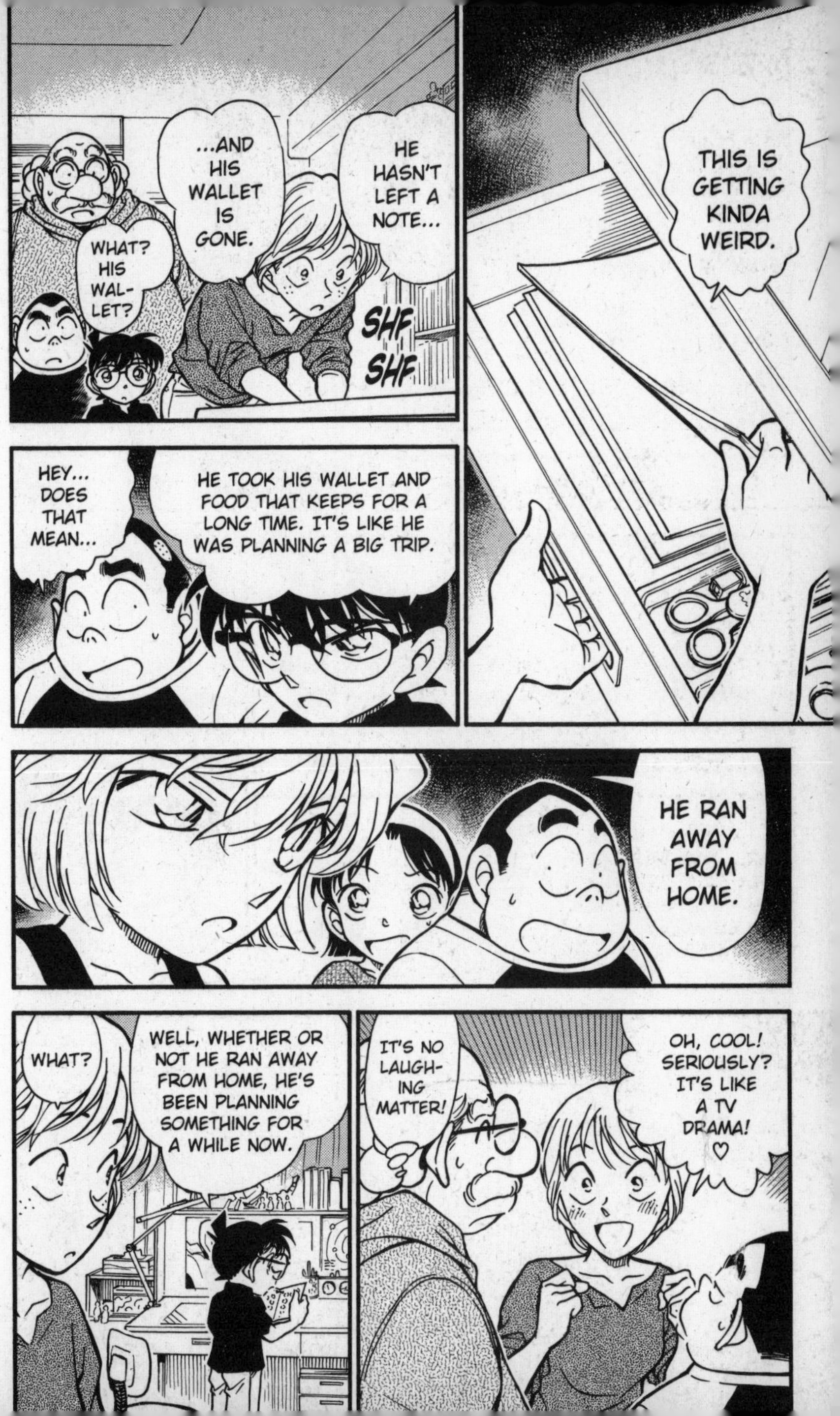
THIS IS GETTING KINDA WEIRD.
HE HASN'T LEFT A NOTE...
SHF SHF
...AND HIS WALLET IS GONE.
WHAT? HIS WAL-LET?
HE TOOK HIS WALLET AND FOOD THAT KEEPS FOR A LONG TIME. IT'S LIKE HE WAS PLANNING A BIG TRIP.
HEY... DOES THAT MEAN...
HE RAN AWAY FROM HOME.
OH, COOL! SERIOUSLY? IT'S LIKE A TV DRAMA! ♡
IT'S NO LAUGHING MATTER!
WELL, WHETHER OR NOT HE RAN AWAY FROM HOME, HE'S BEEN PLANNING SOMETHING FOR A WHILE NOW.
WHAT?

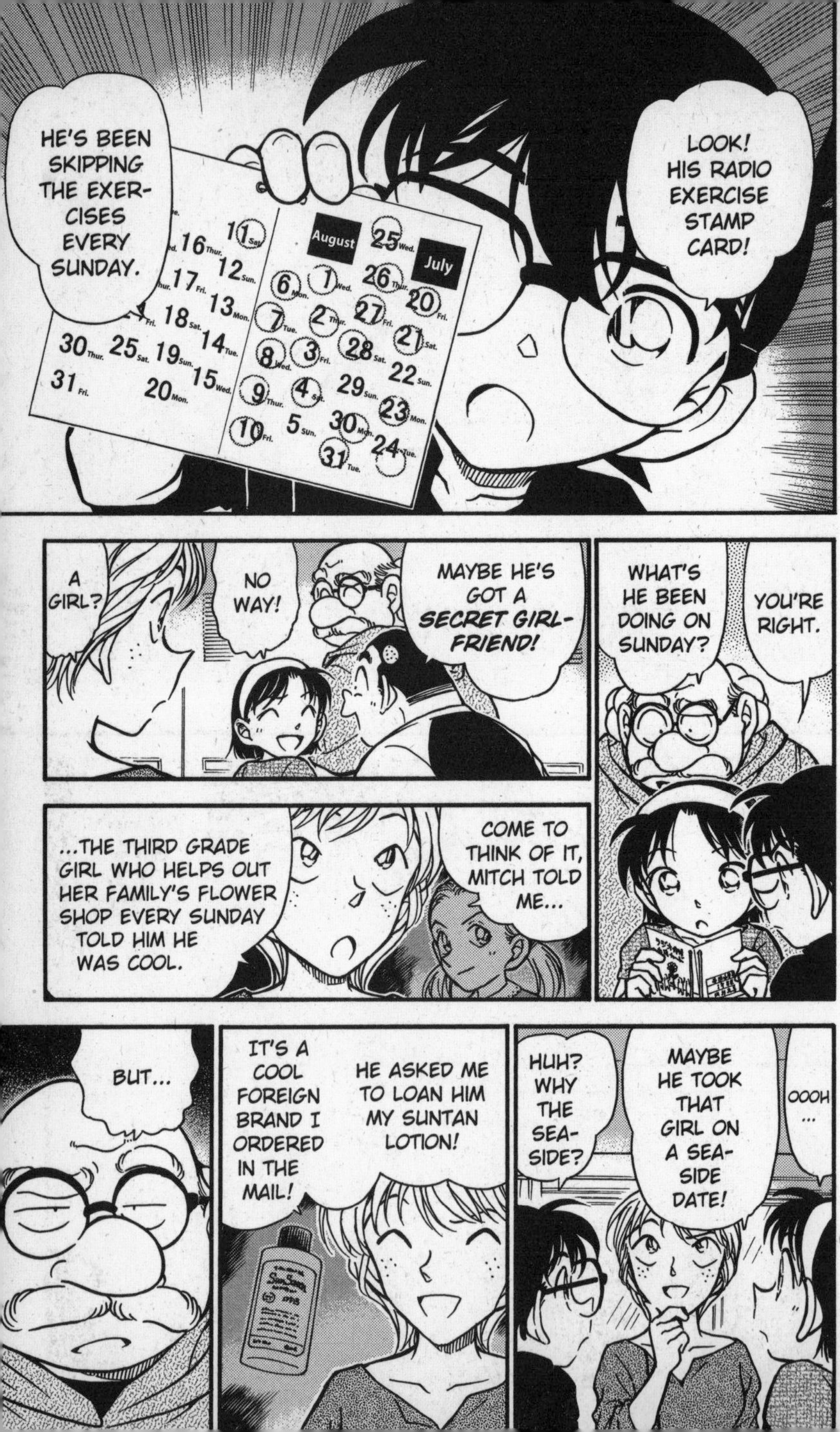
LOOK! HIS RADIO EXERCISE STAMP CARD!
HE'S BEEN SKIPPING THE EXER-CISES EVERY SUNDAY.
July
August
YOU'RE RIGHT.
WHAT'S HE BEEN DOING ON SUNDAY?
MAYBE HE'S GOT A SECRET GIRL-FRIEND!
NO WAY!
A GIRL?
COME TO THINK OF IT, MITCH TOLD ME...
...THE THIRD GRADE GIRL WHO HELPS OUT HER FAMILY'S FLOWER SHOP EVERY SUNDAY TOLD HIM HE WAS COOL.
OOOH...
MAYBE HE TOOK THAT GIRL ON A SEA-SIDE DATE!
HUH? WHY THE SEA-SIDE?
HE ASKED ME TO LOAN HIM MY SUNTAN LOTION!
IT'S A COOL FOREIGN BRAND I ORDERED IN THE MAIL!
BUT...

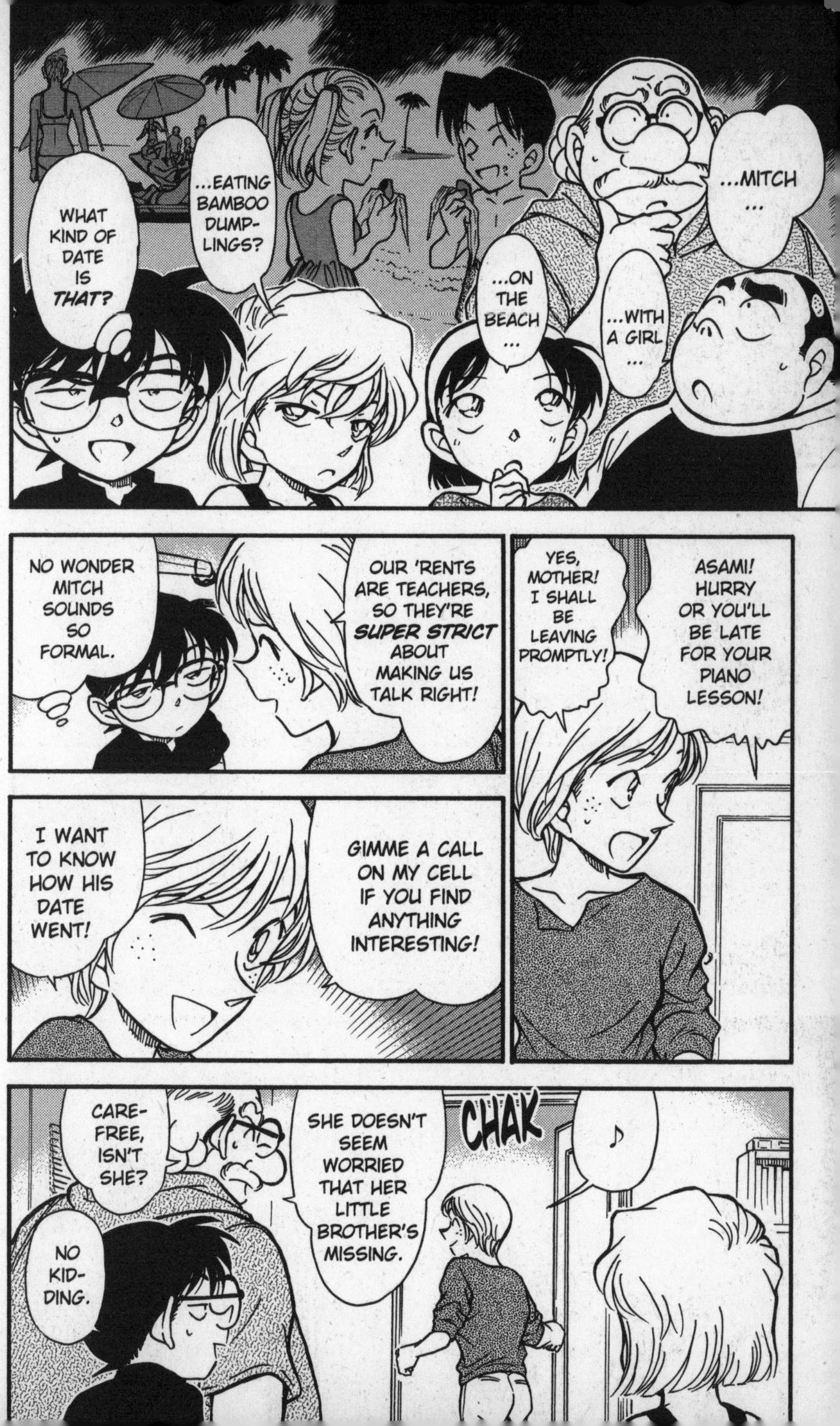
...MITCH ...
...WITH A GIRL ...
...ON THE BEACH ...
...EATING BAMBOO DUMP-LINGS?
WHAT KIND OF DATE IS *THAT?*
ASAMI! HURRY OR YOU'LL BE LATE FOR YOUR PIANO LESSON!
YES, MOTHER! I SHALL BE LEAVING PROMPTLY!
OUR 'RENTS ARE TEACHERS, SO THEY'RE **SUPER STRICT** ABOUT MAKING US TALK RIGHT!
NO WONDER MITCH SOUNDS SO FORMAL.
GIMME A CALL ON MY CELL IF YOU FIND ANYTHING INTERESTING!
I WANT TO KNOW HOW HIS DATE WENT!
♪
CHAK
SHE DOESN'T SEEM WORRIED THAT HER LITTLE BROTHER'S MISSING.
CARE-FREE, ISN'T SHE?
NO KID-DING.

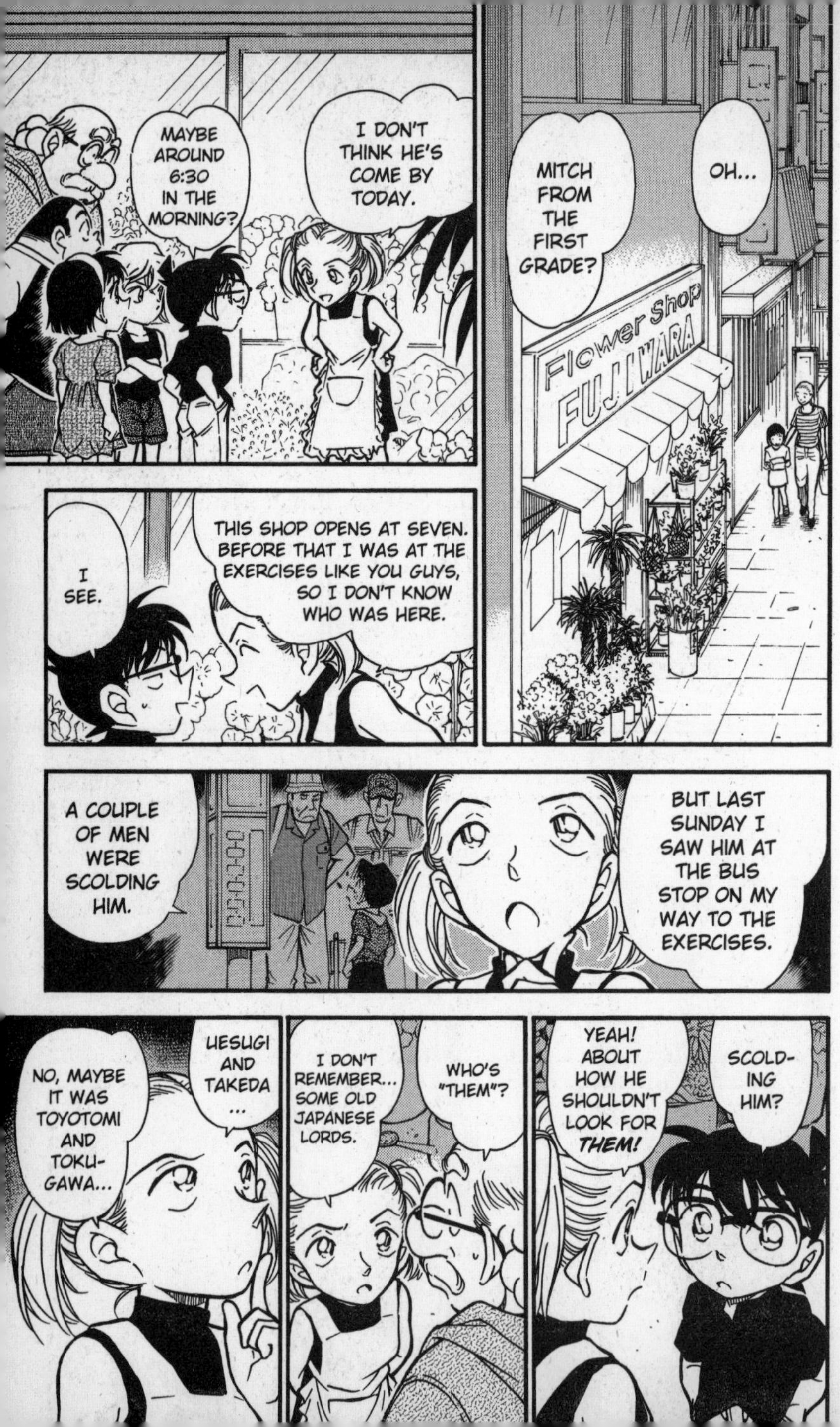
OH...
MITCH FROM THE FIRST GRADE?
Flower Shop FUJIWARA
I DON'T THINK HE'S COME BY TODAY.
MAYBE AROUND 6:30 IN THE MORNING?
THIS SHOP OPENS AT SEVEN. BEFORE THAT I WAS AT THE EXERCISES LIKE YOU GUYS, SO I DON'T KNOW WHO WAS HERE.
I SEE.
BUT LAST SUNDAY I SAW HIM AT THE BUS STOP ON MY WAY TO THE EXERCISES.
A COUPLE OF MEN WERE SCOLDING HIM.
SCOLD-ING HIM?
YEAH! ABOUT HOW HE SHOULDN'T LOOK FOR *THEM!*
WHO'S "THEM"?
I DON'T REMEMBER... SOME OLD JAPANESE LORDS.
UESUGI AND TAKEDA ...
NO, MAYBE IT WAS TOYOTOMI AND TOKU-GAWA...

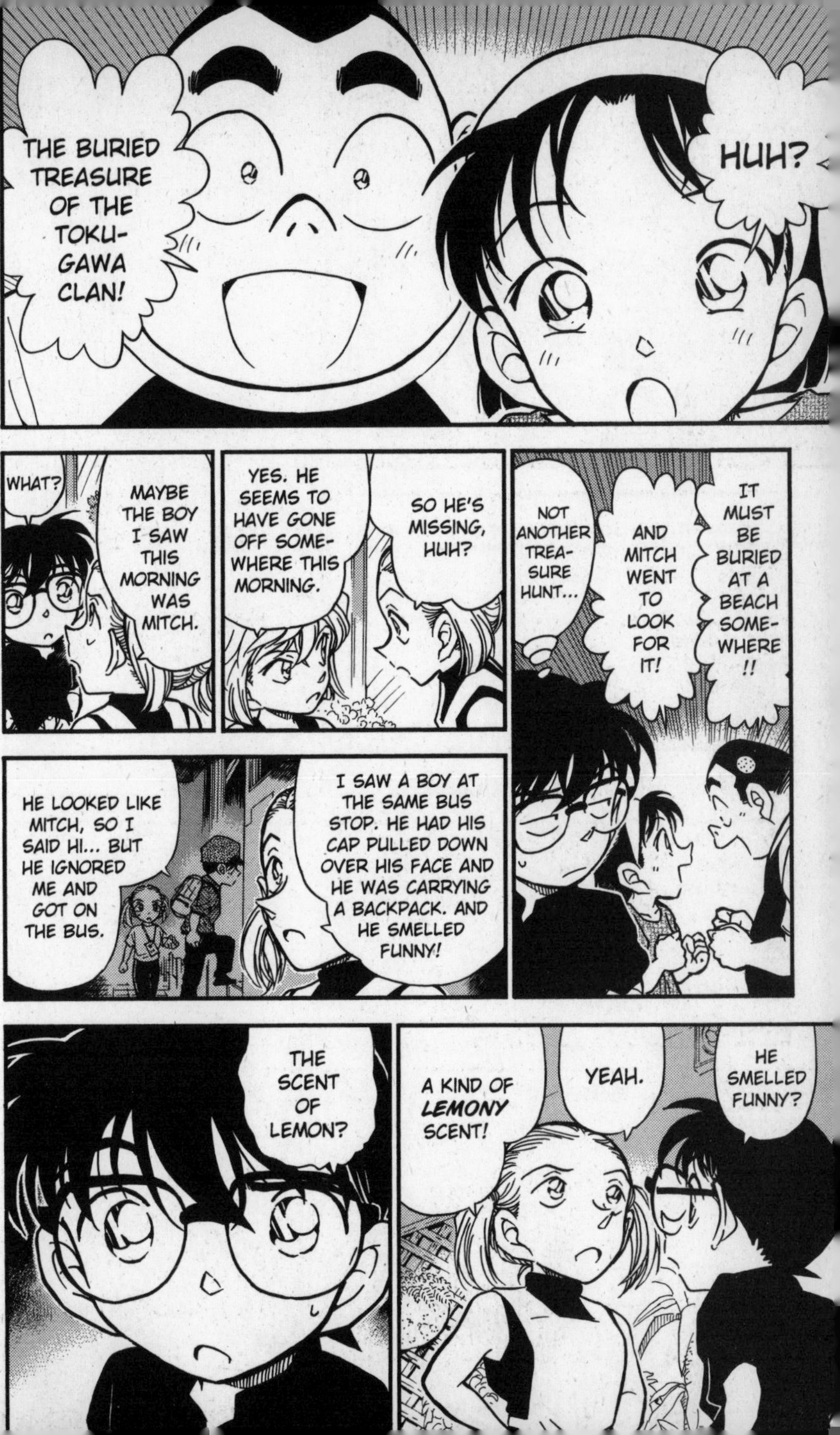
HUH?
THE BURIED TREASURE OF THE TOKU-GAWA CLAN!
IT MUST BE BURIED AT A BEACH SOME-WHERE !!
AND MITCH WENT TO LOOK FOR IT!
NOT ANOTHER TREA-SURE HUNT...
SO HE'S MISSING, HUH?
YES. HE SEEMS TO HAVE GONE OFF SOME-WHERE THIS MORNING.
MAYBE THE BOY I SAW THIS MORNING WAS MITCH.
WHAT?
I SAW A BOY AT THE SAME BUS STOP. HE HAD HIS CAP PULLED DOWN OVER HIS FACE AND HE WAS CARRYING A BACKPACK. AND HE SMELLED FUNNY!
HE LOOKED LIKE MITCH, SO I SAID HI... BUT HE IGNORED ME AND GOT ON THE BUS.
HE SMELLED FUNNY?
YEAH.
A KIND OF *LEMONY* SCENT!
THE SCENT OF LEMON?

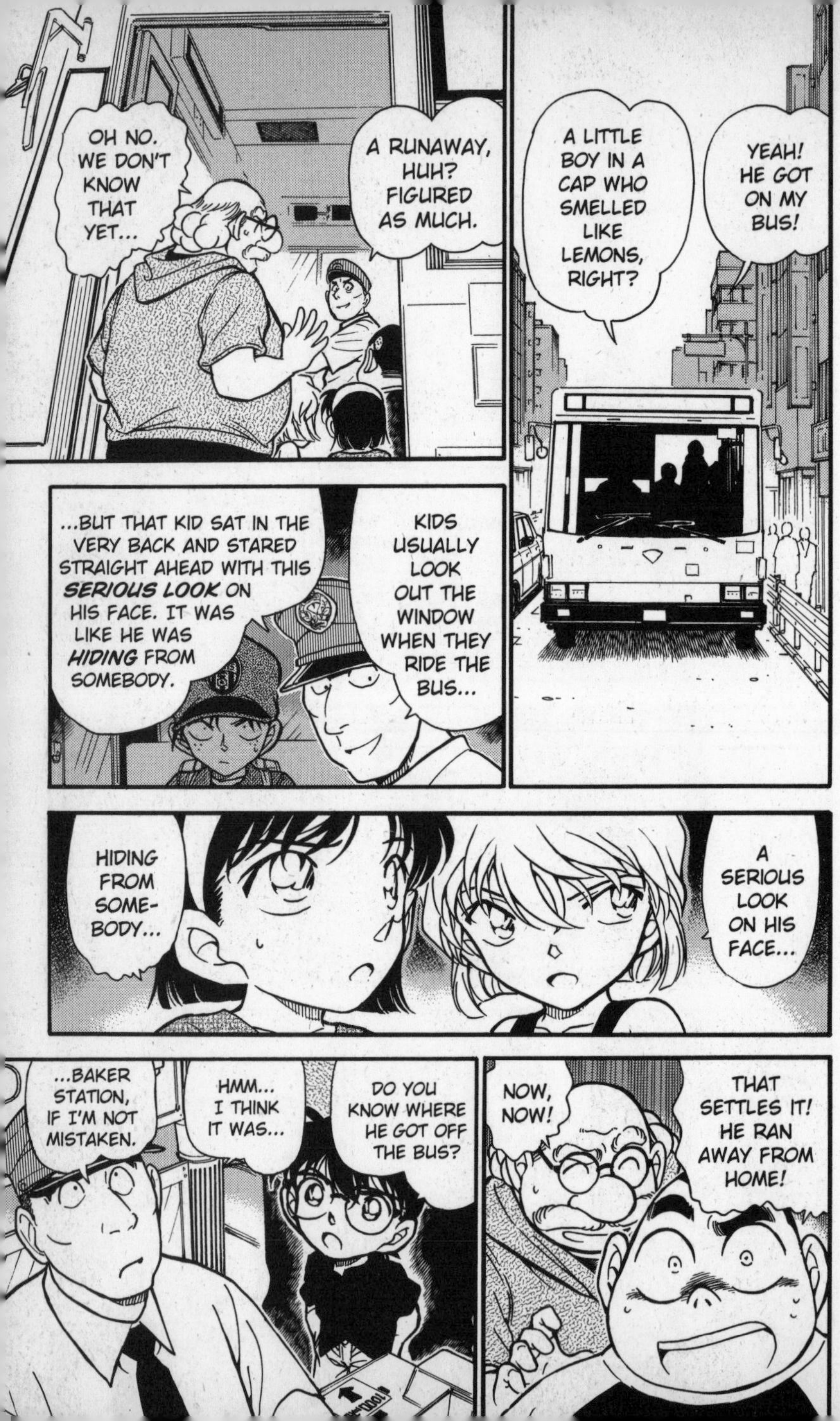
YEAH! HE GOT ON MY BUS!
A LITTLE BOY IN A CAP WHO SMELLED LIKE LEMONS, RIGHT?
A RUNAWAY, HUH? FIGURED AS MUCH.
OH NO. WE DON'T KNOW THAT YET...
KIDS USUALLY LOOK OUT THE WINDOW WHEN THEY RIDE THE BUS...
...BUT THAT KID SAT IN THE VERY BACK AND STARED STRAIGHT AHEAD WITH THIS SERIOUS LOOK ON HIS FACE. IT WAS LIKE HE WAS HIDING FROM SOMEBODY.
A SERIOUS LOOK ON HIS FACE...
HIDING FROM SOME-BODY...
THAT SETTLES IT! HE RAN AWAY FROM HOME!
NOW, NOW!
DO YOU KNOW WHERE HE GOT OFF THE BUS?
HMM... I THINK IT WAS...
...BAKER STATION, IF I'M NOT MISTAKEN.

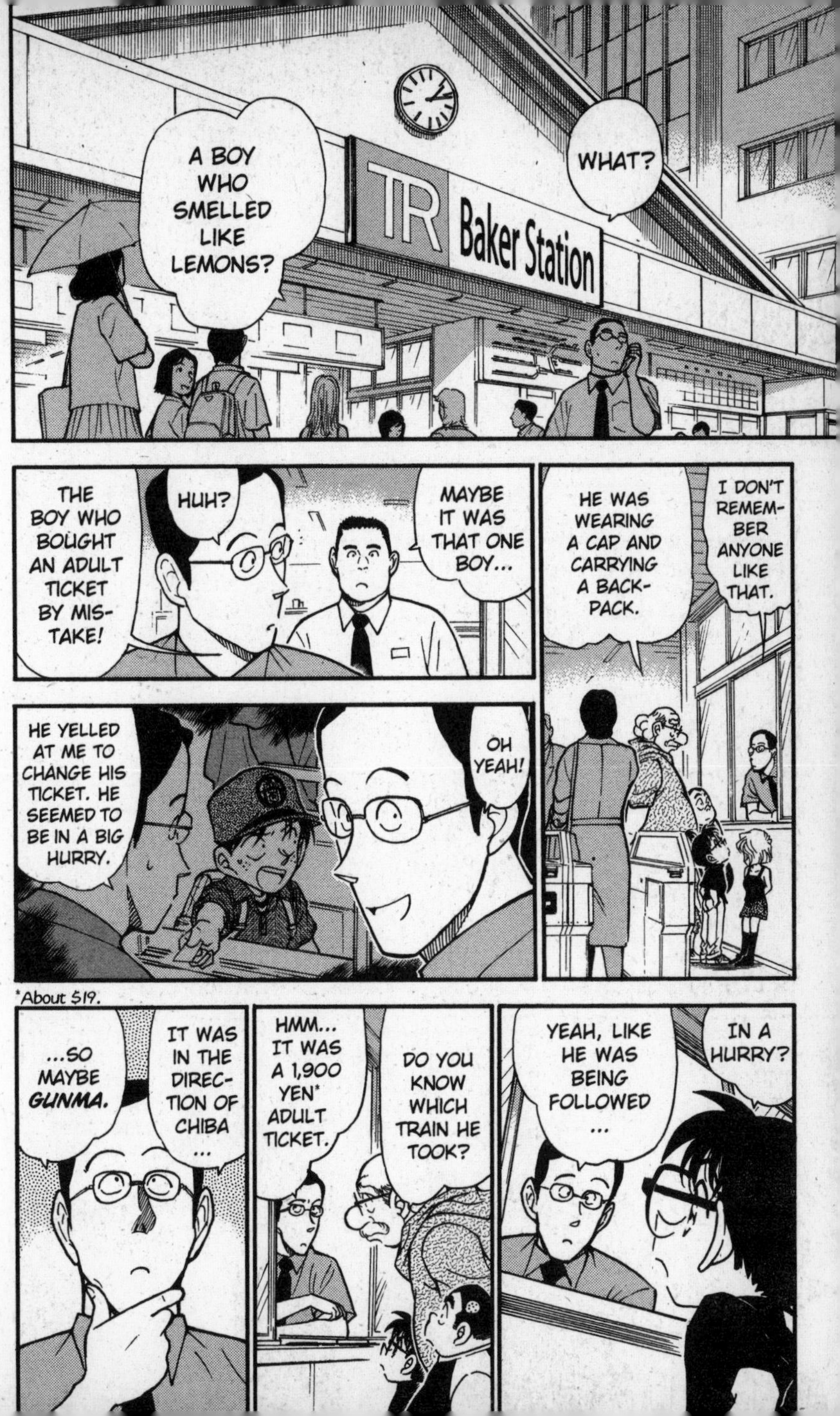
TR Baker Station
WHAT?
A BOY WHO SMELLED LIKE LEMONS?
I DON'T REMEMBER ANYONE LIKE THAT.
HE WAS WEARING A CAP AND CARRYING A BACKPACK.
MAYBE IT WAS THAT ONE BOY...
HUH?
THE BOY WHO BOUGHT AN ADULT TICKET BY MISTAKE!
OH YEAH!
HE YELLED AT ME TO CHANGE HIS TICKET. HE SEEMED TO BE IN A BIG HURRY.
IN A HURRY?
YEAH, LIKE HE WAS BEING FOLLOWED ...
DO YOU KNOW WHICH TRAIN HE TOOK?
HMM... IT WAS A 1,900 YEN* ADULT TICKET.
IT WAS IN THE DIRECTION OF CHIBA ...
...SO MAYBE **GUNMA.**

*About $19.

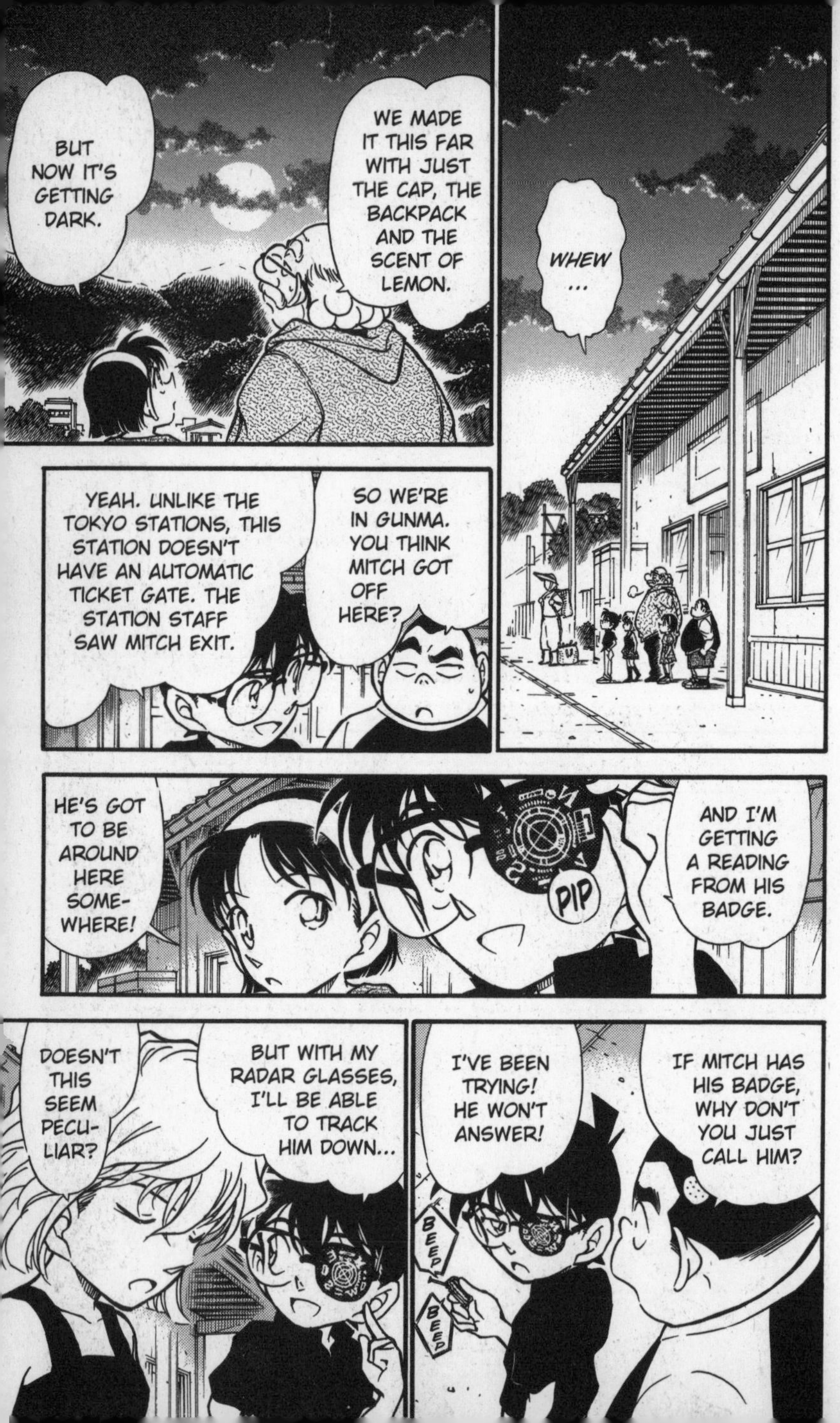
WHEW ...
WE MADE IT THIS FAR WITH JUST THE CAP, THE BACKPACK AND THE SCENT OF LEMON.
BUT NOW IT'S GETTING DARK.
SO WE'RE IN GUNMA. YOU THINK MITCH GOT OFF HERE?
YEAH. UNLIKE THE TOKYO STATIONS, THIS STATION DOESN'T HAVE AN AUTOMATIC TICKET GATE. THE STATION STAFF SAW MITCH EXIT.
AND I'M GETTING A READING FROM HIS BADGE.
PIP
HE'S GOT TO BE AROUND HERE SOME-WHERE!
IF MITCH HAS HIS BADGE, WHY DON'T YOU JUST CALL HIM?
I'VE BEEN TRYING! HE WON'T ANSWER!
BEEP
BEEP
BUT WITH MY RADAR GLASSES, I'LL BE ABLE TO TRACK HIM DOWN...
DOESN'T THIS SEEM PECULIAR?

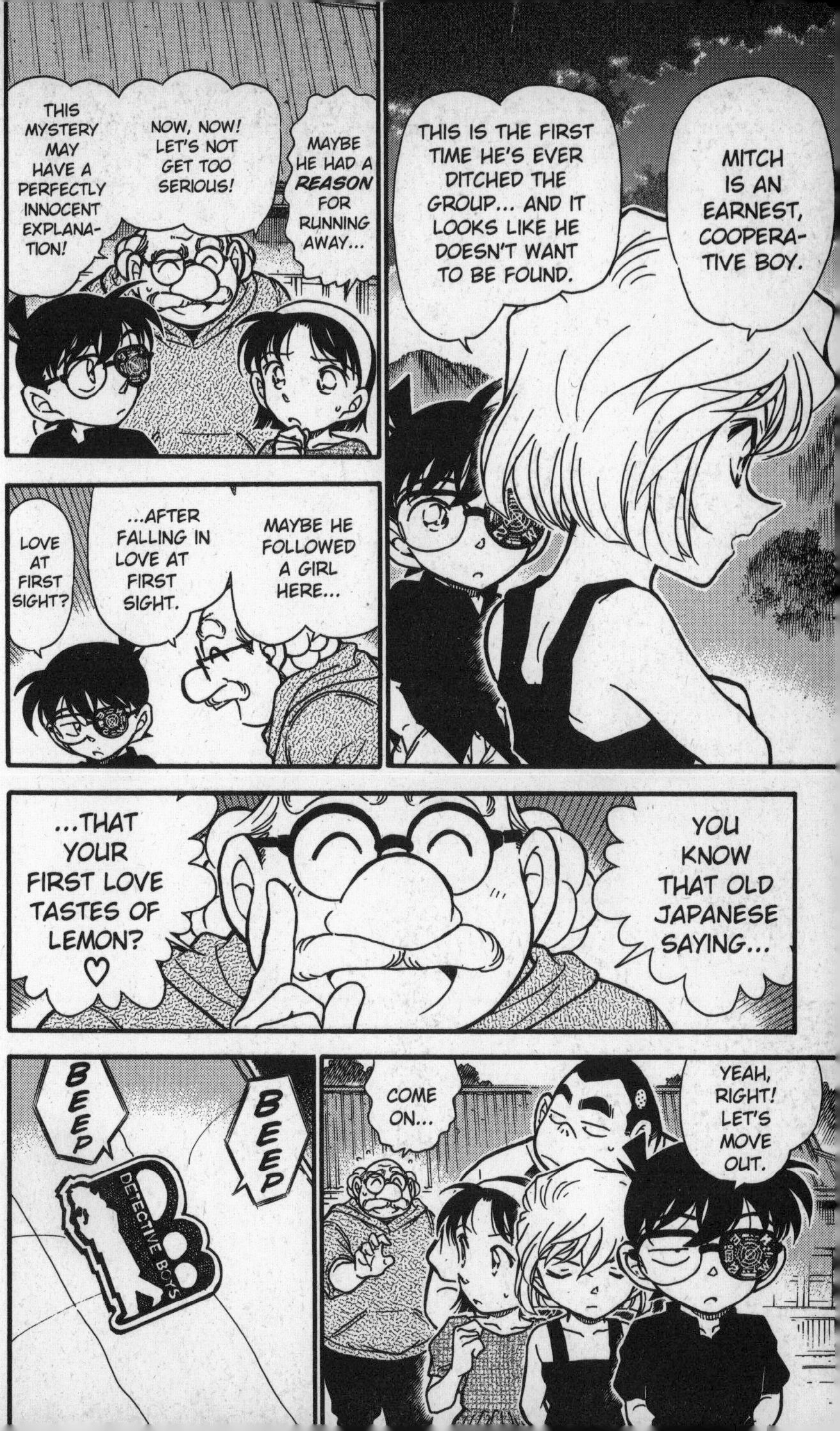
MITCH IS AN EARNEST, COOPERATIVE BOY.
THIS IS THE FIRST TIME HE'S EVER DITCHED THE GROUP... AND IT LOOKS LIKE HE DOESN'T WANT TO BE FOUND.
MAYBE HE HAD A **REASON** FOR RUNNING AWAY...
NOW, NOW! LET'S NOT GET TOO SERIOUS!
THIS MYSTERY MAY HAVE A PERFECTLY INNOCENT EXPLANATION!
MAYBE HE FOLLOWED A GIRL HERE...
...AFTER FALLING IN LOVE AT FIRST SIGHT.
LOVE AT FIRST SIGHT?
YOU KNOW THAT OLD JAPANESE SAYING...
...THAT YOUR FIRST LOVE TASTES OF LEMON? ♡
YEAH, RIGHT! LET'S MOVE OUT.
COME ON...
BEEP
BEEP
DETECTIVE BOYS

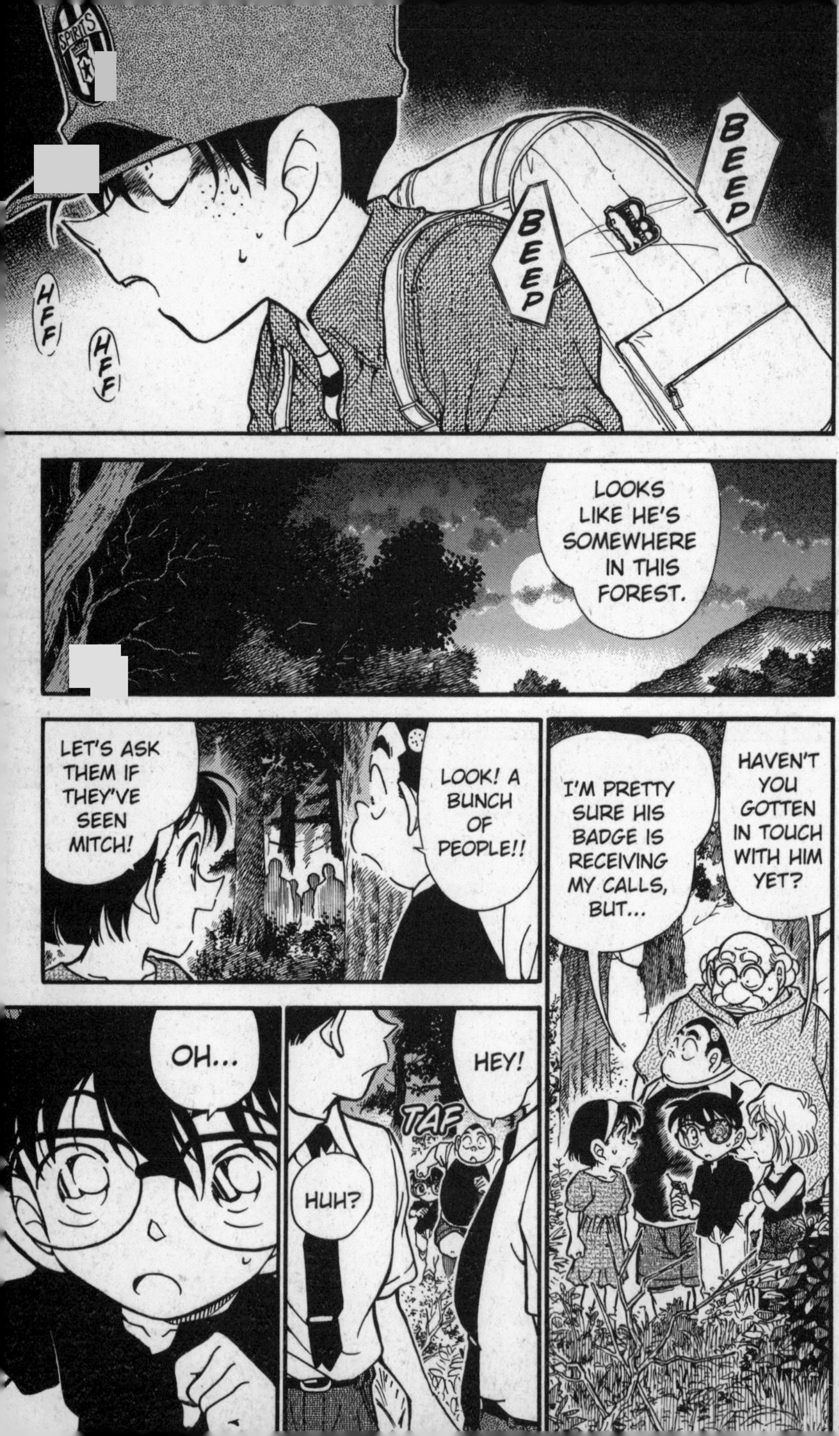
BEEP
BEEP
HFF
HFF
LOOKS LIKE HE'S SOMEWHERE IN THIS FOREST.
HAVEN'T YOU GOTTEN IN TOUCH WITH HIM YET?
I'M PRETTY SURE HIS BADGE IS RECEIVING MY CALLS, BUT...
LOOK! A BUNCH OF PEOPLE!!
LET'S ASK THEM IF THEY'VE SEEN MITCH!
HEY!
TAF
HUH?
OH...

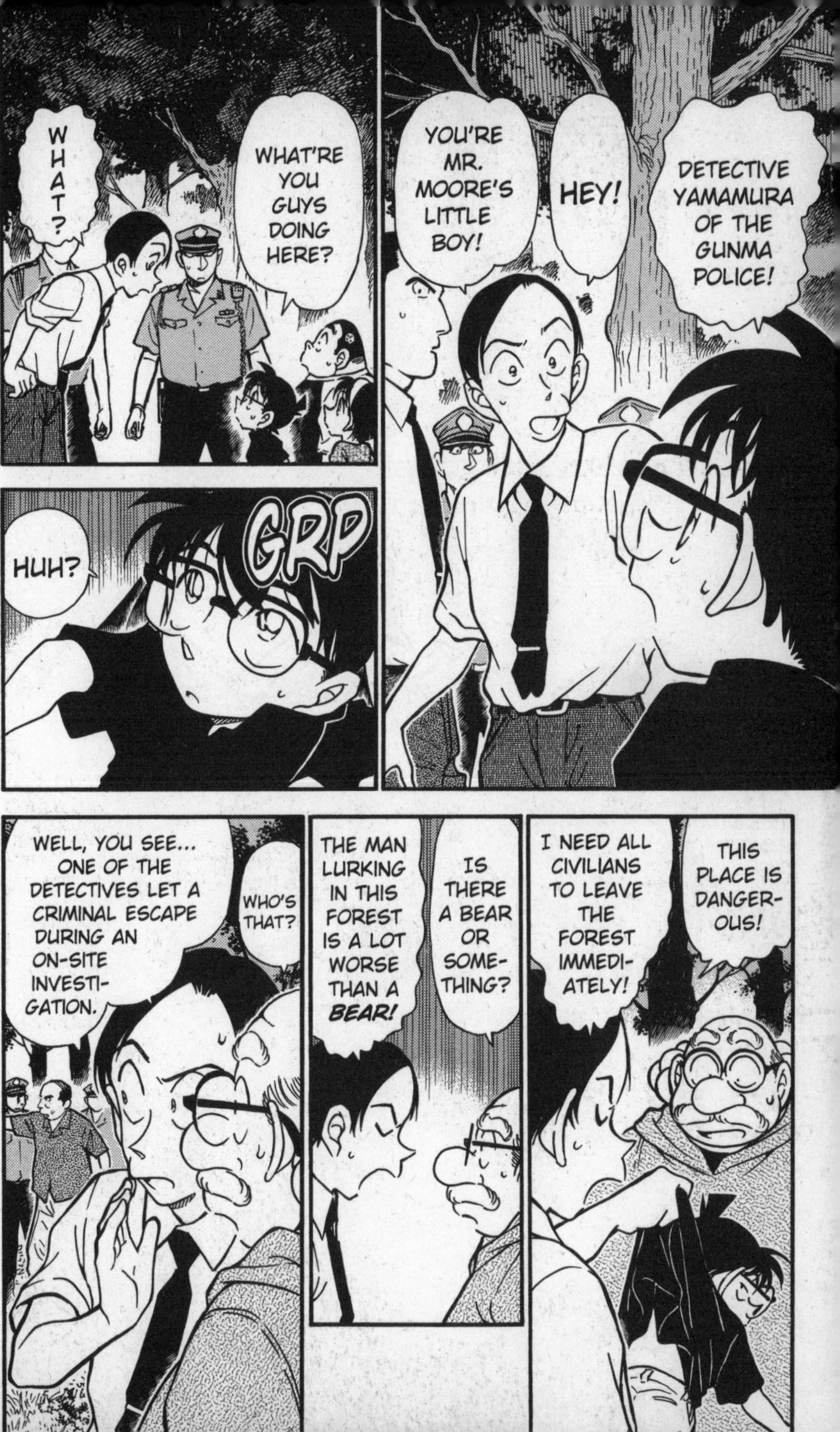
DETECTIVE YAMAMURA OF THE GUNMA POLICE!
HEY!
YOU'RE MR. MOORE'S LITTLE BOY!
WHAT'RE YOU GUYS DOING HERE?
WHAT?
GRP
HUH?
THIS PLACE IS DANGER-OUS!
I NEED ALL CIVILIANS TO LEAVE THE FOREST IMMEDI-ATELY!
IS THERE A BEAR OR SOME-THING?
THE MAN LURKING IN THIS FOREST IS A LOT WORSE THAN A *BEAR!*
WHO'S THAT?
WELL, YOU SEE... ONE OF THE DETECTIVES LET A CRIMINAL ESCAPE DURING AN ON-SITE INVESTI-GATION.

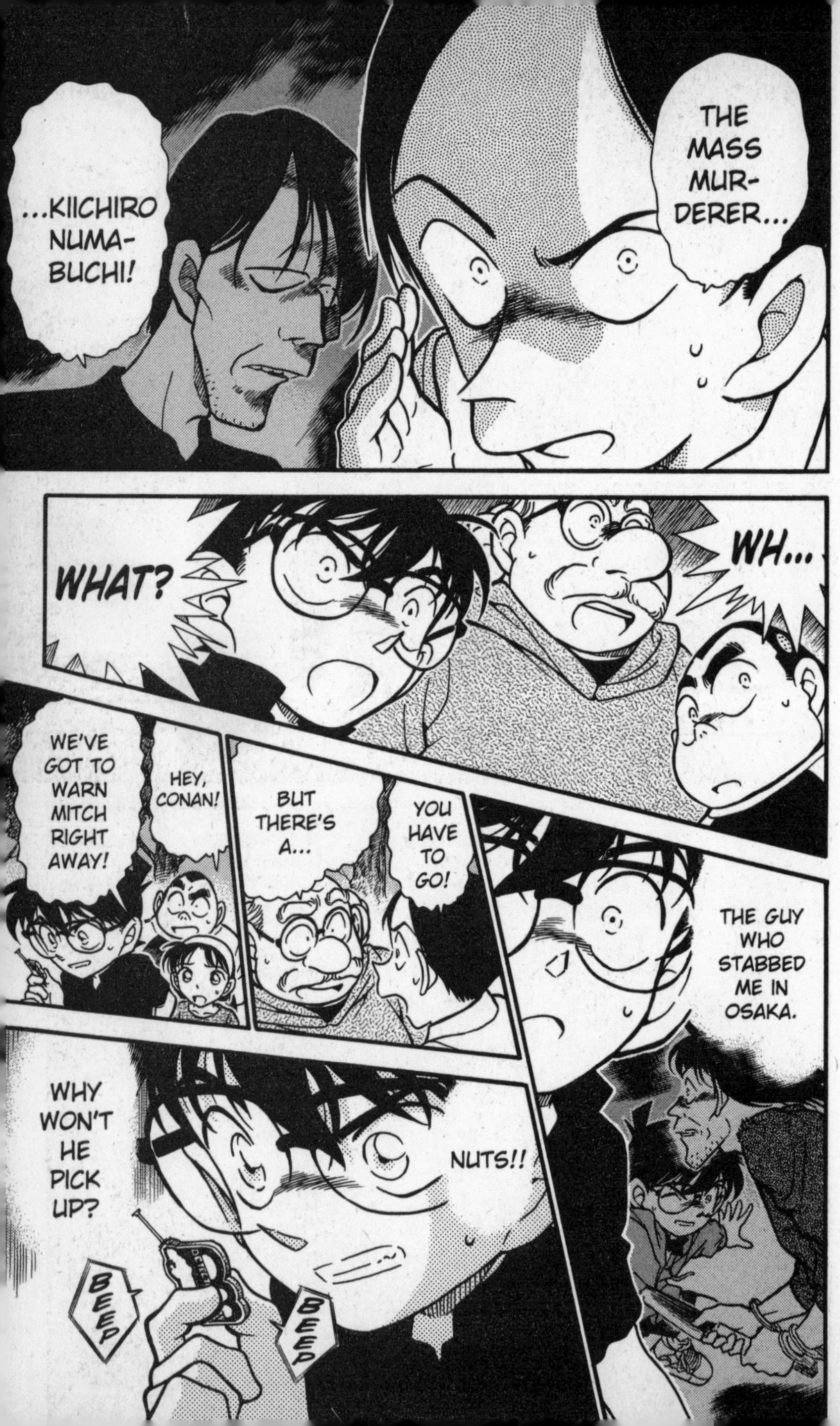
THE MASS MURDERER...
...KIICHIRO NUMABUCHI!
WH...
WHAT?
THE GUY WHO STABBED ME IN OSAKA.
YOU HAVE TO GO!
BUT THERE'S A...
HEY, CONAN!
WE'VE GOT TO WARN MITCH RIGHT AWAY!
NUTS!!
WHY WON'T HE PICK UP?
BEEP
BEEP

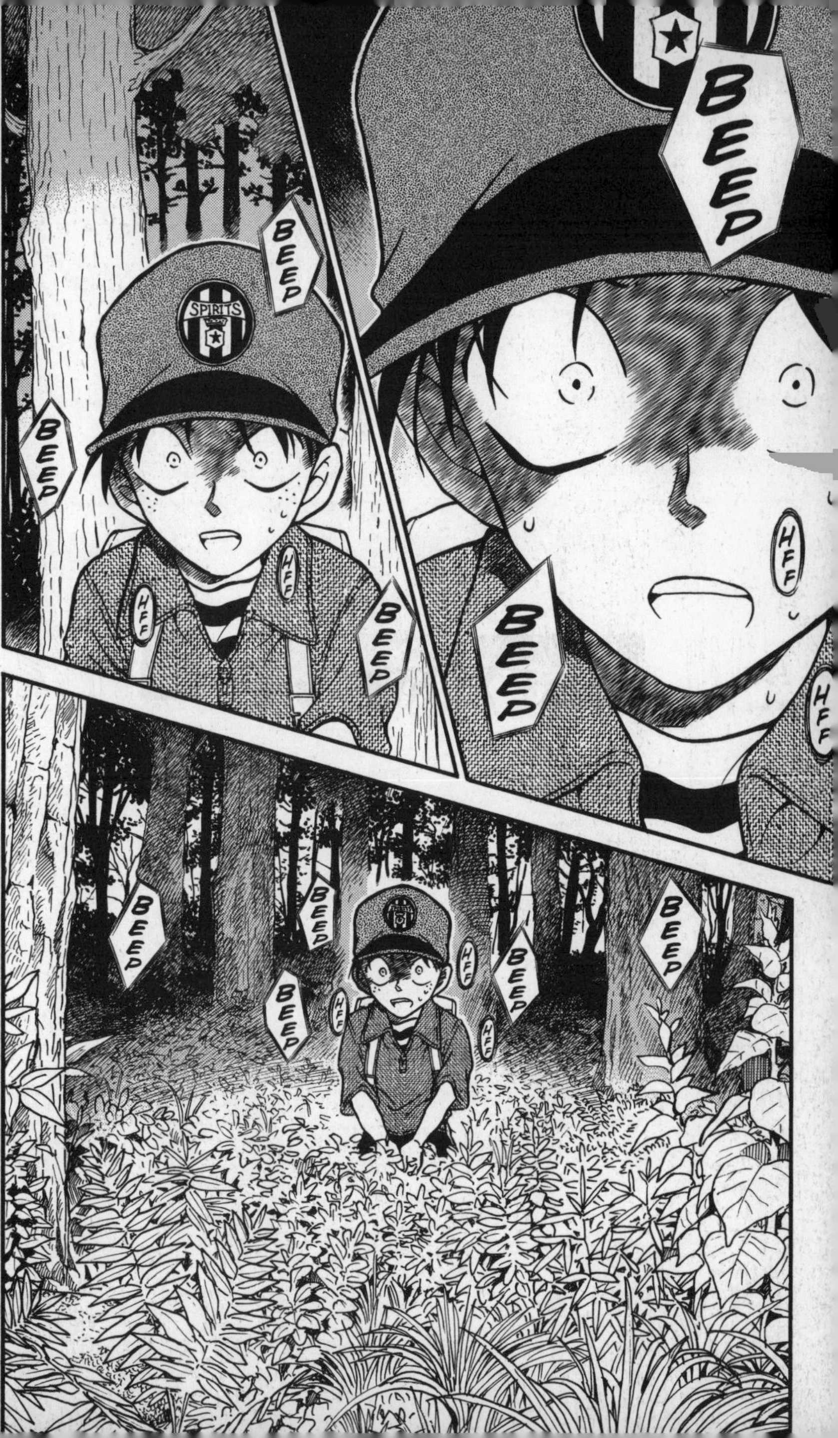
BEEP
HFF
BEEP
HFF
BEEP
SPIRITS
HFF
HFF
BEEP
BEEP
BEEP
BEEP
HFF
BEEP
HFF
HFF
BEEP
BEEP

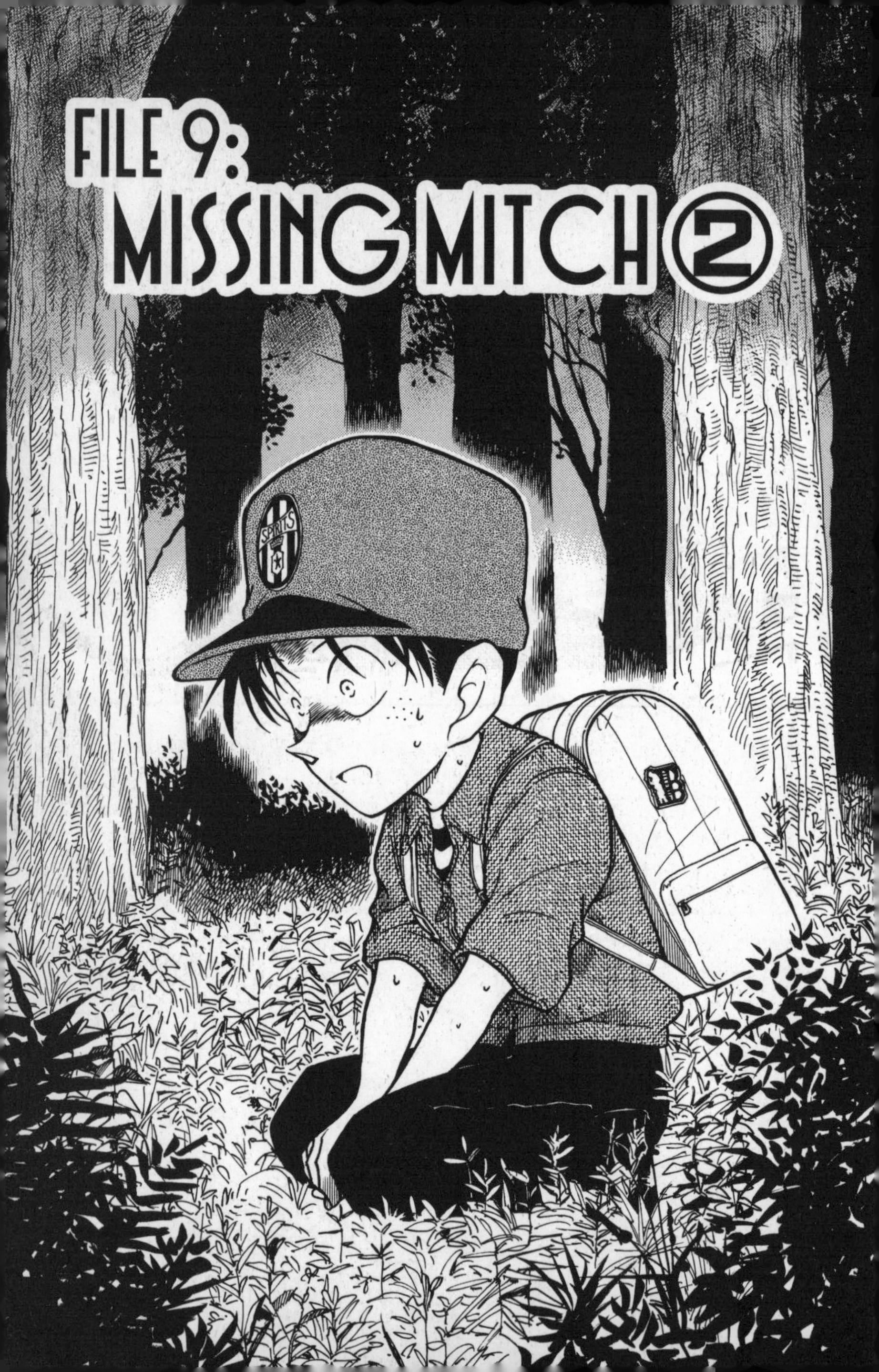
FILE 9:
MISSING MITCH ②
SPIRITS

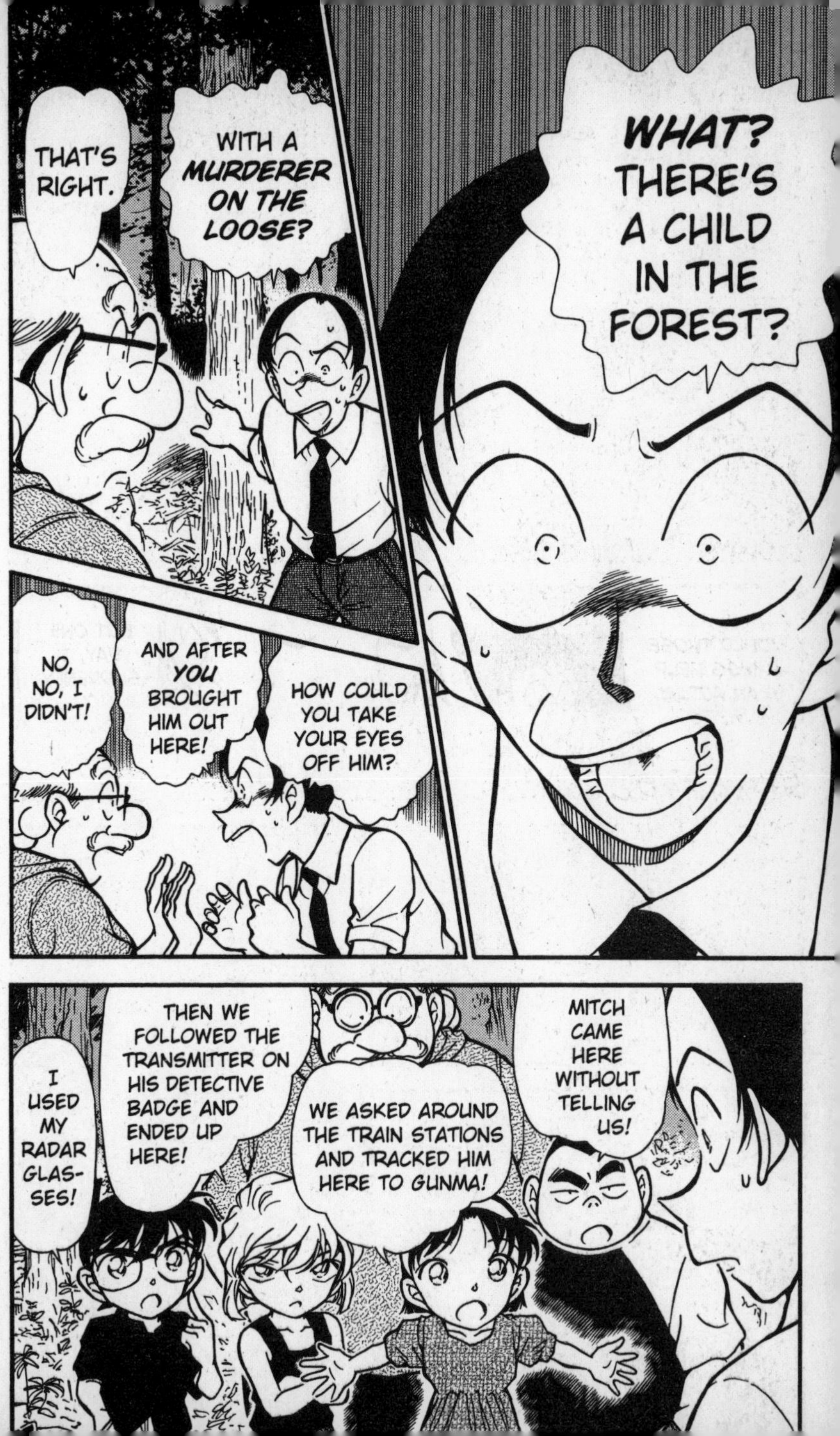
WHAT? THERE'S A CHILD IN THE FOREST?
WITH A MURDERER ON THE LOOSE?
THAT'S RIGHT.
HOW COULD YOU TAKE YOUR EYES OFF HIM?
AND AFTER YOU BROUGHT HIM OUT HERE!
NO, NO, I DIDN'T!
MITCH CAME HERE WITHOUT TELLING US!
WE ASKED AROUND THE TRAIN STATIONS AND TRACKED HIM HERE TO GUNMA!
THEN WE FOLLOWED THE TRANSMITTER ON HIS DETECTIVE BADGE AND ENDED UP HERE!
I USED MY RADAR GLASSES!

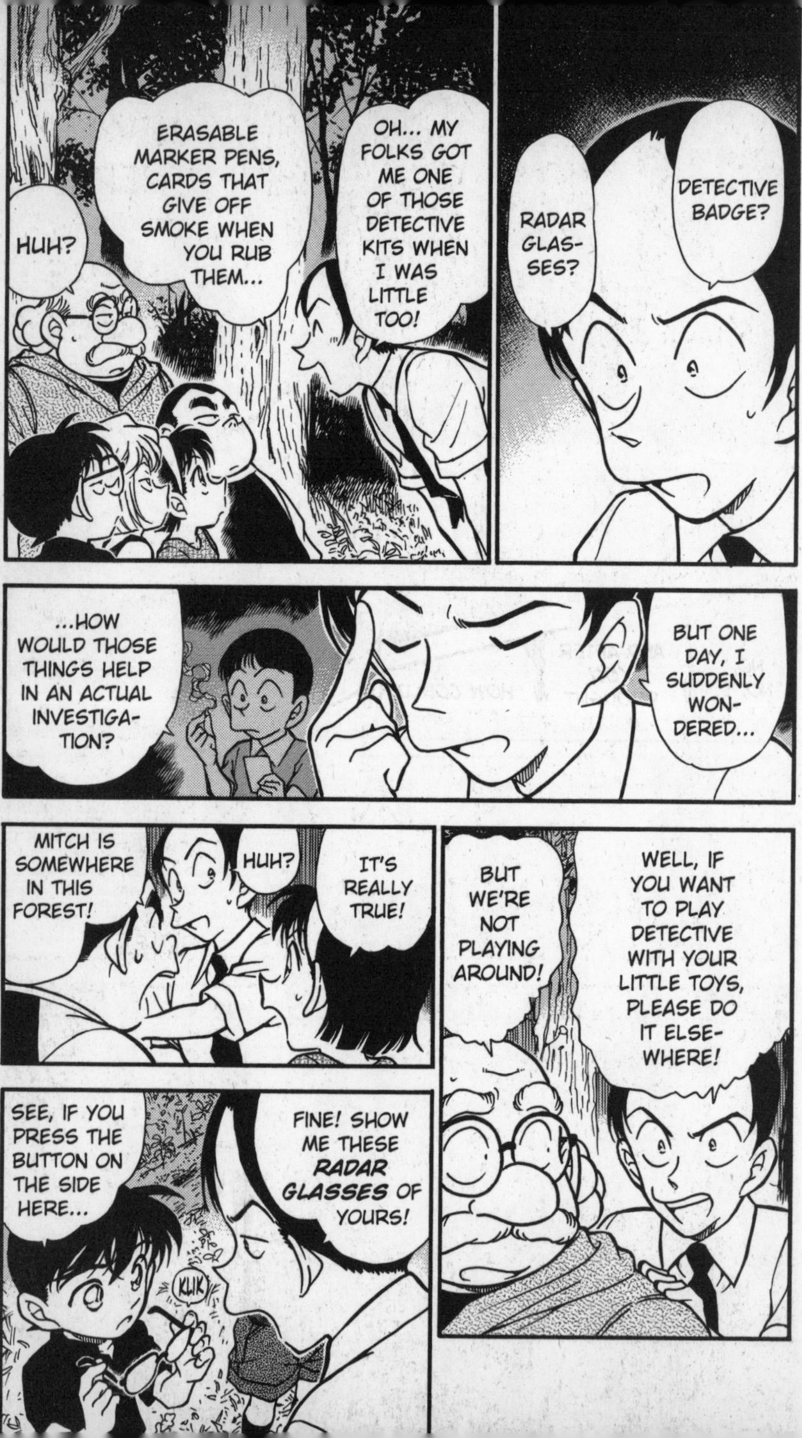
DETECTIVE BADGE?
RADAR GLAS-SES?
OH... MY FOLKS GOT ME ONE OF THOSE DETECTIVE KITS WHEN I WAS LITTLE TOO!
ERASABLE MARKER PENS, CARDS THAT GIVE OFF SMOKE WHEN YOU RUB THEM...
HUH?
BUT ONE DAY, I SUDDENLY WON-DERED...
...HOW WOULD THOSE THINGS HELP IN AN ACTUAL INVESTIGA-TION?
WELL, IF YOU WANT TO PLAY DETECTIVE WITH YOUR LITTLE TOYS, PLEASE DO IT ELSE-WHERE!
BUT WE'RE NOT PLAYING AROUND!
IT'S REALLY TRUE!
HUH?
MITCH IS SOMEWHERE IN THIS FOREST!
FINE! SHOW ME THESE ***RADAR GLASSES*** OF YOURS!
SEE, IF YOU PRESS THE BUTTON ON THE SIDE HERE...
KLIK

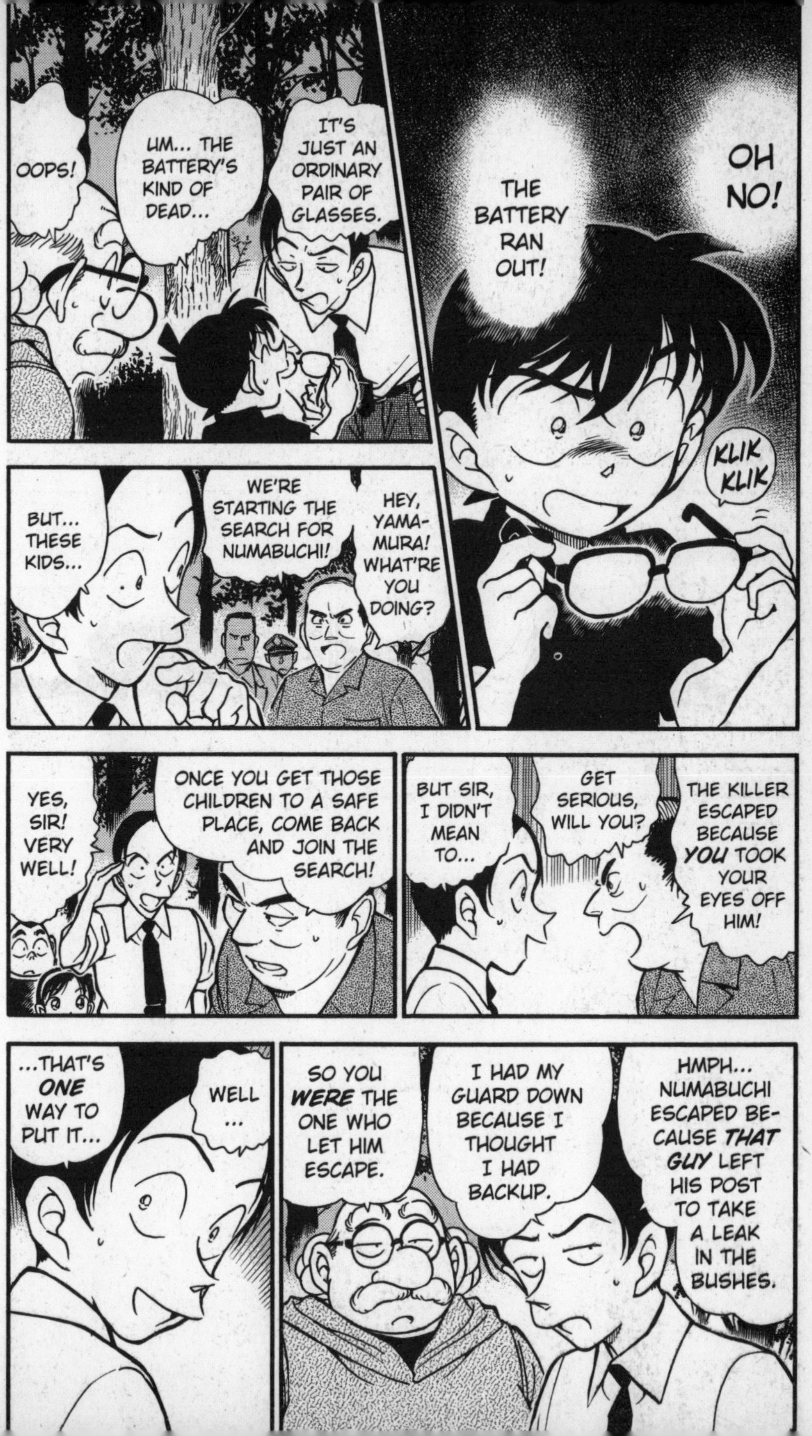

OH NO!
THE BATTERY RAN OUT!
KLIK KLIK
IT'S JUST AN ORDINARY PAIR OF GLASSES.
UM... THE BATTERY'S KIND OF DEAD...
OOPS!
HEY, YAMAMURA! WHAT'RE YOU DOING?
WE'RE STARTING THE SEARCH FOR NUMABUCHI!
BUT... THESE KIDS...
THE KILLER ESCAPED BECAUSE **YOU** TOOK YOUR EYES OFF HIM!
GET SERIOUS, WILL YOU?
BUT SIR, I DIDN'T MEAN TO...
ONCE YOU GET THOSE CHILDREN TO A SAFE PLACE, COME BACK AND JOIN THE SEARCH!
YES, SIR! VERY WELL!
HMPH... NUMABUCHI ESCAPED BECAUSE **THAT GUY** LEFT HIS POST TO TAKE A LEAK IN THE BUSHES.
I HAD MY GUARD DOWN BECAUSE I THOUGHT I HAD BACKUP.
SO YOU **WERE** THE ONE WHO LET HIM ESCAPE.
WELL...
...THAT'S **ONE** WAY TO PUT IT...

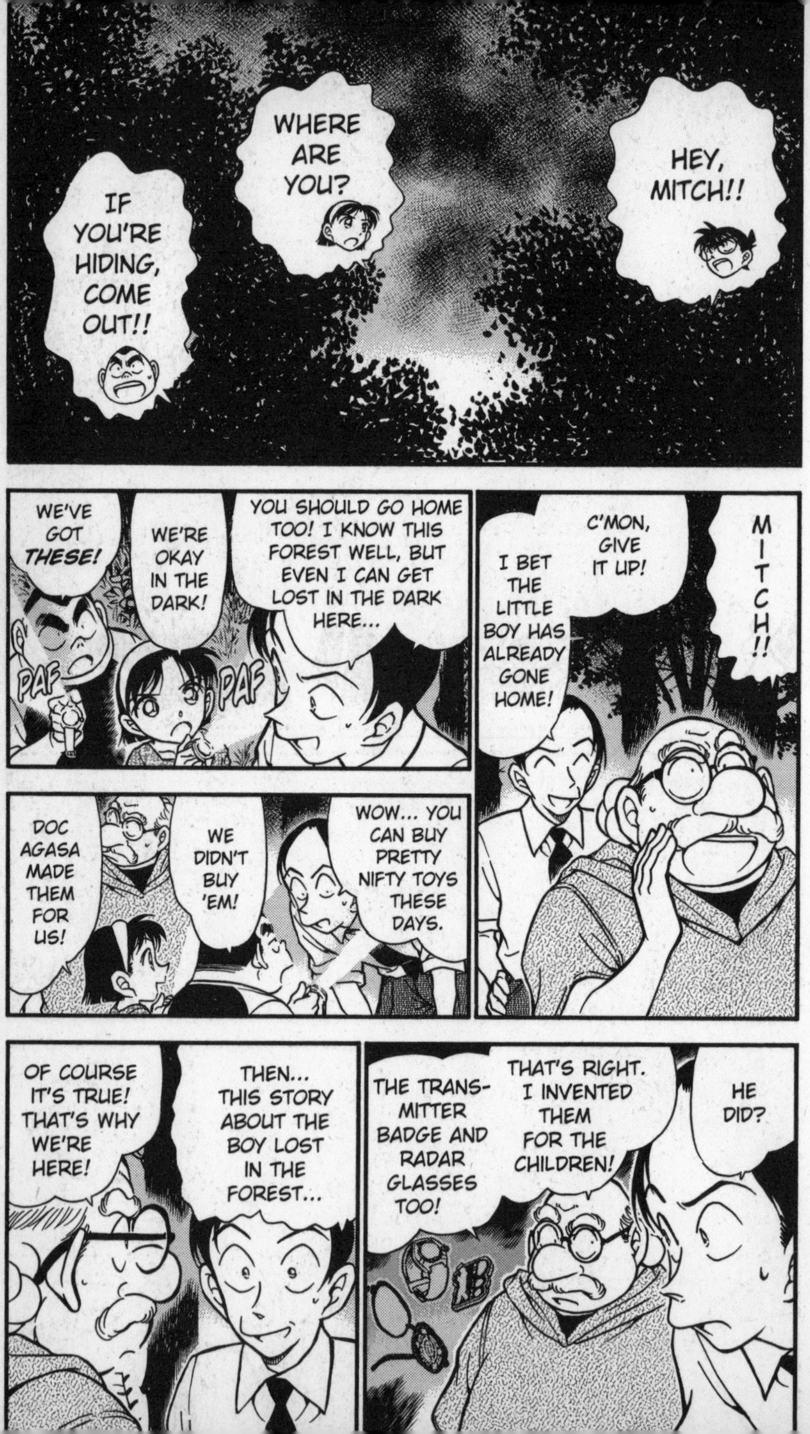
HEY, MITCH!!
WHERE ARE YOU?
IF YOU'RE HIDING, COME OUT!!
MITCH!!
C'MON, GIVE IT UP!
I BET THE LITTLE BOY HAS ALREADY GONE HOME!
YOU SHOULD GO HOME TOO! I KNOW THIS FOREST WELL, BUT EVEN I CAN GET LOST IN THE DARK HERE...
WE'RE OKAY IN THE DARK!
WE'VE GOT *THESE!*
PAF
PAF
WOW... YOU CAN BUY PRETTY NIFTY TOYS THESE DAYS.
WE DIDN'T BUY 'EM!
DOC AGASA MADE THEM FOR US!
HE DID?
THAT'S RIGHT. I INVENTED THEM FOR THE CHILDREN!
THE TRANSMITTER BADGE AND RADAR GLASSES TOO!
THEN... THIS STORY ABOUT THE BOY LOST IN THE FOREST...
OF COURSE IT'S TRUE! THAT'S WHY WE'RE HERE!

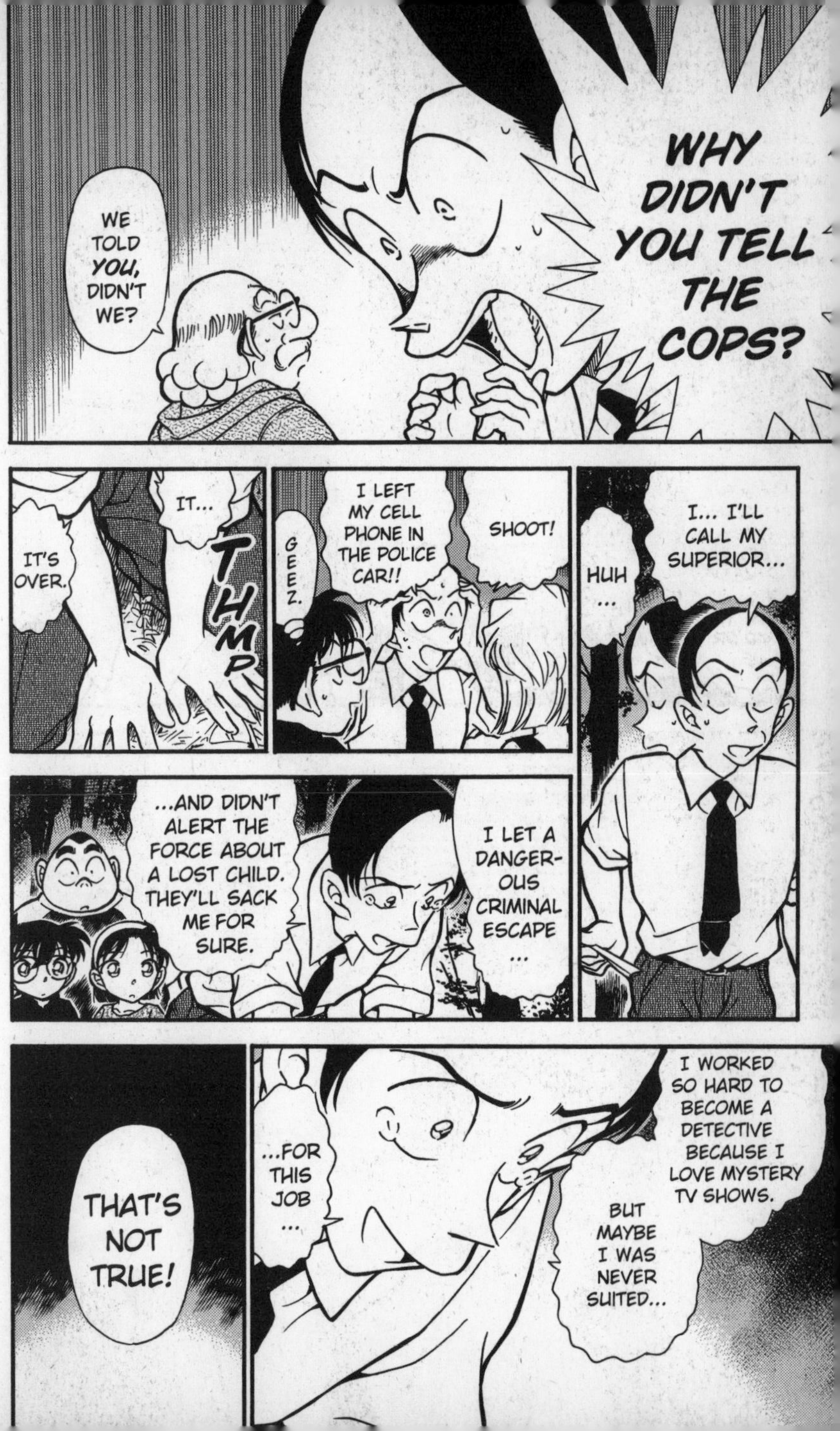
WHY DIDN'T YOU TELL THE COPS?
WE TOLD YOU, DIDN'T WE?
I... I'LL CALL MY SUPERIOR...
HUH...
SHOOT!
I LEFT MY CELL PHONE IN THE POLICE CAR!!
GEEZ.
IT...
THMP
IT'S OVER.
I LET A DANGER-OUS CRIMINAL ESCAPE...
...AND DIDN'T ALERT THE FORCE ABOUT A LOST CHILD. THEY'LL SACK ME FOR SURE.
I WORKED SO HARD TO BECOME A DETECTIVE BECAUSE I LOVE MYSTERY TV SHOWS.
BUT MAYBE I WAS NEVER SUITED...
...FOR THIS JOB...
THAT'S NOT TRUE!

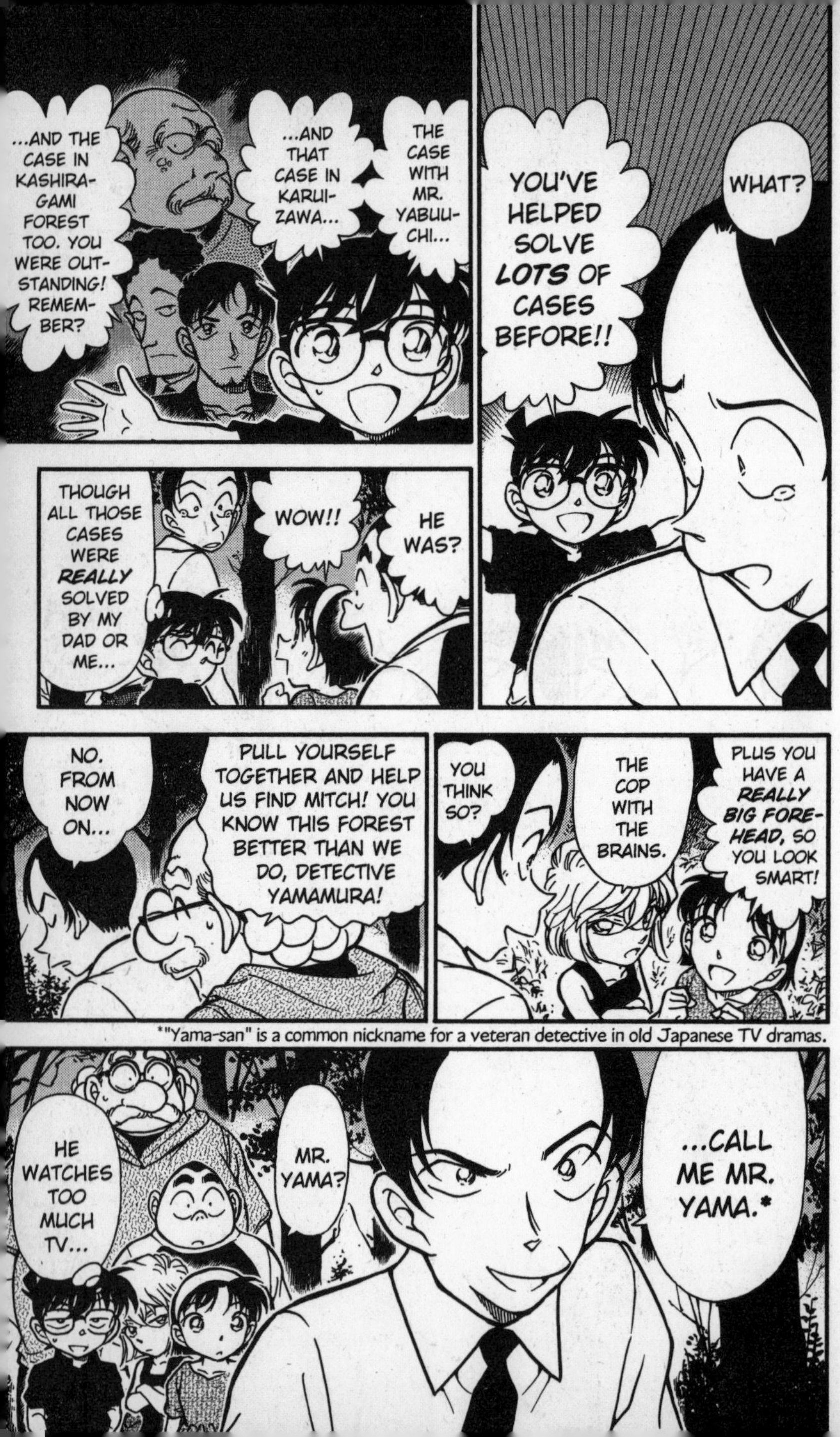
WHAT?
YOU'VE HELPED SOLVE LOTS OF CASES BEFORE!!
THE CASE WITH MR. YABUUCHI...
...AND THAT CASE IN KARUIZAWA...
...AND THE CASE IN KASHIRAGAMI FOREST TOO. YOU WERE OUTSTANDING! REMEMBER?
HE WAS?
WOW!!
THOUGH ALL THOSE CASES WERE REALLY SOLVED BY MY DAD OR ME...
PLUS YOU HAVE A REALLY BIG FOREHEAD, SO YOU LOOK SMART!
THE COP WITH THE BRAINS.
YOU THINK SO?
PULL YOURSELF TOGETHER AND HELP US FIND MITCH! YOU KNOW THIS FOREST BETTER THAN WE DO, DETECTIVE YAMAMURA!
NO. FROM NOW ON...
...CALL ME MR. YAMA.*
MR. YAMA?
HE WATCHES TOO MUCH TV...

*"Yama-san" is a common nickname for a veteran detective in old Japanese TV dramas.

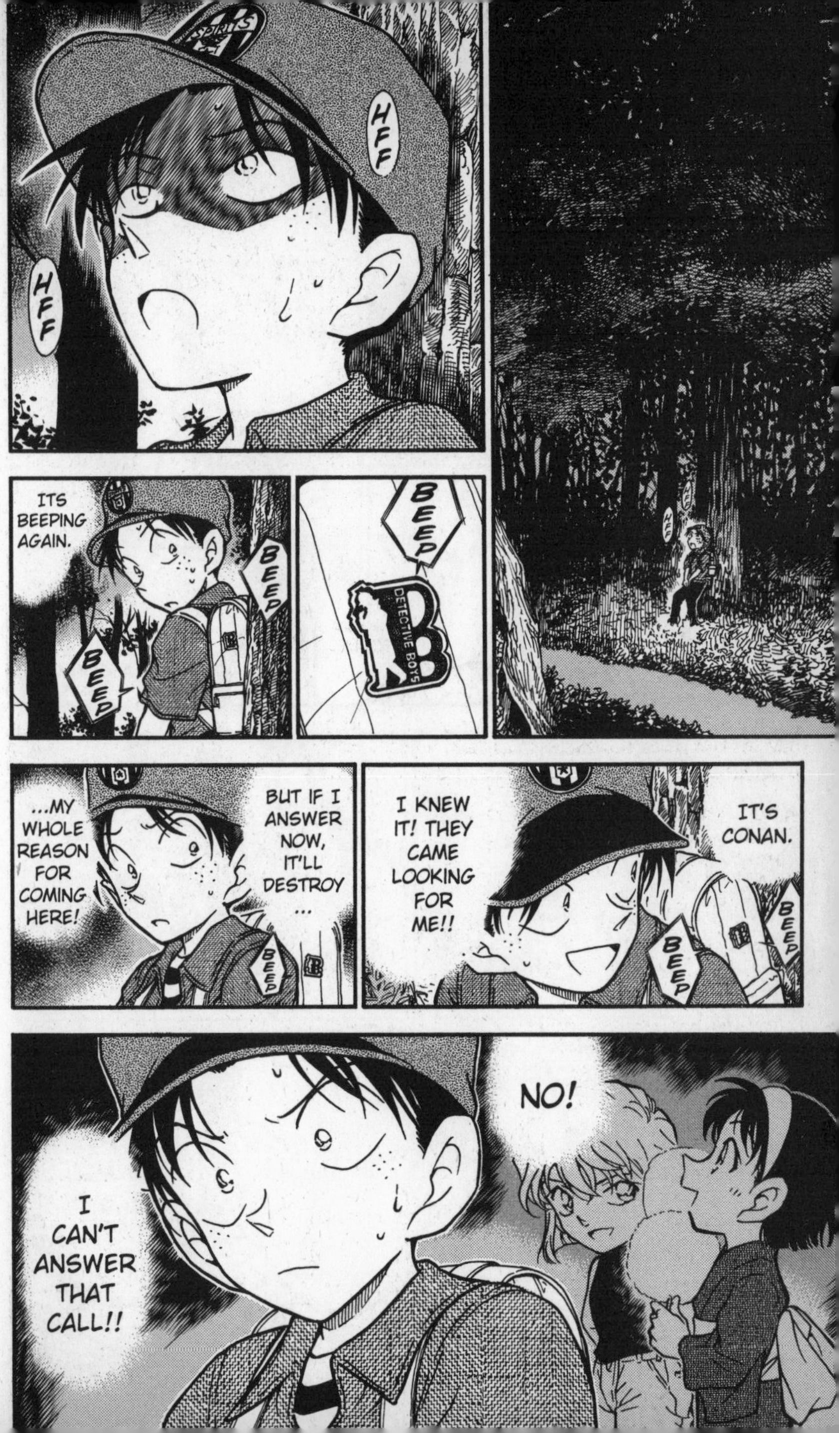
HFF
HFF
HFF
HFF
BEEP
DETECTIVE BOYS
ITS BEEPING AGAIN.
BEEP
BEEP
IT'S CONAN.
I KNEW IT! THEY CAME LOOKING FOR ME!!
BEEP
BEEP
BUT IF I ANSWER NOW, IT'LL DESTROY ...
...MY WHOLE REASON FOR COMING HERE!
BEEP
NO!
I CAN'T ANSWER THAT CALL!!

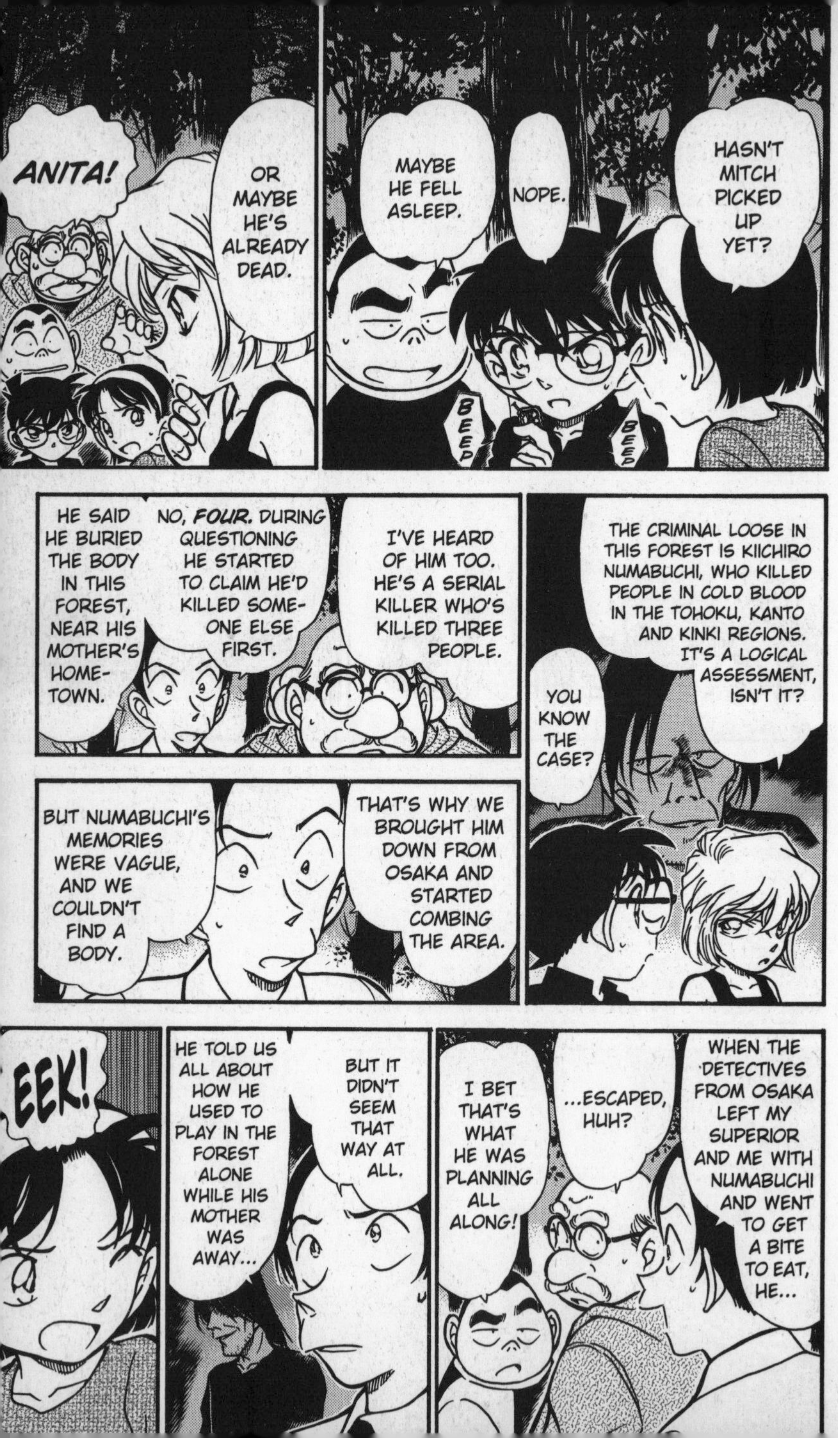
HASN'T MITCH PICKED UP YET?
NOPE.
MAYBE HE FELL ASLEEP.
BEEP
BEEP
OR MAYBE HE'S ALREADY DEAD.
ANITA!
THE CRIMINAL LOOSE IN THIS FOREST IS KIICHIRO NUMABUCHI, WHO KILLED PEOPLE IN COLD BLOOD IN THE TOHOKU, KANTO AND KINKI REGIONS. IT'S A LOGICAL ASSESSMENT, ISN'T IT?
YOU KNOW THE CASE?
I'VE HEARD OF HIM TOO. HE'S A SERIAL KILLER WHO'S KILLED THREE PEOPLE.
NO, FOUR. DURING QUESTIONING HE STARTED TO CLAIM HE'D KILLED SOME-ONE ELSE FIRST.
HE SAID HE BURIED THE BODY IN THIS FOREST, NEAR HIS MOTHER'S HOME-TOWN.
THAT'S WHY WE BROUGHT HIM DOWN FROM OSAKA AND STARTED COMBING THE AREA.
BUT NUMABUCHI'S MEMORIES WERE VAGUE, AND WE COULDN'T FIND A BODY.
WHEN THE DETECTIVES FROM OSAKA LEFT MY SUPERIOR AND ME WITH NUMABUCHI AND WENT TO GET A BITE TO EAT, HE...
...ESCAPED, HUH?
I BET THAT'S WHAT HE WAS PLANNING ALL ALONG!
BUT IT DIDN'T SEEM THAT WAY AT ALL.
HE TOLD US ALL ABOUT HOW HE USED TO PLAY IN THE FOREST ALONE WHILE HIS MOTHER WAS AWAY...
EEK!

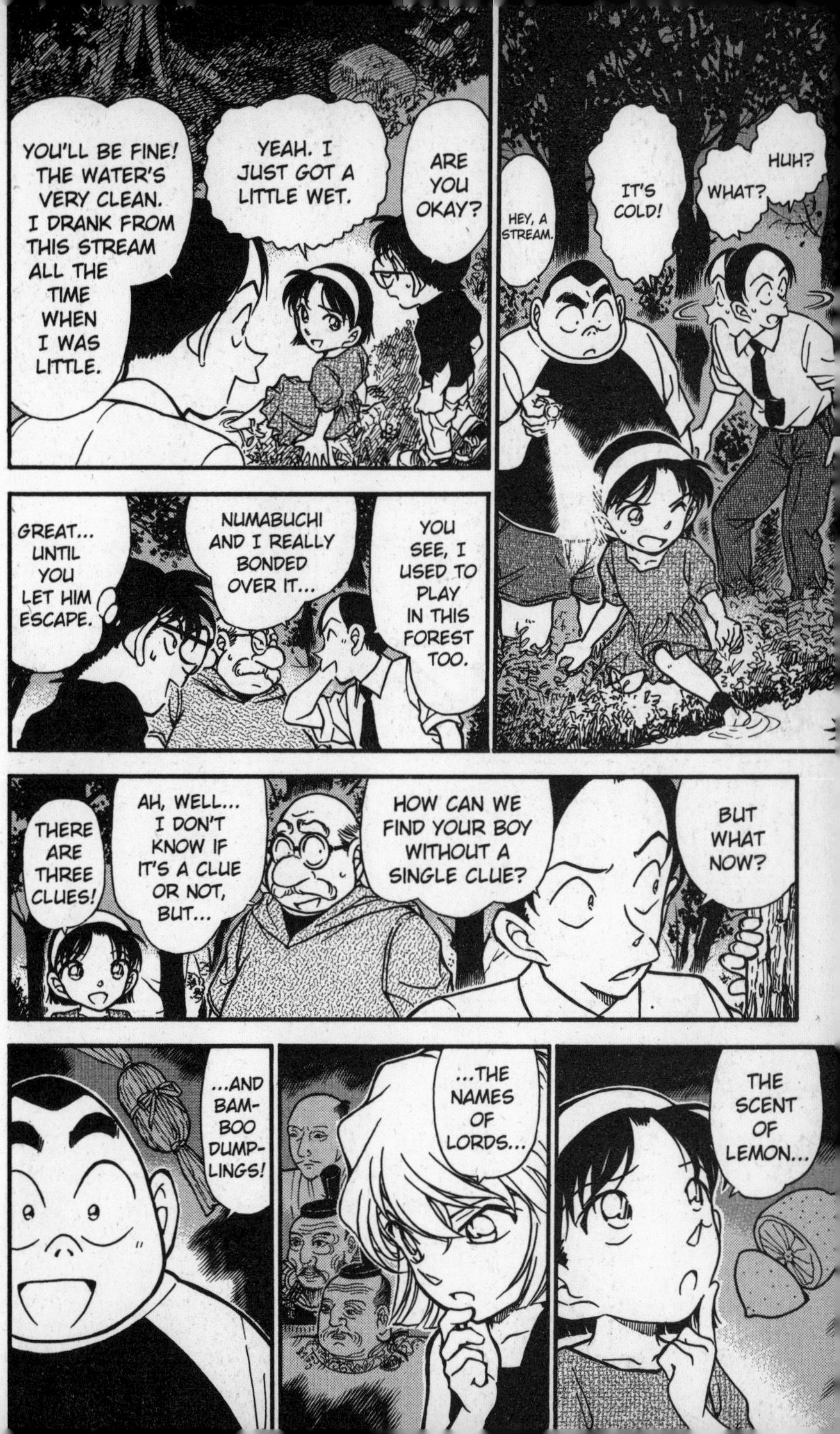
HUH?
WHAT?
IT'S COLD!
HEY, A STREAM.
ARE YOU OKAY?
YEAH. I JUST GOT A LITTLE WET.
YOU'LL BE FINE! THE WATER'S VERY CLEAN. I DRANK FROM THIS STREAM ALL THE TIME WHEN I WAS LITTLE.
YOU SEE, I USED TO PLAY IN THIS FOREST TOO.
NUMABUCHI AND I REALLY BONDED OVER IT...
GREAT... UNTIL YOU LET HIM ESCAPE.
BUT WHAT NOW?
HOW CAN WE FIND YOUR BOY WITHOUT A SINGLE CLUE?
AH, WELL... I DON'T KNOW IF IT'S A CLUE OR NOT, BUT...
THERE ARE THREE CLUES!
THE SCENT OF LEMON...
...THE NAMES OF LORDS...
...AND BAM-BOO DUMP-LINGS!

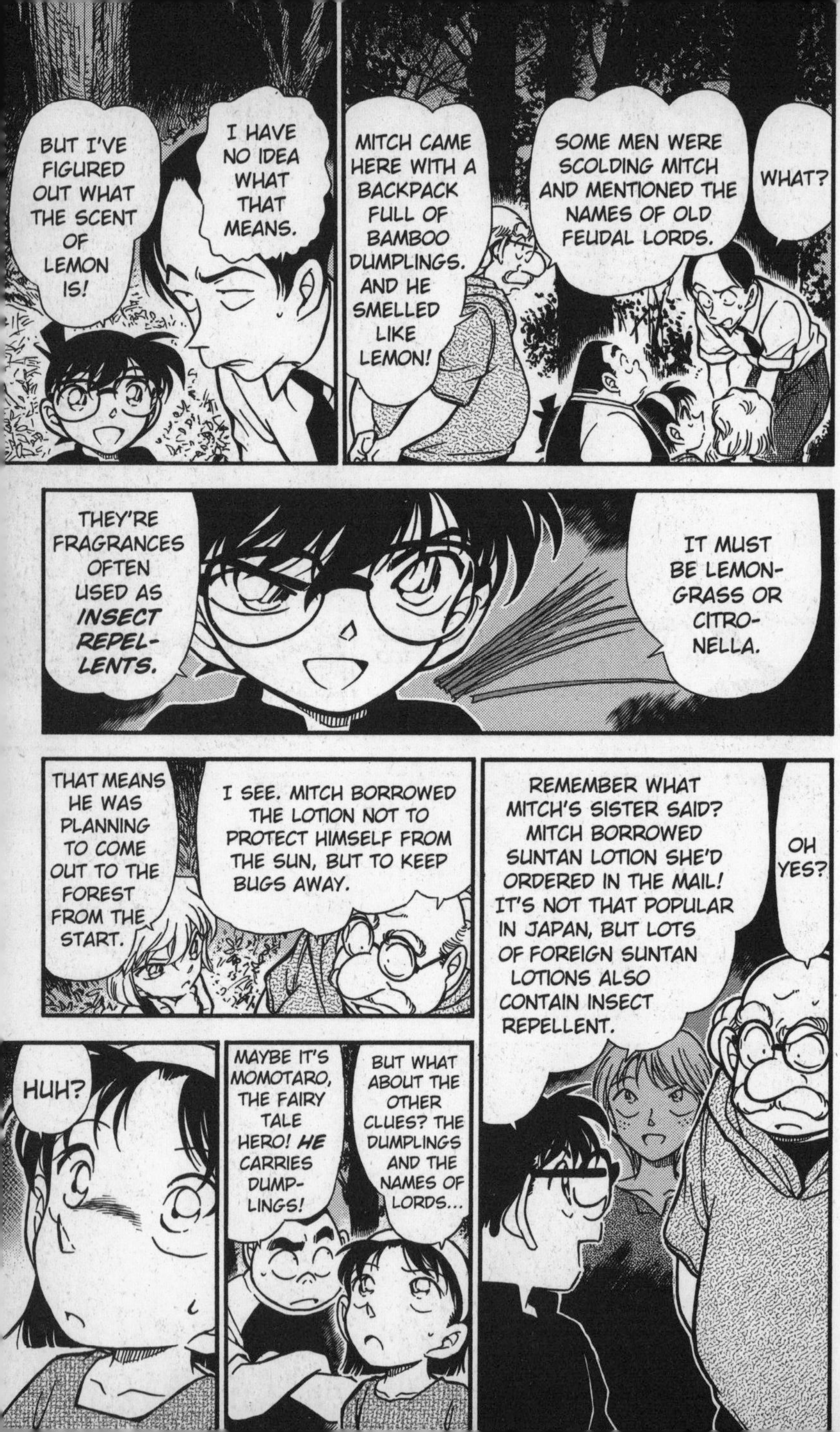
WHAT?
SOME MEN WERE SCOLDING MITCH AND MENTIONED THE NAMES OF OLD FEUDAL LORDS.
MITCH CAME HERE WITH A BACKPACK FULL OF BAMBOO DUMPLINGS. AND HE SMELLED LIKE LEMON!
I HAVE NO IDEA WHAT THAT MEANS.
BUT I'VE FIGURED OUT WHAT THE SCENT OF LEMON IS!
IT MUST BE LEMON-GRASS OR CITRO-NELLA.
THEY'RE FRAGRANCES OFTEN USED AS *INSECT REPEL-LENTS.*
OH YES?
REMEMBER WHAT MITCH'S SISTER SAID? MITCH BORROWED SUNTAN LOTION SHE'D ORDERED IN THE MAIL! IT'S NOT THAT POPULAR IN JAPAN, BUT LOTS OF FOREIGN SUNTAN LOTIONS ALSO CONTAIN INSECT REPELLENT.
I SEE. MITCH BORROWED THE LOTION NOT TO PROTECT HIMSELF FROM THE SUN, BUT TO KEEP BUGS AWAY.
THAT MEANS HE WAS PLANNING TO COME OUT TO THE FOREST FROM THE START.
BUT WHAT ABOUT THE OTHER CLUES? THE DUMPLINGS AND THE NAMES OF LORDS...
MAYBE IT'S MOMOTARO, THE FAIRY TALE HERO! *HE* CARRIES DUMP-LINGS!
HUH?

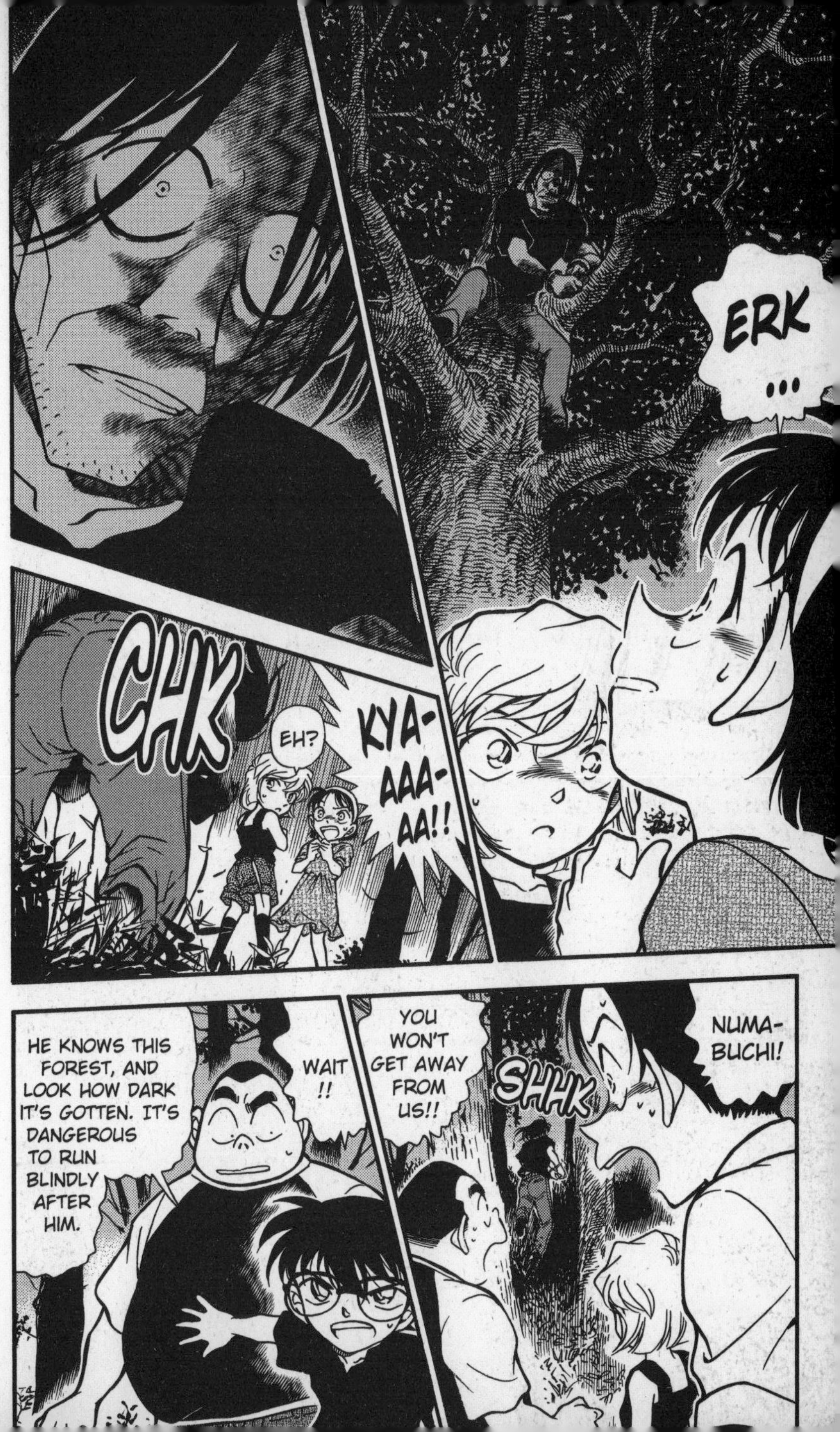
ERK ...
CHK
EH?
KYA-AAA-AA!!
NUMA-BUCHI!
SHHK
YOU WON'T GET AWAY FROM US!!
WAIT !!
HE KNOWS THIS FOREST, AND LOOK HOW DARK IT'S GOTTEN. IT'S DANGEROUS TO RUN BLINDLY AFTER HIM.

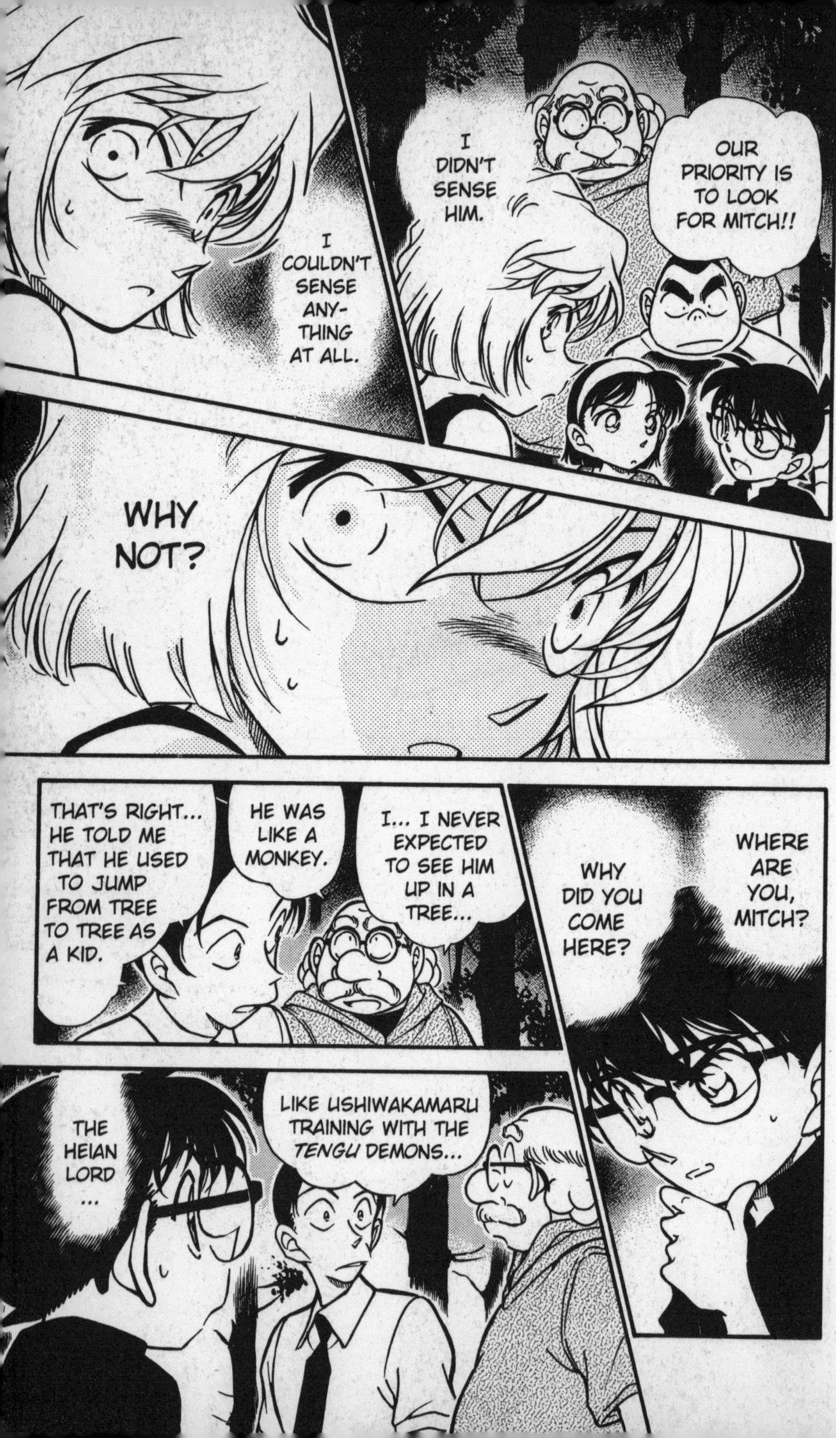

OUR PRIORITY IS TO LOOK FOR MITCH!!
I DIDN'T SENSE HIM.
I COULDN'T SENSE ANY-THING AT ALL.
WHY NOT?
WHERE ARE YOU, MITCH?
WHY DID YOU COME HERE?
I... I NEVER EXPECTED TO SEE HIM UP IN A TREE...
HE WAS LIKE A MONKEY.
THAT'S RIGHT... HE TOLD ME THAT HE USED TO JUMP FROM TREE TO TREE AS A KID.
LIKE USHIWAKAMARU TRAINING WITH THE *TENGU* DEMONS...
THE HEIAN LORD ...

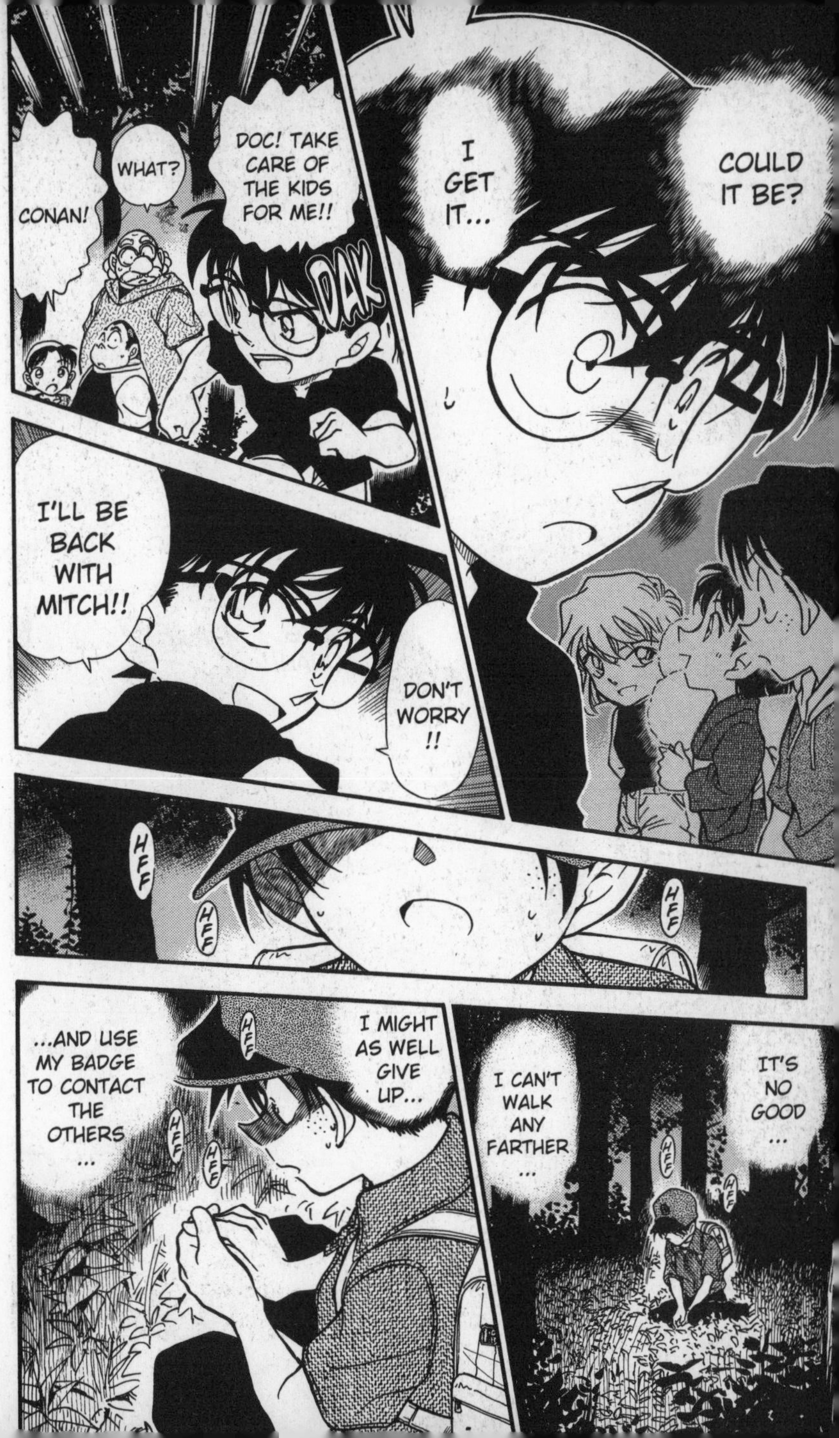
COULD IT BE?
I GET IT...
DOC! TAKE CARE OF THE KIDS FOR ME!!
DAK
WHAT?
CONAN!
DON'T WORRY!!
I'LL BE BACK WITH MITCH!!
HFF
HFF
HFF
IT'S NO GOOD...
HFF
I CAN'T WALK ANY FARTHER...
HFF
I MIGHT AS WELL GIVE UP...
HFF
...AND USE MY BADGE TO CONTACT THE OTHERS...
HFF
HFF

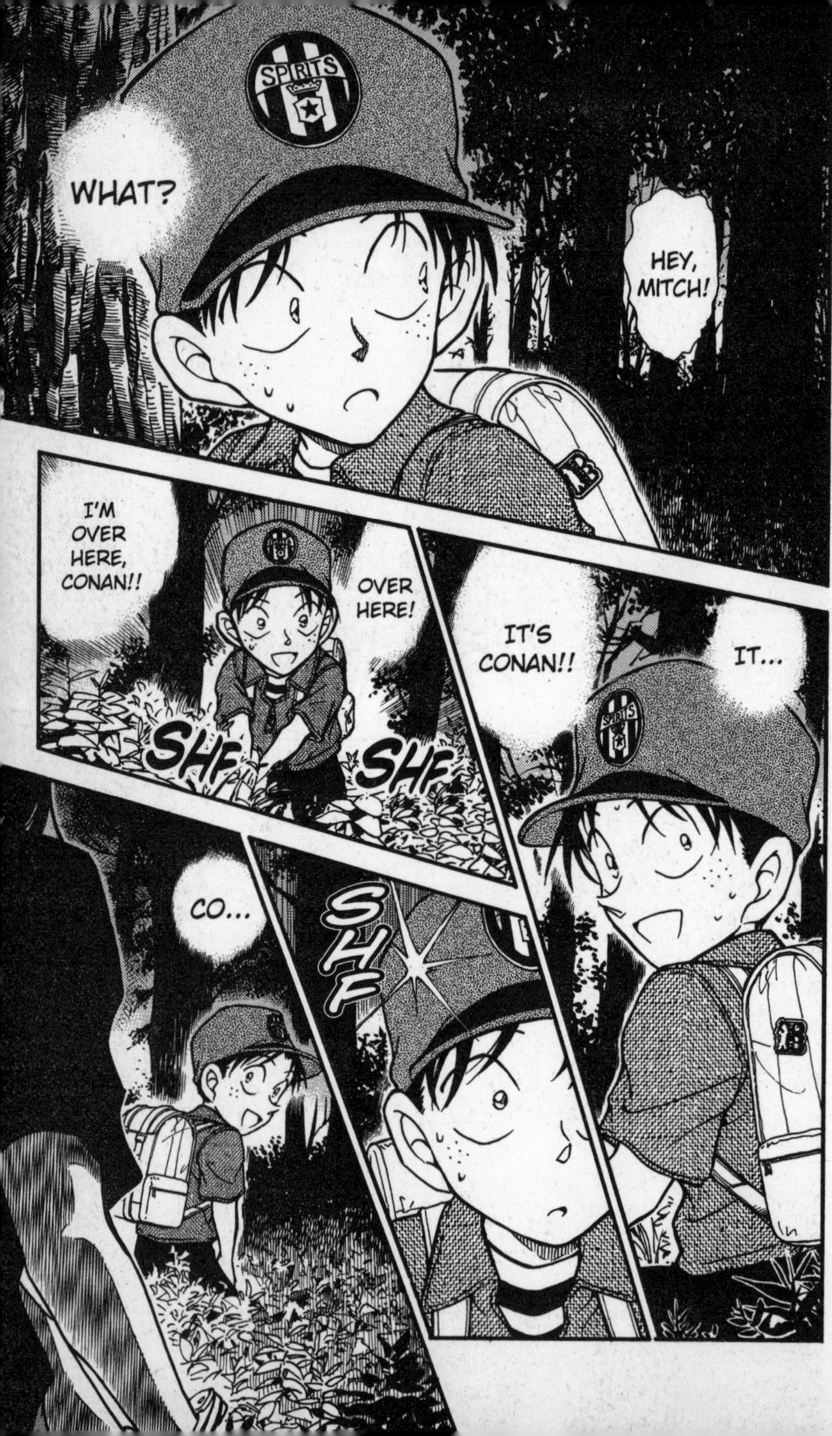
HEY, MITCH!
WHAT?
IT...
IT'S CONAN!!
OVER HERE!
I'M OVER HERE, CONAN!!
SHF
SHF
SHF
CO...

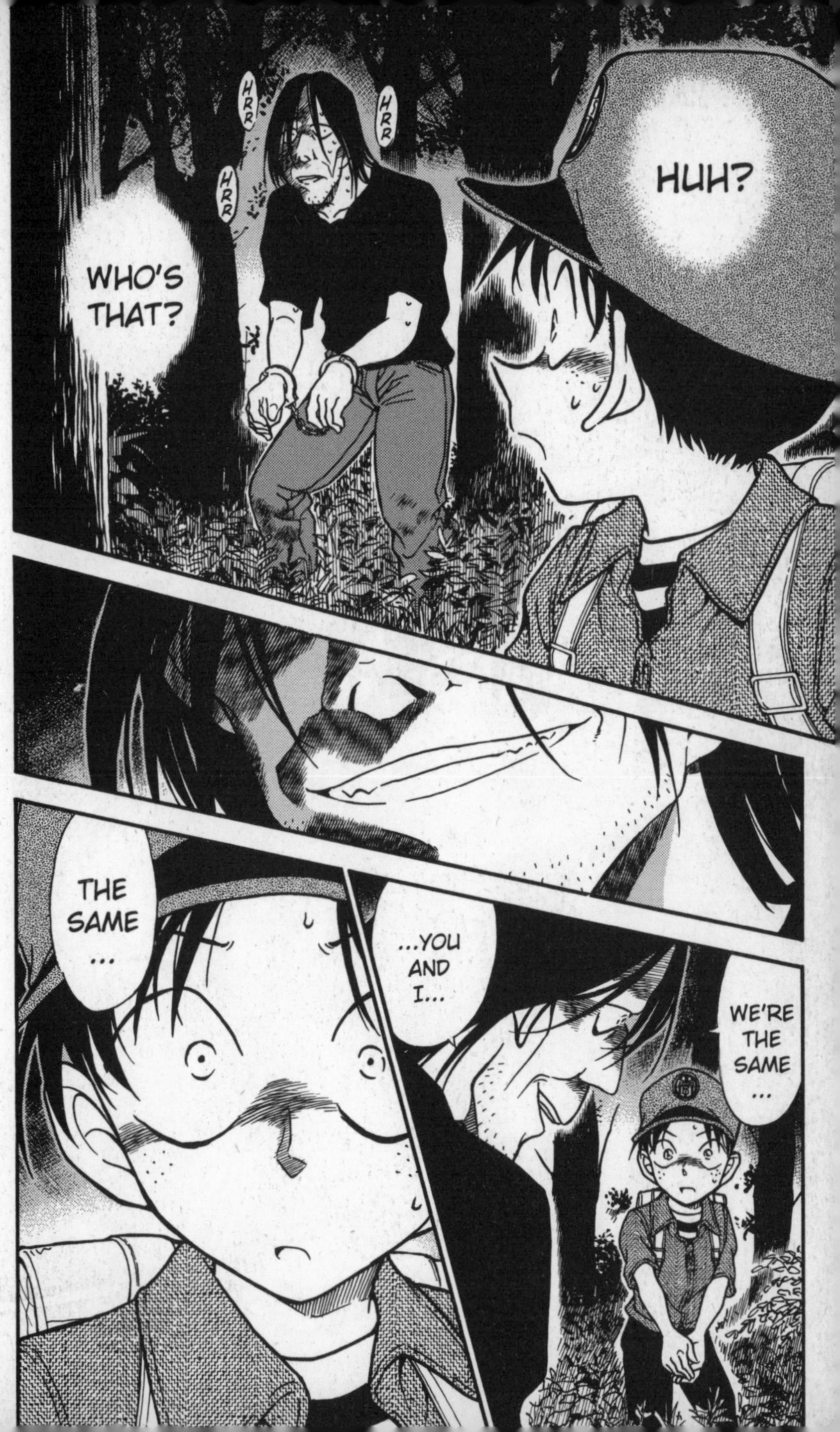
HUH?
HRR
HRR
HRR
WHO'S THAT?
...YOU AND I...
WE'RE THE SAME ...
THE SAME ...

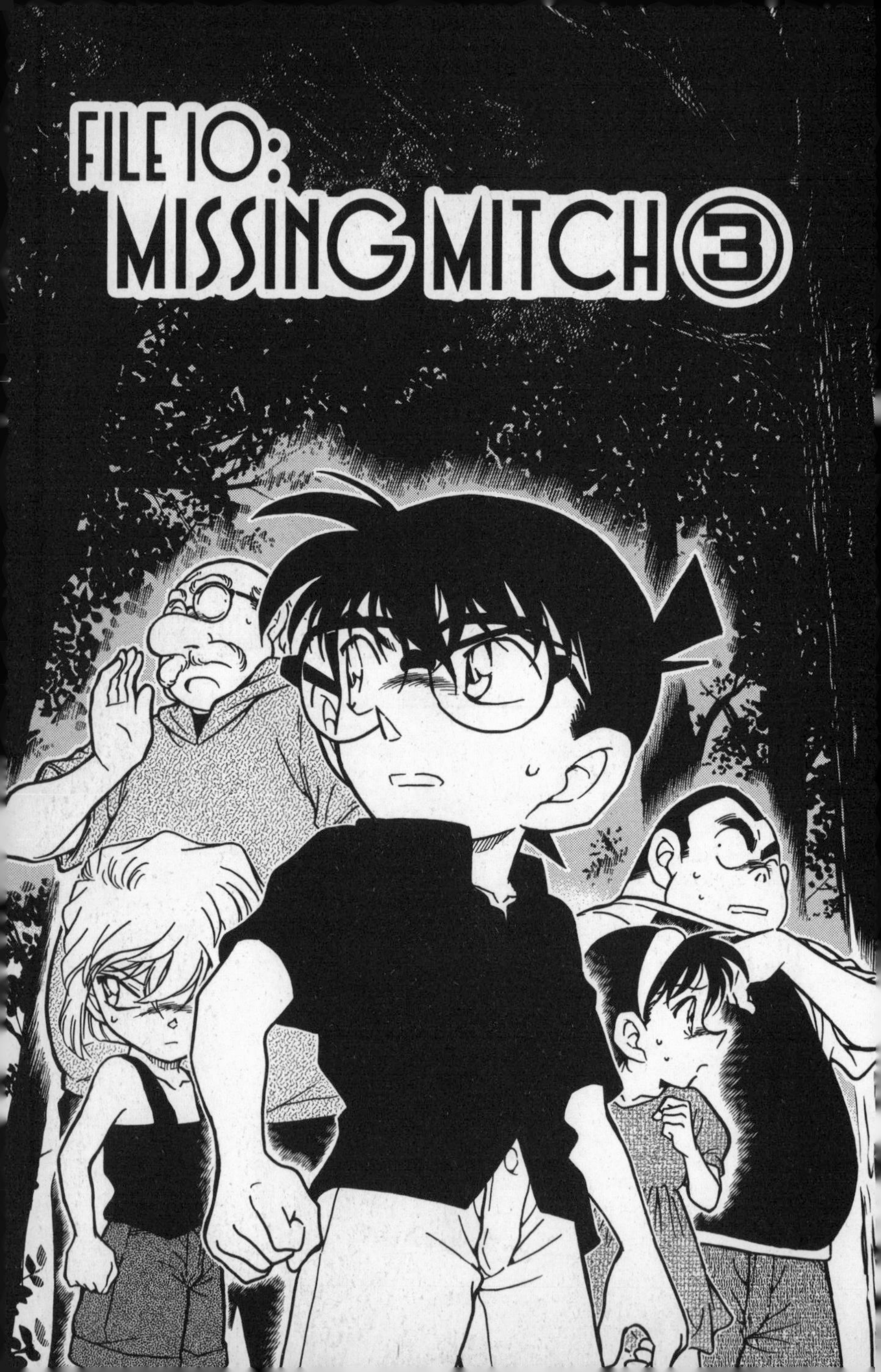
FILE 10:
MISSING MITCH ③

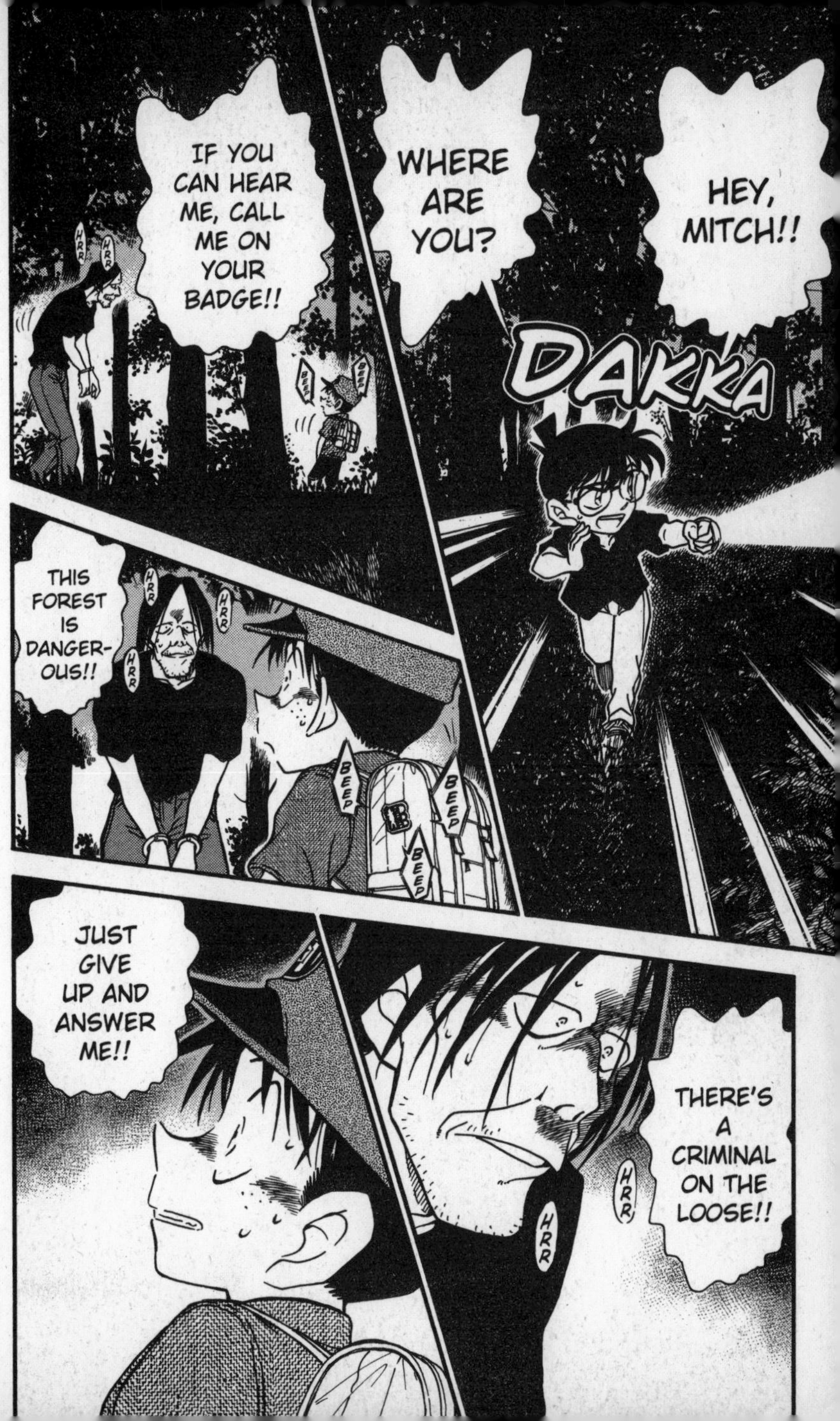
HEY, MITCH!!
WHERE ARE YOU?
DAKKA
IF YOU CAN HEAR ME, CALL ME ON YOUR BADGE!!
HRR
HRR
BEEP
BEEP
THIS FOREST IS DANGER-OUS!!
HRR
HRR
HRR
BEEP
BEEP
BEEP
THERE'S A CRIMINAL ON THE LOOSE!!
HRR
HRR
JUST GIVE UP AND ANSWER ME!!

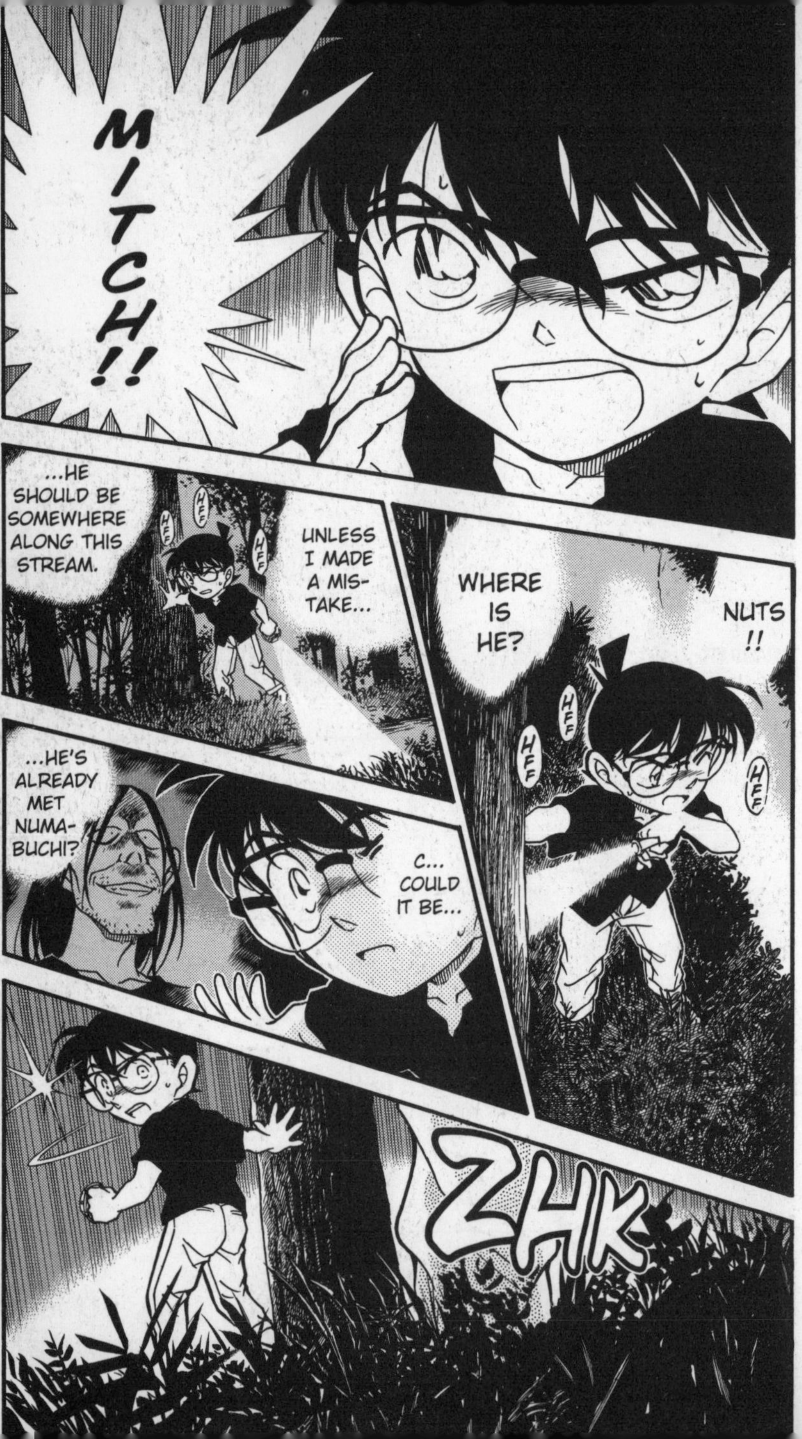
MITCH!!
NUTS!!
WHERE IS HE?
HEF
HEF
HEF
UNLESS I MADE A MISTAKE...
...HE SHOULD BE SOMEWHERE ALONG THIS STREAM.
HEF
HEF
HEF
C... COULD IT BE...
...HE'S ALREADY MET NUMABUCHI?
ZHK

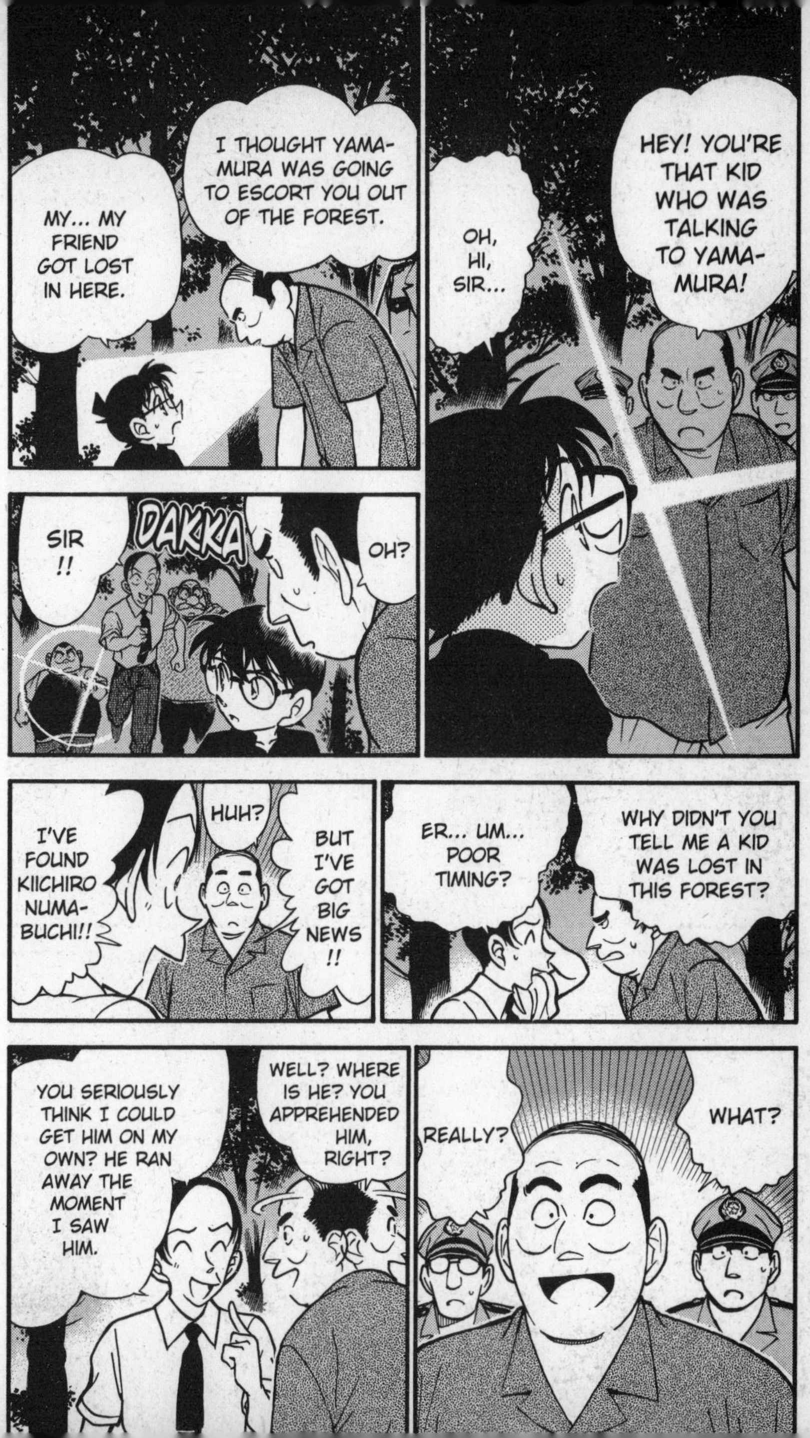
HEY! YOU'RE THAT KID WHO WAS TALKING TO YAMA-MURA!
OH, HI, SIR...
I THOUGHT YAMA-MURA WAS GOING TO ESCORT YOU OUT OF THE FOREST.
MY... MY FRIEND GOT LOST IN HERE.
OH?
DAKKA
SIR !!
WHY DIDN'T YOU TELL ME A KID WAS LOST IN THIS FOREST?
ER... UM... POOR TIMING?
BUT I'VE GOT BIG NEWS !!
HUH?
I'VE FOUND KIICHIRO NUMA-BUCHI!!
WHAT?
REALLY?
WELL? WHERE IS HE? YOU APPREHENDED HIM, RIGHT?
YOU SERIOUSLY THINK I COULD GET HIM ON MY OWN? HE RAN AWAY THE MOMENT I SAW HIM.

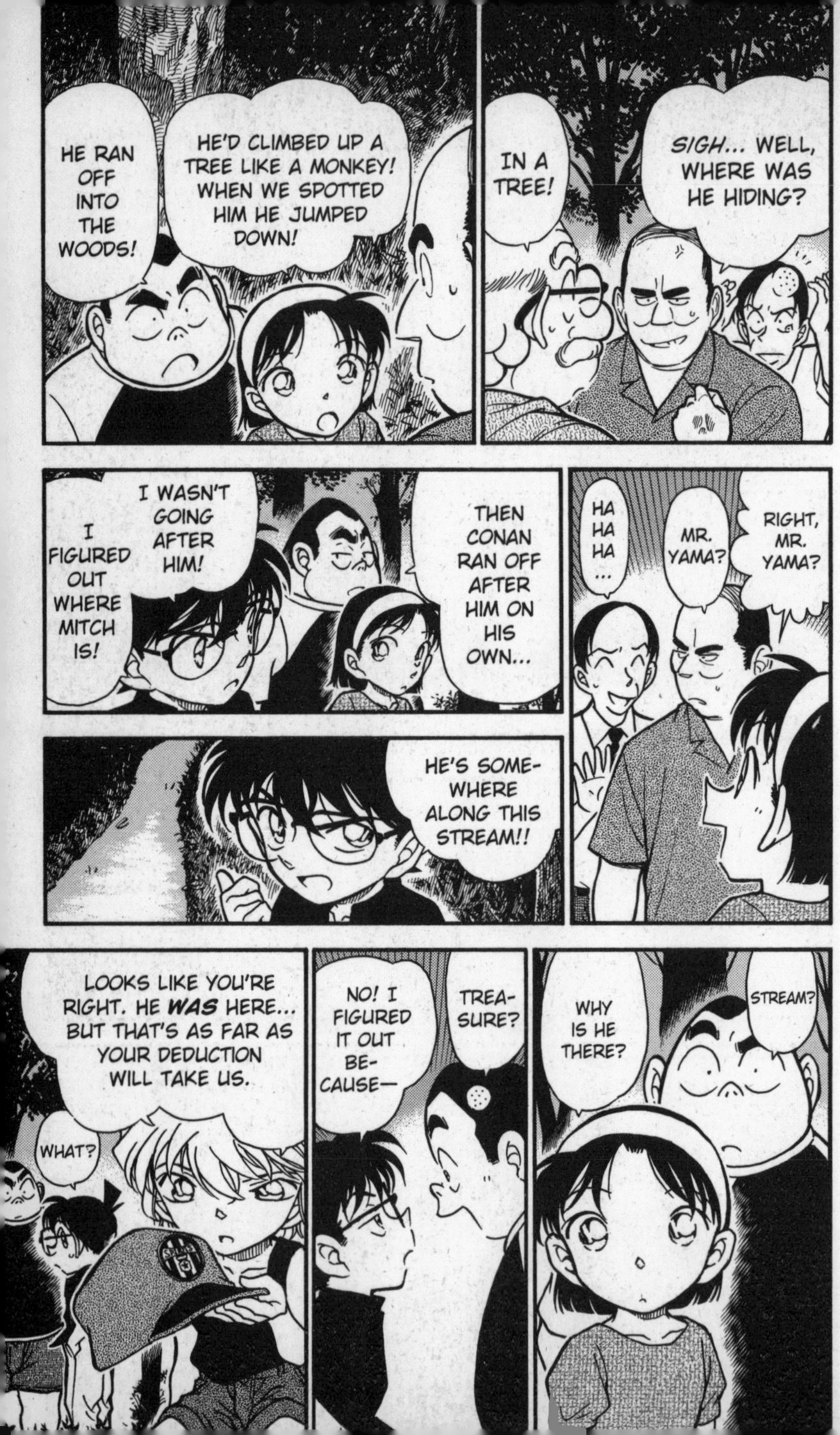

SIGH... WELL, WHERE WAS HE HIDING?
IN A TREE!
HE'D CLIMBED UP A TREE LIKE A MONKEY! WHEN WE SPOTTED HIM HE JUMPED DOWN!
HE RAN OFF INTO THE WOODS!
RIGHT, MR. YAMA?
MR. YAMA?
HA HA HA ...
THEN CONAN RAN OFF AFTER HIM ON HIS OWN...
I WASN'T GOING AFTER HIM!
I FIGURED OUT WHERE MITCH IS!
HE'S SOME-WHERE ALONG THIS STREAM!!
STREAM?
WHY IS HE THERE?
TREA-SURE?
NO! I FIGURED IT OUT BE-CAUSE—
LOOKS LIKE YOU'RE RIGHT. HE *WAS* HERE... BUT THAT'S AS FAR AS YOUR DEDUCTION WILL TAKE US.
WHAT?

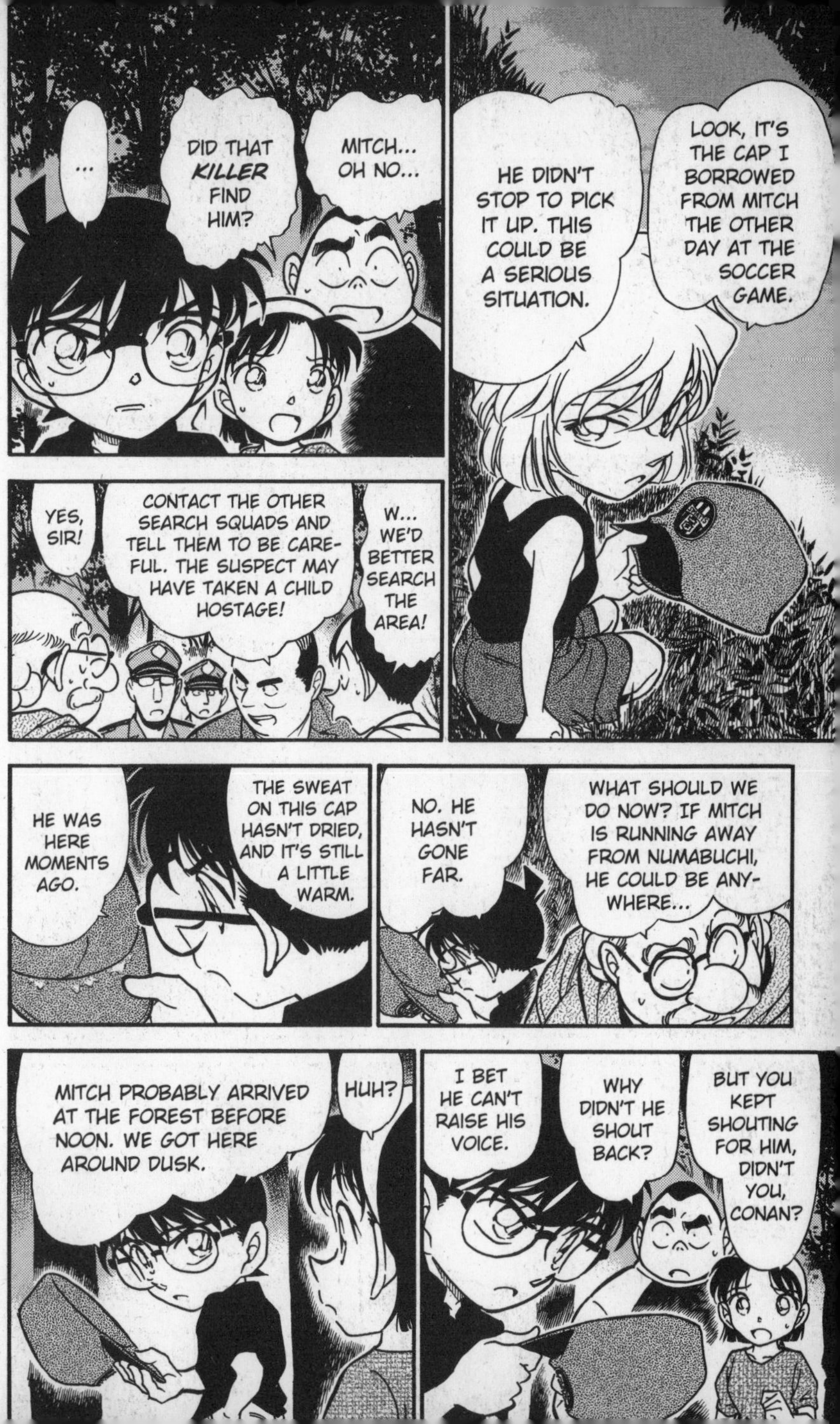
LOOK, IT'S THE CAP I BORROWED FROM MITCH THE OTHER DAY AT THE SOCCER GAME.
HE DIDN'T STOP TO PICK IT UP. THIS COULD BE A SERIOUS SITUATION.
MITCH... OH NO...
DID THAT KILLER FIND HIM?
...
W... WE'D BETTER SEARCH THE AREA!
CONTACT THE OTHER SEARCH SQUADS AND TELL THEM TO BE CAREFUL. THE SUSPECT MAY HAVE TAKEN A CHILD HOSTAGE!
YES, SIR!
WHAT SHOULD WE DO NOW? IF MITCH IS RUNNING AWAY FROM NUMABUCHI, HE COULD BE ANYWHERE...
NO. HE HASN'T GONE FAR.
THE SWEAT ON THIS CAP HASN'T DRIED, AND IT'S STILL A LITTLE WARM.
HE WAS HERE MOMENTS AGO.
BUT YOU KEPT SHOUTING FOR HIM, DIDN'T YOU, CONAN?
WHY DIDN'T HE SHOUT BACK?
I BET HE CAN'T RAISE HIS VOICE.
HUH?
MITCH PROBABLY ARRIVED AT THE FOREST BEFORE NOON. WE GOT HERE AROUND DUSK.

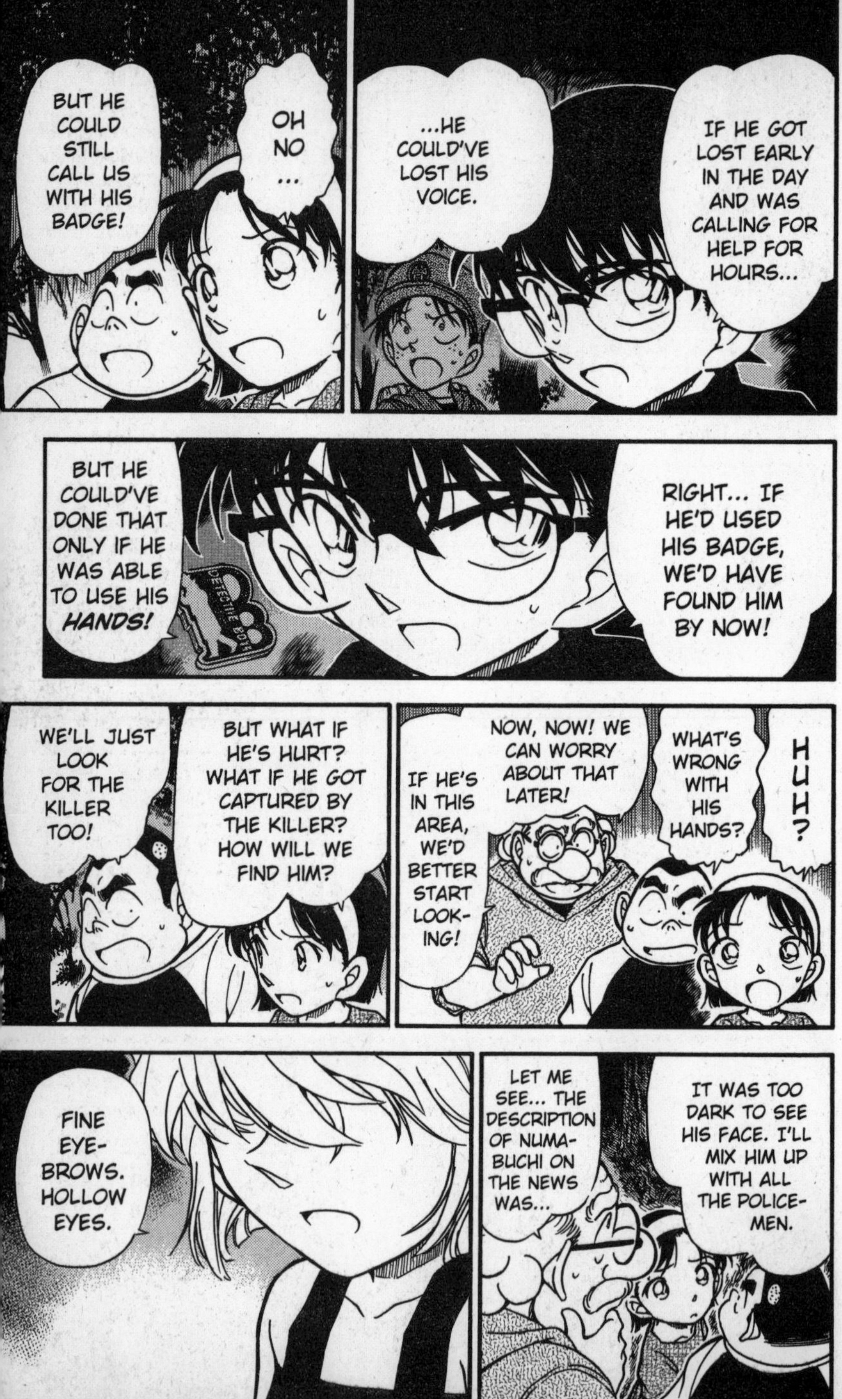
IF HE GOT LOST EARLY IN THE DAY AND WAS CALLING FOR HELP FOR HOURS...
...HE COULD'VE LOST HIS VOICE.
OH NO ...
BUT HE COULD STILL CALL US WITH HIS BADGE!
RIGHT... IF HE'D USED HIS BADGE, WE'D HAVE FOUND HIM BY NOW!
BUT HE COULD'VE DONE THAT ONLY IF HE WAS ABLE TO USE HIS *HANDS!*
DETECTIVE BOYS
HUH?
WHAT'S WRONG WITH HIS HANDS?
NOW, NOW! WE CAN WORRY ABOUT THAT LATER!
IF HE'S IN THIS AREA, WE'D BETTER START LOOK-ING!
BUT WHAT IF HE'S HURT? WHAT IF HE GOT CAPTURED BY THE KILLER? HOW WILL WE FIND HIM?
WE'LL JUST LOOK FOR THE KILLER TOO!
IT WAS TOO DARK TO SEE HIS FACE. I'LL MIX HIM UP WITH ALL THE POLICE-MEN.
LET ME SEE... THE DESCRIPTION OF NUMA-BUCHI ON THE NEWS WAS...
FINE EYE-BROWS. HOLLOW EYES.

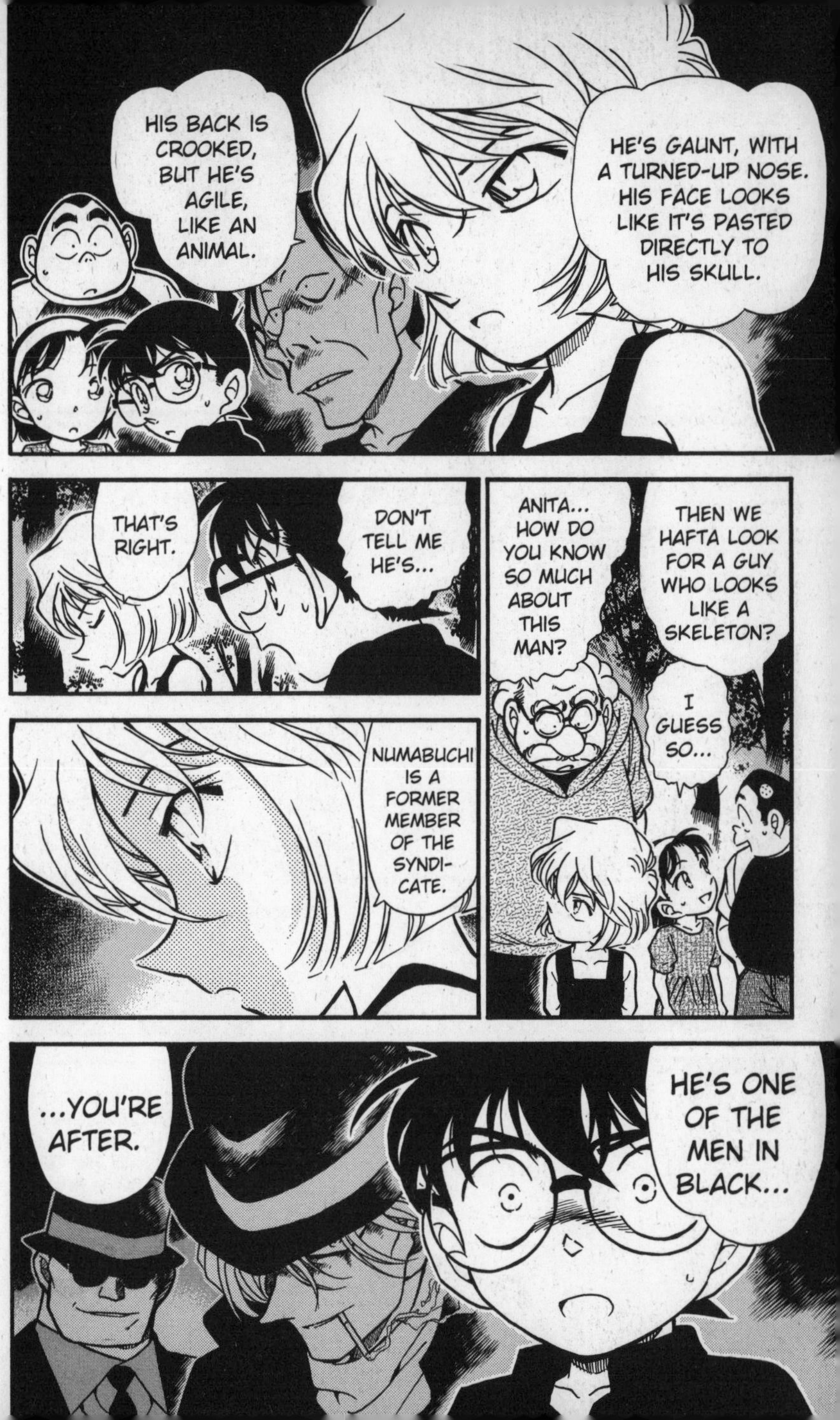
HE'S GAUNT, WITH A TURNED-UP NOSE. HIS FACE LOOKS LIKE IT'S PASTED DIRECTLY TO HIS SKULL.
HIS BACK IS CROOKED, BUT HE'S AGILE, LIKE AN ANIMAL.
THEN WE HAFTA LOOK FOR A GUY WHO LOOKS LIKE A SKELETON?
ANITA... HOW DO YOU KNOW SO MUCH ABOUT THIS MAN?
I GUESS SO...
DON'T TELL ME HE'S...
THAT'S RIGHT.
NUMABUCHI IS A FORMER MEMBER OF THE SYNDICATE.
HE'S ONE OF THE MEN IN BLACK...
...YOU'RE AFTER.

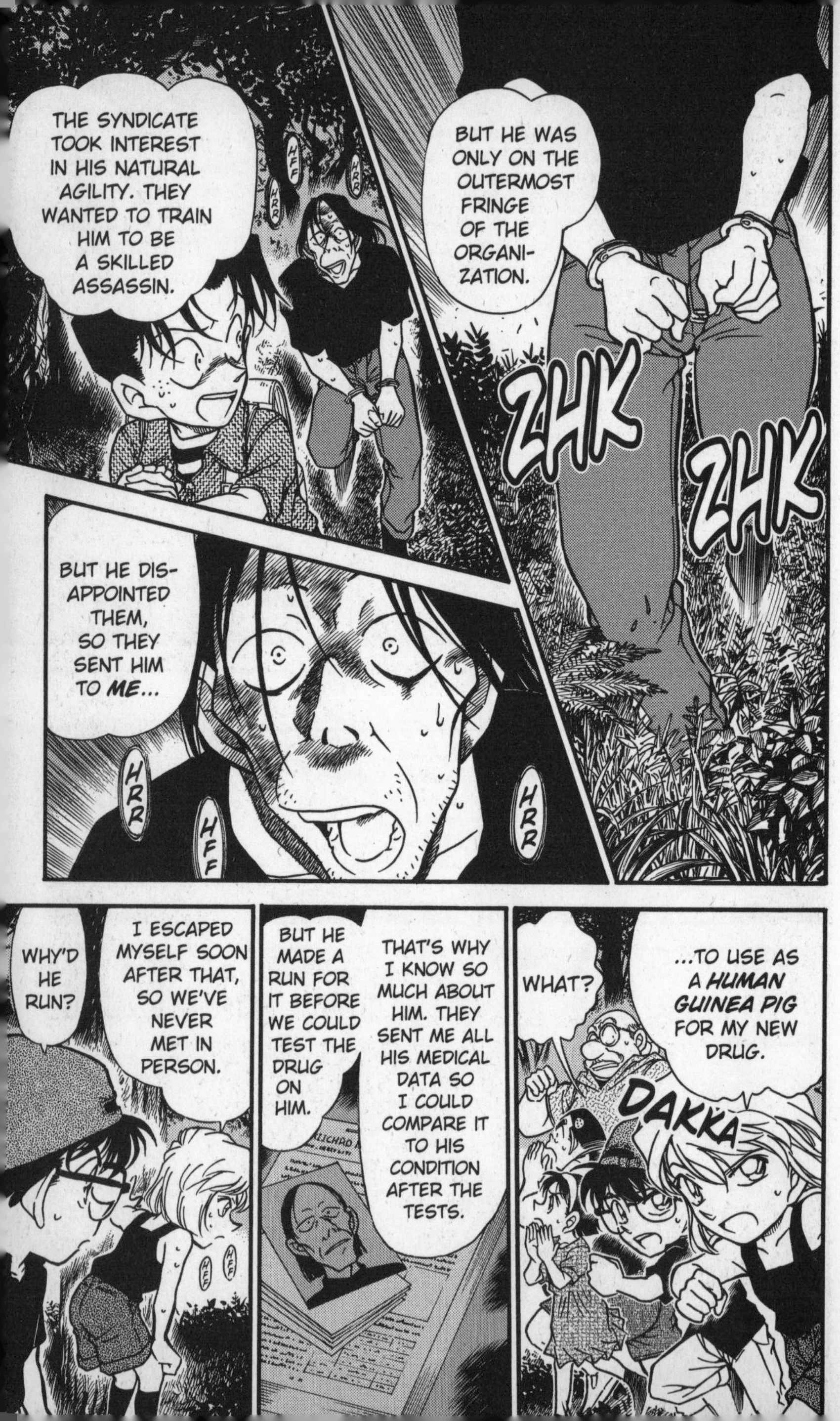
BUT HE WAS ONLY ON THE OUTERMOST FRINGE OF THE ORGANIZATION.
ZHK
ZHK
THE SYNDICATE TOOK INTEREST IN HIS NATURAL AGILITY. THEY WANTED TO TRAIN HIM TO BE A SKILLED ASSASSIN.
HFF
HRR
HRR
BUT HE DISAPPOINTED THEM, SO THEY SENT HIM TO *ME*...
HRR
HFF
HRR
...TO USE AS A *HUMAN GUINEA PIG* FOR MY NEW DRUG.
DAKKA
WHAT?
THAT'S WHY I KNOW SO MUCH ABOUT HIM. THEY SENT ME ALL HIS MEDICAL DATA SO I COULD COMPARE IT TO HIS CONDITION AFTER THE TESTS.
BUT HE MADE A RUN FOR IT BEFORE WE COULD TEST THE DRUG ON HIM.
I ESCAPED MYSELF SOON AFTER THAT, SO WE'VE NEVER MET IN PERSON.
WHY'D HE RUN?
HFF
HFF

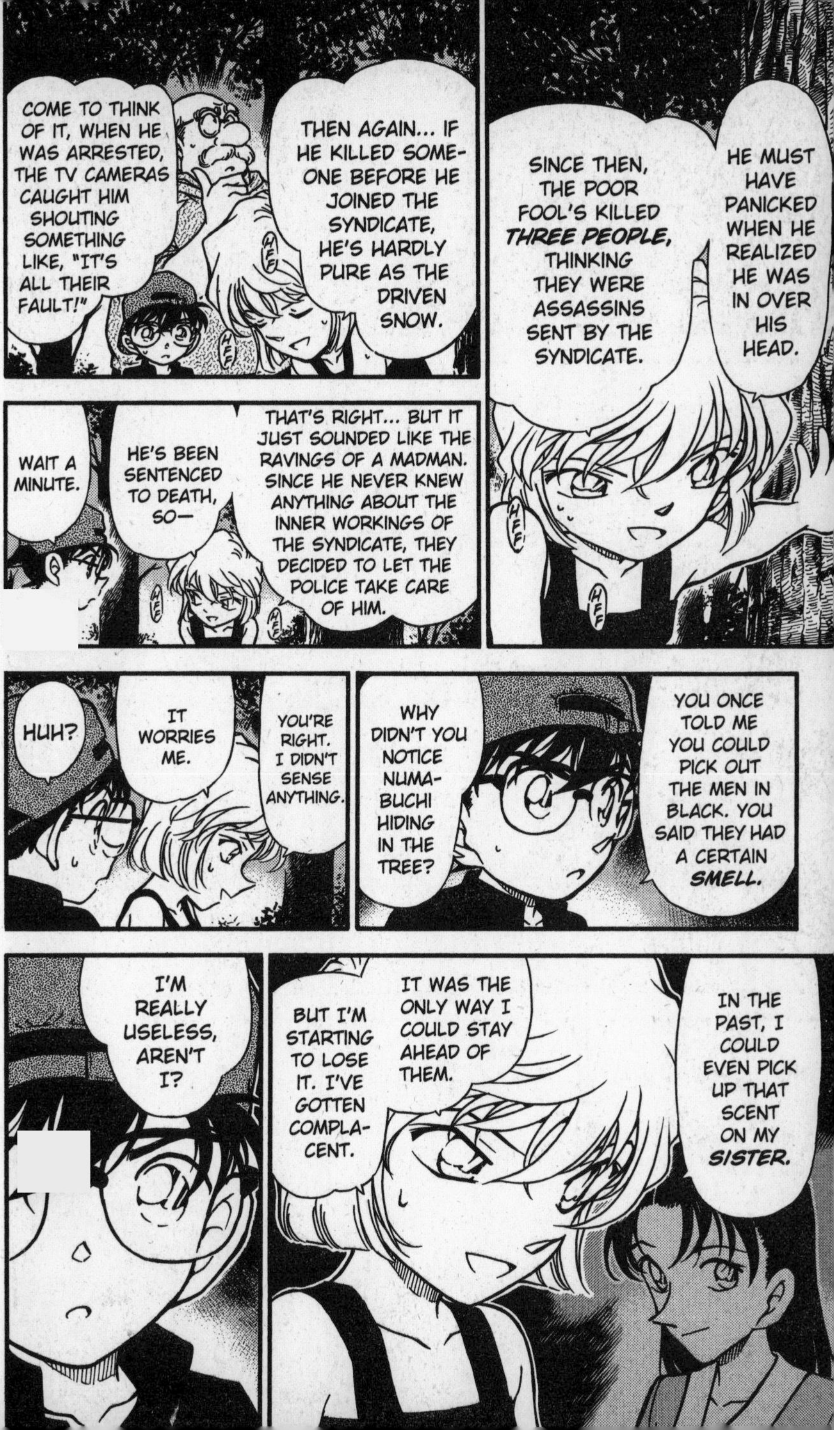
HE MUST HAVE PANICKED WHEN HE REALIZED HE WAS IN OVER HIS HEAD.
SINCE THEN, THE POOR FOOL'S KILLED ***THREE PEOPLE,*** THINKING THEY WERE ASSASSINS SENT BY THE SYNDICATE.
HFF
HFF
THEN AGAIN... IF HE KILLED SOMEONE BEFORE HE JOINED THE SYNDICATE, HE'S HARDLY PURE AS THE DRIVEN SNOW.
HFF
HFF
COME TO THINK OF IT, WHEN HE WAS ARRESTED, THE TV CAMERAS CAUGHT HIM SHOUTING SOMETHING LIKE, "IT'S ALL THEIR FAULT!"
THAT'S RIGHT... BUT IT JUST SOUNDED LIKE THE RAVINGS OF A MADMAN. SINCE HE NEVER KNEW ANYTHING ABOUT THE INNER WORKINGS OF THE SYNDICATE, THEY DECIDED TO LET THE POLICE TAKE CARE OF HIM.
HFF
HFF
HE'S BEEN SENTENCED TO DEATH, SO—
WAIT A MINUTE.
YOU ONCE TOLD ME YOU COULD PICK OUT THE MEN IN BLACK. YOU SAID THEY HAD A CERTAIN ***SMELL.***
WHY DIDN'T YOU NOTICE NUMABUCHI HIDING IN THE TREE?
YOU'RE RIGHT. I DIDN'T SENSE ANYTHING.
IT WORRIES ME.
HUH?
IN THE PAST, I COULD EVEN PICK UP THAT SCENT ON MY ***SISTER.***
IT WAS THE ONLY WAY I COULD STAY AHEAD OF THEM.
BUT I'M STARTING TO LOSE IT. I'VE GOTTEN COMPLACENT.
I'M REALLY USELESS, AREN'T I?

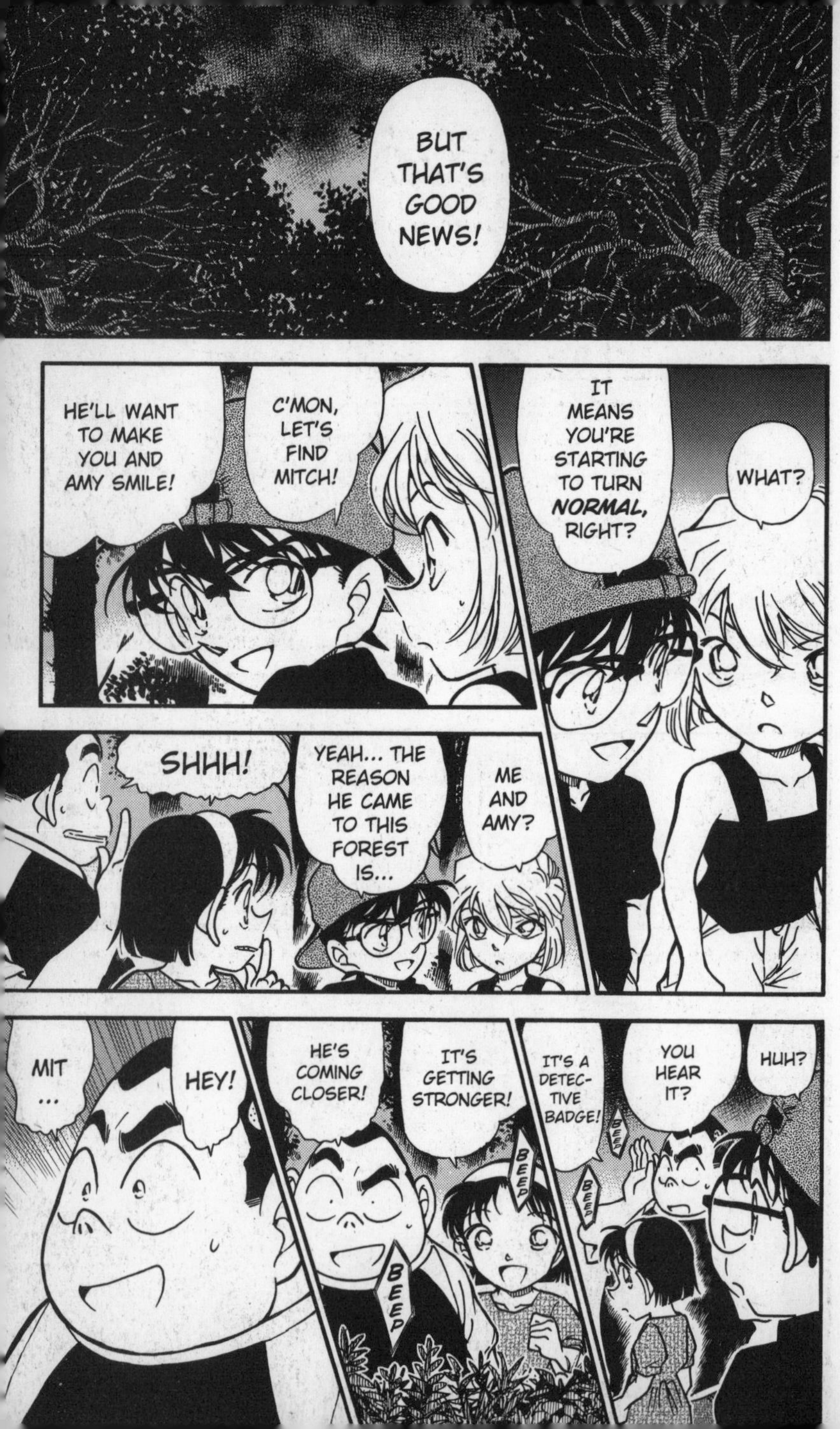
BUT THAT'S GOOD NEWS!
WHAT?
IT MEANS YOU'RE STARTING TO TURN NORMAL, RIGHT?
C'MON, LET'S FIND MITCH!
HE'LL WANT TO MAKE YOU AND AMY SMILE!
ME AND AMY?
YEAH... THE REASON HE CAME TO THIS FOREST IS...
SHHH!
HUH?
YOU HEAR IT?
IT'S A DETECTIVE BADGE!
BEEP
BEEP
IT'S GETTING STRONGER!
HE'S COMING CLOSER!
BEEP
BEEP
HEY!
MIT ...

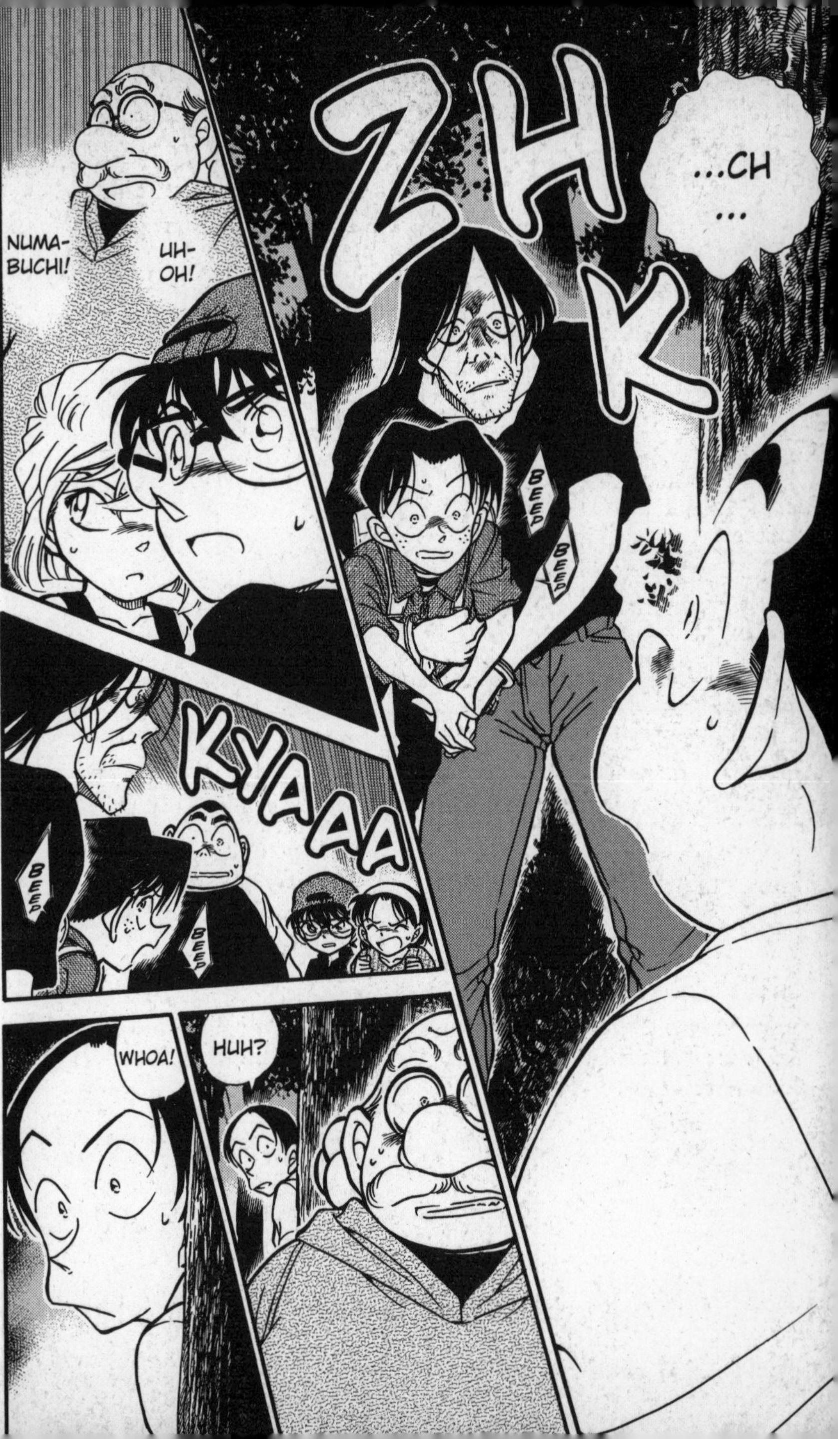
...CH ...
ZHK
BEEP
BEEP
UH-OH!
NUMA-BUCHI!
KYAAA
BEEP
BEEP
HUH?
WHOA!

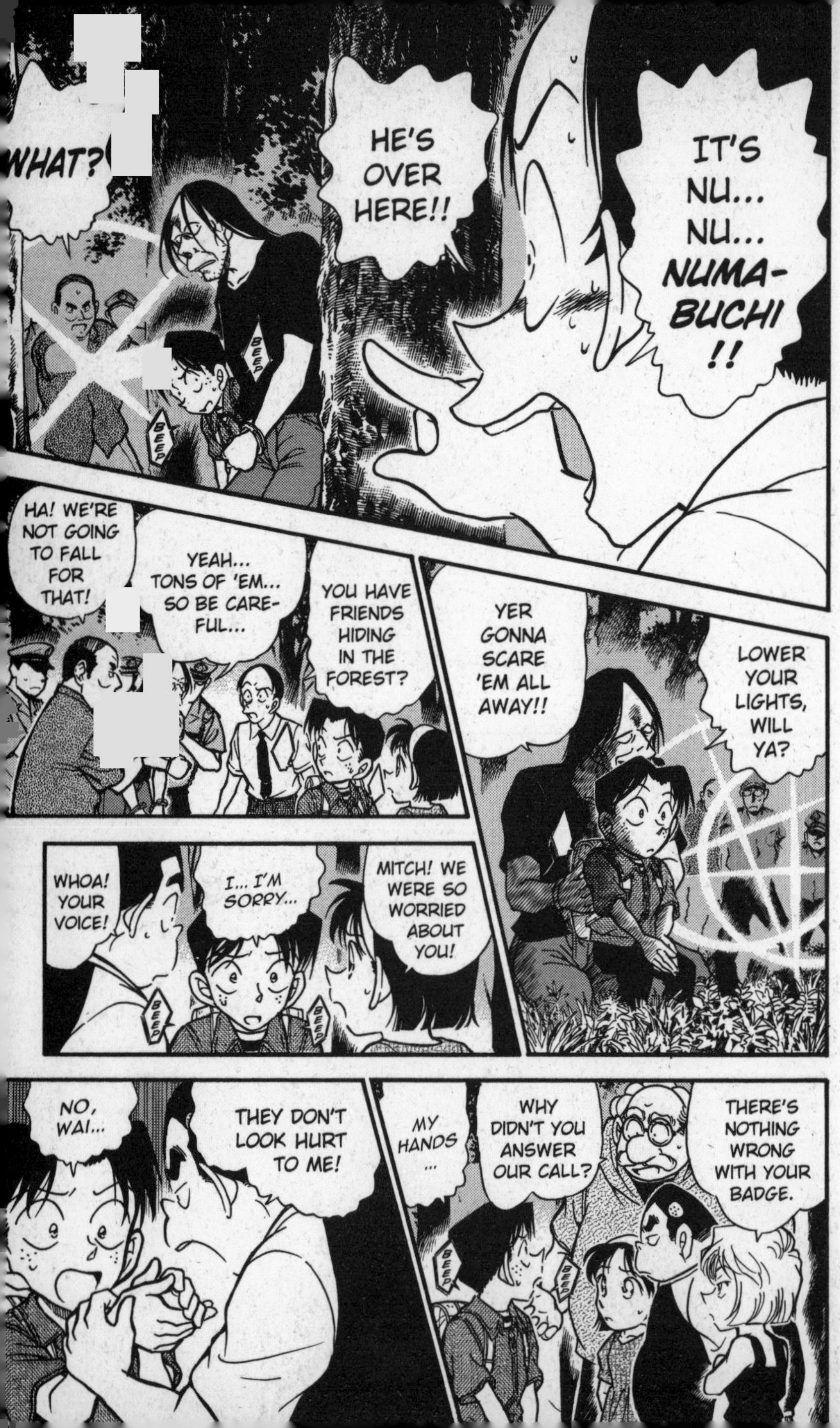
IT'S NU... NU... NUMA-BUCHI!!
HE'S OVER HERE!!
WHAT?
BEEP
BEEP
LOWER YOUR LIGHTS, WILL YA?
YER GONNA SCARE 'EM ALL AWAY!!
YOU HAVE FRIENDS HIDING IN THE FOREST?
YEAH... TONS OF 'EM... SO BE CARE-FUL...
HA! WE'RE NOT GOING TO FALL FOR THAT!
MITCH! WE WERE SO WORRIED ABOUT YOU!
I... I'M SORRY...
WHOA! YOUR VOICE!
BEEP
BEEP
THERE'S NOTHING WRONG WITH YOUR BADGE.
WHY DIDN'T YOU ANSWER OUR CALL?
MY HANDS ...
BEEP
BEEP
THEY DON'T LOOK HURT TO ME!
NO, WAI...

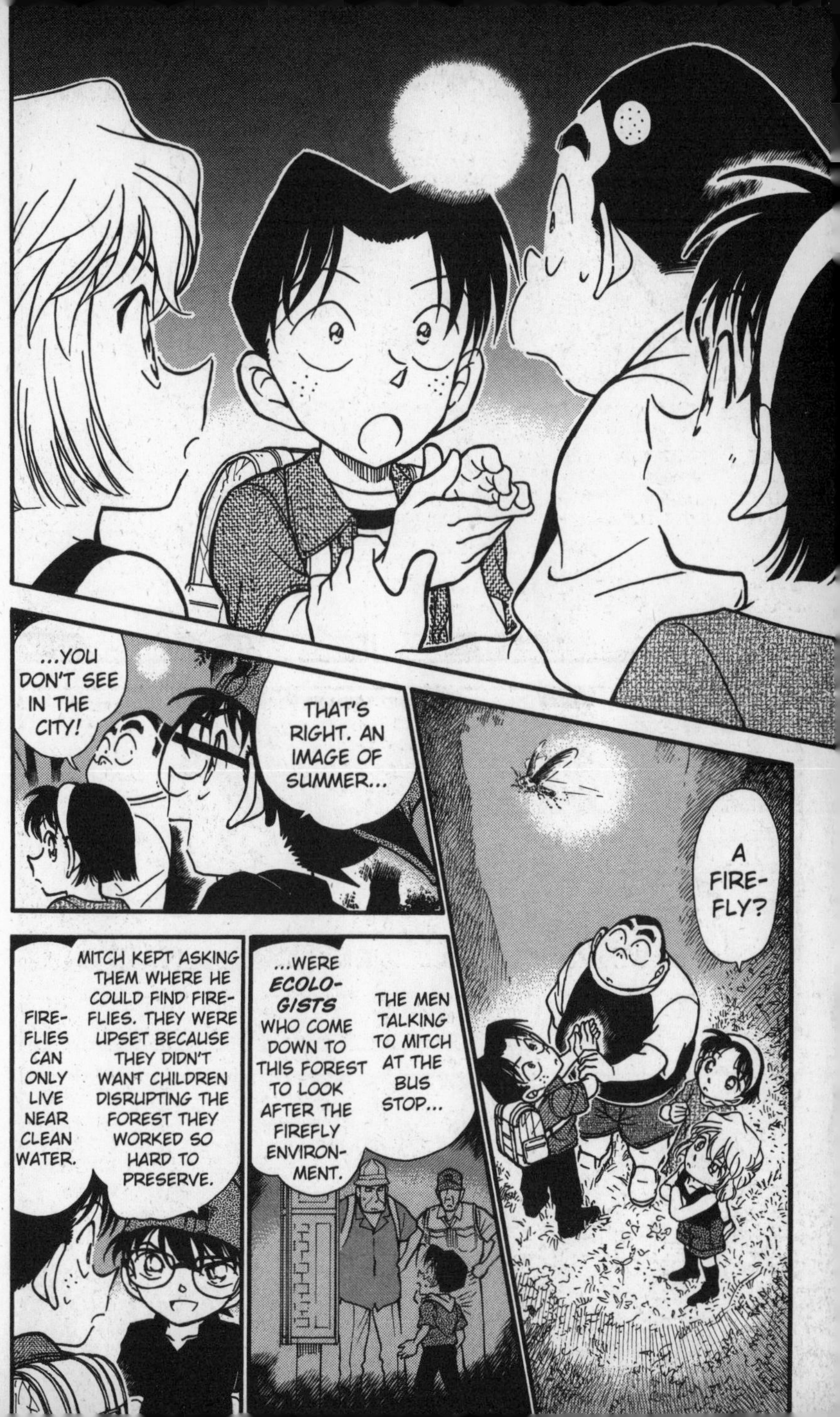
A FIRE-FLY?
THAT'S RIGHT. AN IMAGE OF SUMMER...
...YOU DON'T SEE IN THE CITY!
THE MEN TALKING TO MITCH AT THE BUS STOP...
...WERE *ECOLOGISTS* WHO COME DOWN TO THIS FOREST TO LOOK AFTER THE FIREFLY ENVIRON-MENT.
MITCH KEPT ASKING THEM WHERE HE COULD FIND FIRE-FLIES. THEY WERE UPSET BECAUSE THEY DIDN'T WANT CHILDREN DISRUPTING THE FOREST THEY WORKED SO HARD TO PRESERVE.
FIRE-FLIES CAN ONLY LIVE NEAR CLEAN WATER.

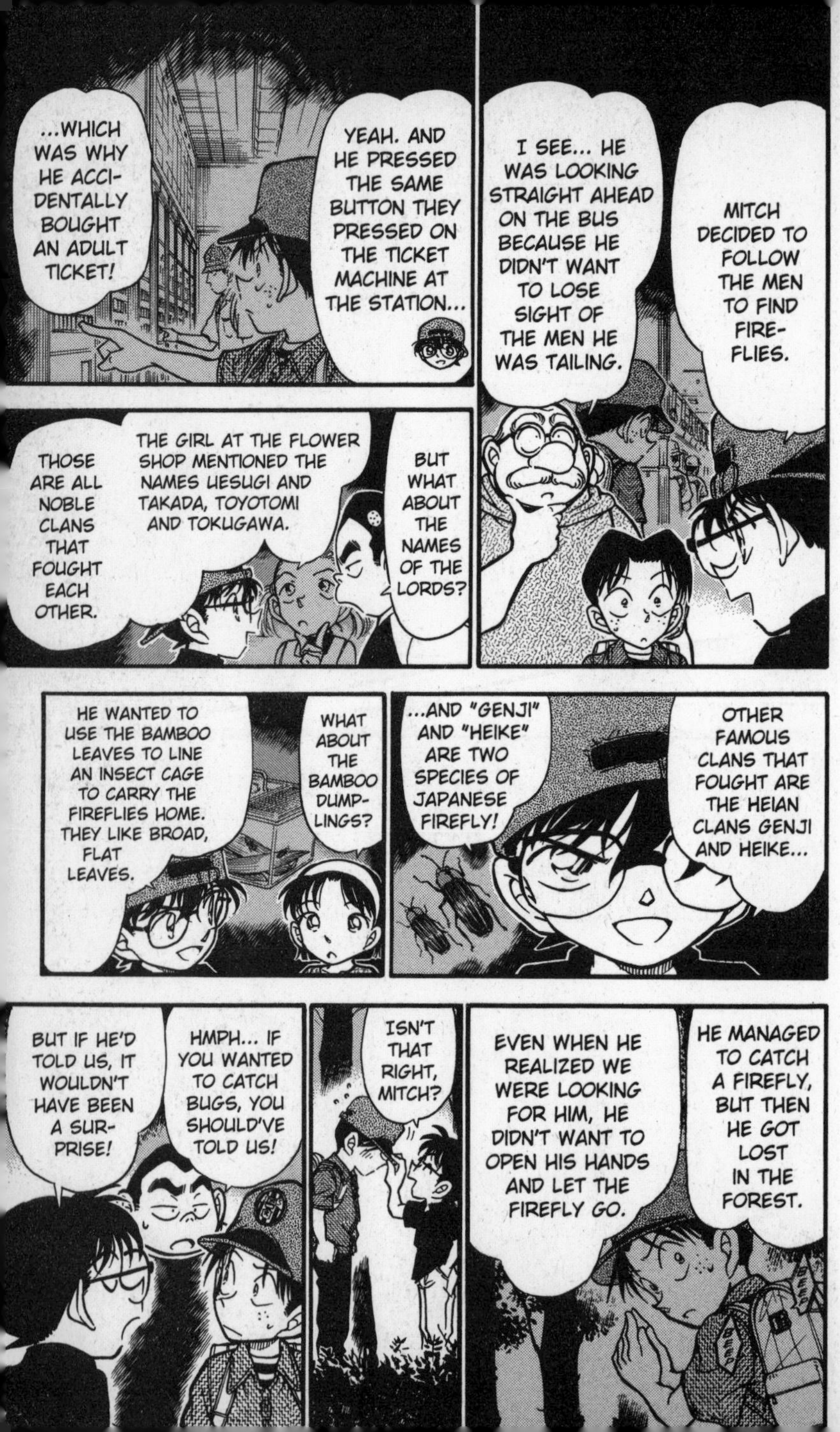
MITCH DECIDED TO FOLLOW THE MEN TO FIND FIRE-FLIES.
I SEE... HE WAS LOOKING STRAIGHT AHEAD ON THE BUS BECAUSE HE DIDN'T WANT TO LOSE SIGHT OF THE MEN HE WAS TAILING.
YEAH. AND HE PRESSED THE SAME BUTTON THEY PRESSED ON THE TICKET MACHINE AT THE STATION...
...WHICH WAS WHY HE ACCI-DENTALLY BOUGHT AN ADULT TICKET!
BUT WHAT ABOUT THE NAMES OF THE LORDS?
THE GIRL AT THE FLOWER SHOP MENTIONED THE NAMES UESUGI AND TAKADA, TOYOTOMI AND TOKUGAWA.
THOSE ARE ALL NOBLE CLANS THAT FOUGHT EACH OTHER.
OTHER FAMOUS CLANS THAT FOUGHT ARE THE HEIAN CLANS GENJI AND HEIKE...
...AND "GENJI" AND "HEIKE" ARE TWO SPECIES OF JAPANESE FIREFLY!
WHAT ABOUT THE BAMBOO DUMP-LINGS?
HE WANTED TO USE THE BAMBOO LEAVES TO LINE AN INSECT CAGE TO CARRY THE FIREFLIES HOME. THEY LIKE BROAD, FLAT LEAVES.
HE MANAGED TO CATCH A FIREFLY, BUT THEN HE GOT LOST IN THE FOREST.
EVEN WHEN HE REALIZED WE WERE LOOKING FOR HIM, HE DIDN'T WANT TO OPEN HIS HANDS AND LET THE FIREFLY GO.
ISN'T THAT RIGHT, MITCH?
HMPH... IF YOU WANTED TO CATCH BUGS, YOU SHOULD'VE TOLD US!
BUT IF HE'D TOLD US, IT WOULDN'T HAVE BEEN A SUR-PRISE!

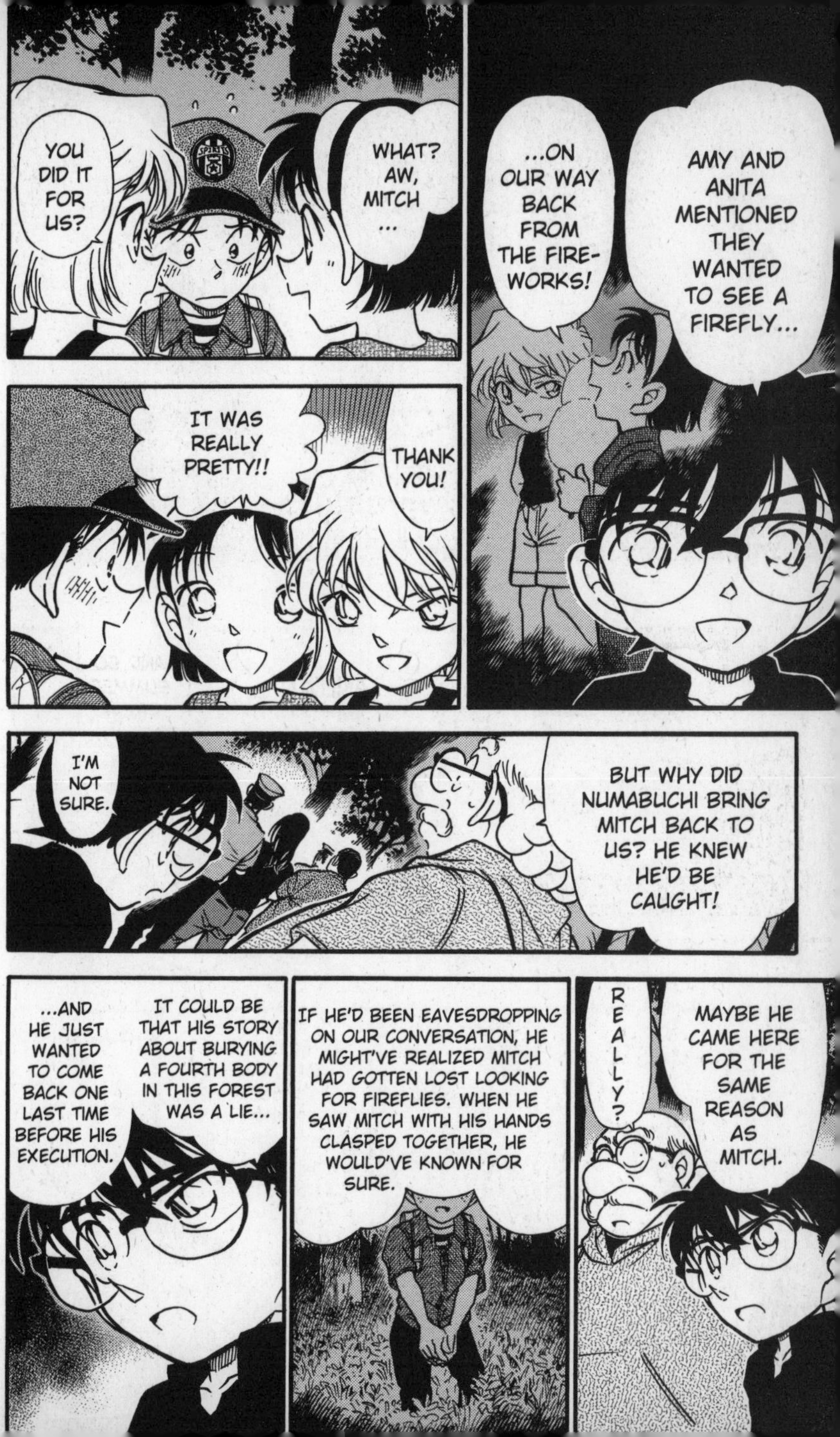
AMY AND ANITA MENTIONED THEY WANTED TO SEE A FIREFLY...
...ON OUR WAY BACK FROM THE FIRE-WORKS!
WHAT? AW, MITCH ...
YOU DID IT FOR US?
IT WAS REALLY PRETTY!!
THANK YOU!
BUT WHY DID NUMABUCHI BRING MITCH BACK TO US? HE KNEW HE'D BE CAUGHT!
I'M NOT SURE.
MAYBE HE CAME HERE FOR THE SAME REASON AS MITCH.
REALLY?
IF HE'D BEEN EAVESDROPPING ON OUR CONVERSATION, HE MIGHT'VE REALIZED MITCH HAD GOTTEN LOST LOOKING FOR FIREFLIES. WHEN HE SAW MITCH WITH HIS HANDS CLASPED TOGETHER, HE WOULD'VE KNOWN FOR SURE.
IT COULD BE THAT HIS STORY ABOUT BURYING A FOURTH BODY IN THIS FOREST WAS A LIE...
...AND HE JUST WANTED TO COME BACK ONE LAST TIME BEFORE HIS EXECUTION.

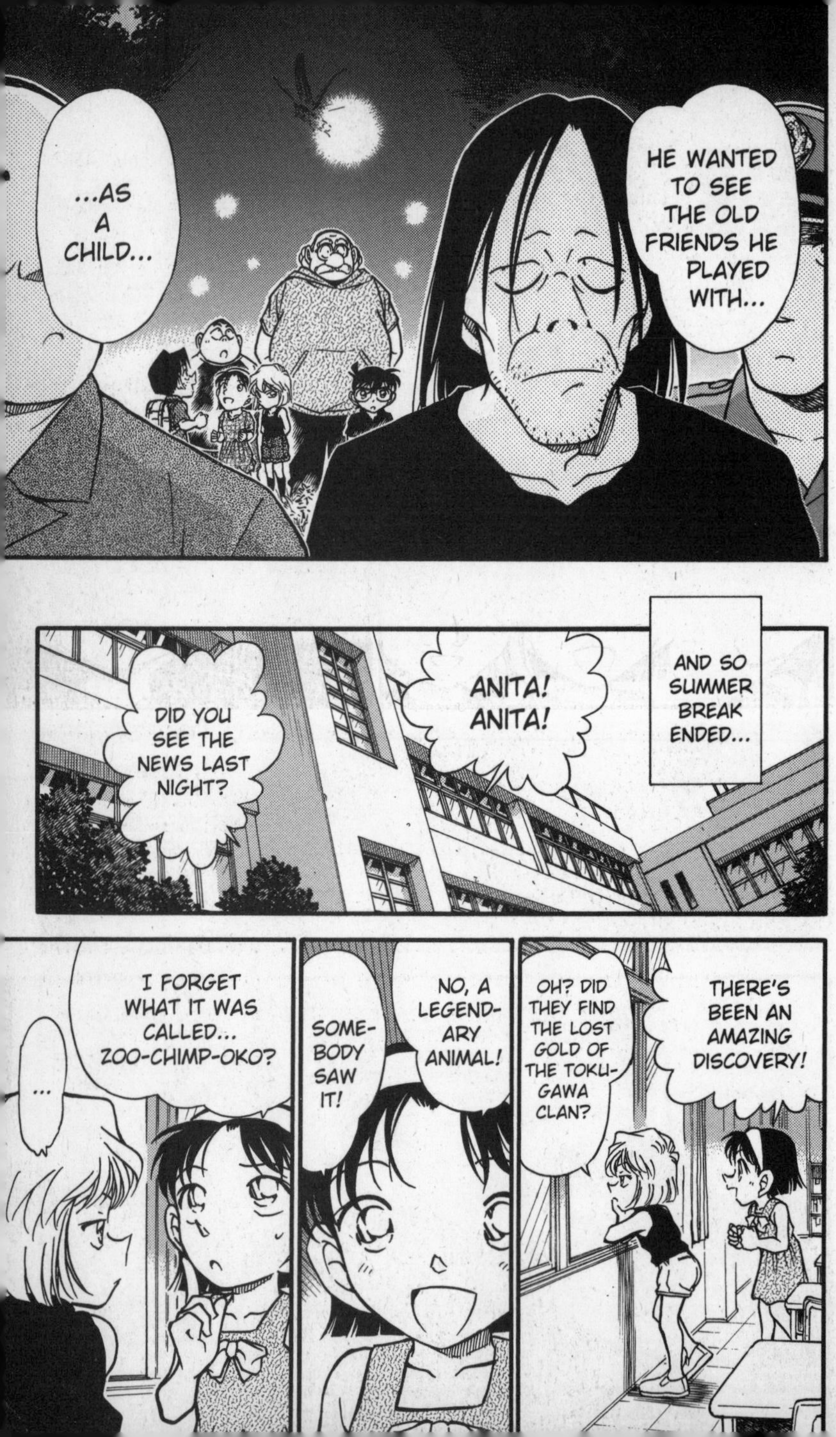
HE WANTED TO SEE THE OLD FRIENDS HE PLAYED WITH...
...AS A CHILD...
AND SO SUMMER BREAK ENDED...
ANITA! ANITA!
DID YOU SEE THE NEWS LAST NIGHT?
THERE'S BEEN AN AMAZING DISCOVERY!
OH? DID THEY FIND THE LOST GOLD OF THE TOKUGAWA CLAN?
NO, A LEGENDARY ANIMAL!
SOMEBODY SAW IT!
I FORGET WHAT IT WAS CALLED... ZOO-CHIMP-OKO?
...

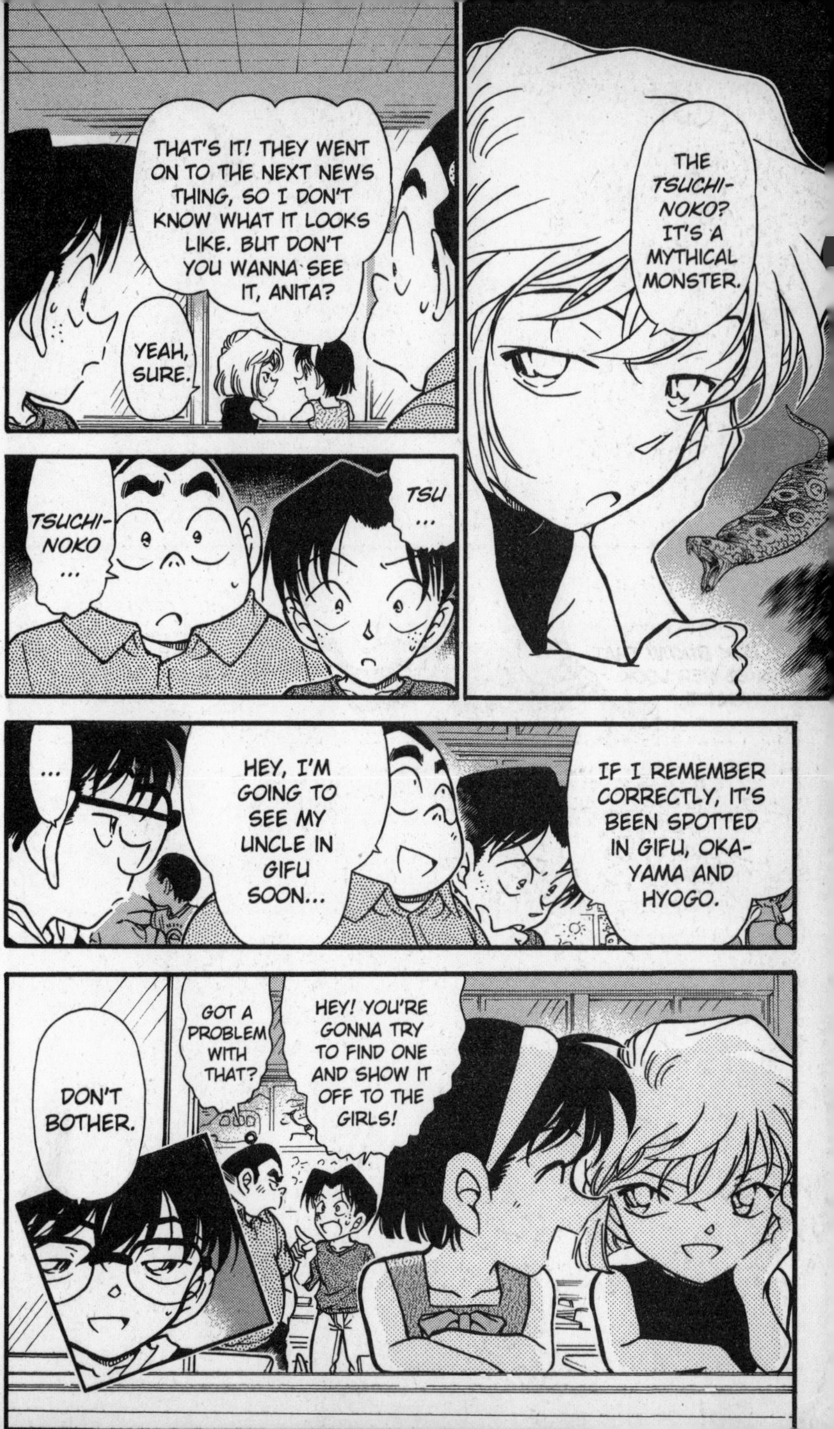
THE TSUCHINOKO? IT'S A MYTHICAL MONSTER.
THAT'S IT! THEY WENT ON TO THE NEXT NEWS THING, SO I DON'T KNOW WHAT IT LOOKS LIKE. BUT DON'T YOU WANNA SEE IT, ANITA?
YEAH, SURE.
TSU ...
TSUCHINOKO ...
IF I REMEMBER CORRECTLY, IT'S BEEN SPOTTED IN GIFU, OKAYAMA AND HYOGO.
HEY, I'M GOING TO SEE MY UNCLE IN GIFU SOON...
...
HEY! YOU'RE GONNA TRY TO FIND ONE AND SHOW IT OFF TO THE GIRLS!
GOT A PROBLEM WITH THAT?
DON'T BOTHER.

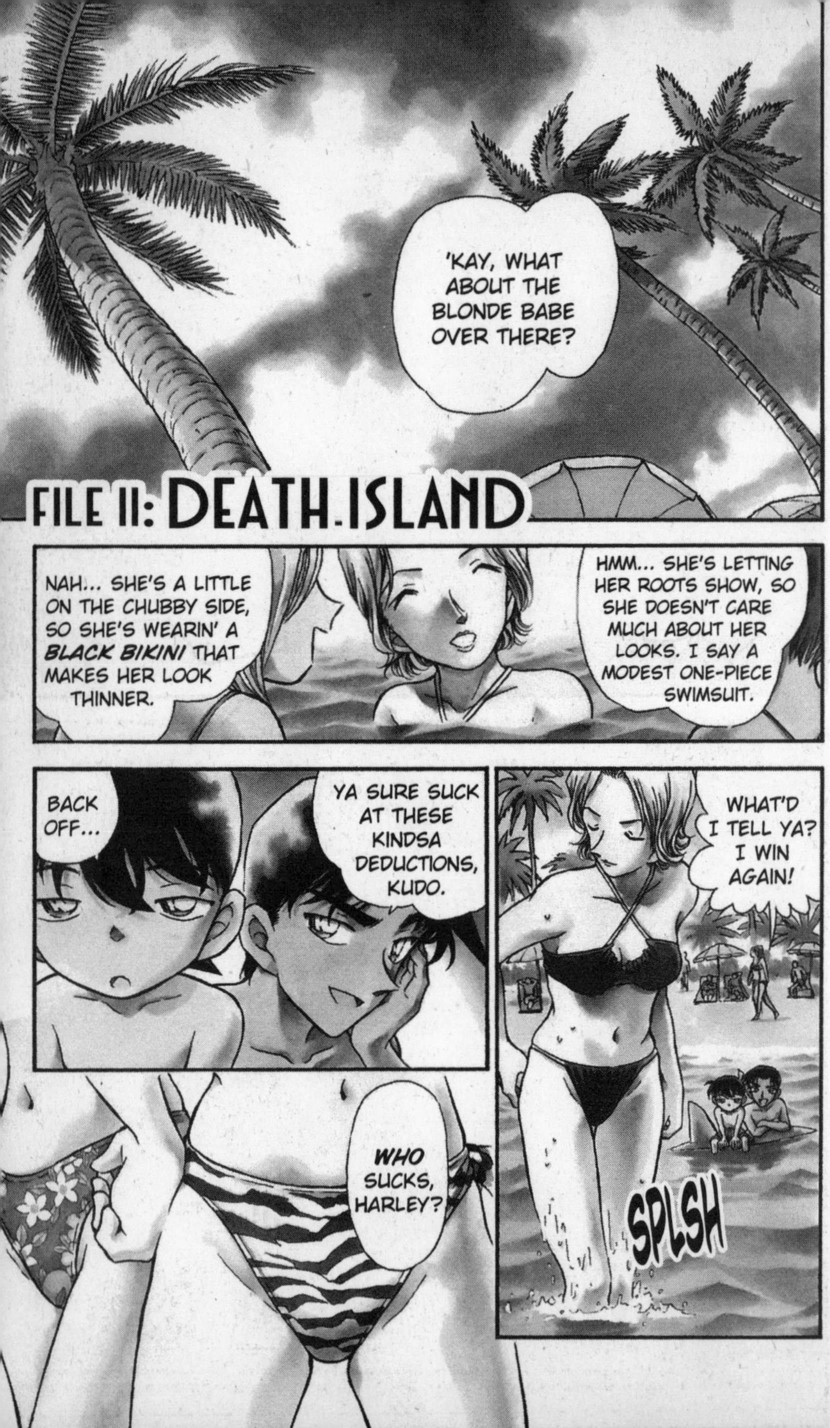
'KAY, WHAT ABOUT THE BLONDE BABE OVER THERE?
FILE 11: DEATH ISLAND
HMM... SHE'S LETTING HER ROOTS SHOW, SO SHE DOESN'T CARE MUCH ABOUT HER LOOKS. I SAY A MODEST ONE-PIECE SWIMSUIT.
NAH... SHE'S A LITTLE ON THE CHUBBY SIDE, SO SHE'S WEARIN' A *BLACK BIKINI* THAT MAKES HER LOOK THINNER.
WHAT'D I TELL YA? I WIN AGAIN!
SPLSH
YA SURE SUCK AT THESE KINDSA DEDUCTIONS, KUDO.
BACK OFF...
WHO SUCKS, HARLEY?

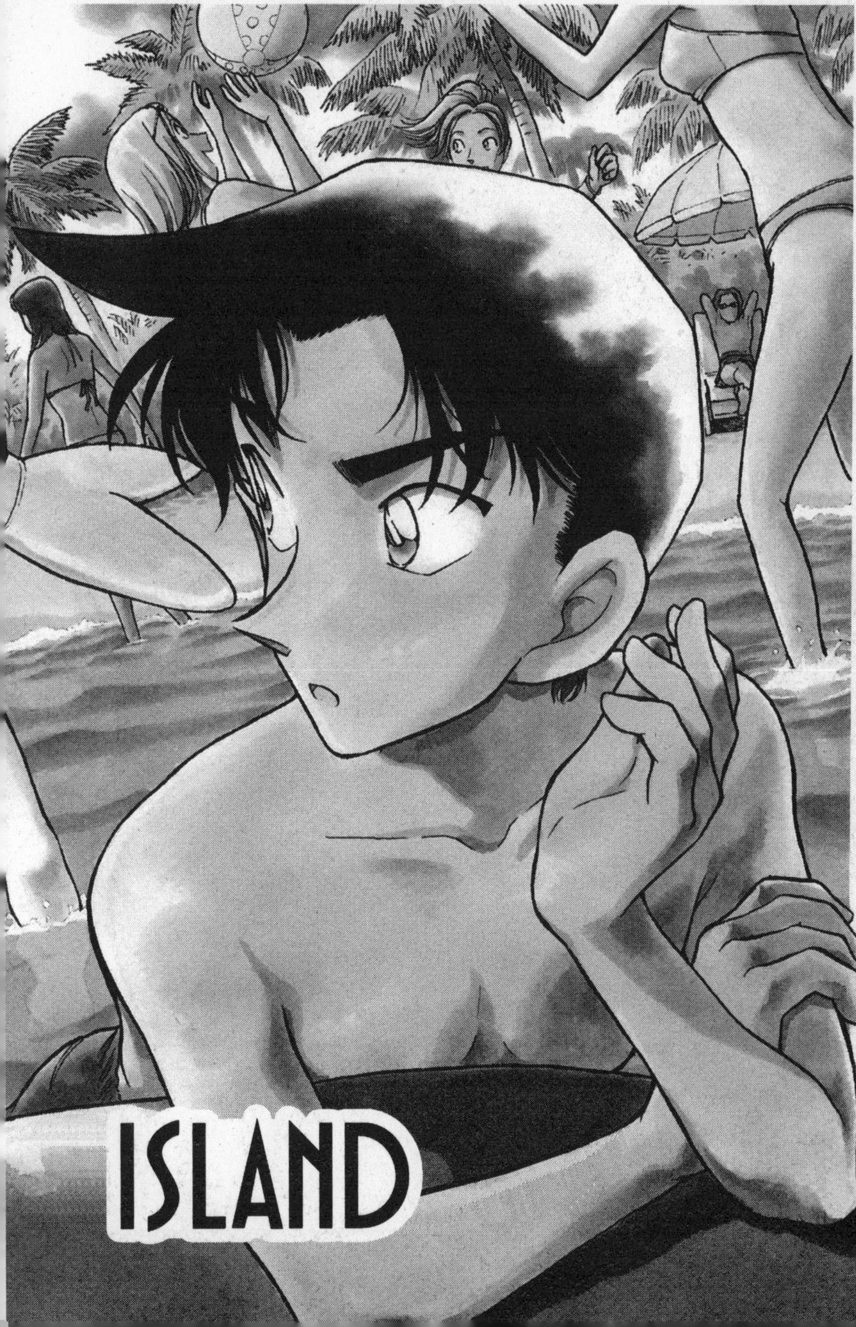
ISLAND

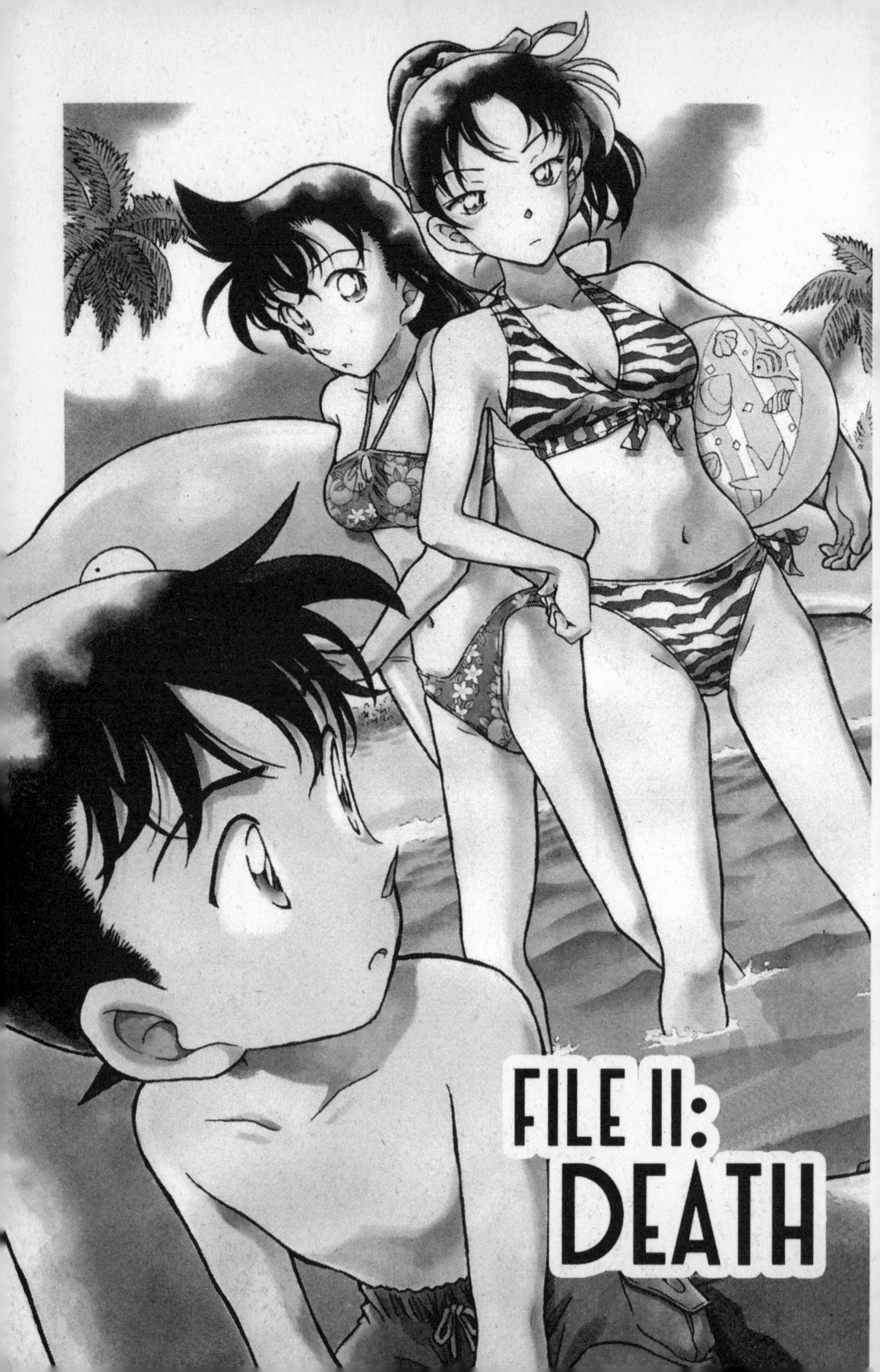
FILE 11:
DEATH

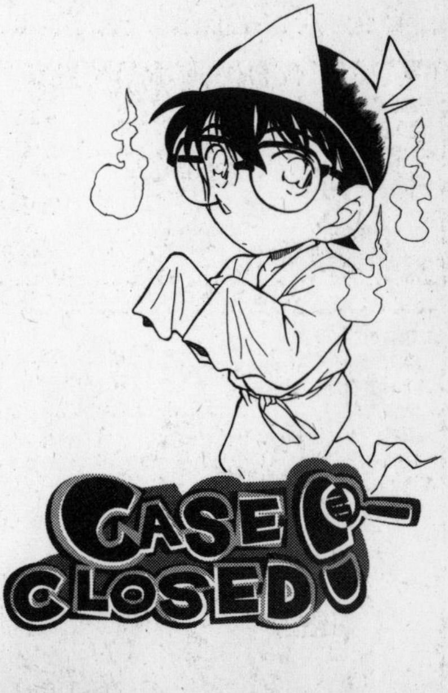
CASE CLOSED

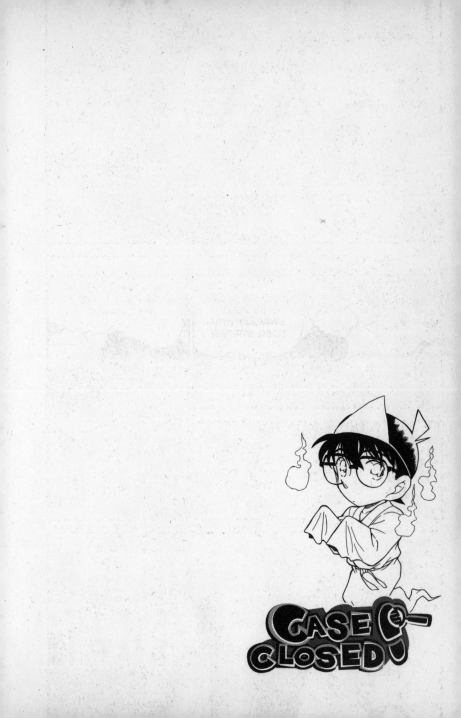

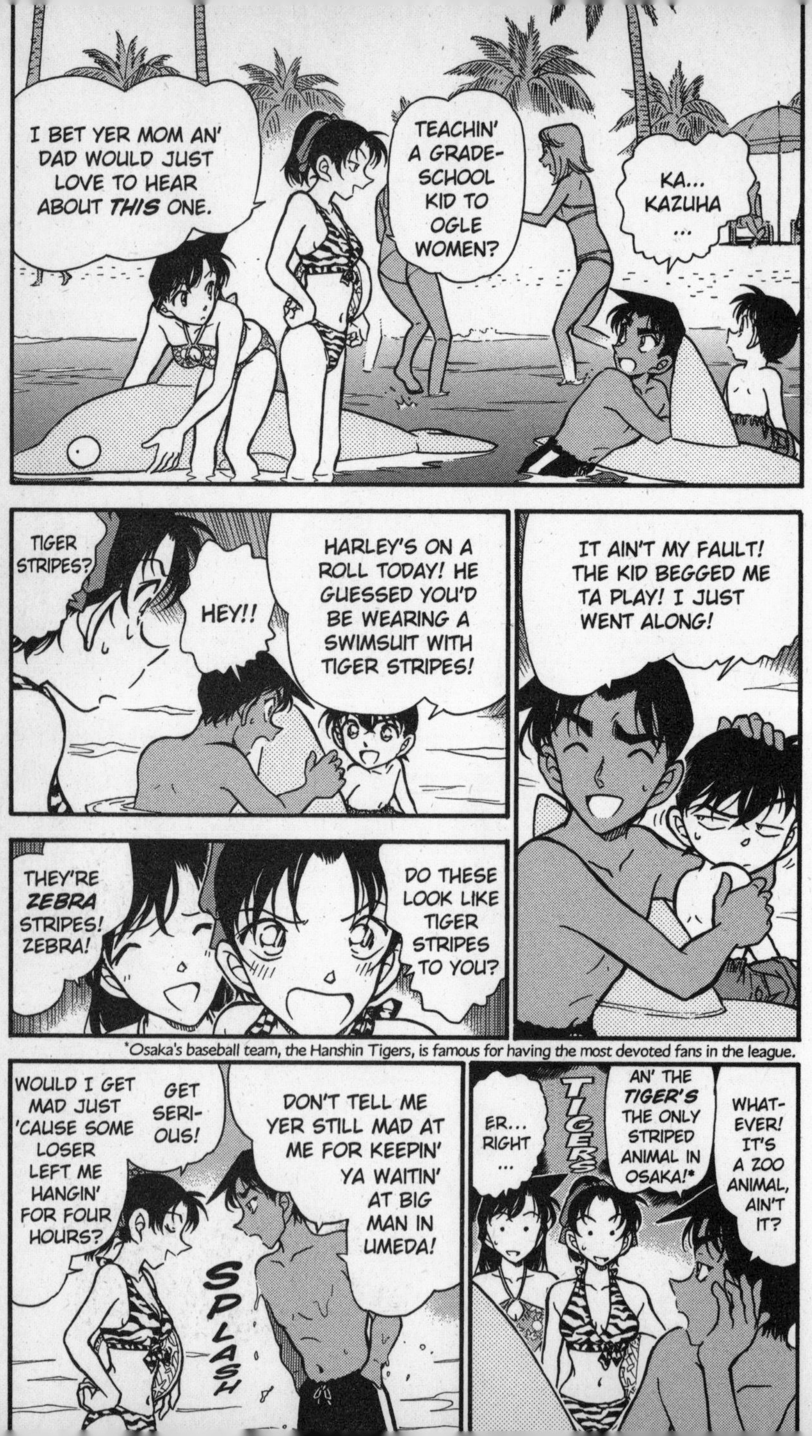
KA... KAZUHA ...
TEACHIN' A GRADE-SCHOOL KID TO OGLE WOMEN?
I BET YER MOM AN' DAD WOULD JUST LOVE TO HEAR ABOUT *THIS* ONE.
IT AIN'T MY FAULT! THE KID BEGGED ME TA PLAY! I JUST WENT ALONG!
HARLEY'S ON A ROLL TODAY! HE GUESSED YOU'D BE WEARING A SWIMSUIT WITH TIGER STRIPES!
HEY!!
TIGER STRIPES?
DO THESE LOOK LIKE TIGER STRIPES TO YOU?
THEY'RE *ZEBRA* STRIPES! ZEBRA!
WHAT-EVER! IT'S A ZOO ANIMAL, AIN'T IT?
AN' THE *TIGER'S* THE ONLY STRIPED ANIMAL IN OSAKA!*
TIGERS
ER... RIGHT ...
DON'T TELL ME YER STILL MAD AT ME FOR KEEPIN' YA WAITIN' AT BIG MAN IN UMEDA!
GET SERI-OUS!
WOULD I GET MAD JUST 'CAUSE SOME LOSER LEFT ME HANGIN' FOR FOUR HOURS?
SPLASH

*Osaka's baseball team, the Hanshin Tigers, is famous for having the most devoted fans in the league.

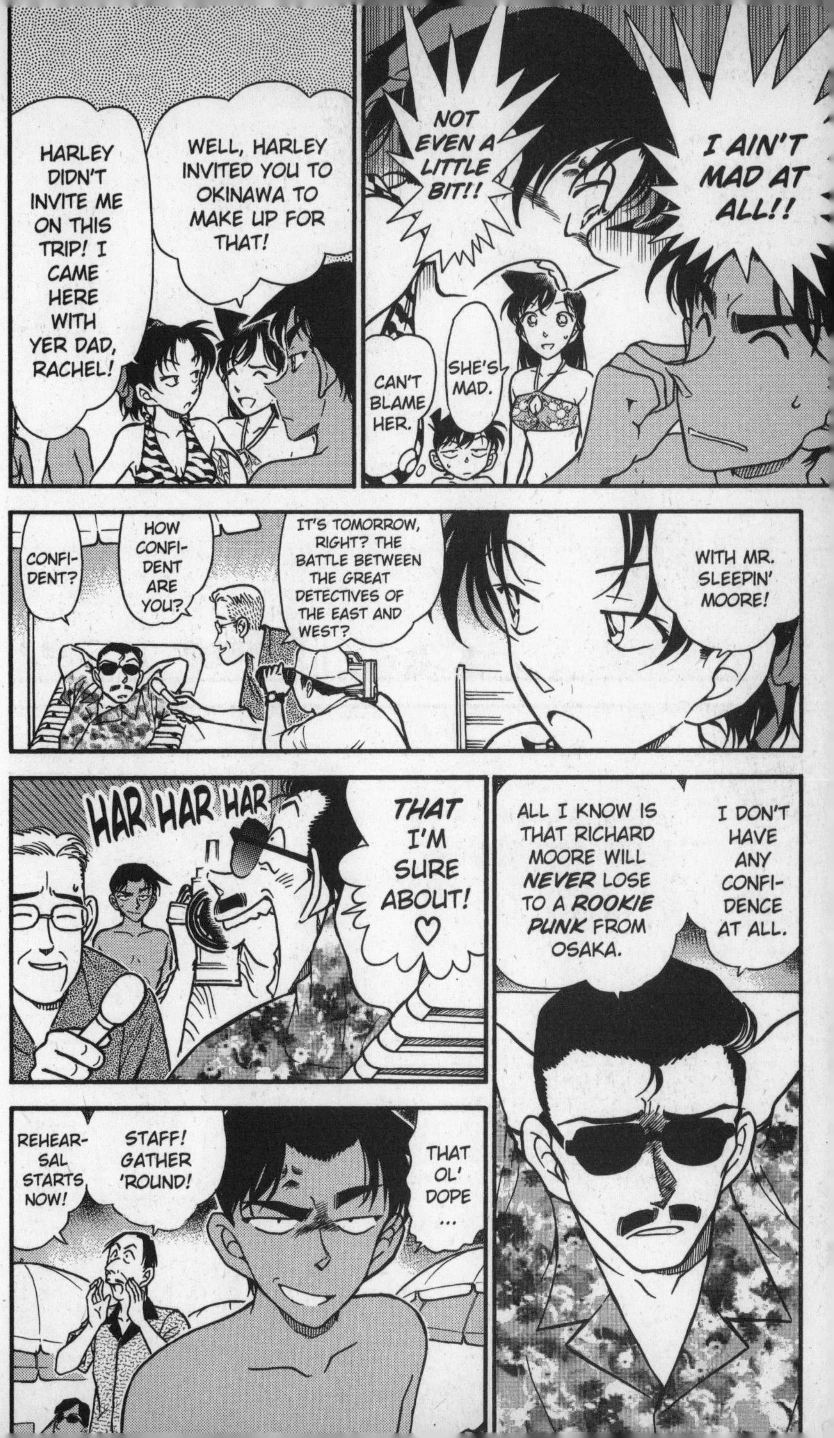

I AIN'T MAD AT ALL!!
NOT EVEN A LITTLE BIT!!
SHE'S MAD.
CAN'T BLAME HER.
WELL, HARLEY INVITED YOU TO OKINAWA TO MAKE UP FOR THAT!
HARLEY DIDN'T INVITE ME ON THIS TRIP! I CAME HERE WITH YER DAD, RACHEL!
WITH MR. SLEEPIN' MOORE!
IT'S TOMORROW, RIGHT? THE BATTLE BETWEEN THE GREAT DETECTIVES OF THE EAST AND WEST?
HOW CONFIDENT ARE YOU?
CONFIDENT?
I DON'T HAVE ANY CONFIDENCE AT ALL.
ALL I KNOW IS THAT RICHARD MOORE WILL ***NEVER*** LOSE TO A ***ROOKIE PUNK*** FROM OSAKA.
THAT I'M SURE ABOUT! ♡
HAR HAR HAR
THAT OL' DOPE ...
STAFF! GATHER 'ROUND!
REHEARSAL STARTS NOW!

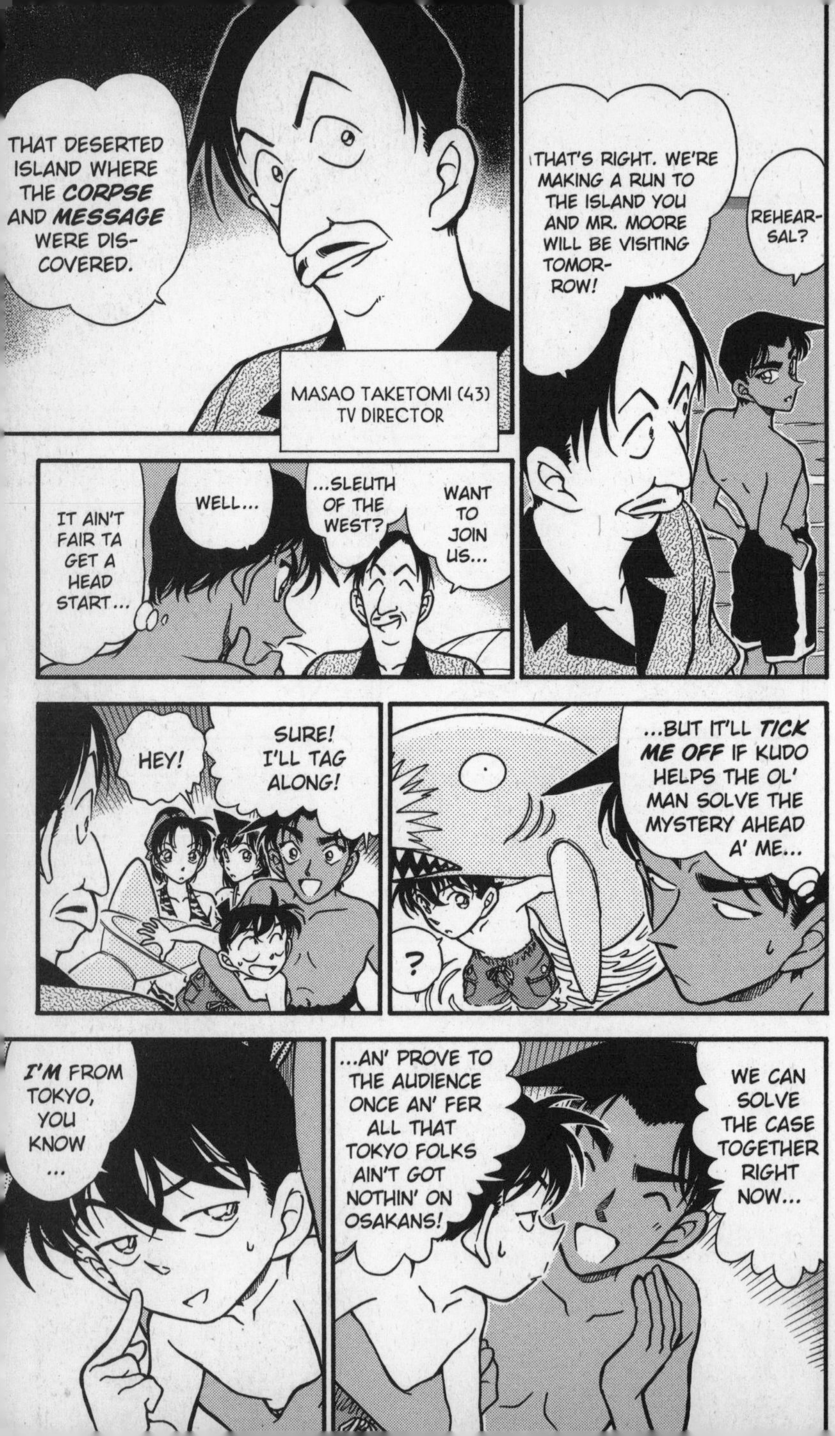
REHEAR-SAL?
THAT'S RIGHT. WE'RE MAKING A RUN TO THE ISLAND YOU AND MR. MOORE WILL BE VISITING TOMOR-ROW!
THAT DESERTED ISLAND WHERE THE CORPSE AND MESSAGE WERE DIS-COVERED.
MASAO TAKETOMI (43) TV DIRECTOR
WANT TO JOIN US...
...SLEUTH OF THE WEST?
WELL...
IT AIN'T FAIR TA GET A HEAD START...
...BUT IT'LL TICK ME OFF IF KUDO HELPS THE OL' MAN SOLVE THE MYSTERY AHEAD A' ME...
?
SURE! I'LL TAG ALONG!
HEY!
WE CAN SOLVE THE CASE TOGETHER RIGHT NOW...
...AN' PROVE TO THE AUDIENCE ONCE AN' FER ALL THAT TOKYO FOLKS AIN'T GOT NOTHIN' ON OSAKANS!
I'M FROM TOKYO, YOU KNOW ...

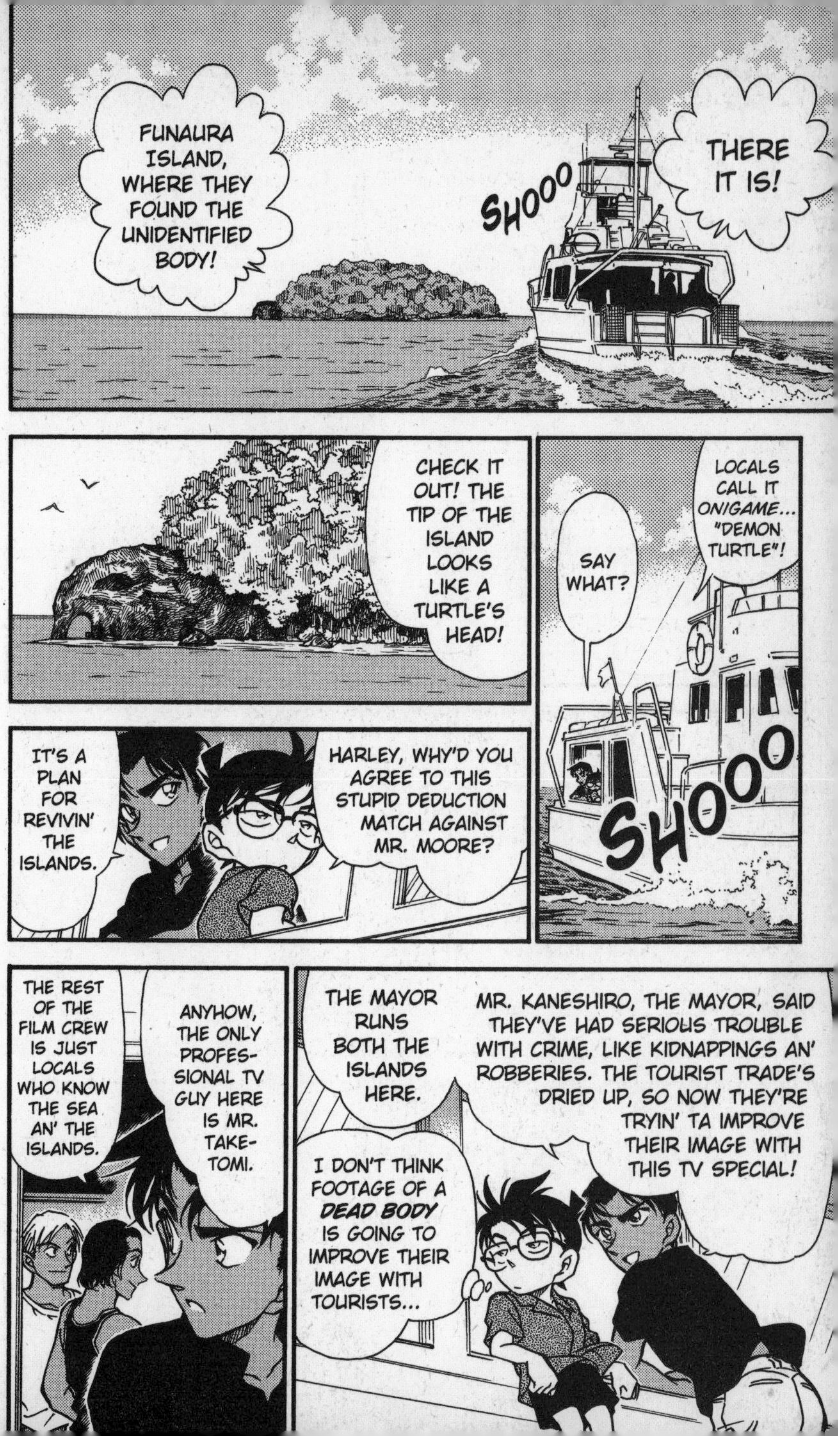
THERE IT IS!
SHOOO
FUNAURA ISLAND, WHERE THEY FOUND THE UNIDENTIFIED BODY!
LOCALS CALL IT ONIGAME... "DEMON TURTLE"!
SAY WHAT?
SHOOOO
CHECK IT OUT! THE TIP OF THE ISLAND LOOKS LIKE A TURTLE'S HEAD!
HARLEY, WHY'D YOU AGREE TO THIS STUPID DEDUCTION MATCH AGAINST MR. MOORE?
IT'S A PLAN FOR REVIVIN' THE ISLANDS.
MR. KANESHIRO, THE MAYOR, SAID THEY'VE HAD SERIOUS TROUBLE WITH CRIME, LIKE KIDNAPPINGS AN' ROBBERIES. THE TOURIST TRADE'S DRIED UP, SO NOW THEY'RE TRYIN' TA IMPROVE THEIR IMAGE WITH THIS TV SPECIAL!
THE MAYOR RUNS BOTH THE ISLANDS HERE.
I DON'T THINK FOOTAGE OF A DEAD BODY IS GOING TO IMPROVE THEIR IMAGE WITH TOURISTS...
ANYHOW, THE ONLY PROFES-SIONAL TV GUY HERE IS MR. TAKE-TOMI.
THE REST OF THE FILM CREW IS JUST LOCALS WHO KNOW THE SEA AN' THE ISLANDS.

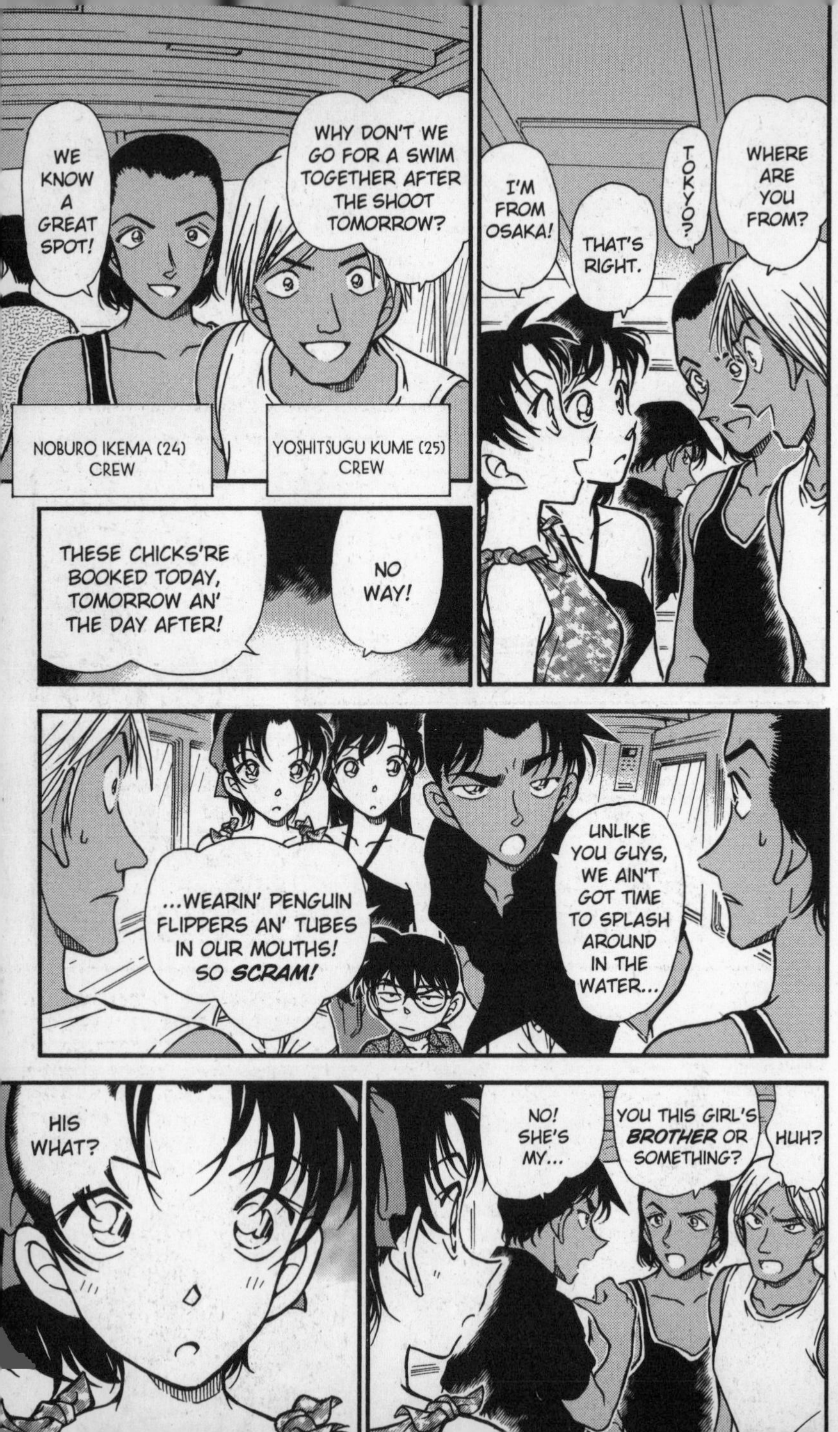
WHERE ARE YOU FROM?
TOKYO?
THAT'S RIGHT.
I'M FROM OSAKA!
WHY DON'T WE GO FOR A SWIM TOGETHER AFTER THE SHOOT TOMORROW?
WE KNOW A GREAT SPOT!
YOSHITSUGU KUME (25) CREW
NOBURO IKEMA (24) CREW
NO WAY!
THESE CHICKS'RE BOOKED TODAY, TOMORROW AN' THE DAY AFTER!
UNLIKE YOU GUYS, WE AIN'T GOT TIME TO SPLASH AROUND IN THE WATER...
...WEARIN' PENGUIN FLIPPERS AN' TUBES IN OUR MOUTHS! SO *SCRAM!*
HUH?
YOU THIS GIRL'S *BROTHER* OR SOMETHING?
NO! SHE'S MY...
HIS WHAT?

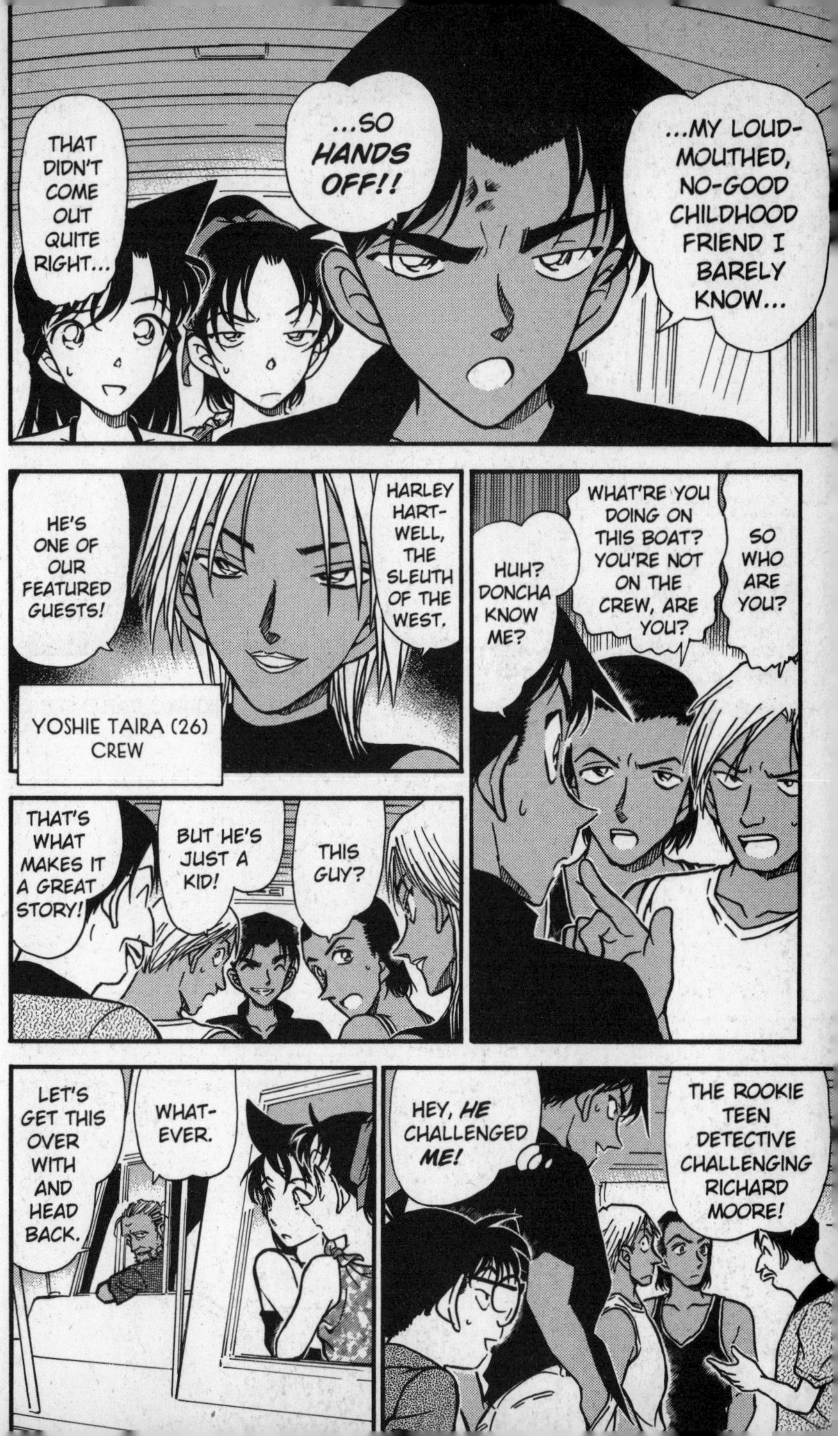
...MY LOUD-MOUTHED, NO-GOOD CHILDHOOD FRIEND I BARELY KNOW...
...SO HANDS OFF!!
THAT DIDN'T COME OUT QUITE RIGHT...
SO WHO ARE YOU?
WHAT'RE YOU DOING ON THIS BOAT? YOU'RE NOT ON THE CREW, ARE YOU?
HUH? DONCHA KNOW ME?
HARLEY HART-WELL, THE SLEUTH OF THE WEST.
HE'S ONE OF OUR FEATURED GUESTS!
YOSHIE TAIRA (26) CREW
THIS GUY?
BUT HE'S JUST A KID!
THAT'S WHAT MAKES IT A GREAT STORY!
THE ROOKIE TEEN DETECTIVE CHALLENGING RICHARD MOORE!
HEY, HE CHALLENGED ME!
WHAT-EVER.
LET'S GET THIS OVER WITH AND HEAD BACK.

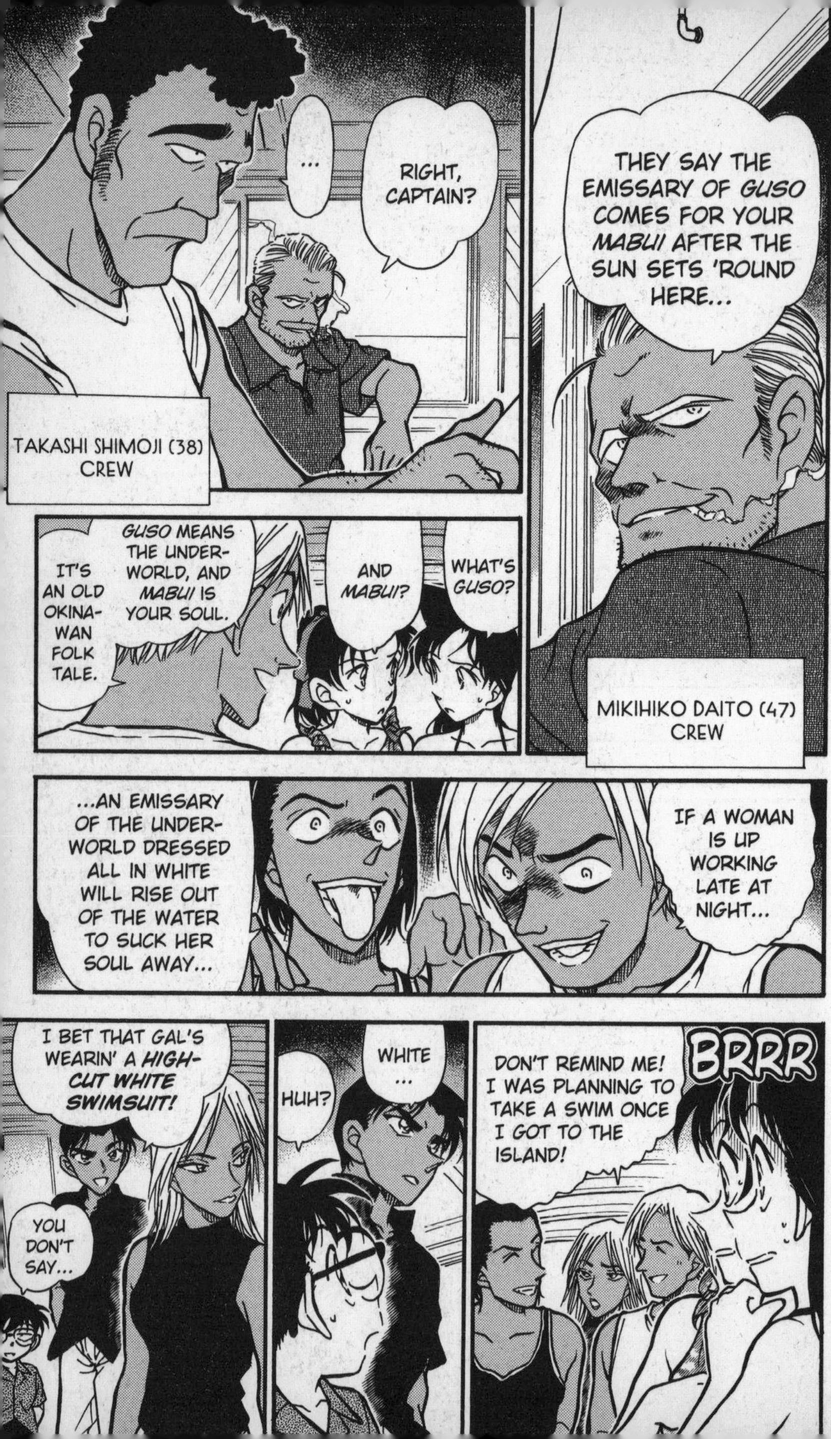
THEY SAY THE EMISSARY OF *GUSO* COMES FOR YOUR *MABUI* AFTER THE SUN SETS 'ROUND HERE...
MIKIHIKO DAITO (47) CREW
RIGHT, CAPTAIN?
...
TAKASHI SHIMOJI (38) CREW
WHAT'S *GUSO*?
AND *MABUI*?
GUSO MEANS THE UNDER-WORLD, AND *MABUI* IS YOUR SOUL.
IT'S AN OLD OKINA-WAN FOLK TALE.
IF A WOMAN IS UP WORKING LATE AT NIGHT...
...AN EMISSARY OF THE UNDER-WORLD DRESSED ALL IN WHITE WILL RISE OUT OF THE WATER TO SUCK HER SOUL AWAY...
BRRR
DON'T REMIND ME! I WAS PLANNING TO TAKE A SWIM ONCE I GOT TO THE ISLAND!
WHITE ...
HUH?
I BET THAT GAL'S WEARIN' A *HIGH-CUT WHITE SWIMSUIT!*
YOU DON'T SAY...

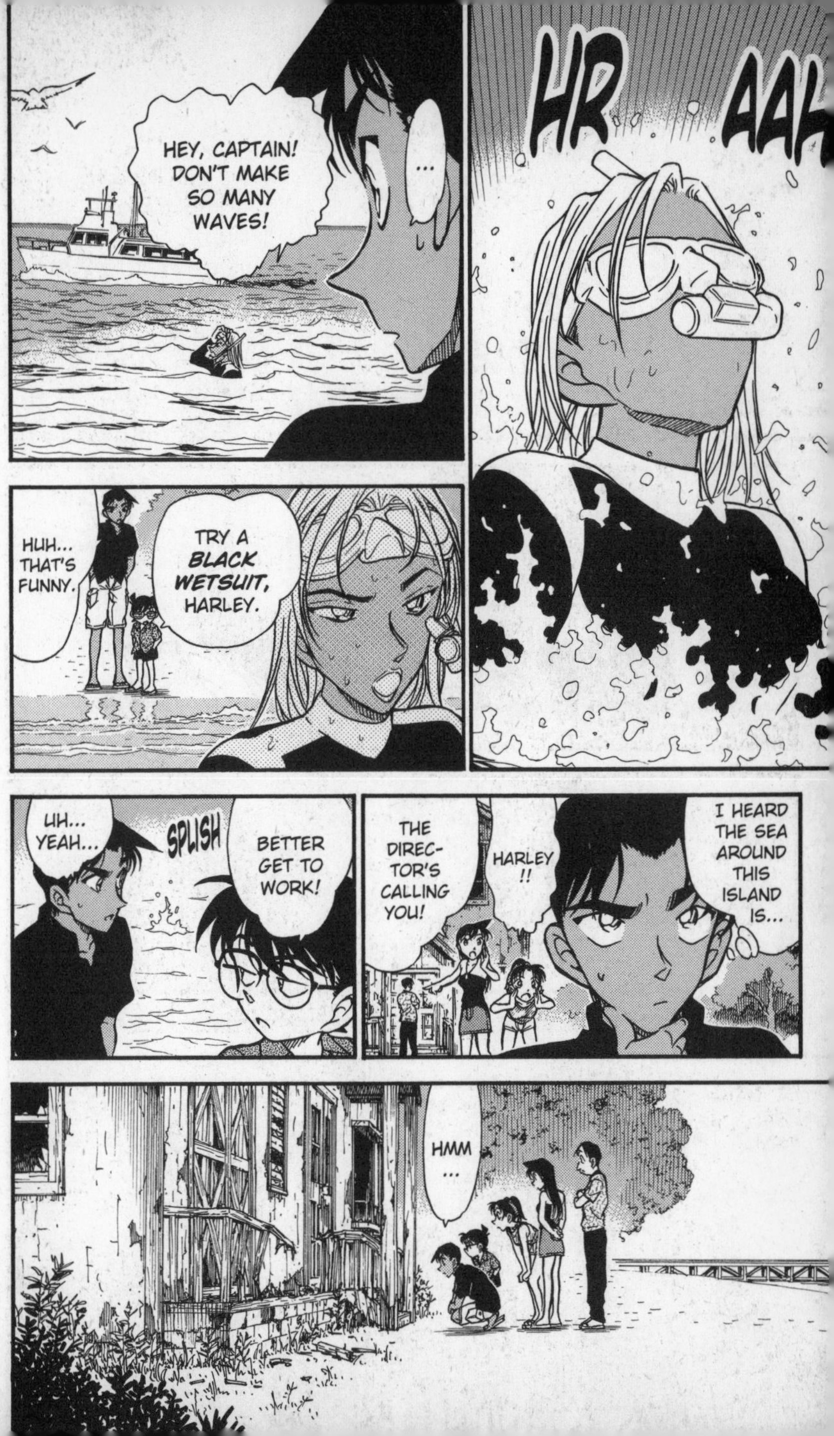
HR AAH
...
HEY, CAPTAIN! DON'T MAKE SO MANY WAVES!
TRY A *BLACK WETSUIT,* HARLEY.
HUH... THAT'S FUNNY.
I HEARD THE SEA AROUND THIS ISLAND IS...
HARLEY !!
THE DIRECTOR'S CALLING YOU!
BETTER GET TO WORK!
SPLISH
UH... YEAH...
HMM ...

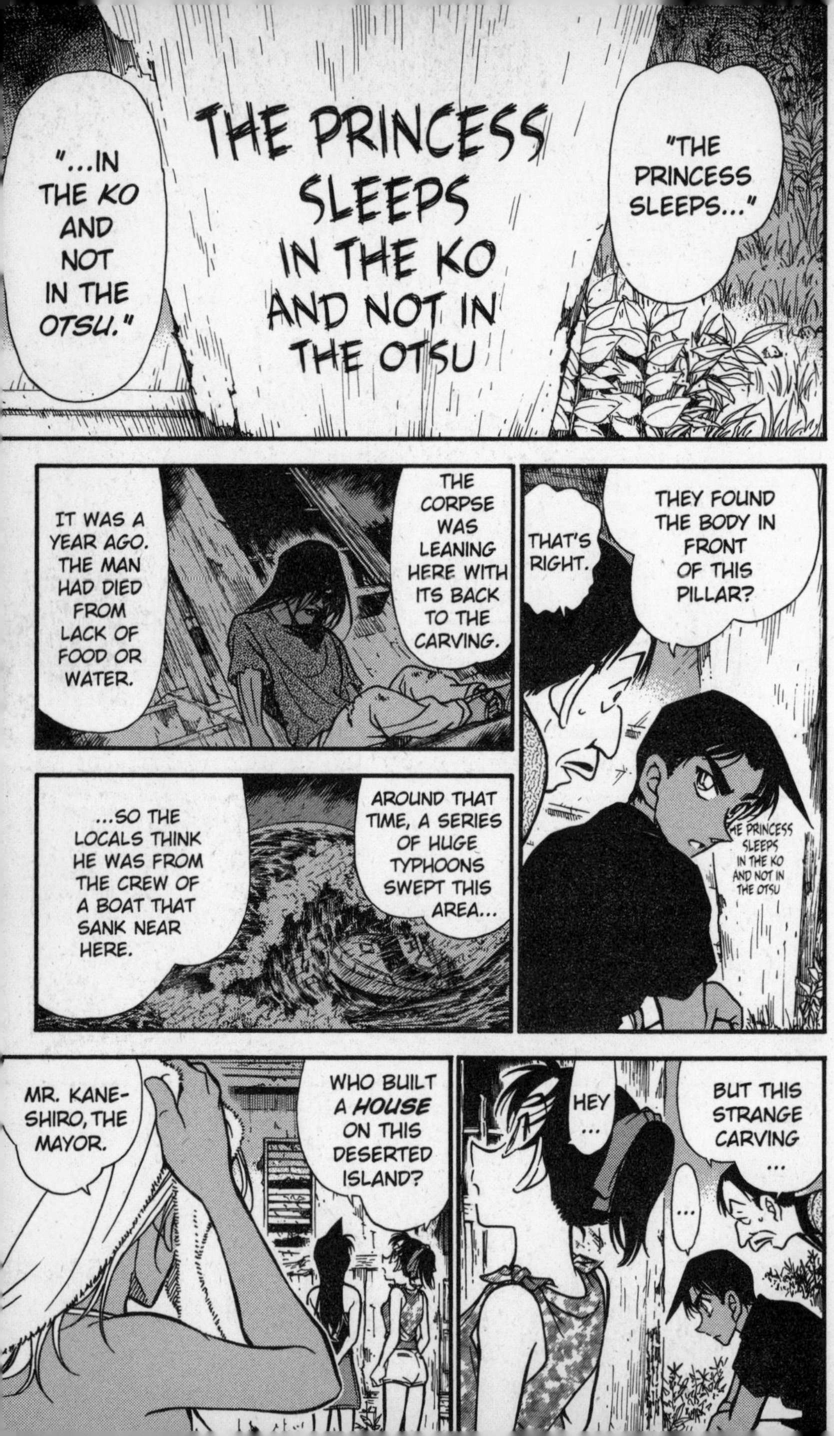
"THE PRINCESS SLEEPS..."
THE PRINCESS SLEEPS IN THE KO AND NOT IN THE OTSU
"...IN THE *KO* AND NOT IN THE *OTSU*."
THEY FOUND THE BODY IN FRONT OF THIS PILLAR?
THAT'S RIGHT.
HE PRINCESS SLEEPS IN THE KO AND NOT IN THE OTSU
THE CORPSE WAS LEANING HERE WITH ITS BACK TO THE CARVING.
IT WAS A YEAR AGO. THE MAN HAD DIED FROM LACK OF FOOD OR WATER.
AROUND THAT TIME, A SERIES OF HUGE TYPHOONS SWEPT THIS AREA...
...SO THE LOCALS THINK HE WAS FROM THE CREW OF A BOAT THAT SANK NEAR HERE.
BUT THIS STRANGE CARVING ...
...
HEY ...
WHO BUILT A ***HOUSE*** ON THIS DESERTED ISLAND?
MR. KANE-SHIRO, THE MAYOR.

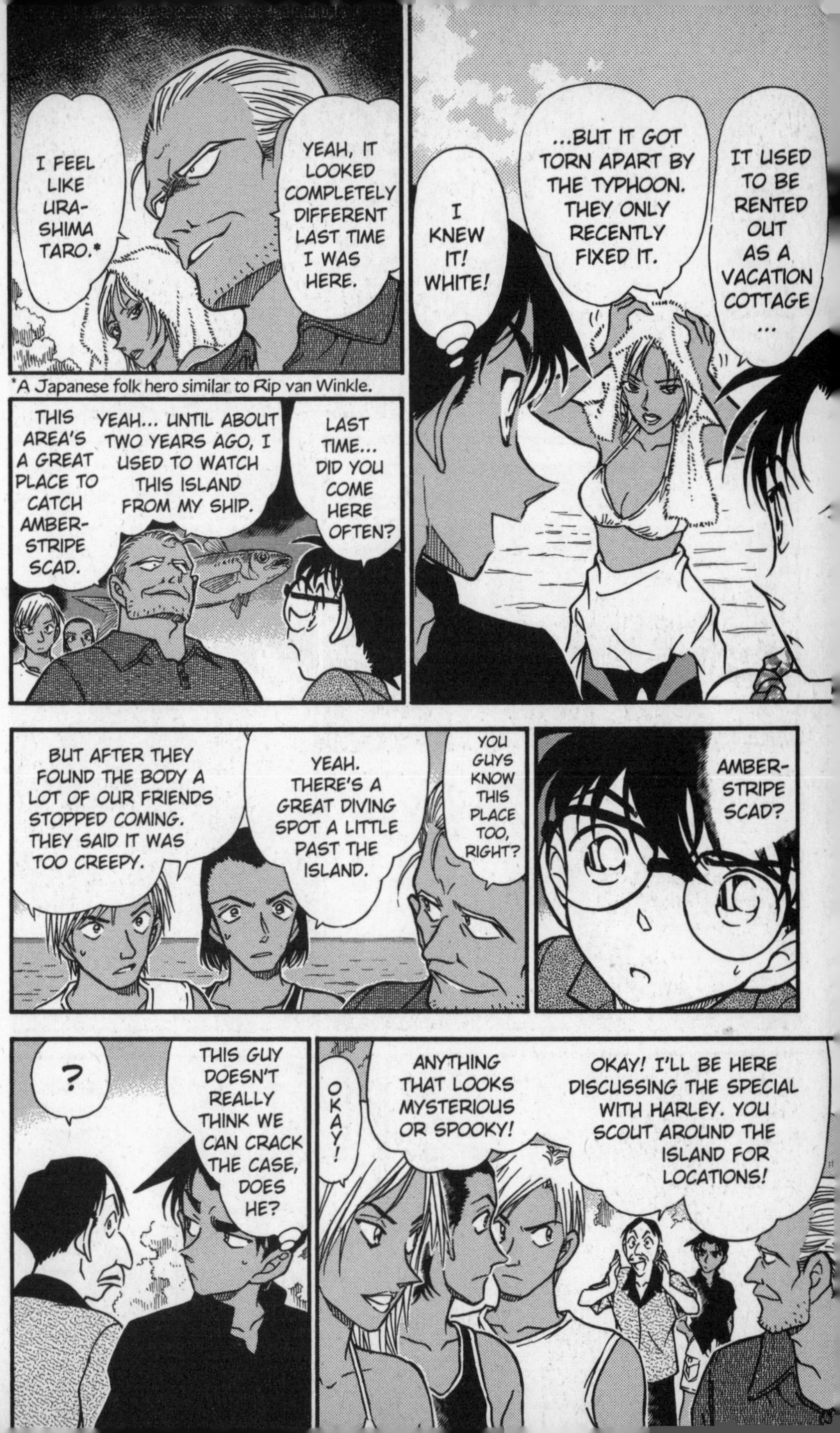
IT USED TO BE RENTED OUT AS A VACATION COTTAGE ...
...BUT IT GOT TORN APART BY THE TYPHOON. THEY ONLY RECENTLY FIXED IT.
I KNEW IT! WHITE!
YEAH, IT LOOKED COMPLETELY DIFFERENT LAST TIME I WAS HERE.
I FEEL LIKE URA-SHIMA TARO.*
LAST TIME... DID YOU COME HERE OFTEN?
YEAH... UNTIL ABOUT TWO YEARS AGO, I USED TO WATCH THIS ISLAND FROM MY SHIP.
THIS AREA'S A GREAT PLACE TO CATCH AMBER-STRIPE SCAD.
AMBER-STRIPE SCAD?
YOU GUYS KNOW THIS PLACE TOO, RIGHT?
YEAH. THERE'S A GREAT DIVING SPOT A LITTLE PAST THE ISLAND.
BUT AFTER THEY FOUND THE BODY A LOT OF OUR FRIENDS STOPPED COMING. THEY SAID IT WAS TOO CREEPY.
OKAY! I'LL BE HERE DISCUSSING THE SPECIAL WITH HARLEY. YOU SCOUT AROUND THE ISLAND FOR LOCATIONS!
ANYTHING THAT LOOKS MYSTERIOUS OR SPOOKY!
OKAY!
THIS GUY DOESN'T REALLY THINK WE CAN CRACK THE CASE, DOES HE?
?
*A Japanese folk hero similar to Rip van Winkle.

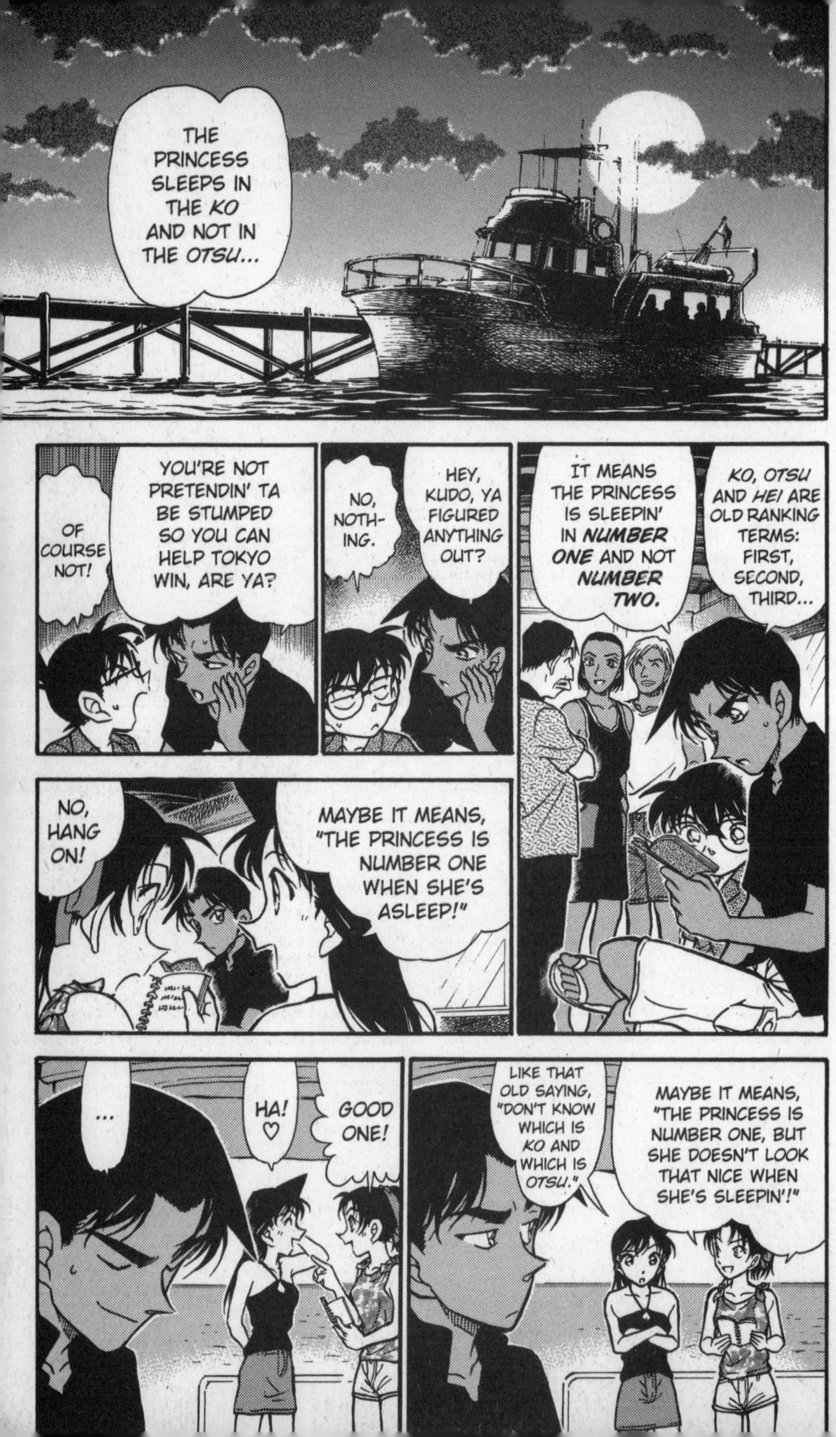
THE PRINCESS SLEEPS IN THE *KO* AND NOT IN THE *OTSU*...
KO, OTSU AND *HEI* ARE OLD RANKING TERMS: FIRST, SECOND, THIRD...
IT MEANS THE PRINCESS IS SLEEPIN' IN ***NUMBER ONE*** AND NOT ***NUMBER TWO.***
HEY, KUDO, YA FIGURED ANYTHING OUT?
NO, NOTHING.
YOU'RE NOT PRETENDIN' TA BE STUMPED SO YOU CAN HELP TOKYO WIN, ARE YA?
OF COURSE NOT!
MAYBE IT MEANS, "THE PRINCESS IS NUMBER ONE WHEN SHE'S ASLEEP!"
NO, HANG ON!
MAYBE IT MEANS, "THE PRINCESS IS NUMBER ONE, BUT SHE DOESN'T LOOK THAT NICE WHEN SHE'S SLEEPIN'!"
LIKE THAT OLD SAYING, "DON'T KNOW WHICH IS *KO* AND WHICH IS *OTSU*."
GOOD ONE!
HA! ♡
...

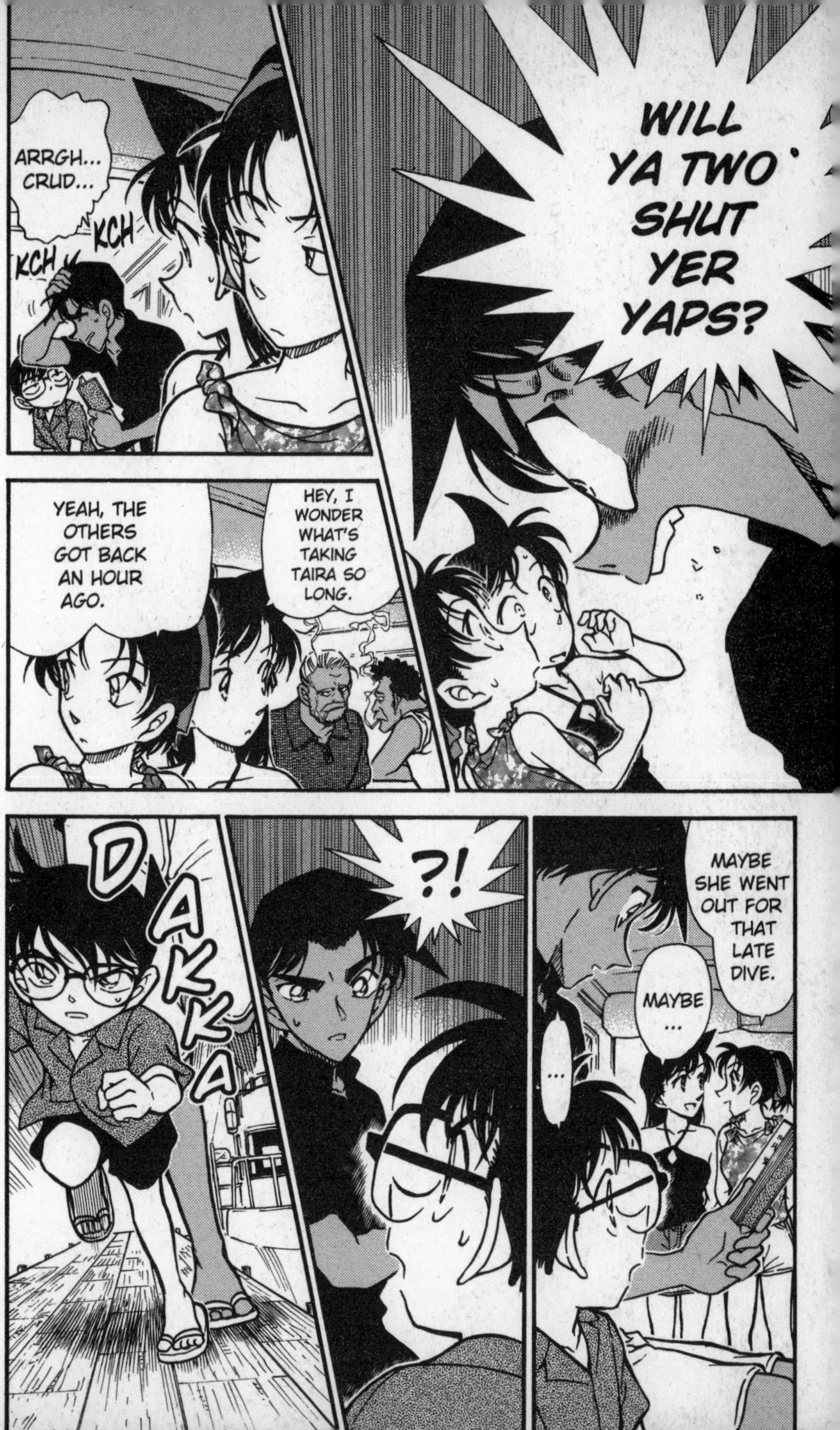
WILL YA TWO SHUT YER YAPS?
ARRGH... CRUD...
KCH
KCH
HEY, I WONDER WHAT'S TAKING TAIRA SO LONG.
YEAH, THE OTHERS GOT BACK AN HOUR AGO.
MAYBE SHE WENT OUT FOR THAT LATE DIVE.
MAYBE ...
...
?!
DAKKA

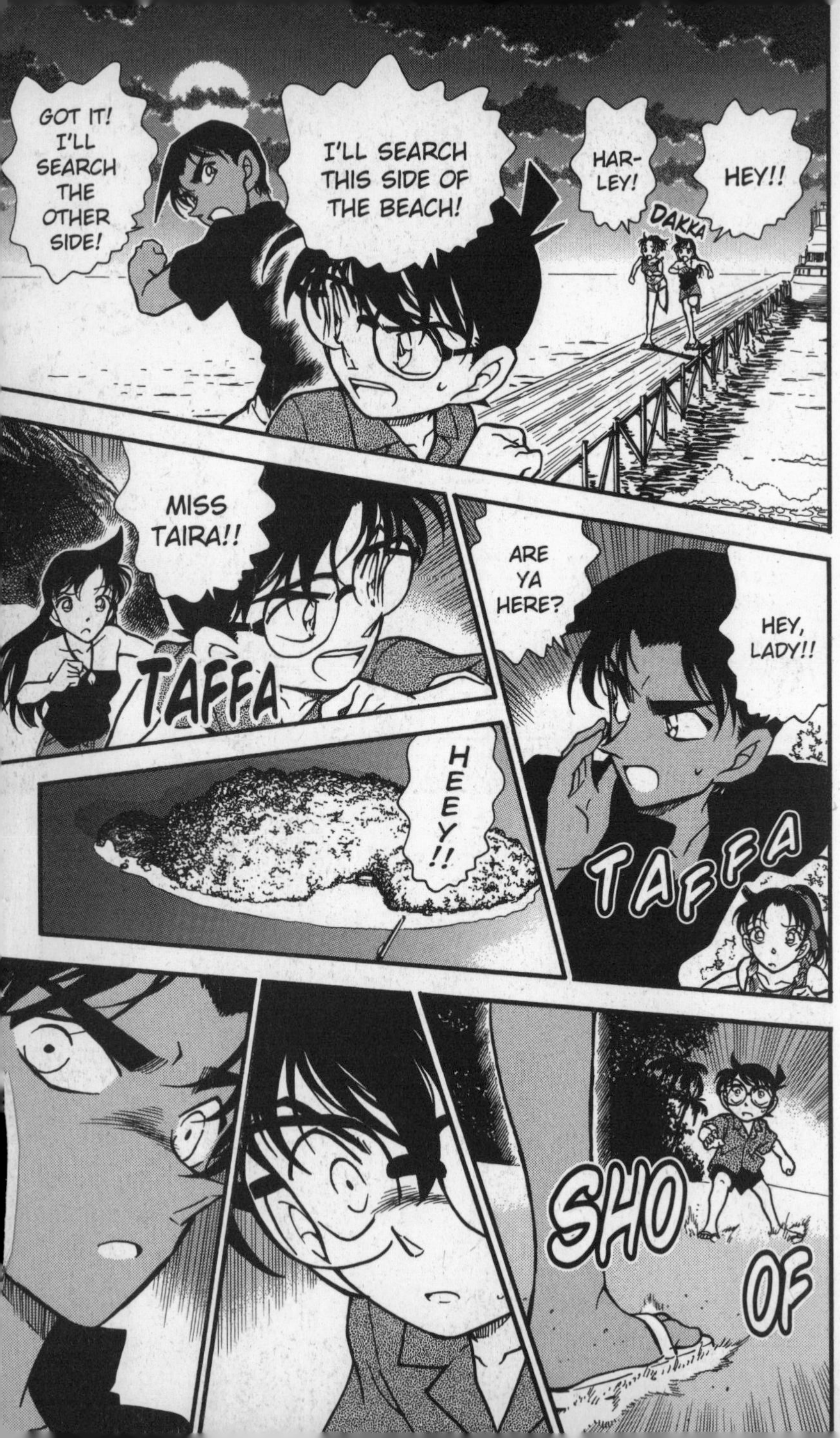

HEY!!
HAR-LEY!
DAKKA
I'LL SEARCH THIS SIDE OF THE BEACH!
GOT IT! I'LL SEARCH THE OTHER SIDE!
HEY, LADY!!
ARE YA HERE?
TAFFA
MISS TAIRA!!
TAFFA
HEEY!!
SHO OF

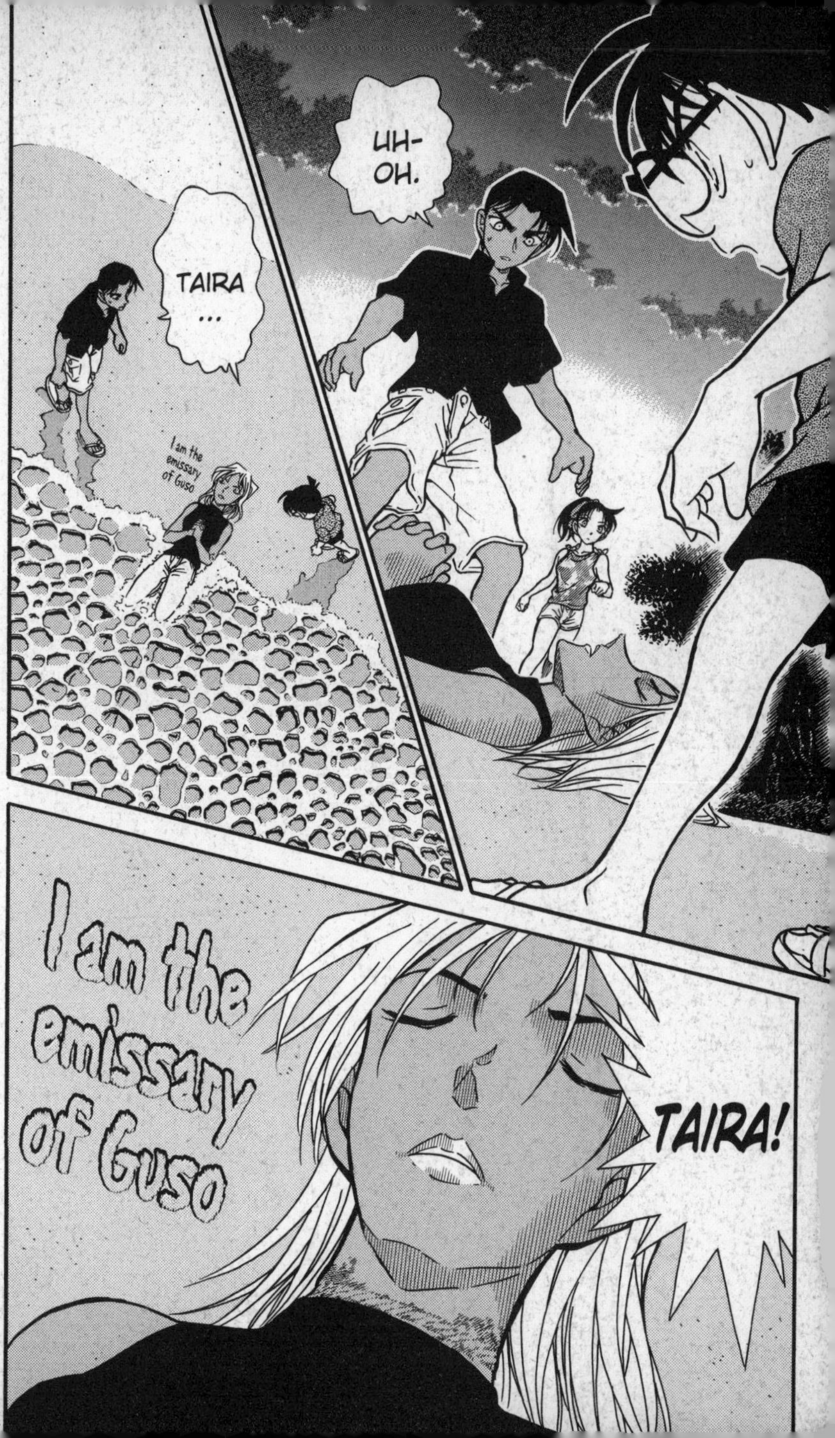
UH-OH.
TAIRA ...
I am the emissary of Guso
TAIRA!
I am the emissary of Guso

Hello, Aoyama here.

I played in a baseball game recently. I hadn't played baseball in four years!

The opposing team was the Whiters, led by sports-manga superstar Tetsuya Chiba! After several foul balls, I managed to get a decent hit. I ran to first base, which was defended by the great Chiba. ♥ I was really hoping to talk to him, but my teammates called in a pinch runner to take my place since I'm so flabby, so the conversation ended there.

Stay in shape, everybody!

[Editor's note: Tetsuya Chiba is a legendary manga artist best known for the boxing manga *Ashita no Joe* (Joe of Tomorrow).]

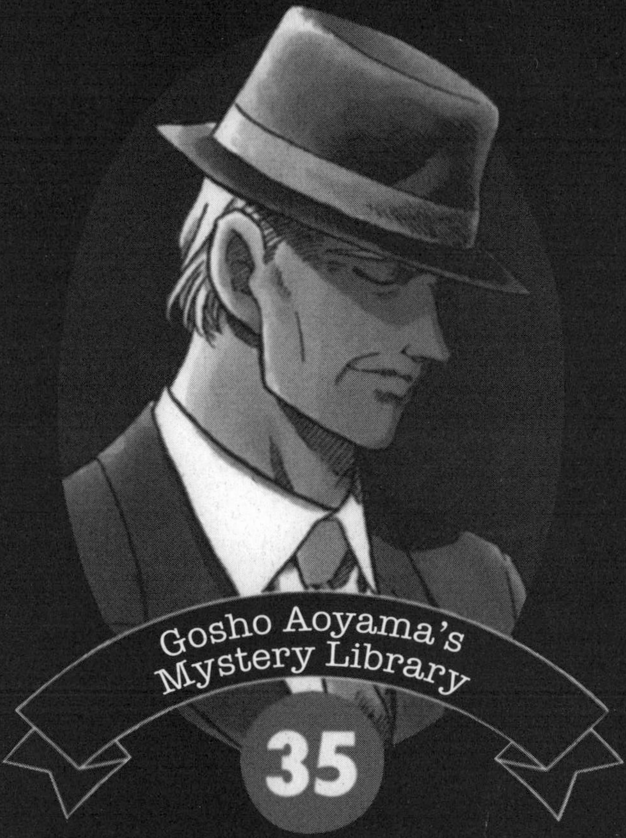
Gosho Aoyama's
Mystery Library
35

DRURY LANE

Disguise is a crucial detective skill, and Drury Lane is a master! A retired Shakespearean actor, he leads a life of ease, but his curiosity leads him to investigate puzzling cases. As an actor, he finds disguises a piece of cake. With his assistant Quacey helping him with makeup, he disguises himself as a police inspector or a suspect. He connects the information he gathers in a logical, mathematical way. He's deaf, but this works to his advantage, since he can concentrate perfectly by closing his eyes.

Drury's adventures were written by Barnaby Ross, a pseudonym of cousins Frederic Dannay and Manfred Lee, a.k.a. Ellery Queen. When the Drury Lane books were first published, Dannay and Lee decided to use a new pen name, and their fans were completely deceived. It's like the time I wrote a manga about a palm-sized detective...except I used my real name. Guess I was too obvious.

I recommend *The Tragedy of Y.*

[Editor's Note: The manga Aoyama refers to is the untranslated miniseries *Tantei Jorji's Minimini-Daisakusen* (Detective George's Mini-Mini Operations).]

InuYasha

Read the action from the start with the original manga series

Full color adaptation of the popular TV series

Art book with cel art, paintings, character profiles and more

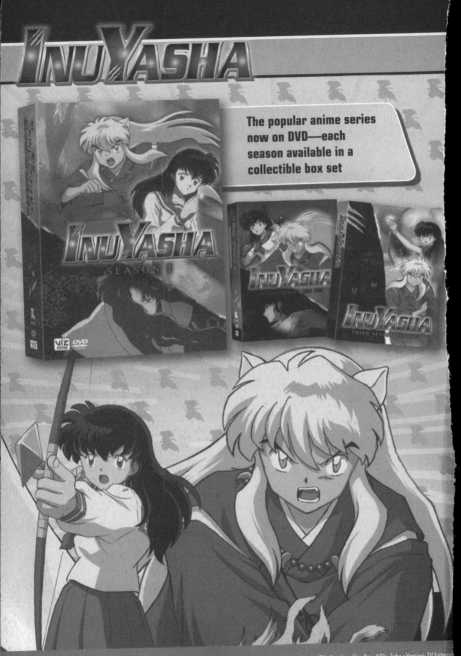

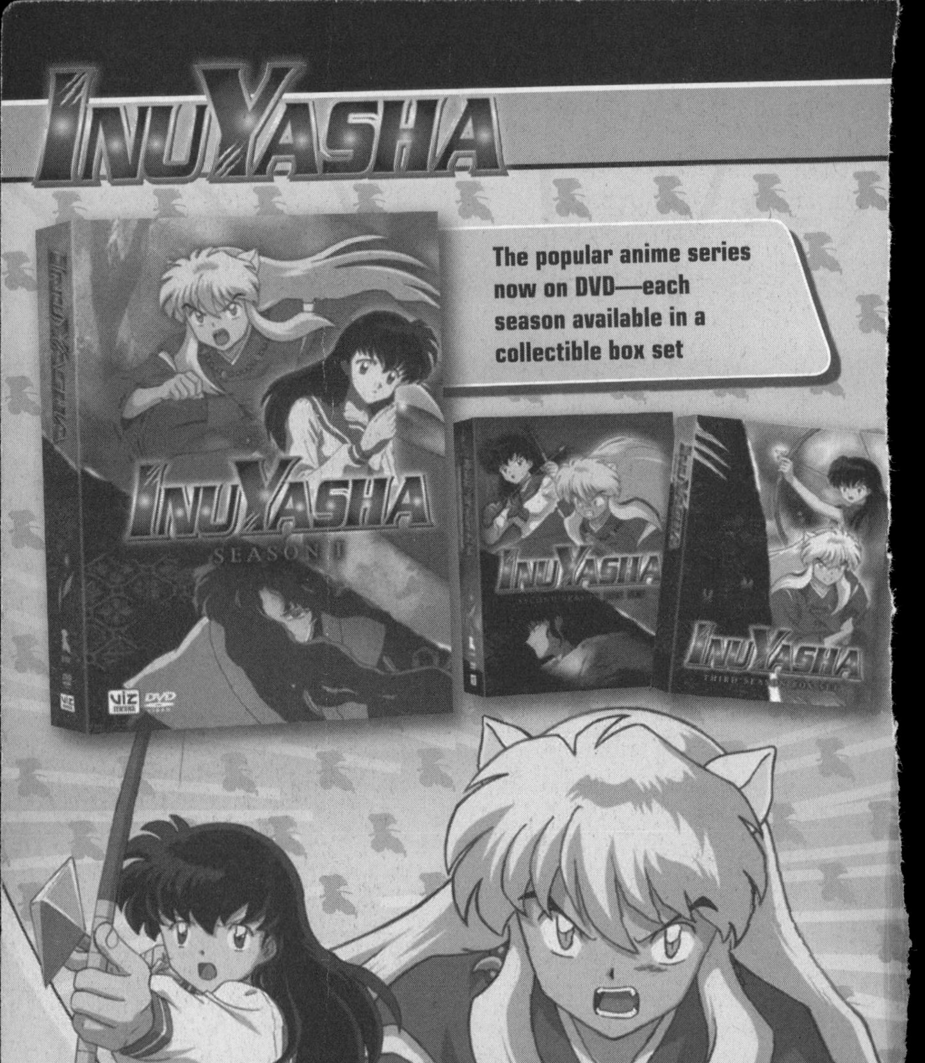
InuYasha
The popular anime series now on DVD—each season available in a collectible box set
InuYasha
Season I
InuYasha
InuYasha

At Your Indentured Service

Hayate's parents are bad with money, so they sell his organs to pay their debts.
Hayate doesn't like this plan, so he comes up with a new one—kidnap and ransom
a girl from a wealthy family. Solid plan… so how did he end up as her butler?

Find out in *Hayate the Combat Butler*—
buy the manga at store.viz.com!

Kenjiro Hata

VIZ MEDIA

www.viz.com
store.viz.com

© 2005 Kenjiro HATA/Shogakukan Inc.

Hey! You're Reading in the Wrong Direction!

This is the *end* of this graphic novel!

To properly enjoy this VIZ graphic novel, please turn it around and begin reading from **right to left.** Unlike English, Japanese is read right to left, so Japanese comics are read in reverse order from the way English comics are typically read.

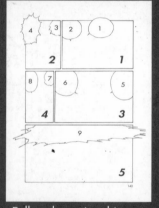

Follow the action this way

This book has been printed in the original Japanese format in order to preserve the orientation of the original artwork. Have fun with it!

MANGA STARTS ON SUNDAY
SHONEN

When ace high school detective Jimmy Kudo is fed a mysterious substance by a pair of nefarious men in black—poof! He is physically transformed into a first grader. Until Jimmy can find a cure for his miniature malady, he takes on the pseudonym Conan Edogawa and continues to solve all the cases that come his way.

CASE CLOSED™

In this exciting volume:

GREEK TRAGEDY

Flash back to one of the cases that made Jimmy Kudo famous before he became Conan! While visiting his actress mother on Broadway, Jimmy discovers some rotten apples in the Big Apple. Someone is trying to kill the stars of *Golden Apple*, a musical based on Greek mythology, and the only clue is a golden apple inscribed "For the Fairest." While Jimmy races to crack the case, Rachel stumbles upon a mystery of her own... and a certain man in a black knit cap!

WWW.SHONENSUNDAY.COM

$9.99 USA $12.99 CAN £6.99 UK

This book reads from right to left.

VIZ media

RATED T+ FOR OLDER TEEN
ratings.viz.com

ISBN-13: 978-1-4215-2886-1
50999
9 781421 528861